Religion Versus Secular Humanism

What the Psychological and Social Sciences Can Tell Us

Religion Versus Secular Humanism

What the Psychological and Social Sciences Can Tell Us

A. Timothy Church

HYPATIA
PRESS

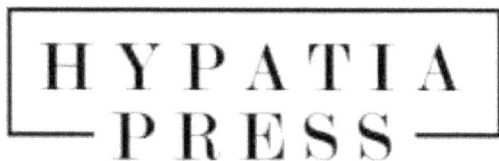

Published by Hypatia Press in the United Kingdom in 2024

ISBN: 978-1-83919-649-2

www.hypatiapress.org

To my family

Great believers and great doubters seem like opposites, but they are more similar to each other than to the mass of relatively disinterested or acquiescent men and women.

– Jennifer Michael Hecht

Contents

Introduction

Never before in history has mankind been of such two minds, so divided into two camps, as it is today. Religions have traditionally been allied with ideas of the supernatural, and often have been based upon explicit beliefs about it. Today, there are many who hold that nothing worthy of being called religious is possible apart from the supernatural…The opposed group consists of those who think the advance of culture and science has completely discredited the supernatural and with it all religions that were allied with belief in it.

        – John Dewey[1]

You may be surprised—given the remarkable relevance of this observation today—that it was offered nearly a century ago by American psychologist and philosopher John Dewey. Indeed, when it comes to the "Big Questions" of human existence—*How did the universe emerge? Why is there something rather than nothing? Is there a meaning or purpose to our lives? How can we live a good and moral life?*—we continue to sense an unbridgeable chasm between those who find their answers in religion and those who are indifferent or even hostile to it. This seems surprising given the deep roots of religion in human history and its continued importance for so many people.

Indeed, from prehistoric times until today, we see ample evidence of the incalculable amount of time and energy expended on religion. Think of the plethora of diverse religious rituals and practices across history and cultures. The centuries of inspirational religious art and music. The multitude of magnificent monoliths, earthworks, cathedrals, mega-churches, temples, and mosques. Unknown numbers of people have sacrificed and been martyred for their religious beliefs. Countless words have been written in sacred texts and commentaries. Centuries have been spent debating the fine points of theology. Religious beliefs and institutions have been

1

deeply ingrained in societies, becoming central to our cultural and personal identities. Religion has provided a framework for understanding the world, consolation during trying times, a sense of meaning in life, and a guide to moral and ethical behavior.

Given these observations, it might seem inconceivable that anyone would question the validity of religious truths or argue that religion is not essential for human well-being. *Is it possible that so many well-meaning, dedicated, and faithful people across human history have been wrong or deluded?*

At the same time, skepticism about religion has existed among a minority of individuals throughout history and has accelerated since the Renaissance and Enlightenment. Today, many critics find religion to be irrational, divisive, and a contributor to violence. For many thoughtful people, the prevalence of suffering and evil calls into question the existence of a benevolent, all-powerful God, as does God's apparent absence or silence. The evolution of religious forms over the millennia in apparent response to changes in ecology and social organization suggests that religions and their gods are human-made rather than a reflection of a divine reality. The diversity of religions also calls into question the truth claims of any particular one. Although religion addresses important psychological needs, economic and psychological well-being are actually greater in the *least* religious nations. As a result, increasing numbers of people, at least in some parts of the world, are now pursuing secular lives without religion, while still finding a sense of meaning and fulfillment.

Statistics reveal a similarly bifurcated picture. On the one hand, clear majorities of respondents in most countries say that religion, God, and prayer play an important role in their lives.[2] Substantial majorities of Americans say they pray to God and believe their prayers are answered.[3] Concomitant with these high levels of religiosity is widespread rejection of key scientific findings such as the general consensus regarding human evolution. Indeed, the proportion of Americans who accept the biblical account of creation has ranged from about 40-50% for years.

On the other hand, although the percentage of Americans self-identifying as atheist or agnostic remains small—perhaps about 10-12%—more than one in four Americans report being unaffiliated with any religion. Indeed, these percentages have been growing.[4] In 2017 survey data, 44% of Americans said they receive no guidance from religion, about one-third do not attend religious services, 20% said they were unsure about the existence of God, and 19% reported that they never pray.[5] The prevalence of nonreligiosity is even greater in many European countries and in Canada and Australia, where from 20-40% of people no longer believe in God or any sort of spirit or life force.[6] As of 2019 in Europe, survey estimates put the percentages of self-identified atheists and agnostics at 10% and 17%, respectively, with much higher percentages in countries such as the Czech Republic, France, Sweden, and the Netherlands.[7]

In short, although worldwide a majority of people describe themselves as religious, a significant minority identify themselves as nonreligious or atheist.[8]

Scholars have pointed to the "cross-pressures," "unstable equilibrium," or "polarization" produced by the expanding gap between religious and secular belief systems. Religious believers are exposed to the growing prevalence of disbelief and perceived threats to their traditional values and standing in society.[9] Within religion itself, tensions and conflicts are percolating between more liberal and conservative communities and believers.[10] Secularists can feel threatened by the intrusion of religion into the public sphere or their personal space. In some cases, they may experience doubts about their disbelief or nostalgia for religion.

In sum, as the writer Paul Elie observed, both believers and nonbelievers are confronted with the same predicament: Whereas religious belief once followed from membership in a particular group or society, the burden of choice—whether to believe or disbelieve—is now back on the individual, where Elie thinks it belongs.[11]

GOALS OF THE BOOK

My work on this book was motivated by this religious-secular gap; the associated cross-pressures and conflicts; my long-standing interest in questions of meaning, values, culture, and worldviews; and my background as a psychologist.

First, to the extent possible, I sought to draw on the psychological and social sciences to address the relative merits and viability of the religious and secular humanist life stances as they relate to the well-being of individuals and societies. Second, I sought to offer some evidence–based proposals to improve the well-being of individuals and societies, while reducing religious-secular conflict. To achieve these goals in a reasonably objective and persuasive manner, it was important to base my analysis and conclusions on a broad, non-polemic, and well-documented synthesis of relevant research on religion and secularity. At the same time, I sought to present relevant thinking and evidence in a way that would be accessible to inquisitive and reflective lay people.

As a psychologist, I do not focus on theological or philosophical arguments for or against religion or secular humanism, although the views of a number of theologians and philosophers are referred to in the book. Instead, my focus is more limited. Given the apparent inability of *either* science or theology to offer definitive evidence for the existence or non-existence of gods, spirits, or other supernatural phenomena, my focus is on a more pragmatic or "down-to-earth" question: *What can the psychological and social sciences tell us regarding the relative merits and viability of religion versus secular humanism with respect to the well-being of individuals and societies?*

At the turn of the 20th century, American philosopher and psychologist William James endorsed such a pragmatic approach. He observed that religion can be judged, not solely by its origins or truthfulness, but by its moral helpfulness, its productiveness in practice, or by "*the way in which it works on the whole.*" In his view, we must all be ready "to judge the reli-

4

gious life by its results exclusively."[12] Similarly, for Dutch-American primatologist Frans de Waal—who views religion as human-made rather than
divinely inspired—the most relevant questions are "What good does religion do for us?" and "What might possibly take its place?"[13] Even the
prominent Catholic theologian Hans Küng argued that a general criterion
for evaluating whether a religion is true or good is the extent to which it
facilitates a meaningful and fruitful existence.[14] In this book, I contend
that the psychological and social sciences can help us answer these pragmatic questions.

CAN SCIENCE STUDY RELIGION?

Historically, and continuing today, religion and science have often been
viewed as conflicting, or, alternatively, as separate spheres of human concern that address different phenomena.[15] From the separate-spheres perspective—which many scholars refute as overly simplistic—science addresses the natural world, physical facts about the universe, or the way the
world "is." In contrast, religion addresses morality and ethics, meaning and
values, spiritual matters, or how the world "ought to be."[16]

Certainly, there are differences between religion and science in the usual methods used to obtain knowledge. Many theologians argue that religious beliefs are rational, warranted, or justifiable by reason.[17] Nonetheless,
religious propositions are frequently accepted based largely on faith, scripture, subjective experience, or religious authorities. Key religious claims
such as the existence of God cannot be directly tested, proved, or falsified
empirically. In contrast, scientific hypotheses or predictions are more readily tested, and research findings can be replicated using systematic observations and experiments. Scientific conclusions are also more susceptible to
revision or refinement based on additional evidence. In contrast, although
various religious doctrines have been elaborated, reinterpreted, or changed
by religious authorities over time, historically such changes have occurred
slowly. Indeed, religious doctrines are often viewed by adherents as unchanging or eternal truths.

5

One potential source of confusion among lay people in evaluating the contributions of science is that scientists and lay people understand the term "theory" in different ways. For many lay people, a theory suggests a possibly unsubstantiated idea, hypothesis, or speculation. In contrast, for scientists a theory typically summarizes or organizes propositions with a degree of empirical support and consensus as a result of replicated scientific tests. Thus, for example, the theory of evolution—which is anathema to some religious people—is widely accepted by scientists, rather than referring to unsupported speculations.

Unlike most religions, science is committed to *naturalism*, the view that the regularities or laws of nature can be revealed through empirical study without reference to gods, spirits, or other supernatural phenomena. Theologians sometimes counter that scientific evidence—because of this *methodological naturalism*—is therefore "radically incomplete" because it fails to take into account divine action and gives inadequate consideration to religious experience as a valid source of knowledge. Indeed, critics sometimes warn scientists about the dangers of *scientism*, that is, the view that science is the ultimate or only standard for knowledge. With this criticism in mind, I acknowledge that it is conceivable—although I believe unlikely—that ultimate reality includes a dimension of "depth" or "mystery" that is beyond the ability of science to detect or investigate.

In any case, as will be evident throughout this book, differences in typical epistemology (i.e., how we obtain knowledge) and methodology between religion and science do not preclude the ability of science to study many aspects of religious behavior. Psychologists and social scientists investigate the behavior of individuals, groups, and societies, and *this can include religious behavior*. Even some Christian psychologists argue that psychological science, if applied properly, can be used to learn more about God and His ongoing creation.[18] This perspective echoes the view of scientists who contributed to the field of *natural theology* during the 17th to 19th centuries, which sought to use investigations of nature to support the existence and attributes of God and the world He created. Today, a number of psychologists, theologians, and organizations continue to promote mutual engagement and sharing of insights between science and religion as equal and complementary partners. The goal? To attain a more complete or enriched understanding of human experience and the universe.[19]

In sum, like many of these scholars, I assume that science can study many aspects of religious behavior, as well as religion's impact on the well-being of individuals and societies. I also make the following assumption: Although scientific research cannot definitively address the *actual* truth status of many religious claims, such research may have an impact on the *perceived* origins, functions, validity, utility, and persistence of religion, and the viability or even preferability of an alternative secular humanistic stance, at least for some individuals.

My analysis in the book has some potential limitations. As already noted, one of the strengths of science is its use of ongoing observation, experiment, and measurement—rather than faith or authority—to derive empirical knowledge. However, this strength of science also introduces some of its challenges. You may observe that the scientific findings reported in this book are not always definitive and sometimes involve complexities or qualifications. Researchers sometimes disagree on the validity of scientific propositions. Also, science, like religion, is not immune from confirmation biases. Scientific conclusions may also evolve over time as findings accumulate and more refined questions are addressed.

These limitations provide an opening for critics who wish to discount the evidence I report or even the ability of science to address the questions I raise about religion and secular humanism. For these reasons, when available, I give greater weight to the results of reviews and *meta-analyses*, which aggregate the results of a large number of studies on a given topic, as well as research findings that have emerged most consistently across studies.

Finally, the perceived persuasiveness of my analysis will likely depend to some extent on one's existing worldview or belief system. My analysis and conclusions are likely to be most persuasive to readers who are open to scientific perspectives and secular values. In contrast, some readers with firm religious convictions, or readers who are skeptical about the value or capacities of science, may view my analysis as incomplete, "reductionist," or misguided. Nonetheless, even for individuals with varying levels of religious commitment, being exposed to naturalistic (vs. supernatural) perspectives on the origins and functions of religion—and scientific findings relating religion and secular humanism to individual and societal well-being—may stimulate reflection regarding the relative merits and viability of these alternative life stances.

I am hopeful that both believers *and* nonbelievers will find the research findings of interest—whether or not their perspective is altered. Certainly, by reading the book, you will get a good sense of the kinds of research that is being conducted on religion and secularity by psychologists and social scientists. If you are a believer, thank you for your openness in engaging with this topic. If you are a nonbeliever or secular humanist, you will be exposed to information on the pros and cons of having adopted such a life stance. For both believers and nonbelievers, an increase in intellectual humility regarding your chosen life stance would be an additional desirable outcome.[20]

DEFINING RELIGION AND SECULAR HUMANISM

It is challenging to define religion in a way that is applicable to religions with gods, religions that lack gods but incorporate alternative supernatural phenomena such as karma and reincarnation, and tribal or "primitive" religions that endorse beliefs in animistic spirits or ancestor worship. No single definition is likely to please everyone. English anthropologist Edward Tylor presented a "minimum definition" as "the belief in Spiritual Beings."[21] However, this definition focuses exclusively on the intellectual or cognitive aspects of religion. French sociologist Émile Durkheim offered a functional definition: "*a religion is a unified system of beliefs and practices relative to sacred things, that is to say, things set apart and surrounded by prohibitions—beliefs and practices that unite its adherents in a single moral community.*"[22] More recently, sociologist Isabella Kasselstrand and colleagues

8

defined religion as *"the amalgamation of ideas, rituals, practices, symbols, identities, and institutions that humans collectively construct based upon their shared belief in the supernatural."*[23]

It is perhaps easier to describe typical elements of religion, which include belief in a supernatural, spiritual, or nonmaterial realm and our relation to it; narratives, myths, or doctrines that elaborate these beliefs; rituals and practices that enact beliefs and contribute to communal bonding; and feelings or experiences that connect one to whatever one views as sacred. Religions may also include moral and ethical prescriptions for behavior; institutions that teach or nurture religious beliefs, practices, and communities (e.g., the church); explanations or accounts of the natural world; and belief in some form of afterlife. These diverse components can be subsumed under four aspects of religion delineated by psychologist Vassilis Saroglou—believing, bonding, behaving, and belonging—which correspond, respectively, to four kinds of psychological needs or functions satisfied by religion: cognitive, emotional, moral, and social.[24]

Despite the definitional challenges, most readers, drawing on their own experiences, will have some conception of what religion typically encompasses. You may be less familiar with how secular humanists define their life stance.

The organization Humanists International offers a "minimum statement on Humanism" that provides a useful starting point for any discussion of secular humanism.

> Humanism is a democratic and ethical life stance, which affirms that human beings have the right and responsibility to give meaning and shape to their own lives. It stands for the building of a more humane society through an ethic based on human and other natural values in the spirit of reason and free inquiry through human capabilities. It is not theistic, and it does not accept supernatural views of reality.[25]

Humanists (at least of the secular variety; see below) endorse a naturalistic worldview that rejects—or is at least highly skeptical of—the existence of supernatural phenomena that transcend ordinary experience such as gods, spirits, karma, or reincarnation. This naturalistic worldview includes acceptance of the reality of our mortality, disbelief in an afterlife, and a focus on the pursuit of human fulfillment in the one lifetime we have. For many if not most secular humanists, the pursuit of personal fulfillment involves the pursuit of personal goals and caring relationships that provide a sense of purpose and happiness; activities and ideals that benefit society; and the valuing and enjoyment of literature, music, and art, which can provide an important source of creativity, as well as aesthetic and emotional experience.[26]

Another core aspect of humanism is ethical principles that are based— not on divine authority as promulgated by religious texts, doctrines, or leaders—but on human needs, values, and experiences; our moral instincts as social animals; and reasoning about the likely consequences of our behavior for people and society. Humanistic ethical principles recognize the inherent worth and dignity of *all* human beings and the right of all people to pursue a life of personal fulfillment through their free and autonomous choices, consonant with an appropriate level of responsibility towards others, society, and the environment. As the British humanist Jim Herrick noted:

> Although humanists do not have a written set of moral rules, and do not believe in absolute good or evil, they are very conscious of an ethical dimension to life. They have principles to guide them and ideals to aspire towards.[27]

Indeed, in lieu of Christianity's Ten Commandments, the American Humanist Association's Center for Education has offered Ten Commitments. These commitments represent the shared humanistic values of its members and provide a guide for teaching values in America's public schools: altruism, empathy, environmentalism, ethical development, global awareness, humility, peace and social justice, responsibility, and service and participation.[28]

Consistent with their naturalistic worldview, humanists generally view reason and scientific inquiry as the best means to gain reliable knowledge and understanding of the world we live in. This often includes endorsement of cosmological theories regarding the origins of the universe (e.g., Big Bang theory) and acceptance of evolutionary theory as the best explanation for the emergence of life, including human beings. The belief that human flourishing requires a healthy and sustainable environment leads many humanists to be concerned about the quality of the environment.

Because of their concern for the dignity and worth of all people, humanists are typically committed to human diversity, support human rights and civil liberties for all, and favor open and democratic processes and societies. They tend to favor political and economic policies that minimize inequality of resources and opportunity, support freedom of choice and opinion, and contribute to social justice, enabling as many people as possible to enjoy a meaningful and satisfying life. Adequate education, including moral education, is seen as essential in building humane, free, and democratic societies.

Although humanism represents a philosophy of life or worldview, it is not a religion and has no formal creed. Humanists hold a range of views regarding the value of religion. A confrontational minority deplores religion. However, others seek to find common ground with religious groups, and would not support undermining the religious beliefs of others or the persecution of religion. Most support freedom of religion, but also the separation of church and state, and many oppose the provision of special privileges to religious groups.

As a comprehensive, nonreligious life stance, secular humanism is a broader and more affirmative worldview than *atheism*, which is simply a belief in the nonexistence of a God or gods; *agnosticism*, the belief that God's existence or nonexistence is unknowable; *skepticism*, an attitude of questioning or doubt regarding knowledge claims that are based on insufficient evidence; and some of the other terms that have been used to label nonreligious individuals.[29] Humanism, but not atheism alone, provides an alternative to religion as a moral framework.[30]

Some humanists prefer not to add adjective modifiers to the humanist label (e.g., secular humanism, religious humanism, scientific humanism, ethical humanism). For example, some view the distinction between religious humanism and secular humanism as unhelpful, while others view the distinction as crucial.[31] I believe it is important to use the secular humanism label in this book in order to be clear that I am referring to a form of humanism that explicitly rejects the supernatural—rather than a religious form of humanism. In doing so, I am aware that the label has negative connotations for some people. Indeed, as some authors have observed, secular humanism has served as the "whipping boy" for the Religious Right, who blame it for many of the world's problems.[32] It has been branded as "a tool of Satan"[33] or a "great godless conspiracy,"[34] and associated with a "whiff of intellectualism that turns people off."[35] I hope, however, that this book will go some way towards communicating the positive perception and identity associated with secular humanism by its advocates.

Finally, in choosing to address the relative merits and viability of the religious and secular humanist life stances, I focus on two contrasting belief systems that can be viewed as points along a continuum ranging from traditional religion to a wholly secular and naturalistic humanism or atheism. In so doing, I give limited attention to an intermediate "third way" along this continuum, which has been referred to as *secular spirituality*, or in more common parlance, "spiritual but not religious" (SBNR). SBNR is typically used to describe individuals who have abandoned traditional or organized religion, but still seek some form of spiritual or transcendent experience that goes beyond observable reality. Such individuals may retain belief in a higher reality or power, or a spiritual (nonmaterial) core to life, whether or not they believe in a conventional God.

I acknowledge the existence and distinctiveness of the SBNR stance. However, I deemphasize it in the book for several reasons. For one, psychologists and social scientists have investigated the SBNR phenomenon less extensively than they have studied conventional religiosity and seculari-ty.[36] In addition, many scholars have noted that the spiritual ideas adopted by SBNR individuals tend to be diverse and idiosyncratic, even diffuse and vague, and thus unlikely to generate a shared or consensus belief system. For many individuals, the activities associated with alternative spirituali-ties—such as yoga, meditation, and mindfulness exercise—are focused exclusively or primarily on pragmatic goals such as health and well-being, and do not represent an alternative or coherent belief system. In addition, unlike religious traditions, these activities tend not to be socialized in their practitioners' children.[37] Finally, other scholars observe that the longer people stay away from traditional religion, the less spiritual they become, suggesting that the SBNR phenomenon may be an intermediate transition point on the way towards a more fully naturalistic and secular worldview.[38] For these reasons, I focus in this book on secular humanism as potentially offering a more promising, coherent, and consensus alternative to tradi-tional religion, although I do address the SBNR stance in Chapter 9.

OVERVIEW OF THE BOOK

The book is organized into two parts. Part I addresses the origin, func-tions, and outcomes of religion from a naturalistic and scientific perspec-tive. In Chapter 1, I provide an overview of early naturalistic accounts of the origin and functions of religion offered historically by selected philoso-phers and by 19th and early 20th century social scientists. Although their theories were somewhat speculative and based on limited evidence, some of them have been supported by subsequent research. In Chapter 2, I address the question of whether we are biologically prepared for religion by focus-ing primarily on interdisciplinary research associated with the cognitive science of religion. This somewhat controversial area of research posits that humans have evolved specific cognitive mechanisms or capacities that pre-pare us to adopt religious ideas.

In Chapter 3, I address evolutionary change in religious behavior, in-cluding the adaptive role of ritual, and the cognitive, emotional, and ecological factors thought to drive this change, leading eventually to the "moralizing high gods" found in the major monotheistic religions. In Chapter 4, I review evidence for the diverse psychosocial functions of religion.

In Chapter 5, I summarize evidence regarding the beneficial psychosocial outcomes of religion, focusing in particular on whether greater religiosity is associated with better physical health, psychological well-being, and prosocial or moral behavior. In Chapter 6, I address the potential harmful impacts of religion, focusing especially on its potential role in promoting prejudice, intolerance, and violence, as well as its mixed impact during the COVID-19 pandemic.

In Part II of the book, I address secular humanism as an alternative to religion as a life stance or belief system. In Chapter 7, I provide an overview of prominent individuals and themes in the history of humanism and religious skepticism. In Chapter 8, I review evidence addressing the contentious issue of whether the world has become more secular, and, if so, why. In Chapter 9, I describe secular living as an alternative to religion, as well as the diverse forms of personal secularity. In Chapter 10, I ask what psychological research can tell us about how to live a fulfilling and meaningful life with or without religion. I then draw on this evidence to make some inferences about the viability of the secular humanist life stance.

At the start of each chapter, I include a brief abstract in which I highlight the chapter's relevance to the overarching question addressed in the book. I conclude each chapter with a Takeaway section in which I discuss any implications for the relative merits and viability of religion, as compared to a more secular life stance. In the book's Conclusion, I revisit the overarching pragmatic question emphasized in the book: *What can the psychological and social sciences tell us regarding the relative merits and viability of religion versus secular humanism when it comes to the well-being of individuals and societies?* I also offer a number of proposals going forward that research suggests will improve the well-being of individuals and societies while also reducing religious-secular conflict—both inherently valuable goals in their own right. Throughout the text, I use endnotes to cite references or studies that support the points I am making. Some endnotes contain additional details or nuance that may be of interest to some readers. It will be apparent to readers that I view secular humanism as a viable alternative to religion for many people. It will also be apparent that most psychologists and social scientists adopt a naturalistic approach to the origins and functions of religion, so my discussion of this work will naturally reflect this perspective. Nonetheless, when I began my research for the book, I had not drawn any definitive conclusions about whether religion alone, secular humanism alone, or some combination of the two was a more likely or desirable future outcome. I was hopeful that my investigation would make possible some conclusions in this regard.

Part I

Religion from a Naturalistic and Scientific Perspective

Chapter 1
Origin and Functions of Religion: Early Naturalistic Accounts

Naturalistic accounts of religion attempt to explain its origins and functions without recourse to gods, spirits, or other supernatural phenomena. To the extent that naturalistic explanations are credible or persuasive they may impact readers' views regarding the cogency of religious versus secular belief systems.

> One [hypothesis] is that these [supernatural] entities really exist only through the human conceptions of them. They are social constructs, corresponding in some way to reactions in social organization. God, then, exists as a human idea, presumably fulfilling some conceptual and emotional needs of man, but without separate existence as an exterior entity. Such is the humanistic view—and one to which all the evidence if rationally considered would seem inevitably to lead.
>
> – Raymond Firth[1]

Is it possible to make definitive conclusions about the origins of religion? Perhaps not, given the vast and largely undocumented history of the human species. That said, religious or proto-religious beliefs and practices likely existed in some form in even the earliest humans and remain an aspect of culture in all societies.

Of course, theological explanations of the origins of religion can be offered. For example, in the Abrahamic traditions of Christianity, Judaism, and Islam, religious experience is attributed to the reality of a transcendent God, who reveals Himself through prophets, the holy word, and other

19

manifestations of the sacred, including personal (e.g., mystical, conversion) experiences. God may also have implanted in humans a *sensus divinitatis* (sense of the divine) and an innate capacity or longing to seek or be "grasped by" a transcendent God.[2]

In contrast to the perspectives of traditional revealed religion, early philosophers—and in recent centuries social scientists—have proposed naturalistic explanations of the origin and functions of religion that could replace divine accounts. I invite you to consider whether aspects of these naturalistic accounts ring true.

Naturalistic accounts of the origins of religion emerged as early as 2400 years ago when the Greek mythographer Euhemerus (330-260 BCE) proposed that "the gods were simply outstanding historical persons who began to be worshipped after their death."[3] Some classical Stoic philosophers contended that the gods were simply personifications of the sky, sea, or other natural forces.[4] For philosophers and writers in the 16th to 19th centuries it was common to attribute the origins of religion in early humans to people's fears and uncertainties regarding the unknown, their ignorance of the natural causes of powerful natural phenomena, and their tendency to personify and animate nature, giving birth to spirits and gods.

For example, the Scottish philosopher David Hume (1711-1776) was pivotal in the historical turn from a theological to a scientific and naturalistic perspective in the study of religion. Hume did not believe it was possible to discern the actual beginnings of religion. However, he attributed the first religious ideas to humans' concerns and anxieties regarding the events of life and future outcomes, their ignorance of the causes of events, and the resulting propensity to turn to invisible powers with human-like qualities. For Hume, the human imagination created the gods rather than the other way around. Thus, religion could be explained within the purview of a science of man.[5]

German linguist Max Müller (1823-1900) was a prominent advocate of the *naturism* or nature-myth theory of religion's origins—which was predominant in Germany during the 19th century. According to this approach, the gods of antiquity represented the personification of powerful and mysterious natural phenomena such as the sun, moon, stars, and mighty rivers that would have aroused strong emotional responses, and served as symbols of the infinite.[6]

Alternatively, English sociologist Herbert Spencer (1820-1903) proposed that ancestor worship was the root of all religions and that the ghosts of ancestors or other superior persons, who appeared as the dead in dreams, became the first supernatural beings. In Spencer's view, which became known as Ghost Theory, "primitive" people believed that all things were inhabited by a sort of phantom or spirit that appears in dreams and becomes permanently detached from the person or thing at death.[7]

Other prominent figures such as Auguste Comte (1798-1857), French philosopher and founder of sociology, attributed the universal emergence of religion to its social functions, particularly its binding moral force. Comte proposed an evolutionary theory of human intellect that proceeded through three stages. During the earliest theological or "fictitious" stage, the mysterious forces of nature are personified as supernatural agents. This stage proceeds through substages of fetishism, polytheism, and monotheism. During a transitional metaphysical stage, the gods are replaced through speculative reasoning about abstract transcendental entities and causes. During a final scientific or "positive" stage, nature and society are understood to be governed by impersonal laws identifiable through science.

Based on Comte's stages, religion should have been left behind with the advancement of science. However, because religion performs indispensable functions in creating moral communities, Comte argued that a new unifying system would be needed as a replacement. Comte believed that a replacement based on science would lack sufficient emotional appeal. Instead, Comte's proposal was to replace traditional religion with a form of humanism, in which we attach our affections to humanity itself as a center of sympathy, mastery, and moral purpose.[8]

21

Some early scholars were less interested in how religion *originated* in human history, and more interested in the related but distinct question of *functions*. For example, when discussing primitive societies, early scholars such as Polish anthropologist Bronislaw Malinowski (1884-1942), English anthropologist Alfred Radcliffe-Brown (1881-1955), American sociologist Talcott Parsons, and Romanian historian of religion (and professor at the University of Chicago) Mircea Eliade (1907-1986) highlighted the emotional and social functions of religion, with rituals playing a central role.[9]

For example, drawing on his work in the Trobriand Islands in Melanesia, Malinowski proposed that religion and its rituals emerged to help primitive peoples cope with the fears, anxieties, and shaken group morale associated with various life crises, especially death. Religion also helped to communicate and maintain traditions that were crucial for the continued cohesion and survival of society. Similarly, Radcliffe-Brown (1881-1955) opined that many religious beliefs and myths are erroneous—and vague and variable in primitive people's minds. However, the social function of religious rituals is central in maintaining group solidarity and continuity.

Better known to most of us are the views of Karl Marx (1818-1883), the German philosopher, economist, and sociologist. He saw religion as persisting because it addresses the emotional needs of people who are alienated and distressed by their economic situation in capitalist societies—thus, his famous depiction of religion as the "opium of the people." In Marx's view, real rather than illusory happiness would be experienced as religion withered away on its own once the capitalist system was overturned through revolution.[10]

Finally, anthropologist Raymond Firth (1901-2002) offered a rather comprehensive early perspective on religion as a projection of the most fundamental human needs and problems.

[Religion] is then seen as a symbolic product of human desires in a social *milieu*. A religious system represents one way of obtaining a framework for handling fundamental problems of social organization—for reducing uncertainly and anxiety, for increasing coherence in human relationships, for assigning meaning to human endeavor, for providing justification for moral obligation. On this rest its power and its capacity for continued adaptation and re-creation.[11]

In Firth's view, empirical evidence argued against the existence of gods. However, he also believed that human societies could not exist "without some forms of symbolic solutions which rest on non-empirical foundations."[12]

I could mention other early scholars—and will do so in a brief history of humanism and religious skepticism in Chapter 7. However, these prominent examples suffice to highlight several points.

First, we see recurring themes in the proposed naturalistic origins of religion—from the early Greek to 19th century philosophers. Religion has been attributed to early humans' anxieties and fears, lack of knowledge, and tendency to personify unexplained natural phenomena, as well as the utility of religion in enforcing social or moral norms. Second, early writers—while offering naturalistic perspectives for so-called primitive religions—were able to retain their own (generally Christian) religious beliefs by exempting the Judeo-Christian tradition from their naturalistic accounts or by adopting the view that primitive forms of religion would eventually progress to modern (i.e., Judeo-Christian) religion under the guidance of divine providence.[13]

Third, early writers such as French political philosopher Jean Bodin (1530-1596) recognized a salient intellectual problem regarding religious claims *that persists today*. Writing in the context of the Protestant Reformation, the religious wars of the 16th century, and the discovery of new religions outside Christianity, Bodin observed that the contradictory claims made by rival religions raised questions about the truth of any particularly one.[14]

23

Finally, in the writings of early scholars we get a glimpse of another debate that continues today. Some viewed religion as irrational and false and thus best abandoned (e.g., Hume, Marx). Some acknowledged religion's faults while advocating the value of its persistence (e.g., Bodin, Herbert, Radcliffe-Brown, Firth). And still others sought a more humanistic or scientific replacement (e.g., Comte).

Naturalistic theories regarding the origins of religion were also offered by early social scientists. In the following, I provide a brief overview of some of the most influential approaches.

TYLOR'S ANIMISM: AN "INTELLECTUALIST" APPROACH

The self-educated Englishman Edward Burnett Tylor (1832-1917) proposed the most prominent early theory of the origins of religion in his two-volume *Primitive Culture* (1871), the first detailed anthropological study of religion. Drawing on his travels and available ethnographic evidence, Tylor proposed that the origins of religion are found in *animism*—the tendency for humans to attribute souls, spirits, or personal powers to all things animate and inanimate. Tylor argued that early humans' experiences with dreams, visions, and death would have led them—or at least some early "savage philosophers"—to believe in an immaterial entity, spirit, or personal soul (i.e., "phantom").[15] Since these spirits or souls can be distinguished from the animate or inanimate objects they inhabit, the idea that pure spirits and eventually supreme gods exist would follow in time. In the cultural evolution of religion, Tylor proposed a three-stage model of religion, with animism coming first, followed by polytheism and eventually monotheism.[16]

Some scholars have found Tylor's account plausible. Others have criticized it. What didn't they like? First, his predominant "intellectual" focus on beliefs in spiritual beings at the expense of religion's emotional aspects. Second, his dualistic distinction between body and soul. Some primitive religions involve powerful entities or forces *without* spirits or souls. Finally, they especially criticized his stage model, which, like other evolutionary

24

models of his time, attributed a pre-logical, irrational, and child-like state of mind to traditional or primitive peoples, while implying the superiority of the Western European mind.[17] Even so, as we will see below, there is solid evidence for the role of animism in many traditional peoples.

PRIMITIVE MONOTHEISM?

Was monotheism present among traditional or primitive peoples? If so, it would be more consistent with biblical accounts. Some early scholars thought the answer was yes.

For example, in 1898, Andrew Lang (1844-1912), a Scottish writer and contributor to anthropology, published *The Making of Religion*, in which he pointed to the apparent presence of a Supreme Being in such primitive tribes as Bushmen, Andamanese, Fuegians, and Australians. This led him to conclude that religion probably got its start "in a kind of Theism."[18] Theism refers to belief in a god or gods, particularly a creator god that intervenes in the universe He created and the lives of its inhabitants.

Similarly, Wilhelm Schmidt (1868-1954), an Austrian linguist, Jesuit scholar, and Roman Catholic priest, argued that a number of existing tribes had a Supreme Being with a monotheistic character and names such as "father," "creator," "sky," and "the old one above." To Schmidt, this implied the existence of monotheism in primitive cultures. Schmidt attributed the purported existence of similar High Gods across diverse primitive groups to a "universal revelation" by God at the dawn of humanity.[19]

Both Lang and Schmidt believed that this original monotheism deteriorated or was obscured by several factors: the differentiation of additional gods across history, the emergence of more human and contemptible traits for the gods, and the worship of ancestral ghosts that interacted more directly with people, among other causes.[20]

Importantly, however, most anthropologists reject the notion that monotheism was an original or early form of religion. The so-called Supreme Beings, High Gods, or "powerful persons" sometimes seen in primitive religions lack the defining characteristics of the God worshipped in modern monotheistic religions, such as omnipotence, omniscience, and moral concerns. Also, even when present in primitive religions, the Supreme Beings typically represent just one of many gods.[21] Indeed, historian of religion Raffaele Pettazzoni argued that the only truly monotheistic religions—Judaism, Christianity, Islam, and Zoroastrianism—all emerged out of polytheistic environments as the result of a reforming prophet—Moses, Jesus, Mohammed, and Zarathustra, respectively.[22]

PRE-ANIMISM AND *MANA*

The British ethnologist R. R. Marett (1866-1943) argued that the first chapter in the origins of religion is largely indecipherable. He also believed that a minimum definition of religion needed to go beyond Tylor's animism theory—with its predominant focus on belief in spirits or souls. Marett offered two reasons for this.

First, more rudimentary forms of magic or religion—involving the attachment of an animating power or force to living and non-animate objects—likely predated the attribution of spirits or souls to such objects.[23] Second, religion involves more than beliefs and ideas. The emotional side of religion, particularly a sense of awe, is central and may be manifested even when religious ideas are vague.[24] Marett believed that the concept of *mana* captured the sense of awe associated with impersonal supernatural powers and forces.[25]

Widespread interest in *mana* towards the end of the 19th century was stimulated by the influential work of the Anglican missionary-anthropologist Robert Henry Codrington, who described *mana* as an elementary religious concept of Melanesians. Codrington concluded that the word *mana* was common throughout the Pacific and that it referred to a universal, spiritual power that attaches itself to persons and things.[26] The geographical distribution of the *mana* concept has been debated. However, comparable terms have been found in many Oceanic languages and some scholars have linked *mana* to terms in Papuan and Austronesian languages beyond Oceania.[27] Analogous concepts have also been attributed to certain

Native American tribes—for example, Algonquin *manitou*, Siouan *wakan*, Iroquois *Orenda*.

A number of 20th century anthropologists, however, questioned Codrington's and Marett's interpretation of *mana* as a spiritual force, power, or medium that attaches itself to persons or things. Rather, such metaphysical interpretations may have reflected the theoretical abstractions of anthropologists more than the native meaning and use of the terms. For example, based on fieldwork among the Tikopia people, New Zealand ethnologist Raymond Firth noted the pragmatic rather than metaphysical use of the *mana* or *manu* concept to describe effective people and things (e.g., "the chief is *manu*," "my uncle, great is his *mana*," "the *manu* canoe").[28] Similarly, in an influential article titled "Rethinking *Mana*," anthropologist Roger Keesing concluded that *mana* refers not to a spiritual substance or power but to the efficacy, potency, or success of human efforts and things. In primitive Pacific societies, humans—hopefully assisted by gods and spirits—contribute to outcomes and only successful outcomes are described as *mana*.[29]

In sum, the idea of *mana* as a supernatural force or power may have played a role in early forms of religion or proto-religion in some societies—particularly in Oceania. Although anthropologists have lamented the concept's diverse meanings across time and contexts, there appears to be some similarity, if not a definitive theme, in the diverse meanings that have been offered for *mana*. *Mana* refers to efficacy, success, vitality, power, generative potency, or force—whether supernatural or not.

Finally, it is noteworthy that mainstream anthropology has continued to address *mana*. However, interest in the concept has lacked the field-defining prominence that characterized the late 19th century and first half of the 20th century.[30]

DURKHEIM'S TOTEMISM: A SOCIAL-FUNCTIONAL APPROACH

Sociologists tend to emphasize the collective experiences and social functions associated with religion. Among early theorists, the French sociologist

27

Émile Durkheim (1858-1917) established this approach in his book titled *Elementary Forms of the Religious Life*. Durkheim dismissed the idea that we could ever identify "the absolute first beginning" of religion.[31] However, he drew on available accounts of aboriginal Australian tribes, augmented by accounts of native tribes in North America, to conclude that *totemism* is the oldest and most elementary form of religion. Indeed, in his view, totemism is more primitive than animism or naturism.[32]

In totemism, the tribal clan, and thus each of its members, is represented by a particular totem, most often an animal or plant. This totem comes to symbolize both the clan and the sacred or divine force or energy experienced by the clan, particularly during periodic assemblies and "effervescent" rituals. Because the totem symbolizes both "god" (however this force or power is defined) and the clan itself, Durkheim believed that worship of the totem is essentially the same as worshipping the clan, which, importantly, serves to reinforce commitment to the clan and social cohesion.[33] Durkheim contended that many of the myths and beliefs associated with religions are superstitious or erroneous. However, such beliefs are secondary to the communal rituals that comprise the essence of religion and account for its historical persistence.

Durkheim's work was considered the most comprehensive effort regarding the origins of religion since Tylor's contribution and a number of scholars have pointed to the insightful and creative nature of the theory. At the same time, significant criticisms have been offered. Perhaps foremost was criticism of Durkheim's limited database. Durkheim based his theory largely on accounts of aboriginal religion in Australia, whose accuracy and generalizability, particularly for ancient conditions, has been questioned. Some cultural groups with religious beliefs and practices place little, if any, emphasis on totems.[34]

Perhaps the most thorough critique of the totemic hypothesis came from the French anthropologist Claude Lévi-Strauss (1908-2009). In his book *Totemism*, Lévi-Strauss traced the rapid early expansion of the totemic hypothesis in ethnology and the history of religion, followed by its subsequent "demolition" by the 1940s.[35] His main criticism involved the diverse and inconsistent forms that totemism exhibits, even in tribal groups with fairly similar social organizations.[36]

In sum, it is clear that some primitive clans or tribes have linked themselves with particular animals, plants, and associated emblems. However, anthropologists have struggled for decades to understand the diverse features of totemism and the extent to which it represents a unitary or coherent elementary form of religious life as proposed by Durkheim.

Might a psychological perspective be more promising?

FREUD'S PSYCHOANALYTIC "WISH-FULFILLMENT" PERSPECTIVE

During the first half of the 20th century, the most prominent psychological theory of the origins of religion was proposed by the Austrian psychoanalyst Sigmund Freud (1856-1939). In *The Future of an Illusion*, Freud argued that religion fulfills one of the oldest and strongest wishes of mankind, the need for protection. Religious belief, he argued, represents a projection onto the external world of a God—who like the father in childhood—can provide security and protection against feelings of helplessness and the inevitable threats and terrors of life, including death. However, just as mature adults should turn away from superstition toward reason, Freud likened religion to an obsessional neurosis involving "a system of wishful illusions together with a disavowal of reality."[37]

The psychoanalytic concepts upon which Freud's theory is based are less widely accepted today, and, in any case, Freud's conception of God as father figure, even if true, would be most directly applicable to monotheism. Monotheism is generally viewed by scientists as a later development in the cultural evolution of religion, rather than an original or early form of religion.

DOES RECENT EVIDENCE OFFER ANY SUPPORT FOR THESE THEORIES?

For most of human history, humans evolved in hunter-gatherer or foraging groups. Thus, I ask here what form religion took in such societies. The ethnographic databases that could help answer this question have limitations. For example, they may underestimate the presence of moralizing gods in less complex, traditional societies.[38] Nonetheless, anthropological studies that draw on these databases provide a window into the plausible earliest forms of religion.[39]

Overall, the results of these studies indicate that animism in some form has been ubiquitous among hunter-gatherer societies. This adds plausibility to Tylor's theory that animism is the earliest and most fundamental feature of religion. More recent proposals that shamanism was an early and perhaps universal form or technique of religion are also supported, as the presence of shamanism is closely linked with the emergence of animism.[40]

In shamanism, a spiritual practitioner or shaman, goes into trance to communicate with animistic spirits for the benefit of the clan or social group—primarily for the purpose of healing, but also for protection, success in hunting, ending bad weather, and so forth. Although shamanism did not feature prominently in early origin theories, some scholars view shamanism as a religion per se, and as the basis for all later religious forms.[41]

Ancestor worship also appears to be widespread among indigenous hunter-gatherer groups. However, it is less clear that it represents a starting point for religion, as proposed by Herbert Spencer. The presence of totemism was not directly coded in these cross-cultural studies. Nonetheless, in the view of some scholars, totemism can also be seen as a form of ancestor worship or reverence.[42]

Finally, monotheism is rare in hunter-gatherer societies according to these studies. These results argue against the ideas of Lang and Schmidt about primitive monotheism.

American psychologist Matt Rossano did his own review of relevant archeological evidence, including burial practices and sites, cave art, and clay-baked animal forms. He concluded that animism, shamanism, and ancestor worship were all present by at least the Upper Paleolithic era (about 35,000 years ago). Indeed, Rossano has suggested that the emergence of these religious forms in anatomically modern humans during the period between 100,000 and 60,000 years ago may have provided the additional social cohesion that enabled modern humans to re-emerge from their African homeland and replace all our human ancestors worldwide.[43]

Similarly, evolutionary psychologist Robin Dunbar has concluded that the earliest religions had a strongly animistic form; that ancestor worship, shamans, and belief in an afterlife were added later, possibly as a cluster; and that the "moralizing high gods" of monotheistic religions only appeared after the introduction of agriculture during the Neolithic period.[44]

TAKEAWAYS

So, what are we to make of these early accounts of the origins and functions of religion? Certainly, some limitations can be noted. For example, the various approaches selectively emphasized the cognitive, emotional, or social aspects of religion, while de-emphasizing other aspects. In addition, critics have pointed to the reductionist nature of these accounts. That is, they attempted to explain (or explain away) religion as "nothing but" the result of psychological or sociological phenomena such as fear, anxiety, wish fulfillment, or social utility.

Even early on, anthropologists such as Mircea Eliade, E. E. Evans-Pritchard, and Clifford Geertz argued that religion should be explained on its own terms and from the perspective of the believer. They also expressed skepticism that broad, general statements about religion could be applied to all humanity. More recently, American psychologist Kenneth Pargament has been a consistent critic of attempts to explain away religion as "nothing but" a psychological or social phenomenon.[45] Indeed, Evans-Pritchard questioned whether scholars lacking some religious commitment could derive valid accounts of religion. He observed that most influential social scientists were atheists or agnostics, and may have sought to use their accounts of early religious forms to refute Christianity.

If primitive religion could be explained away as an intellectual aberration, as a mirage induced by emotional stress, or by its social function, it was implied that the higher religions could be discredited and disposed of in the same way.[46]

In any case, much of what was written by early scholars regarding the origins of religion was somewhat speculative. In part, this can be attributed to the fact that most early accounts relied on secondary analyses of ethnographic reports rather than actual fieldwork with primitive peoples. Also important is the question of whether we can draw inferences about the beginnings of religion from observations of traditional peoples that still exist or did so relatively recently.

Even so...

While acknowledging these limitations, we can ask what initial takeaways might be possible from our consideration of early naturalistic perspectives on religion. A thorough consideration of my overarching question—what the psychological and social sciences can tell us about the relative merits and viability of religion versus secular humanism—must wait until later in this book. Nonetheless, to the extent that readers find these early naturalistic explanations credible or persuasive, it may impact their views regarding the cogency of religious versus secular belief systems.

Anthropologists have sometimes struggled to find consensus around such concepts as animism, shamanism, *mana*, ancestor worship, naturism, and totemism. However, it seems clear that each of these phenomena has played a role in the emergence or development of religion in a range of traditional cultures. Early cultural evolutionary models should be treated with caution—particularly when associated with ethnocentric depictions of traditional or indigenous ways of thinking. Nonetheless, comparative studies of religion clearly suggest a probabilistic link between particular forms of religion and the social ecology of the respective societies (e.g., hunter-gatherer, pastoral, agricultural, or large-scale industrial economies).[47]

At least at first glance, this link seems quite consistent with a naturalistic or human-made explanation of religion, with diverse religious forms reflecting the particular needs of evolving humans in their specific socio-ecological environments. I find such an account at least as plausible, and probably more so, than available theological explanations. For example, one theological explanation is that God intentionally tailored the diverse and evolving forms of religion to fit the developing capacities of humans in a process sometimes referred to as *divine accommodation*. A similar account is offered by theologian John F. Haught:

> Theologically interpreted, not only biblical faith but also the long religious journey of our whole species is a series of responses to an invitation to intimacy by the inexhaustible mystery of God. But since no particular imagery can ever capture the fullness and depth of the elusive infinite mystery, humanity's religious search, including that of Christians, is never conclusive. Hence the many births and deaths of gods and goddesses throughout the ages is logically consistent with the quiet but constant presence and invitation of the Infinite.[48]

I suspect that readers may be skeptical about some aspects of the early origin theories. Nonetheless, they contain some plausible elements and, as noted above, they have received some empirical support in recent cross-cultural studies. Their plausibility should also be weighed against the plausibility of the origin stories offered in various sacred scriptures such as the creation story in Genesis, at least when interpreted literally. Although the ideas offered by early naturalistic accounts may seem questionable to some readers, for other readers the same can be said for many of the myths, doctrines, and "mysteries" of modern-day religions.

Furthermore, for many people, the proposed *functions* of religion offered by early philosophers and social scientists probably ring true. The multifaceted functions of religion include helping us to cope with diverse anxieties and insecurities, including the fear of death; contributing to a sense of meaning, purpose, and even awe in our lives; offering aid in accomplishing valued goals; helping us to understand or explain events in the world around us; providing moral guidance; and contributing to social cohesion in society. As you will see in Chapter 4, the early proposals regarding the functions of religion foreshadow the functions investigated and validated by modern psychologists. These functions persist today and raise the question of whether they can be adequately addressed by secular humanistic perspectives. I will discuss this question later in the book.

In any case, concerns about the limitations of early origin theories contributed to a significant pause in such efforts. Indeed, interest in the anthropology of religion—and origins in particular—waned after the First World War and was relatively stagnant through the 1960s.[49] Anthropologists during the latter 19th and early 20th centuries had felt they were living in a momentous time in which religion had been discredited and needed to be explained. Subsequently, however, anthropology moved towards more systematic fieldwork, which was calling into question elements of the early accounts.

Indeed, in 1993, American anthropologist Stewart Guthrie observed a lack of consensus and little optimism regarding naturalistic or humanistic theories of religion.[50] Recently, however, there has been a rebirth of theory and research on the naturalistic foundations of religion, particularly from cognitive and evolutionary perspectives. I take up these efforts in Chapters 2 and 3.

Chapter 2
Are We Biologically Prepared for Religion?

Despite attention in the popular media, there is no evidence for a dedicated "God gene" or "God spot" in the human brain. However, a number of scientists contend that we all have biologically based cognitive capacities or mechanisms that predispose or prepare us to develop beliefs in gods and spirits, souls, and an afterlife. Indeed, some scholars contend that religious beliefs emerged in human history as an accidental *by-product* of these mechanisms, which evolved for other *nonreligious* purposes. If indeed our adoption of religious concepts is a natural and inevitable artifact of our biological endowment, it may—at least for some people—raise questions about the divine nature and truth status of these concepts, but also help to explain religion's persistence.

...belief in gods comes about through the same mental processes as any other beliefs, using the same mental tools.

– Justin Barrett[1]

[M]any of religion's apparently recurrent features—including, for example, belief in supernatural agents and belief in the efficacy of certain kinds of ritual—are rooted firmly in our uniquely human evolutionary history.

– Leon Turner[2]

Does our biology impact our religiosity? Yes and no. On the one hand, people's genes play very little role in the specific religious beliefs or affiliations they adopt. Socialization and cultural learning are more important for that. On the other hand, our genetic make-up *does* impact the extent to which we endorse religious beliefs generally, view religion as important in our lives, and practice our religion, for example, through attendance at religious services.[3]

Thus, our biological make-up *does* influence some aspects of religious experience and behavior. However, rather than doing so directly, our biology is more likely to impact certain personality traits and cognitive tendencies that, in turn, influence our religiosity. I describe the personality traits associated with greater religiosity in Chapter 5. In the present chapter, I discuss the cognitive capacities or mechanisms that some scientists believe prepare us for religion.

The idea that we might be "biologically prepared" or predisposed for religion is a major focus of an interdisciplinary field referred to as the *cognitive science of religion* (CSR). The field emerged in the 1990s, decades after the early philosophical and social science theories reviewed in Chapter 1. Primary contributors include psychologists, cognitive scientists, anthropologists, neuroscientists, and philosophers. Some scholars see the approach as a highly significant development in religious studies. Others point to the field's many unanswered questions and its limitations in explaining the full range of religious phenomena.

For starters, I offer three forewarnings. First, as with other naturalistic approaches, CSR tries to explain religion without recourse to gods or other supernatural phenomena. Second, as noted in the book's introduction, science is a cumulative and ongoing process and simple or definitive answers are not always readily achieved. Third, the propositions offered by CSR scholars will be novel to readers not immersed in the field. This may contribute to skepticism regarding their validity, particularly for religious believers. In this chapter, I provide an overview and critique of this controversial approach, and consider relevant takeaways for the overarching question addressed in the book.

CENTRAL PROPOSITIONS

Let's begin with some of the central propositions of the CSR approach.

- People in all cultures have an innate or early-emerging tendency, or *preparedness,* to develop beliefs in supernatural agents such as gods and spirits.

- These beliefs arise from a variety of "intuitive" cognitive capacities or mechanisms, which are largely unconscious (or preconscious) and automatic.[4]

- The architecture of the human brain consists of a large number of these intuitive mechanisms—sometimes referred to as modules— each with specialized functions. For example, these functions include detecting *intentional agents* in the environment, including humans, gods, and spirits, and attributing to them intentions, beliefs, desires, and minds.

- These intuitive mechanisms account for why certain religious beliefs come naturally to us—for example, beliefs in gods, souls, and an afterlife. However, more conscious, rational, and deliberate (i.e., "reflective") processing is required to comprehend complex theological doctrines such as the Trinity or transubstantiation, which are more difficult to learn and retain.[5]

Many CSR scholars also incorporate an evolutionary component. That is, the proposed cognitive mechanisms—including those that contribute to religious beliefs—are hypothesized to have evolved through a process of *natural selection.* Natural selection refers to a process whereby human traits or capacities are gradually adopted during the evolution of human beings because they provide advantages for human sexual reproduction and survival. This raises the question of whether religion is directly *adaptive* in human evolution or is a *by-product* of other aspects of human development, an important question I turn to next.

RELIGION AS BY-PRODUCT VERSUS ADAPTATION

There is a persistent debate among scholars who study the evolution of religion. Some believe that religious beliefs and rituals emerged as a *by-*

product of evolved capacities or mechanisms that developed for other non-religious purposes. The by-product view is endorsed by many scholars, including CSR researchers, and is my primary focus in the present chapter. Illustrative is the view of Pascal Boyer, who contends that:

> [t]he building of religious concepts requires mental systems and capacities that are there anyway, religious concepts or not. Religious morality uses moral intuitions, religious notions of supernatural agents recruit our intuitions about agency in general, and so on.[6]

Similarly, sociologist Jonathan Turner and colleagues argue that religion emerged in humans as a by-product of the emotional, cognitive, and behavioral capacities that evolved to strengthen social bonds and the stability of human groups.[7]

In contrast, other scholars believe that religion has been *adaptive* in human evolutionary history, meaning that it has contributed directly to the reproductive success and survival of individuals or groups during human evolution. For example, religion could be adaptive for individuals by alleviating daily anxieties and fears of death, thus contributing to more effective daily behavior and, ultimately, greater reproductive success and survival. For groups or societies, religion could be directly adaptive in strengthening collective identity and social cohesion, thus promoting group success or survival.[8]

The multi-faceted nature of religious experience suggests that both by-product and adaptationist accounts may be needed to account for different aspects of religion. In addition, some aspects of religion may have no evolutionary basis whatsoever. I focus on religion as an adaptation in Chapter 3.

Also significant is the distinction between biological and cultural evolution. Certain genes—for example, genes that help to constitute the cognitive mechanisms associated with religious experience—might have been selected for during the evolution of our biological natures, an example of biological evolution. At the same time, certain religious ideas or *memes* might have emerged and persisted during the evolution of cultures because they contributed to the success and survival of particular groups or societies, an example of cultural evolution.[9] For example, some CSR proponents have argued that the emergence of the "big moralizing gods" of modern-day monotheistic religions is a relatively recent phenomenon in human history, eventually emerging to meet the needs of larger, more complex societies via a process of cultural evolution.[10]

Is the by-product versus adaptationist debate really that important? Indeed, it is—not only scientifically, but also from the standpoint of religious polemics. Some critics of religion, in their attempt to discredit it, have jumped on the contention of CSR proponents that religion is merely an accidental by-product of evolved cognitive capacities. In this view, religion has co-opted normal cognitive processes for its own (in critics' view, maladaptive) purposes. For example, evolutionary biologist Richard Dawkins has argued that children's innate cognitive capacity to rapidly acquire essential information from parents also makes them impressionable and vulnerable to uncritical adoption of religious ideas.[11] In any case, however, *neither* by-product *nor* adaptationist accounts can definitively prove or discredit the truth claims of religions.[12]

Having considered some of the central propositions and issues associated with the CSR approach, let's turn now to the specific cognitive mechanisms or capacities thought by CSR scholars to underlie religion—as a by-product of normal cognitive evolution. CSR proponents contend that religion is a result of the combined operation of all such mechanisms.[13]

AGENCY DETECTION

We can probably agree that in the environments of our early human ancestors, failure to detect a potentially dangerous agent—for example, a carnivorous animal, a human enemy, or a malevolent spirit—could have been fatal. Thus, the ability to readily detect agents would have been adaptive—that is, important for survival and sexual reproduction. Indeed, CSR proponents have proposed the existence of an evolved cognitive mechanism for agent detection, which they refer to as a *hyperactive* or *hypersensitive* *agency detection device* (HADD).[14]

In addition, before scientific explanations were available, it was only natural that our human ancestors attributed uncontrollable events to supernatural agents or spirits. This would include natural phenomena such as floods, thunderstorms, and earthquakes; stress-inducing occurrences such as disease, war, and famine; and critical life-cycle events such as births and death. As succinctly claimed by American-French anthropologist Scott Atran:

> In all cultures, supernatural agents are readily conjured up because natural selection has trip-wired cognitive schema for agency detection in the face of uncertainty. Uncertainty is, and likely will always be, ubiquitous. And so, too, the sort of hair-triggering of an agency-detection mechanism that readily lends itself to supernatural interpretation.[15]

There is some empirical support for a hyperactive agency detection device, primarily from laboratory experiments. As predicted, these studies show that people readily detect human agents with goals and intentions when presented with ambiguous visual or auditory information.[16] Indeed, even infants as young as three-months old are sensitive to agent-like movement in visual stimuli.[17] Also, as predicted, there is some modest evidence that religious people show a greater tendency to detect agents than do nonreligious people.[18] However, it is less clear that the tendency to detect agents is "hypersensitive" or greater under more threatening conditions, as CSR proponents expect.[19]

Overall, it should be acknowledged that evidence for the HADD is somewhat limited, despite its centrality in CSR theorizing. In addition, scholars disagree on the importance that HADD plays in the origin of supernatural concepts.[20]

PERCEIVING PURPOSE AND DESIGN

According to CSR proponents, people also have a cognitive predisposition to perceive purpose and design in people, things, and events. For example, we tend to see events as happening for a purpose or reason. Importantly, according to CSR proponents, this natural *purpose-based* thinking (also referred to as *teleological* thinking) contributes to the emergence and plausibility of supernatural agents and creationist beliefs.[21]

For example, natural disasters may be interpreted as God's retribution for societal sins. Personal tragedies may be seen as divine punishment for personal wrongdoing. Even when natural or physical causes of a phenomenon are acknowledged, both children and adults may see them as also having a divine or supernatural purpose. For example, in explaining the transmission of AIDS, Sesotho-speaking South Africans offered natural explanations involving the AIDS virus, but also supernatural, purpose-based explanations involving witchcraft.[22]

A number of research findings support the proposal that purpose-based or teleological thinking is an innate or early-emerging cognitive tendency contributing to religious beliefs. Here are some examples:

- Across diverse cultures, adults with stronger beliefs in God or karma show a greater tendency towards purpose-based thinking regarding natural phenomena and life events.[23]
- Young children prefer purpose-based explanations of natural phenomena and life events (e.g., mountains are "for climbing"; clouds are "for raining") over more accurate physical or naturalistic explanations, although this tendency may begin to moderate around 9 or 10 years old.[24]
- Even adults will incorrectly endorse unwarranted purpose-based explanations, particularly if they have to make judgments quickly or have little formal education.[25]
- Children and adults from both fundamentalist and non-fundamentalist religious communities readily endorse creationist

(God-created) origins for both animate entities (e.g., the sun, animals, and humans) and inanimate entities (e.g., rocks and crystals).[26]

• Experiential factors are also important, however. For example, children's knowledge of natural history increases their likelihood of endorsing evolutionist beliefs, while their degree of religious interest predicts their endorsement of creationist beliefs.[27]

Based on such findings, some CSR researchers have concluded that our tendency to perceived purpose and design in people, things, and events comes naturally to us and is suppressed, but not replaced, as we learn more scientifically-based explanations.[28] Thus, children who hear about a God who designed the world will find this idea sensible and attractive because it accounts for the purpose and design the children naturally perceive in the world.[29]

PERCEIVING THE MINDS OF PEOPLE AND GODS

Your ability to make inferences about the beliefs, desires, and intentions of other people is clearly central to your ability to navigate everyday social life. CSR proponents refer to this evolved ability as mind perception, mentalizing, or "theory of mind." Importantly, they also argue that this mind perception capacity also underlies our ability and propensity to think about the mental states and intentions of supernatural agents such as gods.[30] As succinctly stated by William Gervais:

> [B]elief in gods is not, at a psychological level, fundamentally different from belief in other human minds. Indeed, gods and minds are perceived in predictably similar ways and processed by the same neural mechanisms.[31]

Indeed, research has shown that people in diverse cultures do tend to attribute to God some of the psychological attributes that characterize human minds, such as beliefs, desires, and intentions.[32] In addition, praying and thinking about gods activate the same brain regions that are active during everyday mind-perception tasks.[33]

Several other lines of research are also generally supportive of CSR perspectives relating mind perception to religion. For example:

- Several studies have found that greater mind perception tendencies predict greater belief in a personal God.[34]

- Believers in the supernatural, as compared to religious skeptics, show greater activation in brain circuitries associated with mind perception.[35]

- There is modest, but not entirely consistent, evidence that autistic individuals—who can have difficulty understanding others' mental states—are, on average, less religious than non-autistic individuals (although many autistic individuals are nonetheless religious).[36]

- Emerging evidence, however, suggests that sociocultural factors—not just innate cognitive mechanisms—can impact conceptions of the minds of humans and God.[37]

Our tendency to attribute human-like desires, intentions, and even physical attributes to God—that is, out tendency to *anthropomorphize*—raises a long-held concern that religion is nothing more than a projection of human characteristics and needs onto God.[38] Historically, even theologians have acknowledged this potential danger for religion. Indeed, theologians such as Paul Tillich have sought to rid religion of anthropomorphism—and reverential terms such as Lord and Father—by devising new conceptions of "God" such as Being-Itself, the Ground of Being, the Unconditional, or Ultimate Concern.[39] However, these non-anthropomorphic conceptions of "God" are incomprehensible to most people and do not reflect the personal God that most people worship.

Some researchers have investigated whether religious people do, in fact, tend to anthropomorphize more than nonreligious people.[40] Other studies have asked whether children naturally conceptualize gods as having unique (beyond human) powers and knowledge such as omniscience, or whether children require further cognitive development and cultural learning to do so. Unfortunately, studies on these topics have produced some inconsistent results, perhaps because of the different research methods used across studies.

Overall, however, research indicates that our evolved ability to reason about the mental states of others likely influences our tendency to attribute human-like mental states and intentions to God. At the same time, cultural learning—including religious exposure and teaching—is an important influence on our emerging conceptions of God's special attributes such as omniscience. Finally, it is clear that religious people do, to some extent, differentiate the minds and attributes of humans and God, at least when asked directly. Therefore, conceptions of God are not *solely* based on our anthropomorphizing tendencies.[41]

MIND-BODY DUALISM AND AFTERLIFE BELIEFS

Do you think of your mind or consciousness as distinct from your physical brain or body? Many, if not most, people *do* make this mind-body distinction. That is, they endorse the idea of *mind-body dualism*. CSR scholars have proposed that this intuitive or natural tendency makes it possible for us to imagine souls without bodies—and hence gods, ancestor spirits, and ghosts.[42] A soul or mind separate from the brain also suggests the possibility that the soul can survive after biological death in an afterlife.[43]

Indeed, some research supports the prevalence of beliefs in mind-body dualism and an afterlife, and the hypothesis that more dualistic thinking is associated with greater religiosity. For example:

- Many studies, in a variety of cultures, have found that people are more likely to view mental processes than biological processes as continuing after death, indicating that people think of the mind and physical brain as distinct.[44] Even adults have difficulty thinking about what it would be like after death, without conscious desires or emotions.[45]

- Cross-cultural data suggests that about 80% of societies have afterlife beliefs and in many countries about 80% of people have some form of such beliefs.[46]
- In both religious and nonreligious societies, belief in the distinctiveness of the mind and brain has correlated with adults' belief in God or karma.[47]

On the other hand:

- Several studies indicate that younger children may not differentiate the continuity of biological and mental processes after death.[48] This suggests that dualistic thinking increases with age—a finding that is less consistent with an innate or early emerging tendency toward mind-body dualism.
- The specific form of afterlife beliefs depends on the cultural context.[49] For example, even within the United States, significant differences have been found in the afterlife beliefs associated with different religious subcultures such as evangelical and mainline Presbyterians.[50]
- Both contemporary neuroscience and biblical scholarship argue against the idea of a mind or soul that is distinct from the physical body or brain, despite our intuitive perception that this is the case.[51]

In short, belief in an afterlife and the specific form of such beliefs are likely impacted by ongoing cultural learning and exposure to religious belief systems. That is, afterlife beliefs likely require some cultural scaffolding and are unlikely to be *solely* the result of an innate or early emerging tendency toward mind-body dualism, as proposed by some CSR proponents.

ARE SOME RELIGIOUS CONCEPTS EASIER TO REMEMBER AND TRANSMIT THAN OTHERS?

Yes, according to some CSR theorists. They argue that our evolved cognitive architecture also includes innate or intuitive conceptual categories or templates that reflect our ideas about persons, animals, and natural objects. Importantly, they further propose that the most memorable and therefore transmissible religious concepts are those that are counterintuitive, but only minimally so, because they incorporate an unexpected or surprising element for their common template.[52]

Take, for example, our conceptual template for PERSON, which does *not* typically include special cognitive powers such as omniscience. Thus, the idea of an omniscient God is counterintuitive because it violates our usual template for PERSON. Similarly, the Christian idea of the virgin birth introduces a counterintuitive physiological property for the PERSON template.

Importantly, these so-called *minimally counterintuitive* (MCI) religious concepts are thought to retain all the typical or default inferences that can be made based on the usual template. For example, we are able to draw inferences about God's thoughts and desires—default inferences from our PERSON template—which are augmented by the minimally counterintuitive idea that God is omniscient. In short, CSR proponents offer an explanation for which types of concepts or ideas are most likely to be retained as religious concepts. It is the concepts that are minimally counterintuitive.

But why then is Mickey Mouse not a strong candidate to be a religious concept? After all, Mickey's ability to talk violates only one property of the ANIMAL template and can therefore be considered minimally counterintuitive. CSR scholars counter that, unlike Mickey Mouse, the Christian God and other viable religious concepts also enable potential inferences about important human concerns.[53] For example, omniscient gods are able to observe, judge, and forgive behavior, but Mickey Mouse cannot.

Given the focus of MCI theory on selective retention and transmission of potential religious concepts, relevant studies have largely focused on memory experiments. Although initial studies provided some support that minimally counterintuitive content is better recalled than entirely intuitive or maximally counterintuitive content,[54] subsequent studies have reported inconsistent results. Other factors are likely equally or more important in the recall of particular religious concepts, such as ease of visualization, relevance to existential concerns, and moral or emotional valence.[55] As Theiss Bendixen and Benjamin Purzycki concluded:

> If MCI—however, defined—has some role to play in the cultural evolution of religious beliefs…this effect is in practice often offset or masked by other more important cognitive, social and ecological forces.[56]

In any case, MCI theory only addresses the content features that are hypothesized to make concepts more memorable, "catchy," and transmissible. It fails to explain why we believe in our own particular gods or religious concepts rather than viable candidates from other religions past or present that also seem minimally counterintuitive. For example, most people today no longer believe in Zeus, Baal, Thor, or various ancestral spirits. To solve this so-called "Zeus problem" some CSR scholars point to the importance of cultural learning of the religious concepts present in our own society.[57] A number of other criticisms of MCI theory have been offered and one recent evaluation concluded that "MCI theory's fate remains as unclear as its defining features."[58]

MORAL INTUITIONS

Do our moral intuitions or judgments have a biological basis? Indeed, CSR researchers and moral psychology scholars have proposed that humans have evolved innate or early emerging moral intuitions that are largely automatic and unconscious. These intuitive moral judgments can be contrasted with the slower, reflective, and generally *after-the-fact* moral judgments we subsequently make to explain or support our initial intuitions.[59] For example, American psychologist Jonathan Haidt defined moral intuition as involving the following:

...fast, automatic, and (usually) affect-laden processes in which an evaluative feeling of good-bad or like-dislike (about the actions or character of a person) appears in consciousness without any awareness of having gone through steps of search, weighing evidence or inferring a conclusion.[60]

Haidt postulated the existence of brain systems or modules associated with five different foundations or dimensions of moral concern—harm versus care, fairness/reciprocity, ingroup/loyalty, authority/respect, and purity/sanctity.[61]

One source of support for the evolved biological basis of moral intuitions comes from the observations of primatologists and ethologists, who see the building blocks of human morality in other primates. For example, in chimpanzees and bonobos primatologists have observed such precursors of human moral sentiments as altruism, empathy for others, desires to belong, and hints of community concern.[62] Based on such observations, the eminent Dutch primatologist Frans de Waal concluded that:

> The moral law is not imposed from above or derived from well-reasoned principles; rather, it arises from ingrained values that have been there since the beginning of time. The most fundamental one derives from the survival value of group life. The desire to belong, to get along, to love and be loved, prompts us to do everything in our power to stay on good terms with those on whom we depend. Other social primates share this value and rely on the same filter between emotion and action to reach a mutually agreeable modus vivendi.[63]

In this view, morality did not originate in religion or rational reflection, but emerged from our background as social animals. Thus, religion's primary contribution may be in endorsing and promoting our natural or intuitive moral tendencies. From this perspective, "Morality came first, and modern religion latched onto it."[64] Or, as argued by psychologist Vassillis Saroglou, "religion does not create but orients morality."[65]

The evolved and biologically adaptive nature of moral or prosocial behavior is also widely accepted by evolutionary biologists. They point to a number of inherited mechanisms that can account for altruistic behavior in humans, despite the paradox that unselfish behaviors might seem at first glance to be at odds with one's own survival and reproductive success. These include (a) *kin selection*—whereby altruistic behavior towards genetic relatives may serve to carry on copies of our own genes; (b) *reciprocal altruism*—whereby altruistic behaviors towards non-related people may be reciprocated directly or enhance our own reputation as a cooperative or moral person; (c) the ability to detect "cheaters" or "free-riders" who do not cooperate with group norms; and (d) empathy, which plays an important role in triggering our moral intuitions. The evolved biological nature of moral intuitions does not, of course, preclude an eventual nexus between religion and morality. For example, religious rituals and practices can trigger and channel our moral intuitions.[66]

Additional support for the innate or early emerging nature of moral intuitions comes from research findings such as the following:

- We all have nearly immediate unconscious reactions to stories or scenes depicting moral violations;
- Our initial emotional reactions are generally good predictors of our subsequent, more reflective moral judgments;
- We sometimes sense or intuit that something is morally wrong, even when we are unable to explain why;
- Proto-moral responses such as empathy and altruism are observed even in babies and toddlers.[67]

Of course, a theological interpretation of such findings can be offered. Our innate or early emerging moral intuitions might be seen as originating in humans' intimations or intuitions regarding God's will.[68] Nonetheless, these findings offer a plausible naturalistic account of moral behavior that is rooted in our evolved biology.

ATTACHMENT RELATIONSHIPS WITH GOD

Do we have an innate or early emerging tendency to form an attachment relationship to God (or gods)? Yes, according to some proponents of *attachment theory*.

British child psychiatrist John Bowlby originally proposed the existence of a universal infant-mother attachment system that evolved as a solution to the adaptive problem of protecting vulnerable infants from predators and other dangers in ancestral environments.[69] Subsequently, American psychologist Lee Kirkpatrick proposed that the attachment system is one of the cognitive mechanisms that comprise our evolved psychological architecture. Importantly, Kirkpatrick argues that religion emerged as a *byproduct* of this attachment system, which evolved for the primary purpose of maintaining protective proximity between young children and their caregivers. Kirkpatrick acknowledges that attachment theory is likely to account for only selected aspects of religion. At a minimum, it can explain why people come to perceive of God as an attachment figure who loves us and provides us with a "safe haven" and "secure base."[70]

Another prominent proponent of attachment theory, Swedish psychologist Pehr Granqvist, also views the attachment system as a genetic disposition or evolved property of the human mind. However, Granqvist also emphasizes the important role of sensitive and responsive caregivers in "co-sculpting" the human mind and in guiding our religious and spiritual development.[71]

CSR and attachment theory approaches can be seen as complementary. While the cognitive mechanisms proposed by CSR scholars make the idea of God "cognitively intuitive," attachment theory emphasizes the relational and affective aspects of believers' conceptions of God. I cite support for this "religion-as-attachment" approach in Chapter 4, which addresses the psychological functions of religion.

INTERIM CRITIQUE

I have already noted some unresolved questions and inconsistent findings associated with some of the cognitive mechanisms proposed by CSR proponents. In addition, critics have raised several more general questions, which are also relevant to my assessment of the CSR approach to religion.

First, the intuitive cognitive mechanisms associated with CSR are variously referred to as innate, early developing, or "maturationally natural." The diverse terminology has led to some ambiguity. Are these mechanisms truly innate or "hard-wired" neural structures whose impact on religious behavior is largely independent of social learning or culture? Or, are they more flexible predispositions that prepare us to process religious ideas, assuming normal development and cultural learning?

CSR proponents have varied in their stance. However, there appears to be general movement away from the former genetic-determinism view towards a "maturationally natural" perspective, which unfortunately is still somewhat ambiguous. Helpfully, Tylor Greenway and Justin Barrett have offered a relatively moderate position, contending that "normal development by no means guarantees religious expression." However, "children are naturally inclined toward religion because of how human minds ordinarily develop during childhood."[72]

Second, CSR proponents have acknowledged that there is limited research on the interconnections among the various cognitive mechanisms. For example, how do they work together to impact religiosity? Such research has been increasing. In general, growing evidence suggests that the cognitive mechanisms are somewhat interrelated and can predict beliefs in the supernatural in varying degrees, although some inconsistencies have been observed across cultures.[73]

Third, some scholars contend that human cognitive architecture is comprised of hundreds if not thousands of specific intuitive mechanisms or modules. However, others argue that more general and conscious central processing mechanisms will also be important in religious cognition.[74] Unfortunately, there is a significant complication in discerning the nature and number of cognitive mechanisms or modules in the brain: Brain science has not advanced to the point where scientists can associate specific neural structures with the proposed cognitive mechanisms.

The question of whether specific brain regions or circuits can be linked to religious experience has been central to an area of research labeled the *neuropsychology of religion* or *neurotheology*. Neuropsychologists, using functional neuroimaging, brain stimulation, and lesion-mapping studies, have linked a number of regions of the brain to religious or spiritual activities such as prayer, meditation, and self-described mystical experiences. However, the neural activity observed during these activities has not been shown to be dedicated or *unique* to religious experiences. Rather, the same brain regions or neural circuits are also implicated in cognitions, motivations, and emotions associated with *nonreligious* activities and events. These brain regions are associated with cognitive control, social reasoning, social motivations, and ideological beliefs.

In short, there is no evidence for a dedicated "God spot," "God module" or "God gene" in the brain, despite the attention received in the popular media.

Rather, the same experience can be interpreted differently—for example, as religious or not—depending on one's personal belief system or interpretive framework, or the context of the experience. In any case, no neurological study of religious experience can prove or disapprove the existence or nonexistence of God or an afterlife.[75]

Finally, perhaps the most significant critique of the proposed cognitive mechanisms is their limited ability to provide a full or rich account of religious experience in specific cultural contexts. The cognitive mechanisms may help to explain a universal receptiveness or preparedness to represent and process religious concepts. However, they are not much help in discerning the *specific* beliefs and practices endorsed by individuals in particular cultures. These specific beliefs result from cultural learning, historical circumstances, and more reflective or conscious processing.[76]

Then How Do We Learn and Adopt Particular Religion Beliefs?

Indeed, why do we believe in the particular God or religious ideas that we do, rather than those of the past (e.g., Zeus) or religions other than our own? For the reflective layperson the answer may seem obvious. People are more likely to believe in those supernatural agents and religious doctrines to which they have been exposed in their learning and cultural environments. Indeed, it is most typical for us to adopt the religious beliefs of our families and surrounding communities.[77]

CSR theorists have proposed a number of cultural learning mechanisms, or so-called *context-based biases,* that explain how we come to believe in particular religious concepts. We tend to adopt those beliefs, including religious beliefs, that are:

- Passed on from parents and close relatives (i.e., *kin bias*);
- Most prevalent in our immediate surroundings (i.e., *conformist bias*);
- Observed in people who are older, skilled, prestigious, or successful (i.e., *prestige* or *success-based bias*);
- Displayed by people in credible and trustworthy ways—for example, through genuine actions, rather than mere talk. These so-called *credibility-enhancing displays* might involve such signals of religious commitment as frequent attendance at religious services; restrictions on diet, dress, and sexual relations; costly tithes or other contributions to one's religious community; and participation in religious rituals.[78]

Indeed, there is substantial evidence that these learning mechanisms or biases can help explain individual and cultural differences in religiosity. Here are some examples:

- In a study involving 53 countries, both individual and cultural differences in belief versus disbelief in God were predicted by whether or not individuals were raised to believe in God, as well as estimates of the rate of regular church attendance in the respective countries (i.e., exposure to credibility-enhancing displays, plus conformist learning).[79]

- Worldwide survey data showed the following: Of those people who reported receiving a religious upbringing, 84% became religious; of those people raised without religion, less than half became religious.[80]

- Exposure to higher levels of credibility-enhancing displays of religion while growing up predicts greater religiosity and more confident belief in God as an adult.[81]

- Childhood exposure to credibility-enhancing displays of religion has a larger impact on adult religiosity than do the cognitive mechanisms proposed by CSR researchers (e.g., anthropomorphism, mind-body dualism, purpose-based thinking, mind perception, and analytic thinking.)[82]

To sum up...

Such findings refute the contention that little cultural exposure or learning is needed to adopt religious ideas. Innate or maturationally-natural cognitive mechanisms might explain our ability and proneness to mentally represent supernatural agents. However, cultural learning mechanisms better explain our actual endorsement of specific religious beliefs and practices.

Available findings also tend to rebut the claim of some CSR scholars that even atheists have a natural, intuitive, or unconscious tendency to believe in God, which must be intentionally overridden through conscious reasoning.[83] The findings also suggest that religion is not innate or inevitable, even if its persistence may be likely. As evolutionary cultural psychologist Will Gervais and colleagues have concluded:

If a learner grows up around religious models, he is likely to become religious. [In contrast] a learner who grows up around people who do not hold religious beliefs—or people who do not exhibit credibility-enhancing displays of their underlying religious beliefs—will come to not hold religious beliefs, even if some natural intuitions, however weakly or strongly, might enable people to easily mentally represent supernatural agents.[84]

TAKEAWAYS

In the context of this chapter, the following question is most relevant: Do the links between religious beliefs and the cognitive mechanisms and learning processes proposed by CSR scholars have any implications for the truth status or persistence of religious ideas? A "yes" answer would have important implications for the relative merits and viability of religion.

As discussed in this chapter, most CSR scholars contend that religious beliefs emerged in human history as an accidental by-product of innate or "maturationally natural" cognitive mechanisms, which evolved for other nonreligious purposes. If our adoption of religious concepts is indeed a natural and inevitable artifact of our biological endowment, it may—at least for some people—raise questions about the divine nature and truth status of these concepts.

In addressing the above question, I should acknowledge that research on some of the proposed intuitive cognitive mechanisms is not as definitive as one would like. Nonetheless, some of them—for example, mind perception and mind-body dualism—would seem to be a prerequisite for our propensity to attribute thoughts and intentions to God and conceive of a separate soul or afterlife. Certainly, the cognitive mechanisms give us the capacity to represent and reason about supernatural agents and their intentions. In addition, in combination, they do show a modest link to individuals' levels of religiosity. It is less clear, however, that these mechanisms push us towards religious beliefs in the absence of specific cultural learning experiences.

Indeed, CSR scholars appear to be moving away from the idea that religious beliefs require little cultural input. Instead, they are moving towards a more interactionist perspective. This perspective sees the proposed cognitive mechanisms as more flexible predispositions that enable us to process and understand religious ideas, assuming normal development and cultural learning in specific religious contexts. In any case, the intuitive cognitive mechanisms probably provide more of a foundation for religious concepts that come to us more naturally—for example, beliefs in gods, souls, and an afterlife—than the more complex theological doctrines that characterize major modern religions. The latter strongly rely on cultural learning. In short, the proposed cognitive mechanisms tell only part of the story when it comes to the emergence and persistence of religion.

Regarding the truth status of religious beliefs, the position taken most often by CSR proponents—at least when they address the issue explicitly—is that CSR theories and studies cannot determine the truth status or justifiability of religious beliefs. Indeed, as Michael Murray and Andrew Goldberg observe, students in introductory philosophy courses all learn that "an account of a belief's origin tells us nothing about its truth."[85] At least in theory, it would be possible for both CSR and religious accounts to be correct. As argued by American philosopher Daniel Dennett:

> [I]t could be true that God exists, that God is indeed the intelligent, conscious, loving creator of us all, and yet *still* religion itself, as a complex set of phenomena, is a perfectly natural phenomenon.[86]

Nonetheless, in the view of most CSR scholars, their proposals provide the basis for a *plausible naturalistic account of religion*. This account views religion as an accidental by-product of normal cognitive capacities and learning processes, while dispensing with the actual existence of gods or supernatural beings. Accordingly, when CSR proponents are explicit in their views about the truth status of religious beliefs, more often than not, they express skepticism, if not outright rejection.

For example, anthropologist Scott Atran refers to the "counterfactual" world of supernatural agents.[87] Psychologist Joseph Bulbulia refers to a *self-deception constraint*, which requires that we truly believe in "religious fictions" if we are to successfully signal our religious commitment.[88] American psychologist Jesse Bering opines that God's existence is both unnecessary and unlikely. In his view, even "the many loopholes of a more humble agnosticism have suddenly become unreasonable places to continue burying our heads."[89] At the same time, Finish philosopher of religion Aku Visala observes that the negative implications of CSR for religious belief are generally assumed rather than spelled out in any systematic or rigorous way.[90]

In contrast, some scholars have suggested that the proposed naturalness of religion—and its link to evolved cognitive and neural mechanisms—is not only unsurprising but consistent with theological perspectives. Among CSR scholars, American psychologist Justin Barrett, an observant Christian, is foremost among those who argue that evolutionary and CSR accounts need not be the enemy of Christianity. God could have guided evolutionary processes to develop the sorts of minds that we have.[91] Or, as succinctly observed by American philosopher Michael J. Murray:

> The theist might then look on these evolutionary accounts as providing us with a description of the way in which God configured evolutionary history to make belief in supernatural reality easy or natural for us.[92]

Indeed, a standard theological view posits that we have an in-born, natural capacity to think about, seek out, and relate to God because God instilled in us a *sensus divinitatis,* or "God-sense," and an inbuilt longing for God.[93] Similarly, God may have given us reasoning abilities so that our "reason might lead us to God."[94] By these theistic accounts, the fact that many people experience God is explained by the *reality* of an omniscient God. We are naturally inclined to adopt religious beliefs because they are true. Each of these theological arguments is consistent with the existence of God, but none can prove it.

In summary, no account of the origin or cause of religious belief—whether naturalistic or theistic—can definitively settle the question of religion's truth status. Nonetheless, to the extent that readers find CSR proposals and supporting research persuasive, it may raise questions in their minds about the validity of religious beliefs. In this sense, the causal origins of religious beliefs *do* seem relevant at least to the *perceived* truth status of religion. Philosopher Michael Ruse goes a bit further when he comments as follows:

> Hence, what I am saying is that, although logically religious beliefs can be held no matter what the causal origins, I am not convinced that the causal origins are entirely irrelevant to the truth status of the religious beliefs.[95]

Finally, we can also ask whether CSR proposals have implications for the persistence, and thus long-term viability, of religion. Given the proposed evolved biological nature of these cognitive mechanisms, most CSR theorists expect religion to persist into the foreseeable future. Some view religion as inevitable. For example, Jesse Bering opines—presumably somewhat tongue-in-cheek—that God is so inherent in our intuitive cognitive systems that to permanently rid ourselves of Him "would require a neurosurgeon, not a science teacher."[96]

One source of support for the CSR view regarding the persistence of religion comes from previous societal efforts to discourage or eliminate religion—for example, in communist countries. These efforts have largely proven unsuccessful in the long run. At the same time, the increasing secularization of some societies (see Chapter 8) suggests that the conditions needed for the eventual elimination of religion might be attained in the future. And, of course, the question of whether religion will persist is separate from whether its persistence would be, on balance, a good or bad thing. I aim to address this question more fully after considering the remaining topics in this book.

In any case, to the extent that religious beliefs and practices do decline over time, I suspect that the more cognitive aspects of religion—that is, specific beliefs and doctrines—will lose their impact more than the social, emotional, and community aspects. The latter aspects are closely connected to ritual, a topic I address in the next chapter. Finally, although CSR proposals generally draw on evolutionary perspectives, they have not actually traced the evolution of religious *forms* over time, which I also address in the next chapter.

Chapter 3
Evolution and Change in Religious Behavior

Religious behavior has changed markedly across human history. Some religious behavior, including its rituals, may have rudimentary precursors in non-human primates, suggesting a role for biological evolution. In addition, many scholars argue that religious rituals and practices culturally evolved in human history because they signaled commitment to one's tribe or community and strengthened group cohesion—important adaptive functions when competing for survival with other groups. Changes in religious forms over time have resulted from human cognitive and emotional development, and ecological and cultural change. Such findings suggest that the diversity of religious forms across human history reflects biological and cultural processes that do not involve divine inspiration or guidance. For some readers, these findings may raise questions about the divine nature and truth claims of any particular religion, while also pointing to which aspects of religion are most likely to persist in the future. In this chapter I address the evolution and adaptive role of religion and its rituals across human history.

Rituals form the bedrock on which most, if not all, religions rest.

– Robin Dunbar[1]

[I]f human societies develop cultural ideas and practices that vary among groups, and have differential effects on the groups' success, then the survival and spread of cultural traits rather than genes—religious beliefs and behavior included—may come to depend on selection acting at the level of groups.

– Dominic Johnson[2]

What is the most important aspect of religion? Its beliefs? Its doctrines? Its rituals or practices? As we saw in Chapter 2, many CSR proponents emphasize the cognitive mechanisms thought to facilitate religious *beliefs*. In contrast, many social scientists, particularly anthropologists, have followed Émile Durkheim's lead in highlighting the critical role of religious *ritual*. For example, as Nathaniel Barrett contends:

[I]f we set aside our modern obsession with belief, it is immediately apparent that the most conspicuous features of popular religious life throughout history are its celebratory aspects: its way of marking major transitions, seasonal changes, and other patterns of life with feasting and festivities, pageantry, dance, music, and so forth.[3]

Indeed, many social scientists emphasize the important adaptive role of rituals in the origin and evolution of religion.

RITUAL AND ITS ADAPTIVE ROLE

First, what do we mean by rituals? The American anthropologist Roy Rappaport defined rituals as performances of "more or less invariant sequences of formal acts and utterances" that serve to communicate acceptance of social norms or conventions with moral or sacred elements.[4] Examples range from the severe initiation rites practiced in some traditional societies to the more routine rituals exhibited in many modern Christian churches such as communion, genuflection, hymn singing, and prayer.

Common features of rituals include synchrony, goal-oriented collaboration, and rhythmic music.[5] The synchrony associated with group rituals has been linked to greater social cohesion, cooperation, and prosocial behavior towards one's ingroup—for example, towards one's kin and co-religionists—but also conformity, tribalism, and aggression towards outgroups.[6] The shared goal of completing a sacred ritual can also promote cooperation and trust among participants. The inclusion of music can facilitate these outcomes by enhancing positive emotions. Indeed, a number of studies have shown that participation in religious rituals, particularly when performed in synchrony, triggers the uptake of endorphins in the brain, which in turn contributes to positive emotions and a sense of communal bonding.[7]

In contrast to the *religion-as-by-product* perspective promoted by many CSR scholars (see Chapter 2), scientists who investigate ritual behavior have most frequently endorsed an *adaptationist* perspective on religion. This latter perspective views religion and ritual behavior as directly adaptive in promoting the survival of individuals and/or groups during human evolution. Like all evolutionary perspectives, adaptationist accounts face the following question: Why have religious practices that are costly in both time and energy—and in some cases painful or dangerous—not been eliminated during human evolution? From an adaptationist perspective there must have been—and continue to be—significant compensating benefits of religious rituals and practices for survival and reproduction.

One adaptive function of rituals is helping people manage anxiety in stressful, threatening, or uncertain situations, thus promoting individual health and survival.[8] For example, one study found that recitation of psalms was associated with lower rates of anxiety for Jewish women exposed to unpredictable rocket attacks in northern Israel during the Lebanon war.[9] Another adaptive function of rituals is signaling commitment to one's religious group. This latter function is central in what anthropologists refer to as *costly signaling theory*.[10]

Here is the essence of costly signaling theory: By engaging in religious practices that are costly in terms of time, effort, resources, or even bodily pain, we signal our commitment to—and willingness to cooperate with—

our co-religionists or group. Costly religious practices also enable members of the group to differentiate genuinely cooperative and trustworthy partners from so-called "free-riders," "imposters," or "cheaters"—that is, individuals who attempt to benefit from the group without making adequate contributions.[11] From the perspective of costly signaling theory, the benefits we obtain as a trusted member of our religious group outweigh the high costs associated with any religious practices. As observed by psychologist Joseph Bulbulia:

> [T]here are many possible ways of signaling one's commitment to coreligionists,...including participation in religious practices, resource expenditure, exhibiting hard-to-learn theological knowledge, displaying various distinctive markers (e.g., headpieces, unusual clothing, masks, charms), and perhaps most basic and ancient, through displays of hard-to-fake emotions such as love, devotion, piety, and fear for the gods.[12]

Among early humans, cohesive and cooperative groups would have been adaptive in several ways: in extracting resources, for example, in group hunting; in protecting against predators and competing groups; and in helping to detect and punish free-riders. In general, the costlier and harder to fake the signal, the more credible the signal should be as an indicator of commitment, and by extension, the greater the resulting social cohesion and intragroup cooperation.[13]

A number of scholars have offered historical examples of the role played by costly signals of religious commitment. For example, American psychologist Matt Rossano noted how many commercial traders in Africa benefited by converting to Islam, despite the high ritual costs of doing so. Costly displays of devotion to Islam—for example, fasting, daily prayers, and abstinence from alcohol—facilitated trust and commitment, enabling co-religionists to develop profitable trade relationships even among strangers.[14]

Similarly, American anthropologist and evolutionary biologist Joseph Henrich traced how sacred oaths, taken in the name of particular gods, were essential in facilitating trust in commercial and trade relationships in ancient Mesopotamia, Greece, and Rome.[15]

In 1994, American economist Laurence Iannaccone documented how the most thriving churches in America, for example, the Church of Jesus Christ of Latter-day Saints (i.e., the Mormon Church) and Seventh Day Adventists, were those with the most demanding requirements—that is, the costliest signals of commitment. In contrast, more liberal and less demanding denominations, for example, mainline Protestant denominations, were showing a continuing loss of membership.[16]

More recently, ordained minister and Professor of Comparative Religion James K. Wellman attributed the greater relative strength and growth of evangelical churches, as compared to mainline Protestant churches, in part to their more absolute truth claims, greater ideological uniformity, and loyalty demands.[17]

Similarly, some sociologists have argued that church attendance and seminary enrollments declined among Catholics after the Second Vatican Council in 1962, which reduced the level of strictness in the church by eliminating some prohibitions.[18]

In short, the logic of costly signaling theory is the following: By reducing participation by "free-riders," stricter religious communities and more "costly" religious rituals increase levels of participation and commitment by the remaining members, and thus the overall benefits of religious engagement, including greater group cohesion and cooperation.[19]

Many empirical studies have offered support for costly signaling theories of ritual and religion. Here are some examples from around the world:

- In a historical study of 30 religious and 53 secular (mostly socialist) communes in the 19th and early 20th century, religious communes imposed more than twice as many requirements on their members as did secular communes, but nonetheless outlived the secular communes.[20]

- In a sample of 14 urban religious congregations (*terreiros*) of the Afro-Brazilian religion Candomblé, religious adherents who exhibited greater religious commitment shared more money into a common pool and also reported giving and receiving more cooperative benefits from their *terreiro*.[21]

- A study of ethnic Tamils in two South Indian villages found that individuals who participated more regularly in religious worship and in costlier public rituals were viewed by others not only as more devout but also as having other prosocial traits such as a good work ethic, good character, and generosity.[22]

- Greater time investments in the Dewali (Indian festival of lights) were associated with greater self-reported social cohesion, positive affect, and perceived health by participants.[23]

- In laboratory experiments with Christian undergraduates in the United States, costly religious signals increased the perceived trustworthiness of both Christians and Muslims, suggesting that such signals can extend trust to adherents of other religions.[24]

- In a study of 60 traditional societies, the costliness of male rites such as tattooing, scarification, piercing, genital mutilations, teeth pulling, and body painting was significantly higher in societies that engage in more frequent warfare. Ritual performances that signal group commitment should be particularly adaptive in warlike societies, given the mortality risks.[25]

- Importantly, the social binding effects of rituals are not *always* positive. For example, in studies of Palestinians, Israelis, and additional religious groups, higher frequency of attendance at religious services—and hence ritual participation—predicted greater support for suicide attacks.[26]

These studies offer good support for costly signaling theories of religion—and the idea that religion is adaptive in human evolution.

Indeed, a persuasive case can be made for the adaptive value of ritual behavior for *both* individuals and groups, as implied by Richard Sosis and colleagues:

High-quality signalers, in other words those committed to the group, are assumed to realize reproductive gains via increased reputational status and group-wide benefits achieved through successful collective action.[27]

In the 1960s, evolutionary biologists largely rejected the idea of group or cultural level adaptation. However, the idea that cultural group differences—including differences in religious rituals and commitments—can have adaptive consequences for group success and survival, is increasingly accepted by evolutionary theorists.[28]

To sum up:

There is fairly persuasive evidence that religion—and costly signals of religious commitment—were adaptive in the survival of individuals and groups in human history. Importantly, this reveals *a naturalistic rather than divine process by which religion emerged and thrived.*

EVOLUTION AND CHANGE IN RELIGIOUS BEHAVIOR ACROSS HUMAN HISTORY

In this section I ask: What is it that evolved or developed during human evolution—biologically or culturally—that can account for the changes observed in religious behavior over human history? If these changes can be attributed to natural processes of biological and cultural evolution, then a religious explanation may be less necessary or persuasive.

The search for answers is complicated by the limited archeological record related to religious behavior during early human evolution, and by ongoing debates about the human lineage itself. Future archaeological findings may lead to further revisions regarding the relationships among different species of the genus *Homo* (human). For my purposes, however, it is sufficient to start from the following premises, which reflect the most common view at present:[29]

- Humans descended from a common ancestor shared with the great apes (gorillas, bonobos, and chimpanzees) about 6 or 7 million years ago.

- The first hominins (human ancestors) of our genus, *Homo*, emerged in Africa, probably about 2½ million years ago.[30]

- In one common view, *Homo erectus* ("upright man"), evolved from the earliest human species, *Homo habilis* ("handy man"), about 1.9 million years ago in Africa and began migrating out of Africa into Eurasia about 1.8 million years ago.

- *Homo erectus* subsequently evolved into a variety of "archaic" human species beginning about 500,000 years ago, including the Neanderthals, who may have existed in Europe and the Middle East from about 250,000 to 30,000 years ago.

- Our own species, *Homo sapiens* ("wise man") evolved in Africa from some species of archaic human around 300,000 years ago, and spread out of Africa around 60,000-70,000 years ago, eventually replacing all earlier human species by between 30,000 to 10,000 years ago according to various estimates.

Not all scholars refer to a taxon of human species when addressing the beginnings and evolution of religious behavior. However, those who do primarily address the likely presence or absence of religious behavior in *Homo erectus*; archaic humans, including Neanderthals; and our own species, *Homo sapiens*.

Precursors Among the Great Apes?

Many religious people object to the idea that human behavior—especially religious behavior—may have evolved from the behavior of non-human primates. In contrast, many scholars, in the search for the beginnings of religious behavior, have looked for evidence of rituals or other building blocks of religious or moral behavior in non-human primates, particularly the Great Apes, our closest relatives. They are looking not for evidence of religion *per se* but for indications of ritual behavior, group cooperation, innate emotions, or cognitive capacities that may have evolved into religious behavior in humans.

For example, can we identify precursors of human religious rituals?

Indeed, American sociologist James McClenon proposed an evolutionary bridge between the ritual behaviors observed by ethologists in non-human primates—for example, grooming and rain dances in chimpanzees—and the rituals of early humans, with their rhythmic drumming and dancing. In primates, such rituals have been observed to help group members deal with group social life by reducing aggression and stress, and promoting reconciliation and cooperation. In early humans, such rituals could also lead to altered states of consciousness and other unusual experiences, which, in McClenon's view, can lead to belief in spirits, souls, and life after death.[31]

Similarly, American anthropologist Michael Winkelman sees parallels between the ritual displays of chimpanzees and other Great Apes and the universal features observed in the shamanistic rituals that emerged during the Middle to Upper Paleolithic transition 50,000 years ago or more.[32]

Other scholars agree that religion has its roots in primate ritual or play behavior. However, they argue that the abstract symbols uniquely associated with human rituals—and their emotional and behavioral significance—would have to be culturally learned. In addition, the sense of group solidarity associated with rituals in early humans would have been vague.[33]

What about precursors of human morality?

Indeed, some scholars view the prosocial emotions and behaviors observed in primates, particularly the Great Apes, as the foundation or precursors of morality and religion in humans.[34] Both in the wild and in captivity, chimpanzees, gorillas, and bonobos exhibit empathic, altruistic, consoling, and nurturing behaviors—for example, with hugs, touching of the arm, pats on the back, grooming, and direct gazes into others' eyes. They also exhibit community concern. For example, high-ranking male chimpanzees regularly serve as arbiters to settle disputes. Similarly, female chimpanzees have been observed pulling reluctant males towards each other to make up after a conflict.[35]

American cultural anthropologist and primatologist Christopher Boehm has also pointed to some of the building blocks of morality, ethics, and conscience—important elements of religion—that can be observed in chimps, bonobos, and apes. These elements include a sense of self, the ability to take the perspective of others, familiarity with rules, and primitive forms of social control. Thus, these building blocks of morality and ethics were almost certainly present in the common ancestor of humans and apes. Although this common ancestor would not have had a sense of right and wrong as understood today, these building blocks would have provided a head start in the evolution of human morality and conscience.[36] Thus, as observed by the primatologist Frans de Waal: "Rather than having developed morality from scratch through rational reflection, we received a huge push in the rear from our background as social animals."[37]

What about some of the cognitive precursors of religion?

Indeed, American evolutionary psychologists Matt Rossano and Benjamin Vandewalle have cited evidence that our primate relatives also exhibit several of the cognitive building blocks of religion, including a hypersensitive tendency to detect agents in the environment, a limited form of mind perception, altered or ecstatic states of consciousness, and primitive imaginative capacities. Thus, these cognitive building blocks of religion were likely present at the outset of human evolution.[38]

In short:

There is ample evidence for the presence of cognitive, emotional, and ritual precursors or building blocks of religion and morality among our closest primate relatives and presumably in the common ancestor of humans and apes.[39] Presumably, this conclusion will be uncomfortable only for people who reject the scientific consensus regarding human evolution.

So, What Evolved or Changed?

There is little question that significant changes in religious behavior have occurred from the time of the early hunter-gathers to modern times. Scientists have concluded this based on ethnographic and archeological evidence, and knowledge of the evolving brain. They have also proposed various cognitive, emotional, behavioral/ritualistic, and ecological bases for these changes. The findings suggest that religious expression, and its changes over time, *may be more about biological and cultural evolution than divine inspiration.*

Cognitive and symbolic capacities

For a number of scholars, what evolved were certain cognitive and symbolic capacities, including language, associated with the evolution of the human brain.[40] For example, Rappaport argued that ritual pre-dates the development of language in early humans. However, only with the emergence of language and the associated increases in communication capacities could religious symbols and concepts arise.[41]

Similarly, American sociologist Robert Bellah argues that prior to the emergence of rapid modern language at least 150,000 years ago, ritual in the earliest human societies (characterized by *mimetic culture*) would have involved only embodied action (e.g., dancing and music) representing oneself and one's group.[42] However, with the development of language—and thus *mythic culture*—rituals were augmented by narratives and stories about the origins of the people, the natural world, powerful beings, and the moral order. Finally, increasing literacy and the creation of alphabetic scripts were central in the emergence of the so-called "Axial Age" and *theoretic culture* (about 800 BCE to 200 BCE). During the Axial Age, increasingly reflective and critical thinking about the relation between individuals, kings, and gods contributed to the emergence of monotheism in ancient Israel, philosophy and questioning of the Homeric gods in ancient Greece, Confucian perspectives in China, and Buddhism in ancient India.[43]

English archeologist Steven Mithen drew on archeological evidence to track the evolution of four domain-specific intelligences from our closest primate ancestors to modern *Homo sapiens*. These included linguistic intelligence, involving language use and complexity; natural history intelligence, involving knowledge and mastery of the environment; technical intelligence, including tool-making; and social intelligence, including mind perception. Mithen argued that all four intelligences were present by the time of *Homo erectus* and the Neanderthals. However, only in *Homo sapiens*, about 30,000-60,000 years ago, did a series of "cultural sparks"— including language and consciousness—result in sufficient cognitive fluidity among the multiple intelligences for religion and art to develop.[44]

Finally, American psychiatrist E. Fuller Torrey drew on several sources—including neuroimaging studies of modern brains, primate brains and behavior, and archeological evidence—to infer the changes in the brain that contributed to the evolution of the specific cognitive skills needed for religious behavior to emerge. He traces the significant increase in brain size and general intelligence in *Homo habilis*; an awareness of self in *Homo erectus*; development of mind perception in archaic *Homo sapiens*; a capacity for introspection, probably in conjunction with language, in early *Homo sapiens*; and the emergence of autobiographical memory in modern *Homo sapiens*. In Torrey's view, once introspection and an autobiographical sense of past and future emerged, questions about the meaning of life and what happens to self and others after death would have become inevitable. This would have provided the original impetus to religious ideas in modern *Homo sapiens* about 40,000 years ago.[45]

In sum, these scholars see both the emergence and evolution of religious behavior as the result of our evolving cognitive and linguistic abilities, and associated changes in the brain, with symbolic religious ideas first emerging most definitively in *Homo sapiens*.

Ritual dynamics and modes of religiosity

Other scholars have emphasized the evolution of ritual behavior across human history. For example, Matt Rossano and Benjamin Vandewalle suggest that singing, chanting, and dancing around campfires was evident in some of humanity's oldest populations—for example, the Australian Aborigines, the Andaman Islanders of Southeast Asia, and the !Kung San of Southern Africa. Thus, these activities may have comprised the earliest form of religious rituals in humans. A brief outline of their evolutionary scenario looks as follows:

- About 1.8 million years ago, group synchrony in ritual behavior first appeared in *Homo erectus*, likely facilitated by increasing brain size.

- About 500,000 to 70,000 years ago, progressive intensification of synchronous rituals promoted "strong social bonding, altered states of consciousness, and potential health and healing effects."[46]

- About 70,000 years ago in Africa, shamanism and the idea of the supernatural arose, further strengthening the positive impact of rituals.

- Subsequently, *Homo sapiens* took shamanism from Africa to Europe, where increasingly costly or intense rituals promoted the emotional bonding and social cohesion that provided a social advantage in outcompeting Neanderthals.

Rossano and Vandewalle presented fairly extensive archeological evidence for their proposed evolutionary scenario, but acknowledged that it remains tentative.[47]

British anthropologist Harvey Whitehouse has presented the most developed model focusing on ritual dynamics and change in the evolution of religion. He distinguishes a much older mode of religion associated with *imagistic rituals* and a later emerging mode associated with *doctrinal rituals* that rely on language and verbal and written communication.

The imagistic mode is characterized by rare but highly arousing rituals capable of leaving behind vivid and enduring episodic memories that bind fellow participants together in highly cohesive groups. Prototypical examples include severe initiation practices, sacrificial rites, and vision quests involving extreme forms of deprivation, bodily mutilation, flagellation, or other shocking actions. Imagistic rituals played a role in ancient religions and in some recent small-scale societies and cults.[48] Unlike religious knowledge in doctrinal traditions—which is summed up in speech or text—the "revelations" that result from imagistic rituals emerge out of collective participation and subsequent long-term private rumination. What emerges is intense small-group solidarity and cohesion among participating group members.

In contrast, in the doctrinal mode of religiosity, rituals tend to be low in arousal but high in frequency. Examples include routine liturgies, blessings, hymn singing, congregational prayers, and communion celebrations—the kinds of rituals that we typically encounter in modern religious communities. Through repetition, teaching by religious leaders, and authoritative written texts such as the Bible and Islamic Quran, religious knowledge in the doctrinal mode is codified in language, successfully learned, and stored in semantic memory. This facilitates standardization, stable reproduction, and transmission of complex religious ideas across time and contexts. As a result, the doctrinal mode of religiosity can become associated with centralized ecclesiastic hierarchies that control the content of religious knowledge and practice. Doctrinal rituals are effective in faithfully retaining and transmitting religious knowledge and practice. However, they can become habituated, even tedious and boring. As a result, they may over time be carried out without much conscious reflection or give rise to periodic imagistic reactions. Many of us can probably relate to the potential for doctrinal rituals to feel repetitive and boring (e.g., think of Catholic rosary prayers).

Some scholars have criticized selected concepts and assumptions of Whitehouse's modes theory.[49] Nonetheless, research has provided empirical support.[50] For example, in initial efforts, experienced anthropologists, historians, and archaeologists were invited to subject the theory to critical scrutiny in the cultures to which they were most familiar. From the resulting observations, Whitehouse concluded that the two modes are indeed globally distributed and ancient features of religious systems.[51]

In addition, extensive examination of prehistoric archeological sites has confirmed Whitehouse's contention that the imagistic mode is much more ancient than the doctrinal mode. Indeed, the earliest societies, which relied on foraging for sustenance, exhibited more imagistic characteristics. In contrast, more recent societies with the highest levels of agricultural intensity showed more doctrinal characteristics. Societies intermediate along this timeline exhibited a blend of imagistic and doctrinal characteristics. This suggests a transitional process between the two modes of religiosity, as well as a strong link between the emergence of the doctrinal mode and the advent of agriculture.[52]

In short, the cultural transition from small-scale hunter-gatherer societies to early states, and subsequently to the large agriculture-based civilizations of East Asia, Mesoamerica, and the Fertile Crescent during the Neolithic period may have been tied to a change from imagistic to doctrinal ritual practices.

Ecstatic or altered states

Some anthropologists link the emergence and evolution of religion to the ecstatic or altered states—and other anomalous experiences such as apparitions or out-of-body episodes—encountered by early hunter-gatherers during repetitive rituals.[53] While the rituals in many modern religious denominations are subdued by comparison, the intense, repetitive, and prolonged dancing, chanting, and singing associated with rituals in hunter-gatherer groups can lead to feelings of ecstasy, altered states of consciousness, and a sense of unity with the universe.[54]

For example, American sociologist James McClenon, in proposing his *ritual healing theory*, presents evidence that repetitive rituals can have therapeutic effects resembling those achieved through hypnosis and placebos. He argues that the ability to benefit therapeutically from such rituals—due to genetically-based susceptibility to hypnosis and altered states—would have been adaptive during human evolution. With the development of rapid language in *Homo sapiens*, evolving rituals would have led to shamanistic healing practices and oral traditions addressing the supernatural. Indeed, McClenon views shamanism and the associated ritual healing practices as the first religion and the foundation for all subsequent religions. McClenon reviews a variety of sources of evidence for his theory. For example, depictions in early cave art do suggest a link between rituals and altered states of consciousness.[55]

Emotions and the need to belong

Other scholars have emphasized the importance of emotions and social bonding in the evolution of religion.[56] For example, American anthropologist Barbara King posits that a universal need for belonging, and its associated emotions, is the foundation of "religious imagination" in humans.[57] Drawing on archeological evidence and inferences about the likely emotions experienced in prehistory, King traces the need for belonging and associated emotions from the great apes to *Homo sapiens*.

King views the evidence of religion as vague and uncertain for *Homo erectus* and as limited and "patchy" for Neanderthals. It is only with *Homo sapiens* that the archeological evidence for sacred ritual and a religious imagination starts to become definitive. This is seen, for example, in elaborate burial sites that suggest social complexity and emotional connection; cave paintings, figurines, and other works of art that suggest symbolic and spiritual rituals and shamanism; and ceremonial buildings and temples that suggest that belongingness was taking on elements of rank and status. In King's view, our human ancestors sought belongingness in their social groups, but only *Homo sapiens* sought out emotional connections with God, gods, or spirits.

An ecological perspective

Last but not least, ecological factors are also crucial in understanding the transformation of religious phenomena over human history. These include subsistence, economic, social, and political aspects of the environment. Archeologist Brian Hayden, in particular, has emphasized such factors in tracing the evolution of religion from the earliest hunter-gatherers to modern humans.

For example, Hayden first describes a generalized "forager" type of religion among the earliest hunter-gatherers that developed from about 250,000 to 35,000 years ago during the Middle Paleolithic period.[58] Humans throughout this period moved in small groups with egalitarian social structures and with limited resources and technology such as simple stone tools. This would have required sharing, mutual help, and alliances, probably leading to the emergence of generalized rituals and initiation rites to strengthen commitment to the group. Drawing on the limited archeological evidence—for example, the use of red ochre, intentional burials, and deep caves—and analogies with more recent hunter-gatherer groups, Hayden draws a picture of this generalized forager type of religion. It would have included initiations, ecstatic rituals, animal totemic cults, concepts of the soul, and some indications of ancestor cults and shamanism, all of which may have combined into a single religious system.[59]

During the Upper Paleolithic period about 35,000 to 10,000 years ago, anatomically modern humans emerged and replaced Neanderthals in Europe. Ecological changes included the emergence of societal elites, improvements in technology, increases in food surpluses, and wealth accumulation among elites. These factors led to new dimensions of religious expression among these more "complex hunter-gatherers," including the following:

- Ritual feasting with lavish displays of ritual objects, for example, in order to establish social, economic, and political advantage for family lineages;

- The emergence of secret societies and initiations among elites, as suggested by the small spaces in caves for rituals, which would only have accommodated small segments of the community;

- Fertility concerns, as revealed in female and phallic figurines and sculptures;

- More definitive evidence of animal cults and shamanism, as revealed in wide-spread depictions of animals and shamanistic features in cave paintings;

- Ancestor cults, as suggested by more elaborate and indisputably intentional burials.[60]

Hayden goes on to describe in detail how ecological changes impacted religious expression during the Neolithic period (about 10,000-4000 BCE) and among Indo-Europeans of the Bronze Age (4000 – 2500 BCE), leading eventually to the features of religious expression in early states—which began to emerge about 3000 BCE.

With the emergence of states, political complexity and the power of elites continued to increase, as did populations and the ability of societies to produce surpluses or obtain them through trade. Under such ecological conditions, we see in early city states the frequent assumption of divinity or supernatural connections by rulers (e.g., the Egyptian pharaohs); the building of imposing temples to communicate kingly power and the legitimacy of divine claims (e.g., the Egyptian pyramids, the ancestral shrine of the Mayan king in Guatemala); and ritual focus on kings and their priests, rather than more general community participation.[61]

Finally, as large multi-ethnic empires emerged, gods from the constituent cultures were typically incorporated by elites into imperial pantheons of gods. However, the very large and diverse populations made it difficult for rulers to control religious developments.[62] As a result, and to address the social and economic isolation of many members of society, various "mystery cults" emerged starting around 500 BCE. These cults emphasized personal, direct, and ecstatic experiences with populist gods and their moral codes (e.g., Isis, Osiris, Dionysus, Cybele, Mithras).

In the Roman Empire, one such mystery cult was Christianity—described by Hayden as an innovative blend of traditional Hebrew beliefs and practices, some new ideas, and fairly heavy borrowing from other mystery cults. With the emergence of Judaism, and then Christianity, we see the first sustained instances of a monotheistic deity in anthropomorphic form that insisted on moral behavior and thought.[63] From Hayden's ecological perspective, the conditions were set for the emergence of what some scholars have referred to as "Big Moralizing Gods" and the prosocial religions of *Homo sapiens*.

THE EMERGENCE OF BIG MORALIZING GODS

Here I am referring to the late-emerging monotheistic God(s) of today's major religions of Judaism, Christianity, and Islam. Scientists have referred to them as "Big Moralizing Gods," "Moralizing High Gods", or just "Big Gods" for short. The terminology reflects the monotheistic God's unique power and moral concerns.

Two important questions have generated substantial debate among scientists interested in the cultural evolution of religion: *When?* and *why?* did such "Big Gods" emerge in human history. Obviously, these questions are relevant in evaluating religious or biblical accounts of the monotheistic God.

Psychologist Ara Norenzayan, an early leader in this effort, argued that religious beliefs and rituals emerged initially as a by-product of normal cognitive mechanisms (see Chapter 2). However, cultural evolution then took over and eventually led to the Big Gods who were capable of monitoring the moral and prosocial nature of human behavior in large-scale societies.[64]

In the small hunter-gatherer groups that characterized most of human history, powerful and omniscient spirits or gods were not needed to detect, reward, or punish moral or social transgressions. Transgressions were difficult to hide and group members could readily monitor reputations. According to this perspective, local gods or spirits might require rituals and sacrifices. However, they were typically unconcerned with the transgressions and sins that preoccupy the gods of major world religions.[65] Similarly, evolutionary biologist Joseph Henrich describes the gods of small-scale human communities such as hunter-gatherers as "weak, whimsical, and not particularly moral." Their concerns were "local, even idiosyncratic" and their interventions were "generally unreliable and ineffective."[66]

Things changed, however, with the emergence of large-scale societies. Most people were increasingly unknown to each other. Opportunities to behave in selfish and antisocial ways without detection or punishment increased significantly. Additional mechanisms were therefore needed to monitor and punish antisocial behavior. The idea of supernatural monitoring by a powerful and omniscient God—who knows everything, cares about human morality, and is willing to punish transgressors—provided one such mechanism.[67] Indeed, the God of Abraham is described in the Hebrew Bible, the New Testament, and the Islamic Quran as seeing everything. Similarly, throughout villages in Tibet and Nepal, "Buddha Eyes" are displayed and Lord Buddha is known as the "Eye of the World" in Buddhist scriptures.[68]

Importantly, religious believers in these larger-scale cultural groups—fearing supernatural punishment for antisocial behavior—would have exhibited greater cooperation, trust, and self-sacrifice for the group than would religious believers in groups with morally indifferent or less omniscient gods. This would have contributed to group success in competition and conflict with other social groups—for example, in warfare, demographic expansion, and economic competition.[69]

Is there support for this so-called "Big God Hypothesis"? Support would include evidence that belief in Big Moralizing Gods is largely associated with—or even a prerequisite for—the emergence of larger, more complex societies. Research in this area is active and evolving, and debates have sometimes been heated.[70] In the following, I summarize some of the main points of discussion.

First, regarding the "when" of Big Moralizing Gods, there is general consensus that their emergence is a relatively recent phenomenon in the grand scope of human evolution. However, estimates of precisely when they emerged vary significantly, ranging from as early as 10,000 BCE with the dawn of agriculture,[71] to the so-called Axial Age (i.e., the first millennium BCE),[72] to as late as 500 BCE.[73]

Some recent analyses suggest that Big Gods made their first appearance in Egypt around 2800 BCE and subsequently appeared sporadically in local religions throughout Eurasia, including in Mesopotamia (around 2200 BCE), Anatolia (around 1500 BCE), and China (about 1000 BCE).[74]

Differences in these estimates likely reflect differences in how Big Gods are defined. The Big Gods that emerged during the Axial Age and are worshipped in today's major religions are more definitively concerned about morality than the "Big Gods" of more archaic religions.[75]

Second, regarding the "why" of Big Moralizing Gods, there is growing evidence that their emergence usually *followed* rather than *preceded* large increases in sociopolitical complexity. They may have primarily served to maintain cooperation in societies once they had already exceeded a certain size.[76]

Indeed, recent analyses indicate that Big Moralizing Gods followed sociopolitical complexity by about 300 years, on average. In the same analysis, the best predictors of the emergence of both sociopolitical complexity and Big Moralizing Gods were intergroup warfare intensity and agricultural productivity.[77] The rise of animal husbandry or pastoralism also had a significant influence on the emergence of moralizing religions.[78]

Finally, it is probably important to distinguish the Big Moralizing Gods that emerged late in human evolution from the "lesser" supernatural agents that are common across human societies. These lesser gods also exhibit moral concerns—albeit typically covering a narrower range of social behaviors than the Big Moralizing Gods of the major monotheistic religions.[79]

Indeed, some scholars have presented support for a *broad supernatural punishment hypothesis*. This hypothesis proposes that the emergence of large-scale societies was fostered—not by the evolution of Big Moralizing Gods—but by belief in supernatural punishment more broadly conceived. This would include punishment by ancestral spirits, multiple lesser gods, or inanimate processes such as karma.[80] For example, these broader forms of supernatural punishment might have fostered the evolution of political complexity because political leaders elevated their ancestral spirits to augment their own political authority, which, in turn, contributed to the emergence of large-scale, complex societies.[81]

In summary, although questions remain regarding the cultural evolution of Big Moralizing Gods, there is general consensus that their emergence was a relatively recent phenomenon in the grand scope of human evolution. At least for some people, such findings may raise questions about the truth and divine status of the major monotheistic religions. The findings suggest that the monotheistic God was not originally or eternally present, but rather a late arrival in human cultural evolution.

Takeaways

I draw on the information in this chapter to address several questions: What is the most likely timeline for the emergence of religion in human history? What, if anything, does the diversity of religious forms across human history imply about the truth claims of religion? Is religion adaptive in the survival of individuals or groups? Are there implications for the truth and persistence of religion? The answers to these questions are clearly relevant to perceptions of the cogency and viability of the religious worldview, part of the overarching question addressed in this book.

When Did Religion Emerge?

As noted earlier, many scholars have described parallels between the rituals, emotions, cognitive capacities, and moral instincts of non-human primates and humans. This suggests some biological continuity between the behaviors of our primate ancestors and the proto-religious behaviors of early humans. Even so, the rituals of the earliest humans would have lacked the symbolic meanings and narratives that we generally associate with religion. Such shared meanings and narratives would have awaited the emergence of language and symbolic thinking.

Thus, although a minority of scholars entertains the possibility of some early forms of religious experience among Neanderthals, and even more speculatively among *Homo erectus*, the plausibility of this position depends on how we define religious experience. Should pre-linguistic mimetic rituals or various altered states be considered spiritual or religious? If our definition of religion includes symbolic concepts and narrative myths, then religion should probably be considered unique to *Homo sapiens*, with the most definitive evidence suggesting its emergence around 40,000-60,000 years ago. As argued by evolutionary psychologist Robin Dunbar, religion in its fully modern sense—incorporating communal beliefs—would have required the language skills and higher-level mind perception abilities of anatomically modern humans.[82]

In addition, some scholars view the time period around 10,000 BCE as an important transition point, involving the co-evolution of agriculture, more permanent settlements, the doctrinal mode of religiosity, and (a minority view) Big Moralizing Gods. As previously noted, scholars offer different opinions about precisely when Big Moralizing Gods emerged. However, more recent evidence suggests that they generally *followed* rather than preceded or caused the rise of large, sociopolitically complex societies. They may have merely helped to sustain such societies once they developed. In any case, the gradual evolution of religious expression suggests that it may be more about biological and cultural evolution than divine guidance or inspiration.

What Does the Diversity of Religious Forms Imply?

In addressing the truth claims of religion, the precise time periods during which different forms of religious expression emerged may be less important than the clear evidence that conceptions of supernatural agents and their powers have changed significantly over human history. These changes have reflected, in large part, changing ecological and cultural contexts. For example, we see a gradual transition from the typical local and ancestor spirits with limited powers in smaller hunter-gatherer groups to the Big Moralizing Gods observed in the larger-scale societies associated with some of today's major religions.

To account for such changes, a religious or theistic account would have to postulate an evolutionary process in which earlier forms of supernatural beliefs such as animism and ancestor worship emerged under God's guidance or plan. For example, sociologist of religion Rodney Stark points to the Judeo-Christian idea of *divine accommodation*, which posits that "*God's revelations are always limited to the current capacity of humans to comprehend.*"[83] From this perspective, the monotheistic God was present even among early animists and ancestor worshippers, but early humans lacked the ability to understand His revelations.

An alternative theological perspective would explain the prevalence of these "primitive" forms of religious experience as a degeneration from the original conception of the Supreme Being due to human error or sin—for example, as proposed in Lang and Schmidt's (largely refuted) theory of primitive monotheism (see Chapter 1). Indeed, Christian psychologist Justin Barrett appears to adopt a degeneration theory when he suggests the possibility that "a perfectly adequate concept of God does come as part of our biological heritage" and that the "diversity in god concepts we see is a consequence of human error and not divine design."[84]

However, given available archeological evidence, an ecological perspective on the cultural evolution of religion provides, in my view, a more persuasive and straightforward explanation for the diversity of religious forms across human history. Across time and cultures, the particular supernatural beings that we worship—through a diversity of imagistic and doctrinal rituals—have depended, not on divine revelation, but on our biological, ecological, and cultural histories. This conclusion also seems more plausible than the argument that the particular god or gods that we personally believe in are the only ones that are real, while the plethora of other spirits and gods worshiped over human history were all false.

As noted in Chapter 1, this religious pluralism dilemma was pointed out long ago by the French political philosopher Jean Bodin (1530-1596), among others, and remains a quandary for the reflective believer today. In addition, the status and interpretation of various religious doctrines has been frequently debated and modified over time by fallible and interested theologians and scholars, raising further questions about their divine origin or inspiration.[85]

Is Religion Adaptive in the Survival of Individuals or Groups?

Having reviewed by-product and adaptationist views regarding the evolutionary origins of religion, can we draw some interim conclusions about the adaptiveness of religion for individuals or groups?

On the one hand, if we adopt a cautious position, we should perhaps conclude that scientists have not yet definitively resolved whether religion is adaptive or not, or whether it is best explained by biological or cultural evolution. On the other hand, as summarized earlier in this chapter, a plausible case can be made for the adaptive value of ritual and religion for both individuals and groups. Religion and its rituals can help individuals manage anxiety in stressful, threatening, or uncertain situations, thus promoting individual health and survival.[86] Religious expression also signals commitment and trustworthiness while inhibiting behavior that could damage one's reputation. For groups, religion promotes social cohesion and success in inter-group competition and conflict. Both biological and cultural evolution are likely involved, supporting what scientists refer to as *multilevel selection* or *gene-culture co-evolution*.

As alluded to earlier, some scholars remain skeptical about the reality of adaptive selection processes at the cultural or group level. However, given available evidence, American biologist Peter Richerson and colleagues argue that the conditions required for natural selection at the group level are met. Indeed, human groups differ culturally. Cultural variation—for example, in religion—is transmitted via social learning across generations. And, success in intergroup competition is frequently impacted by such cultural differences. Across human history, cultural groups with particular religious features could have replaced other groups, for example, by growing at a faster rate, better overcoming resource constraints, avoiding internal conflict, and succeeding in war and other intergroup conflicts.[87]

Finally, it is worth noting that the adaptiveness of religion does not preclude the possibility that atheism or religious skepticism is also adaptive in the evolution of cultures. Indeed, as psychologist Vassilis Saroglou has suggested, the presence of *both* religion and atheism—rather than either alone—may be most adaptive for societies. While religion may promote the cooperation and social cohesion that helps societies succeed, atheists may tend to possess the kinds of traits—such as nonconformity and analytic thinking—that facilitate needed change or development.[88]

Implications for the Truth and Persistence of Religion

Finally, we can ask: Does evidence of the evolution of ritual and religion have any implications for the truth and persistence of religion?

First, regarding the truth status of religion:

On the one hand, the adaptive nature of religion in human evolution does not necessarily tell us whether religious claims are true or false. One can still argue that the beliefs, doctrines, and rituals adopted by various religions have divine origins, for example, as communicated by prophets and in sacred texts. On the other hand, the plausible adaptiveness of religion in cultural evolution reveals the plausibility of a naturalistic, as opposed to divine, process by which religion emerged, changed over time, and survives.

For example, fear of supernatural monitoring and punishment can be effective and adaptive, as suggested by available research (see Chapter 4), without it being a real phenomenon. Indeed, in most anthropologists' discussions of the evolution of religion one finds an implicit assumption that the associated beliefs and doctrines are not actually true. That is, the plethora of spirits and gods that have appeared in human history, including those that we worship today, have not actually existed, but rather evolved to meet the needs of individuals and societies.

Regarding the persistence of religion:

I speculated in Chapter 2 that religion's more cognitive aspects—that is, specific beliefs and doctrines—might be less persistent or stable over time than the emotional and community-bonding aspects. Indeed, the diversity of supernatural beings and doctrines in human history suggests that these cognitive elements can be readily replaced or discarded over time. In contrast, the emotional and social needs of individuals and groups that are met by religion seem more difficult to abandon or ignore. Even in relatively secular societies and among atheists, rituals—often with a religious element—continue to be used to celebrate major events and transitions such as weddings and funerals. And, of course, rituals will continue to be used to communicate and reinforce whatever beliefs or doctrines are retained.

Research on the potency of the imagistic mode of religiosity, costly signals of religious commitment, and the differential success of strict versus liberal denominations, might also provide clues to which religious forms will better persist—or at least be more vibrant—in the future. This might include those religious forms that take on more emotive, imagistic, or "effervescent" forms and that adopt beliefs and practices that more effectively bind religious communities together. If so, we may find increasing bifurcation between individuals or societies that practice more vibrant or strict forms of religion versus those that endorse increasingly secular orientations.

In any case, the persistence of religion will depend, in large part, on its continuing ability to fulfill the functions of religion for individuals and societies. I address these psychosocial functions in the next chapter.

Chapter 4
The Psychosocial Functions of Religion

Religion can address a variety of psychological needs. These include ameliorating existential anxieties, including the fear of death; instilling a sense of meaning and purpose in life; coping with uncertainty, for example, by enhancing feelings of control and predictability; and satisfying needs for belonging and connection. Religion can also serve societal functions by contributing to social cohesion and by monitoring or "policing" moral or prosocial behavior. The finding that religion functions to meet certain psychosocial needs does not preclude a divine origin or basis for religion. However, for some people, this finding may raise the question of whether religion is "nothing but" a projection of human needs. In this chapter I review the relevant evidence and take an initial look at whether a fully secular perspective might be able to compete with, or substitute for, these functions of religion.

For starters, if you consider yourself religious, please take a moment and try to articulate your reasons for religious belief and the functions that religion serves in your life. If you are not religious, take a moment to consider the purpose or functions that religion might play in the lives of believers. In this chapter you will learn what psychologists and social scientists have found about the psychosocial functions of religion. I encourage you to consider whether these functions ring true in your own experience or in the experience of religious believers you know.[1]

I first discuss the most frequently investigated psychological functions of religion. I then turn to the moral monitoring or "policing" function of religion in society.

REDUCING EXISTENTIAL ANXIETIES

Fear, first of all, produced gods in the world.
— Statius[2]

In every calm and reasonable person there is hidden a second person scared witless about death.
— Philip Roth[3]

Is there any meaning in my life that will not be destroyed by my inevitably approaching death?
— Leo Tolstoy[4]

Historically, many scholars and writers have noted the important role of religion in ameliorating the inevitable existential anxieties associated with living, particularly the fear of death.[5] Written evidence of humanity's fear of death dates back to at least 2100 BCE with the *Epic of Gilgamesh*, an ancient Sumerian text that recounts the king of Uruk's quest for immortality.[6] Across human history—or at least since humans developed self-awareness—people have been plagued by existential questions and anxieties such as the following: How do I cope with my injury or disease? Are there gods or forces that I can turn to for safety? Am I loved or valued by others? What is the meaning and purpose of my life? What will happen to me when I die?[7]

In much of today's world, existential anxieties have been made even more salient, as traditional economic, political, and community structures and opportunities seem threatened, and health fears have been heightened by a deadly pandemic. In such contexts, religion provides a powerful means of reaffirming one's self and collective identity in the face of existential insecurity and anxiety.

Indeed, a number of international surveys have shown that individuals, regions, and countries that experience greater insecurity exhibit greater average religiosity.[8] For example, drawing on global survey data, political scientists Pippa Norris and Ronald Inglehart have shown that religious practices such as prayer and attendance at religious services are more frequent in societies characterized by greater existential insecurity, as assessed by income, literacy, education, health care, and life expectancy. Conversely, in societies with greater security, the rated importance of God and religion in people's lives is reduced, which, in turn, reduces the frequency of religious practices. In the same study, a poverty index—which assessed individuals' insecurity in relation to food and shelter, running water and electricity, and perceived standard of living and health—was also related to stronger religious values within countries.[9]

In general, findings relating existential insecurity to greater religiosity are stronger and more consistent when comparing countries rather than individuals. This suggests that individuals' *perception* of the existential security of their *society as a whole* may be more important than their *personal* level of security in determining their level of religiosity.[10]

One form of insecurity—related specifically to physical health—is the presence of pathogens or diseases in one's environment.[11] Readers are probably not consciously aware of the role that pathogen avoidance has played in religious behavior. However, research has shown that one function of religion—at least historically and in traditional societies—has been the avoidance and management of infectious diseases. Religion does so by better demarcating ingroup members from strangers or members of outgroups, thus avoiding exposure to unfamiliar pathogens to which one has not developed an immune response.

The idea that religion evolved, in part, as a disease-avoidance strategy can also account for the prevalence of rituals aimed at cleansing or moral purification in each of the major world religions. Examples include washing before praying; crossing oneself with holy water; avoidance of food substances that might contaminate the body, for example, in kosher laws; and using incense to purify spaces. Indeed, a fair amount of research has related the historical prevalence of pathogens in different environments to overall religiosity and to a variety of conservative, ethnocentric, and xenophobic traits that would serve to reduce contact between members of different groups.[12]

Among the existential anxieties we experience as humans, the most profound is probably the fear of death, at least when our mortality is brought into conscious awareness. Fear of death is the special focus of *Terror Management Theory* (TMT)—a significant line of psychological research since the 1980s. TMT was inspired by the writings of American cultural anthropologist Ernest Becker. For example, in his influential book *The Denial of Death,* Becker argued that:

> ...the idea of death, the fear of it, haunts the human animal like nothing else; it is a mainspring of human activity—activity designed largely to avoid the fatality of death, to overcome it by denying in some way that it is the final destiny for man.[13]

TMT proposes that as we grow up, we become aware of the inevitability of death and the limits of our parents' ability to provide security and protection. This awareness, coupled with our instinct for self-preservation, creates the potential for debilitating anxiety or terror. To defend or buffer against this death anxiety, we must believe that some aspect of us will continue after death, either *literally* through an afterlife or *symbolically.* Symbolic immortality may take many forms. This could include making lasting achievements in business, art, and science, or, on a more modest scale, having children or being remembered with fondness by friends and family after our death.

Indeed, obituaries often contain content relevant to both literal and symbolic immortality. For example, we read that the deceased has gone home to God or rejoined loved ones in heaven (i.e., literal immortality), as well as lists of life contributions or family members who will fondly remember the deceased (i.e., symbolic immortality).

According to TMT, to achieve literal or symbolic immortality and protect against death anxiety, we all seek security and protection in *cultural worldviews*. For many people, religion—for example, the Christian or Islamic belief systems—provides such a cultural worldview. Secular humanism, as described in this book, can also be considered a cultural worldview.[14] *Both* religious and secular worldviews provide means or standards by which one can achieve *symbolic* immortality. However, religions may be particularly well suited as a buffer against death anxiety because they alone provide a means to achieve *literal* immortality. Judaism, Christianity, and Islam offer the possibility of literal immortality in heaven, while some Eastern religious traditions describe a process of rebirth after death.

At the same time, both religious and secular worldviews are potentially fragile social constructions that must be continually buttressed or defended in order to remain effective as a buffer against death anxiety. Thus, according to TMT, we all seek to defend or buttress our worldviews—in some cases by denigrating competing worldviews—when reminded of our mortality or when our worldviews are challenged. For example, if the idea of eternal life was challenged by an atheist, a Christian might respond to this perceived threat to their immortality by vigorously defending their Christian belief system and/or by disparaging atheism.

Research support for the propositions of TMT is extensive. For example, after the September 11 terrorist attacks in the United States, a short-term increase in church attendance, Bible sales, and Internet religion was observed. This suggests that religious worldviews were being buttressed, at least temporarily, in the face of a reminder of mortality.[15] Similarly, the devastating 2011 earthquake in Christchurch New Zealand led to an increase in religious faith among those directly affected.[16] More recently, after the invasion of Ukraine by Russia, demand for Bibles, and access to the Bible online, increased dramatically in Ukraine.[17]

Similarly, when the mortality of research participants has been made salient in laboratory settings—for example, by asking them to describe the emotions they experience when they think about their own death—they tend, as expected, to defend their worldview and/or denigrate competing worldviews.[18] For example, in studies with North Americans, participants whose mortality was made salient reported greater religiosity, belief in God, and belief in divine intervention than participants whose mortality was not made salient.[19] In a study of Islamic students in Iran, students whose mortality was made salient expressed greater endorsement of religiously motivated martyrdom attacks against the United States.[20]

For my purposes in this book, the most relevant questions on this topic are the following:

- *Do people who are more religious—for example, because they anticipate literal immortality in an afterlife—experience less anxiety about death and thus less need to defend their (religious) worldview when reminded of their mortality?*

- *Do people necessarily respond in a defensive manner when reminded of their mortality, or are more positive responses, including those of a more secular nature, also effective in reducing existential anxieties?*

In answering the first question, the distinction between *intrinsic* and *extrinsic* religious orientations is important. People with an intrinsic religious orientation have deeply internalized religious beliefs that serve as a "master motive" or guide for their behavior and approach to life. In contrast, people with an extrinsic religious orientation adopt a more utilitarian approach to religion, in which religion is used primarily for such ends as protection and comfort, relationships, and social standing.[21]

Several studies have found that people high in intrinsic religiosity *do* report lower levels of death anxiety and reduced need to defend their religious worldview when reminded of their mortality. However, this is not the case for people who are high in extrinsic religiosity, who may even report *greater* fear of death.[22] Overall, however, the average relationship between most indicators of religiosity and death anxiety is actually very small and the results across studies are not entirely consistent.[23]

Importantly, there is some evidence that death anxiety is lowest among people who are *either* very religious *or* nonreligious (e.g., atheists), and highest among people with less definitive beliefs.[24] One interpretation of this finding is that nonbelievers have relatively low death anxiety because they focus on their present lives and are not worried about their salvation or fate after death.

Regarding the second question above, some research indicates that awareness of one's mortality can indeed motivate people in positive ways. For example, we may strive to enhance our physical health or personal growth, prioritize our goals in more meaningful directions, or build supportive relationships and communities.[25] In addition, some research findings suggest that a secular worldview that includes belief in social-moral progress may also protect against existential anxieties such as the fear of death.[26] These studies are important because *they suggest ways in which secular or nonreligious individuals can ameliorate death anxiety or awareness of their mortality.*

FINDING MEANING IN LIFE

> There is nothing in the world, I venture to say, that would so effectively help one to survive even the worst conditions, as the knowledge that there is a meaning in one's life.
>
> — Victor Frankl[27]

> Being religious means asking passionately the question of the meaning of our existence and being willing to receive answers, even if the answers hurt.
>
> — Paul Tillich[28]

Drawing on his experiences in Nazi death camps during World War II, the Viennese psychiatrist Victor Frankl concluded that a key to survival in the camps was the ability to find and retain a sense of meaning or purpose in the face of such extreme suffering. Even under such severe conditions, one might find meaning by seeking to survive for the sake of a loved one, to complete unfinished life tasks, to report to the world what had happened, or to maintain courage, dignity, and unselfishness before others, oneself, or God. Frankl concluded that all humans require a sense of meaning or purpose in their lives and that striving to find such a meaning—which he termed the *will to meaning*—is the primary motivational force in human beings.[29]

Unlike existentialist philosophers such as Jean-Paul Sartre, who argued that people must define or invent their own "essence" and meaning, Frankl argued that the meaning of our lives is not so much invented, but discovered or detected—for example, as we perform work or deeds, experience someone or something, or encounter difficulties, suffering, or death.[30]

Ultimately, man should not ask what the meaning of his life is, but rather must recognize that it is *he* who is asked. In a word, each man is questioned by life; and he can only answer to life by *answering for* his own life; to life he can only respond by being responsible.[31]

Subsequently, numerous psychologists have observed humans' need for meaning, their *meaning making* tendencies in all domains of their lives, or the unique role that religion can play in finding meaning in life.[32] Not surprisingly, theologians have also addressed the importance of meaning in life. Indeed, for theologian Paul Tillich, the search for meaning in life is the very essence of the religious attitude.

So, what do we *mean* by "meaning in life?"

The need for meaning can be described as a motive to understand or make sense of one's experience and to feel that one's life has significance or purpose.[33] Psychologists also talk about our *meaning systems*, which include the beliefs and expectations we have about ourselves, the nature of the world, and the relationship between the two.[34] Such meaning systems may be necessary for humans to function in the world. They guide our perceptions. They contribute to a sense of mastery, control, and self-identity. They facilitate adaptive functioning amidst uncertainty. And they address existential concerns such as the awareness of our eventual death. Given the apparent universality of the need for meaning, some psychologists have proposed that the need is an evolved adaptation important for human survival.[35]

How does religion address this universal need for meaning in life? In a now classic work titled *Meanings in Life*, American psychologist Roy Baumeister described the role that religion can play in addressing four basic needs for meaning:

- *Purpose*: Major religions such as Christianity offer definitive ideas about the ultimate purpose in life. We should seek salvation and fulfillment through goals and activities that accord with a divine or sacred plan. Even suffering becomes more bearable if understood within such a divine plan or purpose.

- *Value*: Religions provide the ultimate value base, with God's will providing the ultimate criterion of right and wrong. Indeed, religious systems are typically closely tied to ideas of morality.

- *Efficacy*: Religions provide a feeling of efficacy or control in situations or events involving uncertainty. For example, we use prayer to enlist divine assistance or support in bringing about desired outcomes. Alternatively, we can experience a degree of indirect or secondary control by leaving important life outcomes in God's hands.

- *Self-worth*: For example, in Christianity, believers are assured of God's love and grace. In addition, participation in a community of believers can provide the esteem and respect of others.[36]

Religious meaning systems may be particularly advantageous in interpreting stressful circumstances and even death, which can be interpreted as having occurred for a reason, as beyond our understanding, or as leading to heaven and reunification with loved ones. In some cases, such circumstances may lead us—through deepened spirituality—to posttraumatic growth.[37] Indeed, a number of studies support the role and importance of religious meaning making in dealing with such traumas as natural disasters, terrorist attacks, personal illness, or the death of a loved one. Here are some examples:

- Survivors of Hurricane Katrina in the United States and survivors of the 2010 major earthquake in Chile commonly explained the event as an "act of God," thus attributing a sense of meaning or purpose to an uncontrollable event.[38]
- In a U.S. national sample, greater intrinsic religiosity and religious participation prior to the 9/11 terrorist attacks were associated with better health outcomes over the three years following the attacks. Religious people were able to find meaning in the event and to interpret it collaboratively within their religious communities.[39]
- Among parents who had recently lost a child to sudden infant death syndrome, more religious parents reported greater cognitive processing of the loss, greater social support, and greater perceived meaning in the child's death. In turn, these outcomes were associated with greater psychological well-being 18 months after their child's death.[40]

Of course, we can engage in forms of meaning making that do not involve religion. However, available studies indicate that religion is a common and effective way to imbue significant events—perhaps especially significant misfortunes—with a sense of meaning or purpose.

Other studies have addressed the relationship between religious beliefs and perceived meaning in life more generally, that is, not simply in relation to traumatic experiences. For example:

- In many studies, people who report greater religiosity tend to report a greater sense of meaning or purpose in their lives.[41]
- The positive relationship frequently found between religiosity and psychological well-being can be accounted for, at least in part, by the greater perceived meaning in life of religious people.[42]

- Religious people tend to report more strivings or goals they see as having spiritual or sacred qualities. This, in turn, has been associated with greater happiness, life satisfaction, and marital adjustment, and less depression and neuroticism.[43]

The distinction between *presence* of meaning in life—that is, feeling that your life has meaning—and the *search* for meaning in life is important. Individuals with firm religious commitments are more likely to report the presence of meaning in their life. Individuals who are still searching for meaning tend to have a more open, flexible, and questioning approach to religion.[44]

Finally, there is also a strong association between religiosity and meaning in life when comparing countries. For example, using Gallup World Poll data in 132 nations, one study found that people in poorer nations averaged higher in perceived meaning in life than people in wealthier nations, in part, because of the greater average religiosity of people in poor nations. Thus, even under objectively poor living conditions, individuals can attain a sense of meaning or purpose, with religion playing an important role in doing so. The researchers concluded that as societies become wealthier, religion becomes less central in some people's lives, leading more people to lose their sense of meaning or purpose.[45]

ADDRESSING UNCERTAINTY AND THE NEED FOR CONTROL

…the prevalence of beliefs in God may reflect, at least in part, a psychological process set in place to help relieve the anxious uncertainty associated with the threat lowered personal control poses to belief in an orderly world.

– Aaron Kay and colleagues[46]

An important, and perhaps primary, function of religion is to provide a buffer or shield against the inevitable uncertainties in life, thus satisfying our inherent need to feel a sense of control over events and experiences.

Without such a shield the world can be experienced as chaotic, unpredictable, and stressful.[47]

One prominent approach views religion as a source of *compensatory control*. That is, when our own ability to control events is uncertain or under threat, the belief that events will unfold in accordance with God's will can provide a comforting sense that things are nonetheless under control.[48]

Another approach, referred to as *uncertainty-identity theory*, describes how we deal with self-uncertainty—that is, uncertainty about who we are, how we should think and behave, and our futures. We do so by identifying with groups. Such groups provide a sense of personal identity; guidance on how we should think, feel, and behave; feelings of belonging; and consensual validation of a worldview.[49] Although identification with a variety of secular cultural, ethnic, political, or community groups could serve these uncertainty-reducing functions, religious groups may be particularly well suited for this purpose.

A final approach describes how personal uncertainty can induce people to bolster or defend their cultural norms and values, including their religious values, while denigrating the norms and values of others.[50]

A significant application of uncertainty-identity theory has been to explain the emergence and appeal of religious extremism. When self-uncertainty is acute, for example, during adolescence, unemployment, or widespread economic or societal uncertainty, extremist groups can become especially attractive. They offer a strong source of social identity, self-esteem, and belonging, while providing answers and ideologies for an uncertain and unpredictable world.[51]

A variety of studies have provided support for the role of uncertainty as a religious catalyst. Here are several examples:

- A number of studies have demonstrated that even temporary threats to personal control increase the strength of religious commitments or the idea that events in the world unfold according to God's plan.[52]

99

- Consistent with the uncertainty-reducing function of religion, some evidence suggests that people with greater needs for certainty average higher on religious values than people with greater openness to uncertainty, ambiguity, and new knowledge.[53]

- A number of laboratory studies support a link between self-uncertainty and elevated religious zeal or extremism, as revealed by greater willingness to support a war in defense of one's religious convictions and greater derogation of a different religious group.[54]

- In field studies conducted with Palestinian Muslims and Israeli Jews, some evidence has linked greater self-uncertainty to greater support for suicide bombings among Palestinians and more aggressive military action among Israelis when national identity was central to self-definition.[55]

- People who endorse more traditional or fundamentalist forms of religion have higher *needs for closure*—that is, they prefer order, structure, and predictability in their lives, and dislike ambiguity and uncertainty.[56]

There are practical implications of these findings linking religiosity to needs for certainty and control. For example, sociologist of religion James Wellman and colleagues have argued that the success of evangelical megachurches in the United States can be attributed, in part, to their ability to create "certainty enclaves" of "sanctuaries of certitude" for their members.[57]

Are there secular alternatives to religion in reducing uncertainty and increasing feelings of control? Indeed, there are. A significant finding in compensatory control studies is that government institutions can serve as a secular alternative to religion as a compensating source of perceived order, stability, and control.[58] For example, in survey data from 67 countries, people who chronically experienced lower levels of personal control in their countries tended to indicate stronger support for government control in their lives, particularly if the respective governments were not associated with corruption.[59] The compensatory role of government as an alternative to religion was further supported in a study of 155 countries, which found that the provision of better government services was associated with lower religiosity across countries, as well as across states in the United States.[60]

Additional studies indicate that active engagement in personally important *secular* goals can substitute for religious zeal in coping with an uncertain world. Secular beliefs in scientific progress can also serve as a source of compensatory control and perceived order in coping with uncertainty.[61]

In short, a number of laboratory and real-world studies support the view that religion serves an important function in addressing feelings of personal uncertainty and needs for closure, predictability, and control. At the same time, there is evidence that these outcomes can also be attained through effective governments, belief in scientific progress, pursuit of meaningful secular goals, and perhaps other secular means.

MEETING NEEDS FOR BELONGING AND CONNECTION

[H]uman beings have a pervasive drive to form and maintain at least a minimum quantity of lasting, positive, and significant interpersonal relationships.
—Roy Baumeister & Mark Leary[62]

[G]od (and other divine figures) function like symbolic attachment figures to whom believers actively strive to obtain or maintain a sense of being connected.
– Pehr Granqvist & Lee Kirkpatrick[63]

According to psychologists, we all have a need to maintain close interpersonal relationships or bonds. For many people, religious communities or a relationship with God can meet this need.

For example, the humanist psychologist Abraham Maslow included "love and belongingness" in his hierarchy of human needs.[64] Psychologists Roy Baumeister and Mark Leary described the need to belong as a fundamental human motivation and reviewed a broad range of research studies supporting this *belongingness hypothesis*.[65] According to *attachment theory*, the human need for belonging or connection can be extended or generalized to explain the desire for a personal relationship with God, at least for believers.[66]

From the perspective of attachment theory, believers seek to establish and maintain a sense of closeness to God—for example, through prayer—with God providing both a *safe haven* (i.e., someone they can turn to in the face of suffering or uncertainty) and a *secure base* (i.e., a source of confidence and support) as they explore and navigate the challenges of everyday life.[67] Thus, God can serve as a companion who remains "by one's side," functioning psychologically much like other close interpersonal relationships.[68] In some cases, one's relationship with God may be a substitute for limited or unsatisfactory relationships with others. However, belief in God is more typically accompanied by social support and a sense of belonging and identity with a community of fellow believers.

Indeed, a number of studies indicate that meeting needs for belonging and connection is one function of religion and that people seek a relationship with a loving and accepting God.[69] Here are some examples:

- In a study of Swedish university students, those who lacked a current romantic relationship averaged higher on a number of religious phenomena, including having a personal relationship with God.[70]

- A study of American university students found that, at least for women, greater religiosity was related to lower levels of loneliness, regardless of the level of perceived social support from other sources.[71]

- In a survey of church-goers in the United States, people who reported receiving more emotional support from fellow church members tended to experience a greater sense of belonging in their congregation, which, in turn, was associated with greater satisfaction with their health.[72]

- Turkish immigrants in Germany reported greater religiosity than Turks living in Turkey. This was consistent with the immigrants greater need to compensate for lower levels of belonging and acceptance in German society.[73]

- When loneliness, social exclusion, separation from others, or abandonment by God have been made salient in laboratory studies, participants have reported stronger beliefs in supernatural agents, increased religiosity, or increased desires to be close to God.[74]

In sum, by providing a faith community and a perceived relationship with God, religion can contribute to the satisfaction of human needs for belonging and connection—an important function of religion for many people.

MONITORING MORAL OR PROSOCIAL BEHAVIOR

Religion doesn't just meet individuals' psychological needs. It also serves societal functions. For example, in Chapter 3, I reviewed evidence supporting the adaptive role of rituals and other costly religious practices in signaling group commitment and enhancing societal cohesion. In addition, religion can play an important societal role in monitoring or "policing" moral or prosocial behavior.

Indeed, evolutionary biologist and political scientist Dominic Johnson cites evidence that the idea of supernatural punishment has been a universal feature of all cultures. However, it takes on different forms depending on the prevailing ecology of the cultural group. In indigenous and ancient cultures, supernatural agents lack the omnipresent and omniscient powers of the Abrahamic God. However, they still have the capacity to facilitate cooperation by detecting and punishing selfish or antisocial behavior.[75] In Eastern religions such as Hinduism and Buddhism the potential for punishment is incorporated in concepts such as karma and reincarnation.[76] As long as people fear supernatural punishment—in the present or in an afterlife—it can impact behavior, whether supernatural punishment is a real phenomenon or not.[77]

Indeed, a number of studies have demonstrated the ubiquity of beliefs in supernatural monitoring and punishment across societies, as well as the relationship of such beliefs to greater moral or prosocial behavior. Here are some examples:

- In a study of 48 indigenous societies, researchers examined the perceived presence of supernatural sanctioning in communities that practiced cooperative management of natural resources such as forests and fisheries. Community members viewed religion as playing a role in sanctioning uncooperative behavior in 81% of the cases. Perceived sanctions included disease, death, and misfortune, as well as material, social, and spiritual sanctions.[78]

- In a field experiment with Hindus in Mauritius, participants who viewed the Hindu god Shiva as a watchful God who rewards and punishes behavior cheated less in allocating money that benefited their local village or themselves.[79]

- In a study of eight communities practicing Christianity, Hinduism, Buddhism, animism, or ancestor worship, the more participants viewed their moralistic gods as punitive and knowledgeable about people's behavior, the more generous they were in allocating coins to geographically distant strangers who shared their religion (i.e., co-religionists).[80]

- Studies in a variety of cultures have shown that making gods or supernatural agents salient in research participants' minds—for example, by asking them to read verses from the Quran or think about God or karma—leads to more prosocial behaviors or intentions.[81]

- Interestingly, several studies suggest that fear of supernatural punishment is more effective than supernatural benevolence or forgiveness in inducing moral or prosocial behavior. Perhaps people's belief in a more forgiving God enables them to "cleanse their moral palate, and thereby feel more licensed to transgress again."[82]

From a secular humanist perspective, the following question is important: Can secular sources of monitoring and punishment of behavior be as effective as the monitoring associated with supernatural agents (e.g., God, karma)?

Some studies offer clues. For example, when government (rather than supernatural) authority or punishment is made salient in people's minds—for example, by exposing them to terms such as civic, jury, court, police, and contract—similar effects on prosocial behavior have been found. This suggests that secular institutions may be as effective as religion in eliciting prosocial behavior, at least in societies with respected secular institutions.[83]

In addition, several studies reveal that people are willing to personally punish free-riders or non-cooperators to enforce prosocial norms of behavior, although these tendencies may function differently across cultures.[84] Of course, punishing others requires one to sacrifice time and energy, and risks the possibility of angry retaliation. The cultural evolution of belief in supernatural monitoring and punishment is thought to have provided at least a partial solution to the costliness and risks of punishment by humans.

Indeed, Canadian psychologist Kristin Laurin and colleagues found that people who believe in powerful Gods who employ divine punishment showed less willingness to engage in punishment themselves or to support secular state-sponsored punishment. These results suggest that there is a compensatory relationship between different forms of monitoring and punishment of behavior. As the researchers concluded:

> By demonstrating that people perceive a psychological trade-off between earthly and divine punishment options, the current findings support theories suggesting that beliefs in punishing supernatural agents emerged, in part, because they offered societies a way to avoid some of the costs associated with earthly punishment.[85]

In short, it is possible that secular institutions can substitute for religion's social function in monitoring moral behavior. Indeed, the fact that relatively secular countries are among the most peaceful and functional in the world suggests that this is the case.[86]

TAKEAWAYS

Before addressing the overarching question of this book—the relative merits and viability of religion versus secular humanism from the perspective of the psychological and social sciences—it is worth pointing out the following: Many of the functions of religion posited by early philosophers and social scientists based on limited ethnographic evidence and philosophical speculations (see Chapter 1) find support in current psychological research, as reviewed in this chapter.

These interrelated functions of religion include providing consolation and support; coping with fears and anxieties, especially death; dealing with uncertain and uncontrollable events; attaining a sense of meaning and purpose in life; experiencing a sense of belonging, identity, solidarity, or cohesion with larger social groups; and monitoring moral or prosocial behavior. The general convergence of proposals and findings over time suggests that the primary psychosocial functions of religion have been understood for centuries. Nonetheless, believers likely differ in the extent to which they are consciously aware of—or able to articulate—the psychological bases of their faith.

The fact that religion serves these functions does not preclude the possible truth of religious beliefs. That is, knowing that religion satisfies certain psychological needs does not establish that religion is "nothing but" a projection of such needs. Many if not most believers attribute their faith to the actual existence of God and His perceived presence in their lives, even though their religious faith may nonetheless be serving one or more of these psychological functions.[87] On the one hand, the finding that people seek a comforting or loving attachment relationship with God is consistent with theological interpretations. On the other hand, for some people, the realization that religion serves certain psychological needs may diminish their perception that religion has a divine basis.

In any case, we observe these functions of religion regularly and poignantly in our daily lives. For example, when we see news coverage of significant natural disasters such as wildfires, damaging storms, and earthquakes, we commonly see survivors express thanks to God for their survival and that of their loved ones. Or, we observe people find comfort and meaning in the death of a loved one through their belief that the loved one is now in heaven or "a better place" with other loved ones, presumably for an eternity.

However, a skeptic might understandably wonder how the thankful survivors of various tragedies explain the fate of the many good people who did not survive. Or, we can ask why an omniscient God did not prevent the catastrophic event in the first place (i.e., the theodicy problem in religion). Interestingly, research reveals that religious people tend to credit God for positive outcomes, while protecting God from blame for negative outcomes. They do so by attributing negative outcomes to bad luck, human error and sin, or Satan—or by justifying them as part of God's larger plan.[88]

Or, as a more mundane example, we frequently see athletes thank the Lord, give glory to God, or note their "blessings" in winning a game or event. They do so without apparent awareness of the irony that many of their deserving competitors were also praying for victory but did not experience such blessings. We may reasonably ask how and why God selected among these deserving competitors, or—even more to the point—whether athletes or their fans should expect God to get involved in the outcome of athletic events in the first place. As it turns out, about one-fourth of Americans believe that "God plays a role in determining which team wins sporting events." There is also some evidence that religious people attribute a greater role for God when they win than when they lose.[89]

Returning to the overarching question of this book, the most pertinent question for this chapter is the following: Can a fully secular or nonreligious worldview compete with, or substitute for, religious worldviews in dealing with existential anxieties; our needs for meaning, control, and belonging; and society's need to monitor moral or prosocial behavior? This question may be especially relevant in those societies where the role of religion in daily life has clearly decreased in recent times, as reflected in reduced church attendance, largely public sector education, policies of church-state separation, and the limited role of religion in the business and government sectors. I will consider this question more thoroughly later in this book. However, I can offer an initial glimpse of an answer here based on the type of studies cited in this chapter.

For starters, however, there are several reasons why we might expect secular perspectives to fall short of religion in reducing existential anxieties and uncertainties and in achieving a sense of meaning, control, and belonging.

First, secular science, philosophy, and the humanities can provide relevant information regarding the origins of the universe, potential sources of personal meaning and control, moral and ethical principles, and the nature and determinants of behavior and well-being. However, it is fair to ask whether any secular meaning system can compete with the explanatory reach of religious meaning systems, which address ultimate questions of existence, meaning, and morality that—in the view of believers—transcend earthly experience.

For example, psychologist Roy Baumeister posited that a sense of meaning serves two general functions—predicting and controlling the natural environment and helping people regulate their emotional states, for example, during traumas or misfortunes. Science is clearly more effective than religion for the former function, but science may fall short of religion for the latter function.[90]

Similarly, philosopher Steven T. Asma, in his book *Why We Need Religion*, argues that religion is better than science at helping us manage our emotional lives. By comparison, he argues, secular contributions to well-being—lacking metaphysical commitments—will fall short.[91] Indeed, for many believers, naturalistic or scientific explanations have limited value in answering existential questions about the purpose of their lives, why they and the universe exist, and whether they will continue to exist in some form after their physical death.

Second, in addition to their explanatory reach, religions typically present their doctrines as eternally true. In this way, they have an apparent advantage over scientific perspectives, which evolve to some extent over time as new findings emerge. Unfortunately, however, religion's claims of permanent truth can lead to inflexibility in religious doctrines and intolerance toward alternative religious or secular perspectives. In addition, even a cursory look at theology reveals a level of historical discord and selective change and reinterpretation over time. This suggests that the purported immutability or permanent truth advantage of religion over science is not as great as might be claimed.[92]

Third, secular perspectives offer a variety of means to seek and achieve a degree of symbolic immortality, for example, through lasting achievements or being remembered by friends and family. However, only religious belief systems offer the opportunity for literal immortality in an afterlife. Furthermore, as pointed out by Baumeister, the prospects for even symbolic immortality are generally illusory, with little likelihood of being remembered in any meaningful way even by relatives beyond about 70 years after one's death.[93] This sad reality likely contributes to the appeal of religious beliefs in an afterlife.

While acknowledging these potential advantages of religion over secular perspectives, some evidence—reviewed in this chapter—suggests that secular perspectives may be able to compete as an alternative in serving the proposed functions of religion, at least for some people. For example:

- A number of Terror Management Theory (TMT) studies have revealed that buttressing *secular* worldviews—not just religious worldviews—can buffer against reminders of mortality.
- A variety of positive secular responses to the awareness of mortality may be effective alternatives to belief in an afterlife. These include working to maintain one's health or making the best use of

one's limited time on earth through one's goals, values, and relationships.

- Regarding religion as an antidote to uncertainty, a study in Canada found that the experience of uncertainty did *not* increase religious zeal in university students that reported high engagement in, and personal control over, important secular goals.[94] That is, feelings of uncertainty and needs for control can also be addressed through secular or nonreligious means.

- Indeed, there is some evidence that three potential sources of perceived control—personal, religious, and governmental—can be largely substituted for each other in meeting needs for order, structure, and reduced uncertainty in our lives.

- There is also some evidence that secular institutions may be as effective as religion in monitoring and eliciting moral or prosocial behavior, at least in societies with respected secular institutions.

- Studies of people with life-threatening illnesses, as well as healthy college students, reveal that having a sense of meaning in life is more important than religion per se for one's psychological well-being or equanimity.[95]

Importantly, this last finding suggests that *if a sense of meaning and purpose can be achieved via secular means*—for example, via career, friendships, family, or involvement in meaningful causes—*religious commitments may not be necessary for psychological well-being.*

In fact, most people seem to experience plenty of meaning in their lives (see Chapter 10), even though they may not have conceptualized a coherent or explicit philosophy of life, religious or secular.

Of course, people who find themselves unable to believe in the supernatural, or in the various promises of religion, will have little choice but to seek secular means to reduce existential anxieties and uncertainties and to attain a sense of meaning, belonging, and control. In this regard, a number of prominent psychologists, among them Gordon Allport, Roy Baumeister, William James, and Robert Emmons, have considered whether psychological science might offer a scientific substitute for religion, for example, in helping individuals cope with anxieties and traumas, find direction and meaning in life, and achieve self-understanding.[96] I am not promoting psychological science as a substitute for religion. Nonetheless, in Chapter 10, I will discuss what psychological science can tell us about how to lead happy, meaningful, and fulfilling lives with or without religion.

But first, in the next two chapters, I review some of the more thoroughly investigated psychosocial outcomes of religion, both good (Chapter 5) and bad (Chapter 6). These outcomes are particularly relevant in assessing the relative merits of religion versus secular humanism as alternative life stances.

Chapter 5
The Psychosocial Benefits of Religion

Any assessment of the relative merits and viability of religion and secular humanism should be based, in part, on an evaluation of the psychosocial benefits of religion. In this chapter I summarize evidence of the proposed benefits of religion for physical health, psychological well-being, and prosocial or moral behavior. I also address the individual and societal factors that might account for and impact these positive outcomes. Finally, I offer some preliminary answers to the following question: Are religion's positive contributions to well-being and prosocial behavior unique and irreplaceable or are secular means to these outcomes equally viable?

[R]eligion can be understood as double-edged in nature; it can be both a source of problems and a source of solutions.
  – Hisham Abu-Raiya, Kenneth Pargament, & Neal Krause[1]

It is no contradiction to invoke religion to explain both terrible massacres and extreme generosity, both ethical integrity and moral apathy.
  – Samantha Abrams, Joshua Jackson, & Kurt Gray[2]

If religion serves the psychosocial functions discussed in Chapter 4, we should expect religious commitment to lead to positive psychosocial outcomes, such as better functioning and well-being. However, historic and present-day experience reveals that religion can be both beneficial and detrimental to individuals and societies, depending on the nature of the associated beliefs and practices. On the one hand, religion can be a source of joy, comfort, meaning, and prosocial behavior. On the other hand, it can promote personal guilt and anxiety, spiritual struggles, prejudice and intolerance, and, in the worst instances, extremism and violence. In this chapter, I address the proposed beneficial psychosocial outcomes of religion that have received the most attention in psychological research.

DOES RELIGION BENEFIT PHYSICAL HEALTH?

Over the past 30 years, hundreds of studies have related aspects of religion to physical health and psychological well-being. Fortunately, a number of reviews provide a good sense of the extent of the relationships. These reviews have concluded that greater religious involvement often, but not always, has a positive impact on physical health and mortality outcomes.[3] For example, in a majority of studies, greater religiosity has been associated with lower rates of suicide, alcohol use/abuse, heart disease, cancer, and overall mortality, as well as better immune functioning.[4]

In addition, some research has found that members of faith traditions that prescribe more demanding health habits, such as prohibitions on smoking, alcohol, drugs, and sex outside of marriage, live longer, on average, than members of other faith traditions.[5] Additional research suggests that religious people, on average, exhibit more positive outlooks toward their age-related disabilities; higher rates of screening for early detection of diseases (e.g., mammography, pap smears, HIV testing, prostate exams); and greater compliance in taking medications, thus obtaining greater benefits from treatment.[6]

I should note three qualifications to these overall findings, however. First, the strength of the relationship between religiosity and physical health is generally only weak or moderate, in part, because so many other factors, such as genes, aging, environmental factors, and one's religious orientation, also impact physical health. Second, poor health may lead one to turn to religion and prayer as a coping mechanism, thus reducing any positive relationship between religiosity and good health. Third, as addressed later in this chapter, negative forms of religious coping or spiritual struggles can have harmful effects on the course of physical illness and mortality.

What aspect of religion best predicts better physical health and mortality outcomes? Regular attendance at religious services. Regular participation in religious communities can encourage mutual assistance, emotional and moral support, volunteerism, and attitudes and beliefs that are conducive to healthy lifestyles.[7] Indeed, epidemiologist Tyler VanderWeele has estimated that attending religious services at least weekly is associated with 25% to 35% lower mortality over 10 to 15 years.[8]

There is some evidence, however, that the benefits of religion for longevity hold only in relatively religious cultural contexts. For example, one study found that in relatively religious U.S. counties, religious people lived 2.2 years longer, on average, than did nonreligious people. However, in relatively secular counties, religiosity did not confer any longevity benefits. Indeed, in the most secular counties, religious people actually lived an average of 1.72 *fewer* years than nonreligious people.[9]

In short, whether religion contributes to longevity appears to depend on whether religion is normative or socially valued in the cultural context.

DOES RELIGION BENEFIT PSYCHOLOGICAL WELL-BEING?

Reviewers have typically concluded that the relationship between religion and psychological well-being is often positive but generally modest.[10] Beneficial outcomes have included reduced likelihood of, and better recovery from, anxiety disorders, depression, and substance abuse; reduced emotional distress; greater marital stability; and greater happiness, life satisfaction, and optimism.[11] For example, various large-scale meta-analyses of studies have found that:

- Greater religiosity is, on average, modestly associated with fewer depression symptoms, although there is considerably variability in the strength of the relationship across studies;[12]

- In adolescents and emerging adults, greater religiosity is modestly associated with fewer risky behaviors, including less alcohol or substance abuse, smoking, delinquent behaviors, and premarital sex, as well as increased psychological well-being;[13]
- In cancer patients, greater religiosity has overall positive but modest effects on patient mental health;[14]
- In longitudinal studies—which enable stronger conclusions about whether religion causes or predicts *future* well-being—religiosity or spirituality has shown very modest positive effects on subsequent psychological health.[15]

Recently, however, sociologist Ryan Cragun and social psychologist David Speed expressed skepticism that religiosity matters for well-being or happiness. They examined large representative samples in 60 countries and found that the relationship between religiosity and happiness is neither universal nor robust across cultures. Indeed, happiness is better predicted by demographic variables than by religiosity. While acknowledging the possibility that religiosity can contribute to the happiness of *some* individuals, they concluded that, in general, "happiness is not reliant upon religiosity."[16]

Both religion and well-being are complex and multifaceted, however, and we might expect some aspects of religious experience to relate differently to various aspects of well-being. For example, regular attendance at religious services may be more important than other aspects of religious experience such as beliefs and prayer in predicting certain aspects of well-being.[17] Indeed, by one estimate, religious service attendance is associated with an approximately 20% to 30% reduction in rates of depression and a three- to six-fold reduction in rates of suicide.[18]

The nature or fervency of one's beliefs may be particularly important. For example, it appears that an *intrinsic orientation* to religion is more conducive to psychological well-being than either an *extrinsic* or *quest* orientation, both of which may actually be associated with reduced well-being.[19] Recall that for individuals with an intrinsic orientation, religion is a master motive guiding their lives and an end in itself. For individuals with an extrinsic orientation religion is a means to other ends, such as social relationships, status, or comfort. For individuals with a quest orientation, religion involves a flexible, questioning search for existential meaning that accepts doubt and the absence of firm answers.

I would argue that the quest orientation—with its searching focus, openness to doubts, and lack of definitive answers—is a particularly intellectually humble or honest approach to religious belief. Nonetheless, to the extent that people seek order and answers in their lives, the quest to resolve religious doubts and uncertainties may lead to discomfort and reduced well-being, at least while individuals are still searching. At the same time, based on a compilation of findings from 91 studies, social psychologist C. Daniel Batson and colleagues concluded that the quest orientation to religion promotes greater open-mindedness, flexibility, and possibly self-actualization.[20]

Regarding the fervency of belief, a national on-line survey in the United States replicated the usual modest positive relationship between religiosity and self-reported well-being. However, only the most fervent believers reported greater subjective well-being than atheists, agnostics, and religiously unaffiliated individuals. Religiously affiliated individuals with only low to moderate levels of religious commitment actually averaged *lower* in well-being than these nonreligious individuals.[21] A similar on-line survey of respondents in Germany, Switzerland, and Austria found that only those religiously affiliated respondents who were actually *practicing* their religion reported modestly higher life satisfaction and meaning in life than individuals with no religious affiliation.[22]

In short, these large-scale studies suggest that the benefits of religious belief and practice for psychological well-being may be largely limited to those individuals with the most intrinsic, fervent, and definitive beliefs. In addition, as discussed in the next section, the relationship between religiosity and well-being apparently depends on the cultural context.

Do the Psychological Benefits of Religion Depend on a Country's Overall Religiosity and Circumstances?

Yes. Several large-scale studies have found that the positive relationship between religiosity and psychological well-being is stronger—although still modest—in those countries, states, and counties in which religion is more normative or socially valued.[23] For example, in a comparison of 65 countries, greater religiosity was modestly associated with greater self-esteem for individuals in the most religious countries such as Pakistan, the Philippines, Egypt, Saudi Arabia, Indonesia, India, El Salvador, United Arab Emirates, and Malaysia. In contrast, the weakest—and generally trivial—associations between religiosity and self-esteem were found primarily in the secular countries of Scandinavia and Western Europe.[24] The authors of another multinational study with similar findings concluded that:

> [I]n religious countries, religious people are psychologically better off, partially because they enjoy greater social respect and recognition. Their non-religious counterparts are worse off, as they report being treated with less respect. Conversely, in non-religious countries, religious people do not feel more highly respected than their non-religious counterparts, which explains why there is little to no difference in the subjective well-being between these two groups in non-religious countries.[25]

Similarly, the benefits of religiosity for psychological well-being are greatest in countries around the world (and in U.S. states) that are experiencing the most difficult circumstances—for example, those with lower average incomes and education, and poorer health and health prospects. These are also the most religious states and countries. Apparently, people in more secular societies are able to more readily attain a sense of well-being without formal religion.[26]

Finally, the relationship between religiosity and well-being may be stronger among people from lower socio-economic backgrounds, in racial/ethnic minority communities, and among other marginalized people. This is consistent with sociological theories that see religion as a compensatory source of comfort and aid for people from marginalized communities.[27]

In summary, we can conclude that religion often has positive, albeit generally modest, benefits for both physical health and psychological well-being. However, the extent of these benefits will likely vary depending on the nature and strength of one's religious commitments, the social norms and values regarding religion in various cultural contexts, and the difficulty of one's life circumstances.

Importantly, there is also some indication that secular or nonreligious people may actually experience higher levels of well-being than religious people with low to moderate levels of religious commitment,[28] a possibility that I will revisit in Chapter 9.

Finally, the impact of religion on well-being also depends on whether one applies positive or negative methods of religious coping, as described in the next section.

RELIGIOUS COPING AND RELIGIOUS STRUGGLES

Stimulated by American psychologist Kenneth Pargament's 1997 book titled *The Psychology of Religion and Coping*, many studies have investigated the specific religious coping methods that people use to deal with daily stressors, and especially more significant traumas or life events.[29] Pargament and colleagues sought to identify the full range of positive (beneficial) versus negative (harmful) religious coping methods, and delineated 21 such methods.

For example, you are using *positive religious coping* methods when you search for comfort and reassurance through God's love and care; seek control through a problem-solving partnership with God; or engage in religious activities to shift focus from a stressor. In contrast, you are using *neg-*

ative religious coping methods when you redefine a stressor as a punishment from God for your sins; passively wait for God to control the situation; or express confusion and dissatisfaction regarding your relationship with God.[30]

Other psychologists have referred to negative religious coping as *religious/spiritual struggles* or *religious strain*.[31] Some of these researchers have identified six types of religious struggle: divine (e.g., feeling as though God has abandoned you); demonic (e.g., worrying that your problems are the work of the devil or evil spirits); interpersonal (e.g., concern that other people do not respect your religious beliefs); moral struggle (e.g., worrying that your actions are morally or spiritually wrong); ultimate meaning (e.g., feeling as though your life has no deep meaning); and doubt (e.g., feeling troubled or worried by questions about your religious or spiritual beliefs). Researchers have begun to investigate the different ways in which people might respond to their religious struggles, which may have implications for spiritual growth or decline.[32]

Fortunately, people use positive religious coping much more frequently than negative religious coping. Also, a significant amount of research with college students, community adults, or medical patients has revealed that positive religious coping is associated with a variety of indicators of better psychological and physical well-being, as well as greater spiritual growth, better compliance with medical recommendations, and reduced death concerns.[33] In contrast, negative religious coping or religious struggle has been associated with poorer psychological well-being, including depression and anxiety; higher mortality risk among ill elders; poorer adherence to medical recommendations; and increased death concerns.[34]

Such results remind us that religion can be a double-edged sword. It can serve as a source of comfort, particularly when positive coping methods are applied. However, when religious worldviews break down, as revealed in negative religious coping or spiritual struggles, religion is potentially harmful to physical and psychological well-being. In addition, for some people, the process of leaving religion to become more secular can itself be traumatic, particularly for those leaving behind more conservative or "high-control" religious communities.[35]

Given the overarching question addressed in this book, another important issue is whether religious methods of coping are superior, or add something unique, to nonreligious or secular means of coping. For example, secular coping might include seeking support from others or doing some cognitive restructuring—for example, by taking a new angle on the situation or asking oneself what is really important. Some studies do suggest that religious coping may contribute something unique in the prediction of adjustment to such stressful events as surgery, divorce, and serious illness.[36] At least for religious individuals, religious coping methods may have the advantage of being imbued with the sacred.

DOES RELIGION LEAD TO MORE PROSOCIAL OR MORAL BEHAVIOR?

Most of us are familiar with The Golden Rule to "do unto others as you would have them do unto you." The Golden Rule, or something comparable, is prescribed by all of today's major world religions. Indeed, religions are intimately concerned with our "prosocial" or moral behavior.

Prosocial behavior encompasses such actions as altruism, generosity, cooperation, forgiveness, tolerance, and trust, as well as proscriptions against selfishness, dishonesty, prejudice, aggression, and violence. History is filled with heroic and noble examples of religion-inspired prosocial contributions to society and humankind. Examples include involvement in the anti-slavery and civil rights movements, disaster and poverty relief efforts, refugee settlement, and the founding and operation of hospitals, orphanages, charities, schools, and universities.

Beyond these notable examples, the most relevant question for my purposes is the extent to which religion promotes prosocial behavior *in everyday believers*. Psychologists investigating this question refer to the *religion-prosociality hypothesis*, and seek to determine the extent to which religion inspires or elicits prosocial or moral behavior, while inhibiting antisocial, immoral, or unethical behavior.

Recall that moral instincts are likely deeply rooted in our evolutionary heritage and thus likely predate, in some limited form, religiously-motivated morality or prosocial behavior. Thus, although religion might promote and shape prosocial behavior, it is probably not its sole or original cause. Nonetheless, several of the findings reported in previous chapters suggest that religion can play a role in prosocial behavior. For example, recall that:

- Prosocial tendencies, including those encouraged by religion, could have evolved through cultural group selection, as more co-operative and prosocial groups outcompeted less cooperative groups;

- Belief in, or reminders of, supernatural monitoring or punishment is associated with greater prosocial behavior or intentions;

- Costly requirements and rituals in religious communities can promote greater cooperation among their members.

Overall, however, research on the religion-prosociality hypothesis has revealed a mixed and complex picture.[37] When people are asked in survey studies to *self-report* their level of religious involvement, greater religiosity has been modestly to moderately associated with *self-reported* prosocial values, traits, or behaviors. That is, people who describe themselves as more religious also tend to describe themselves as more prosocial. Nonetheless, there continues to be disagreement among scientists about how to interpret these findings, particularly in light of the failure of many studies to demonstrate a consistent link between religiosity and *actual* prosocial behavior—that is, how people actually behave as opposed to how they *say* they behave.[38]

For example, although religious people tend to report having values and traits associated with forgiveness—a key tenet in monotheistic religions—and seem to understand that they are *supposed to be* forgiving—religious involvement appears to play at best a modest role in determining who will and will not forgive in specific instances.[39] Indeed, sociologist Mark Chaves, in his 2009 Presidential Address at the annual meeting of the Society for the Scientific Study of Religion, observed that we should not expect that greater religiosity will or should lead to more prosocial behavior in general. This is because religious phenomena are very situation-specific and "people's religious ideas and practices generally are fragmented, compartmentalized, loosely connected, unexamined, and context dependent."[40]

I will first summarize the results of self-report survey studies, which have provided the most consistent support for a link between religiosity and prosociality.

Self-report Surveys

Charity, volunteering, and civic engagement

Some international surveys, as well as national surveys of Americans, provide evidence that, on average, more religious individuals, as compared to more secular individuals, report greater donations to charity, greater volunteering, and greater involvement in civic and political life. However, there are complexities and potential qualifications in these findings.[41]

For example, there remains some debate on the extent to which religious charity and volunteering extends beyond one's own religious community. A number of studies suggest that the more religious people are—particularly conservatively religious—the greater their tendency to concentrate their giving and volunteering toward their own religious group rather than toward secular community causes.[42] In addition, recent survey evidence in the United States suggests that only religious people who attend religious services regularly show greater civic engagement (e.g., in voting) than atheists and agnostics.[43]

Indeed, to the extent that religious people become more engaged in volunteer and civic activities, it could be accounted for, at least in part, by the tendency of religious organizations to organize such activities rather than because of their religious beliefs or values per se. Involvement in religious institutions can act as a feeder mechanism leading to greater opportunities for secular volunteering.[44] Indeed, based on a recent national survey of Canadians, researchers concluded that "atheists likely have fewer opportunities to volunteer but are similarly inclined to volunteer."[45]

In addition, it is less clear that members of religious communities will be more generous in charitable giving or volunteering than members of secular groups that have a humanistic worldview or social outreach focus. Indeed, there is some evidence that atheists view charity and social justice activism as important goals of secular groups and that such activism is an important aspect of atheists' identity.[46]

At least in the United States, more religious individuals tend to prefer private charity over governmental action and are thus somewhat *less* supportive, on average, of government policies and actions dealing with poverty and inequality.[47] This is especially the case for individuals with conservative religious identities and culturally conservative values, despite the prosocial value of these programs in helping people in need.[48] In contrast, secular individuals are more likely to support government intervention and taxes over charitable giving to reduce inequality. Thus, studies of charitable giving may largely reflect differences between religious and secular individuals in their preferred forms of prosocial generosity.[49]

David E. Campbell, an expert on religion's role in American politics, and his colleagues have pointed to some of the complexities in comparisons of civic engagement by religious and nonreligious Americans. In particular, they note that *nonreligiosity* can be distinguished from *secularism*. They described nonreligious Americans as those who are low in religiosity *and* also lack an affirmative secular worldview or identity such as secular humanism. In contrast, secularists are those with affirmative secular worldviews that value reason, objective evidence, human knowledge, and free thought, *irrespective* of their level of religiosity. The researchers then used this distinction to define four groups of Americans:

- *Religionists*—above average in religiosity and low in secularism;

- *Nonreligionists*—low in both religiosity and secularism;
- *Secularists*—low in religiosity but high in secularism;
- *Religious Secularists*—combine religious belief with a secular worldview.

Nonreligionists reported the least political and nonpolitical civic engagement. Secularists reported somewhat greater amounts of political engagement than Religionists, but less nonpolitical engagement. Interestingly, the Religious Secularists reported the greatest amount of both political and nonpolitical civic engagement.

Based on these findings, the authors concluded that the United States should not be unduly worried about its civic health, even as the country is becoming more secular.[50] Rather, "growth in nonreligiosity is counterbalanced by an accompanying rise in secularism which, as we have seen, leads to greater civic engagement."[51] In short, nonreligiosity and secularism, as defined by Campbell and colleagues, are not the same thing and only the former is associated with civic disengagement.

Values and morality

Comprehensive reviews have found that religious people tend to favor values that support conventionality, tradition, order, and benevolence towards known others. In contrast, they tend to devalue openness to change, autonomy, and pleasure-seeking.[52] The strength of the relationships between religiosity and these values is modest to moderate in size. Regular churchgoers are also more likely to condemn violations of traditional or conventional morality, including premarital sex, pornography, divorce, homosexuality, gambling, and cheating on taxes.

One finding is of special interest: Greater religiosity is modestly linked to *benevolence* values, but not *universalism* values—which refer to valuing the welfare of *all* people and nature. This has suggested to some reviewers that religion-based prosociality—despite Christian prescriptions to love one's neighbors *and* one's enemies—is typically aimed toward close others, rather than toward humanity or nature more generally.[53] However, there is some evidence that religious Buddhists do tend to endorse universalism values.[54]

In addressing the question of whether religion leads people to be more moral or not, a potential dilemma arises. It may depend on how we define morality.

For example, psychologists Jonathan Haidt and Jesse Graham identified five different aspects or foundations of morality. Religious people show particular concern for loyalty to the ingroup, respect and obedience to authority, and sanctity and purity—the so-called "socially binding" foundations of morality. However, religious people, as compared to more secular people, do *not* show greater concern for fairness and justice or for compassion.[55] Moral perspectives differ most in the sexual and reproductive domains, for example, with regards to abortion, sexual orientation, and casual sex.

Also, a number of studies have found that religious people tend to endorse absolutist or rule-based (i.e., *deontological*) moral styles in which the distinction between right and wrong looks definitive over more relativist and outcome-based (i.e., *consequentialist*) moral styles in which the distinction between right and wrong is more complex and context-dependent.[56]

Personality traits

Do more religious people report higher levels of prosocial personality traits? To a modest extent, yes. The relevant studies have generally examined five broad traits associated with the so-called *Five Factor* or "*Big Five*" *model* of personality. This model proposes that most personality characteristics can be encompassed at a high level of generality under five broad personality dimensions, typically labeled Neuroticism (vs. Emotional Stability), Extraversion, Openness to Experience, Agreeableness, and Conscientiousness.[57]

Relevant reviews have consistently found that people who report greater religiosity show a modest tendency to report greater Agreeableness and

Conscientiousness, both of which can be viewed as prosocial traits.[58] People who report greater Agreeableness describe themselves as trusting, cooperative, compassionate, altruistic, helpful, modest, and straightforward (as opposed to aggressive and antagonistic). People who report greater Conscientiousness describe themselves as organized, self-disciplined, responsible, planful, and achievement-oriented (as opposed to careless, irresponsible, and spontaneous).[59] In addition, there is some evidence that slightly stronger relationships between religiosity and personality can be found when more specific prosocial traits such as altruism, fairness, forgivingness, and self-discipline are examined—facets or traits that may be more specifically linked to religiosity.[60]

We see interesting findings with the Openness to Experience trait. Openness to Experience describes people who are open to ideas, emotions, and values; intellectually curious; imaginative; unconventional; and aesthetically sensitive. Research indicates that the relationship between religiosity and Openness to Experience depends on one's religious or spiritual orientation. People with a more fundamentalist or tradition-oriented religious orientation tend to average *lower* on Openness to Experience. In contrast, people with a more "spiritual" orientation—that is, one that is more nontraditional, individualized, or mystical—tend to average *higher* in Openness to Experience.[61] People with a religious upbringing who subsequently become nonreligious also tend to show higher levels of Openness to Experience, particularly its unconventionality aspects.[62]

Overall, the relationships between religiosity and personality traits noted here have held up well across different religious traditions and cultures, although the strength of the relationships depends on how normative religiosity is in a given country.[63] Religiosity and personality may impact each other. On the one hand, involvement in a religious community could promote greater Agreeableness and Conscientiousness. On the other hand, research indicates that our personality traits in youth can impact how religious we become as an adult.[64]

To sum up:

There is considerable evidence that greater religious involvement is positively associated with *self-reported* prosocial values, personality traits, and behavior. However, the frequent failure of religiosity to predict greater prosociality in *actual behavior* has fueled questions about the validity or meaningfulness of the findings in self-report studies. Studies have found that religious people tend to average higher in *impression management*—that is, the tendency to describe themselves in a socially desirable or enhanced manner—particularly in those domains that are central to their self-concept, such as religion.[65] This finding has led a number of scholars to conclude that the apparent association between religiosity and self-reported prosocial behavior may be an artifact of the stronger impression management tendencies of religious individuals.[66]

This possibility remains under debate. A reasonable conclusion is that impression management tendencies inflate, but do not fully account for, the relationship between religiosity and self-reported prosocial behavior. But what about the relationship between religiosity and *actual* behavior?

Behavioral Studies

As foreshadowed above, studies of *actual* behavior—rather than *self-reported* behavior—have largely failed to show a reliable relationship between greater religiosity and more prosocial or moral behavior. On the one hand, there is some *indirect* behavioral evidence for such a relationship. For example:

- In 19th century America, religious communes, as compared to secular communes, exhibited greater cooperation and trust, as inferred from the greater longevity of the religious communes.[67]
- People in more religious kibbutzim in Israel showed more cooperation in a "behavioral economics game" (see below) than people in secular kibbutzim.[68]
- Reviews most frequently conclude that greater personal religiosity is at least modestly associated with reduced crime, although there

127

are some complexities in this research.[69] For example, there is some indication that strongly religious *and* nonreligious individuals may be more similar in their levels of crime than individuals who are less committed in either direction.[70]

On the other hand, more controlled studies, in and out of the laboratory setting, have *not* shown a consistent relationship between levels of religiosity and prosocial behavior. Rather, social scientists have described the relationship as limited, generally weak, and dependent on the context or situation.

For example, one study found that religious, as compared to nonreligious, participants were more responsive to appeals for charity only on Sundays. This suggested that religious individuals are not more charitable in general, but "only when their religion is made salient to them."[71] Also, in a study of adults in the United States and Canada, researchers found no discernible difference in the frequency of moral and immoral acts reported by religious and nonreligious people in their daily lives. However, religious people did express more intense self-conscious emotions in response to their actions, for example, guilt and embarrassment in response to immoral acts and pride and gratefulness in response to moral acts.[72]

The most common type of behavioral study has involved laboratory interactions in which participants take part in "behavioral economic games" meant to assess their actions under more controlled conditions. In these tasks, participants' generosity, trust, or cooperation are assessed, for example, by allocating a certain amount of money to participants and determining how much of their allocation they are willing to share with other participants, or by examining participants' willingness to reciprocate the gifts of others by returning money under various conditions. In general, these studies have found that religious people are *not* more prosocial than nonreligious individuals toward other study participants unless the other participants are known to share a religious or other ingroup identity with the focal participant—that is, when "the situation calls for maintaining a favorable social reputation within the ingroup."[73]

The greater importance of the situational context—as compared to the general religiosity of the person—in eliciting prosocial behavior has also been documented in so-called religious *priming studies*. In the typical religious priming study, participants are first exposed to religious cues or primes—consciously or unconsciously—to determine whether doing so increases prosocial attitudes or behaviors, at least temporally. Because the religious priming occurs first under controlled conditions, such studies are thought to provide a firmer basis for inferring the direction of causality—that is, religious cues presented first are thought to "cause" any prosocial behavior that follows.

A variety of priming methods are available. For example, if you were a participant in such a study, you might be asked to read passages from the Bible or answer questions about your religious beliefs (i.e., explicit priming). You might be asked to unscramble sentences containing religious words (i.e., implicit priming). You might be exposed to rapid, unconscious visual displays of religious concepts (i.e., subliminal priming). Or, you might be asked to complete the research tasks in a naturalistic or everyday setting with religious cues, such as in a church or while listening to background calls for prayer (i.e., contextual priming).[74]

Does such religious priming increase prosocial behavior? A widely cited meta-analysis of 25 such studies found that religious priming has, on average, small to moderate effects on prosocial behavior for religious people. Perhaps not surprisingly, religious cues or primes do not have reliable effects on the prosocial behavior of nonreligious people. Importantly, when religious cues or primes are *absent*, religious people do *not* show greater prosocial behavior than nonreligious people in these studies. These results suggest that in the absence of situational cues or reminders of one's religion, religious people are *not* generally more prosocial than nonreligious people, at least on the kinds of measures of prosocial behavior used in these priming studies.[75]

Contextual priming tends to have the largest impact on prosocial behavior in these studies. In addition, contextual priming simulates more realistically the types of religious cues and environments experienced *in everyday life*. Thus, it is worth highlighting a few typical studies of this type, which I think readers will find intriguing. It is also noteworthy that researchers have conducted these studies in a variety of religious and cultural contexts.

- In a study in Chile, students showed more cooperation with other participants in their assigned task, and anticipated greater cooperation from others, when the task was conducted *in a church setting* as compared to a lecture hall (i.e., in a religious context as compared to a secular context). Importantly, the religiosity of the students did *not* predict participants' level of cooperation or their expectations of others' cooperation.[76]

- In a study in Mauritius, people showed more cooperation when their assigned task was completed *in a Hindu temple* rather than in a restaurant, irrespective of their self-reported religiosity.[77]

- In a study of shopkeepers in Marrakech, Morocco, participants behaved in a more charitable manner *when a Muslim call to prayer was audible*, although the effects on charity dissipated rapidly after the call to prayer ended.[78]

- In a study of Catholics in Mauritius, participants donated more money anonymously to a charity when the study was completed *in either a Catholic Church* or a *Hindu temple* than when it was completed in a restaurant.[79]

These illustrative studies further support the view that, for religious people, it is the situational context—not the participants' general level of religiosity—that largely induces prosociality. In addition, religious cues or primes impact religious people more reliably than they impact nonreligious people. Based on findings such as these, psychologists Ara Norenzayan and Azim Shariff concluded that "[t]he religious *situation* is more important than the religious *disposition* in predicting prosocial behavior."[80]

WHAT FACTORS UNDERLIE RELIGION'S (GENERALLY MODEST) BENEFITS?

Finally, we can ask, what is it about religion that might contribute to well-being or prosocial behavior? Among the most commonly mentioned factors are the following.[81]

- *Health-related behaviors* – religious prescriptions can lead to fewer health-risk behaviors (e.g., smoking, substance abuse, risky sexual practices) and the "sanctification" of one's body (i.e., treating one's body as sacred), which in turn leads to better physical health.

- *A cognitive framework of meaning* – religion provides a cognitive framework and sense of meaning and purpose in life, which in turn can contribute to greater life satisfaction, self-esteem, optimism, and positive affect.[82]

- *Social networks and support* – Active participation in religious communities can increase social networks—both religious and secular—and the amount and quality of social support,[83] which in turn can contribute to greater life satisfaction, reduced stress, and various positive health outcomes.[84] Religious social networks can also contribute to prosocial behavior by promoting charitable activity, volunteering, and civic engagement.[85]

- *Self-regulation*—Religion promotes self-regulation or self-control, and in turn well-being and prosocial behavior.[86] Longitudinal studies suggest that religion promotes self-control over the long-term and that self-control may, at least for some people, have a reciprocal effect on their religiosity.[87]

- *Positive affective states*—Religious services, prayer, and "expansive" worship postures—as well as the hopeful outlooks associated with religion and its rituals—can induce various positive emotional states, including feelings of gratitude, awe, peacefulness, and love.[88]

131

- *Positive virtues or traits*—To the extent that greater religiosity leads to such virtues as forgiveness, altruism, humility, and gratitude, this could contribute to religion's impact on prosociality and well-being.[89] One comprehensive model proposes that the Christian virtues of forgiveness, compassion, and beneficence are instrumental in explaining religion's impact on health and well-being.[90]
- *Religious coping styles*—Religious people can draw on a number of positive religious coping styles (see above) to deal with stressors.[91]
- *Moral cues or reminders*—Religious cues or reminders can promote prosocial behavior by reminding people of moral prescriptions or by activating awareness or fears of supernatural monitoring.[92]

These factors help to explain how religious beliefs and practices can promote well-being and prosocial behavior, at least to the modest or limited extent found in extant research. A question for later chapters in this book is how secular humanists can achieve these positive psychosocial outcomes.

TAKEAWAYS

An assessment of the psychosocial benefits of religion is central to my pragmatic comparison of the relative merits and viability of religion versus secular humanism. What can we now conclude, based on available evidence, about the impact of religiosity on well-being and prosocial or moral behavior?

Regarding well-being, the evidence reveals that the impact of religion can be double-edged. When applied in a positive manner, for example, through positive religious coping methods, it can have a positive, albeit generally modest, beneficial impact on physical health and psychological well-being. The relationship between religion and well-being is stronger for people with more intrinsic and committed religious orientations and in cultural contexts in which life circumstances are more challenging and religion is more valued and normative. In contrast, when applied in a negative manner, for example, through negative religious coping methods, religion can also be a source of strain, guilt, and spiritual discontent, contributing to anxiety, depression, and a perceived loss of meaning and control. Fortunately, people more often apply positive rather than negative religious coping methods.

Given that religion and well-being are most frequently assessed by researchers at a single point in time, it is often not definitive whether greater religiosity *causes* enhanced well-being or, inversely, whether people who already feel better about themselves are more likely to become involved in religious activity. Indeed, both directions of causation might be operating.

And what about the relationship between religiosity and prosocial behavior? I should first acknowledge potential limitations of some of the research on this topic.

For example, some scholars have questioned whether one-time religious cues or primes—whether presented in or out of the laboratory setting—can adequately simulate the more persistent, realistic, and powerful encounters provided by participation in actual religious rituals and communities. Indeed, continuous cues or reminders of one's religion can be provided by regular attendance at religious services, calls for charity and community involvement, emotional and community-binding rituals, and other routine religious practices such as daily prayer and grace before meals. Such ongoing religious cues or reminders are probably not well-captured by the cues or primes used in psychological studies of prosociality.

Similarly, the behavioral tasks—typically behavioral economics games—used to assess prosocial behavior in these studies may not adequately reflect the variety of prosocial behaviors observed in everyday experience. Also, they may not induce the level of investment or satisfaction elicited by performing prosocial behaviors in one's daily life.

Given these limitations, we might be justified in largely discounting the results of many of the behavioral studies relating religiosity to prosocial behavior.

Nonetheless, while acknowledging the limitations of such studies, most psychologists believe that they tell us something important about the situational or bounded nature of religious prosociality, which has been referred to as the *minimal model of religious prosociality*, or as *parochial altruism*.[93] For example, psychologist Vassilis Saroglou summarizes what he thinks most scholars have concluded about religious prosociality:

- It is minimal and limited in extent, typically involving low-cost behaviors towards ingroup members such as relatives, friends, and other members of one's religious community;
- It is frequently motivated by egoistic concerns regarding self-image and social reputation rather than altruistic motivations;
- It is conditional on contextual variables such as situational reminders or cues that can activate or inhibit it;
- It varies greatly depending on one's religious orientation (e.g., intrinsic vs. extrinsic) and the specific aspects of religion activated (e.g., group identity vs. personal devotion).[94]

On the one hand, the typical focus of prosocial behavior on ingroup members should not be surprising, given our evolved tribal instincts and the costs of further expanding our circle of moral concern or empathy.[95] On the other hand, it may be premature to conclude that religion's impact on prosocial behavior is so modest and limited. Indeed, some scholars have recently expressed more optimism that religiously motivated prosocial behavior extends *beyond* one's ingroups to people more generally.[96]

For example, a few recent studies have shown that when religious people are asked to think about God it can increase their generosity, or decrease dehumanizing attitudes, towards members of other religious groups.[97] However, these studies again suggest that religious cues or reminders (e.g., thinking about God) may be necessary to increase—at least temporarily—prosocial behavior towards people beyond one's religious ingroup.

In any case, prosociality that is directly largely or exclusively towards ingroup members should not be too readily disparaged. If religion reliably contributes to greater generosity, cooperation, and empathy, and less intolerance or aggression, towards ingroup members, this nonetheless argues for the merits of religious involvement—even if the ideal of a more universal altruism that extends to all people is not commonly achieved.

Are Religion's Positive Contributions Unique or Irreplaceable?

In addressing the overarching question of this book, the most important question for this chapter is the following: Is religion unique or irreplaceable in its positive contributions to well-being and prosociality—or, are secular means to these goals substitutable and equally viable? Although I will address this question more completely in Part II of this book, some initial inferences are possible based on the research summarized in this chapter.

First, recall that the relationship between religion and well-being is, on average, modest, and most applicable to individuals who have strong beliefs or actively practice their religion. People with relatively weak or uncertain religious commitments may average no higher in well-being, and perhaps even lower, than committed secular humanists. Furthermore, as noted earlier, religious people may accrue well-being advantages only in those countries in which religion is normative and highly valued or in which life circumstances are difficult. This is consistent with evidence that people in well-off, secular countries report higher levels of psychological well-being than people in poorer countries, which also tend to be more religious.[98]

Second, researchers do not fully understand the mechanisms by which religion contributes to well-being—although some likely factors were noted in this chapter. From a religious perspective, a greater sense of well-being could be viewed as the result of religious faith or God's grace. However, might secular mechanisms serve equally well? Religious prescriptions can lead to behaviors that are conducive to health and well-being—for example, prohibitions against smoking or alcoholic drinks, or dietary restrictions. However, these benefits can also be attained by secular individuals who are conscientious about their health. Similarly, while religion can contribute to a sense of purpose and meaning, secular individuals can presumably find such purpose and meaning through nonreligious goals and activities. I address this presumption in Part II of this book.

Third, both religious and secular people can experience positive emotions such as joy, awe, and wonder. For religious people, such emotions can be experienced during religious encounters, ranging from the relatively mundane to the mystical. However, secular people can also experience comparable emotions when encountering natural phenomena such as the expansiveness of the cosmos; the grandeur of oceans, canyons, and mountains; inspiring music or art; or scientific discoveries.

Fourth, it is less clear that secular networks or organizations such as social groups, political organizations, service clubs, athletic teams, and so forth, can adequately replace religious communities as a source of social and emotional support. Indeed, some scholars have suggested that religious support may be qualitatively different and more impactful on well-being than other sources of social support. Committed members of religious communities typically share important beliefs and values, feelings of social belonging, intimate emotional connections over time, and assurances of mutual help.[99]

Indeed, an interview study of a nationally representative sample of Americans found that the relationship between church attendance and greater life satisfaction was largely accounted for by the number of close friends in one's congregation, particularly for those with a strong religious identity.[100] In considering whether secular sources of social support might be equally impactful on peoples' life satisfaction, the authors offered the following opinion:

Even if social networks in non-religious contexts could have a similar effect on life satisfaction as that of congregational friendships, it is difficult to think of any non-religious organizations in the United States that are comparable to congregations in scale and scope of membership base, intensity of member participation in collective rituals, and strength of identity that members share. Even if social networks and identities forged in non-religious organizations could have benefits comparable to those we found here, congregations are nevertheless unique among American voluntary organizations as a source of life satisfaction.[101]

Later in this book, I will consider the possibility that certain secular congregations (e.g., Sunday Assemblies) can offer levels of social support, emotional connection, and feelings of shared values comparable to those provided by religious congregations. It should also be noted that in many countries, people have largely turned away from organized religious communities. Instead, they adopt more personal religious, spiritual, or nonreligious perspectives and cultivate secular sources of social and emotional support.

Fifth, regarding religion and prosociality, it is important to recall that moral or prosocial behavior did not originate solely in religion, although religion can channel, reinforce, shape, or elaborate such behavior. In addition, secular individuals can behave as morally as religious individuals, but for different reasons. For example, as noted previously, secular people are as motivated as religious people by compassion and concerns for fairness and justice, which can provide sufficient secular bases for moral or prosocial behavior.[102] There is a modest tendency for religious people to report higher levels of the prosocial personality traits of Agreeableness and Conscientiousness. However, the full range of Agreeableness and Conscientiousness—including high levels of these traits—is also seen among secular individuals.

Sixth, prosocial behaviors such as charitable donations are more closely associated with the community aspects of religion than the belief aspects.

This raises the possibility that membership in organized secular groups might be equally conducive to such behaviors. Indeed, there is some evidence that active members of secular organizations are as likely to make charitable contributions, and in comparable amounts, as members of religious organizations. What is important is organizational involvement and social connections.[103]

In sum, as psychologist Ara Norenzayan has noted, religion is not the "only game in town" when it comes to promoting prosocial behavior. There are secular incentives and institutions that also serve this function, which likely become more important as the role of religion in society decreases.

Secular societies with effective institutions promote strong cooperative norms, and this is precisely where the vast majority of atheists live. Moreover, these institutions have replaced religious sources (and in some cases such as Northern Europe, much more effectively), and given birth to secular humanism, or a set of norms grounded in morality without reliance on gods.[104]

Other researchers offer comparable conclusions. For example, Azim Shariff observes that "the evidence clearly points to a positive effect of religion on prosociality, but against it being the only—or even best—path to prosocial behavior."[105] Similarly, psychologist Jordan Moon and colleagues have concluded that "there is little evidence to suggest that religion is a unique driver of prosociality." They note that the various factors that promote prosociality can also be achieved via secular means.[106]

Finally, it is important to acknowledge that not all religion-inspired behavior is healthy, prosocial, or beneficial. In the next chapter I address evidence of the harmful outcomes of religion—especially its potential contributions to prejudice and violence. I then revisit the main takeaways from research on the outcomes of religion—both positive and negative.

Chapter 6
Is Religion Harmful?

An assessment of the relative merits and viability of religion and secular humanism should also consider religion's potential harmful effects. In this chapter I highlight religion's role in prejudice and intolerance towards various marginalized groups; its potential association with terrorism and violence, but also peace-making and transitional justice efforts; and its mixed impact during the COVID-19 pandemic. I discuss some practical implications and methods for reducing religion-based prejudice or violence.

While reading the previous chapter on the psychosocial benefits of religion, some readers, particularly critics of religion, were probably exclaiming "But what about the harmful effects of religion?" If you are among these critics, you are in good company. In a recent survey in 27 countries, an average of 47% of respondents agreed that "Religion does more harm in the world than good." In several countries, more than 60% expressed this opinion.[1] Indeed, we should acknowledge a variety of potentially harmful effects of religion for individuals and societies.

For example, as noted in the previous chapter, some people experience religious or spiritual struggles. In addition, the patriarchal structures of some religious communities have been linked to forms of domestic violence, including wife-battering, child abuse, and honor killings.[2] Indeed, persistent patterns of child abuse have been revealed in a number of prominent religious communities. A research team in the United States identified fifty-six megachurch scandals between 2006 and 2017, in most cases involving sexual abuse by the senior pastor.[3] In some countries, religious leaders and institutions have been involved in additional scandals involving money laundering, embezzlement, and drug dealing.[4]

Historically, religious institutions have made significant contributions to science. However, they sometimes inhibit scientific innovations that can improve individual and societal well-being, for example, by opposing stem cell research, vaccines, and actions that can address climate change.[5] In some cases, religions may prevent individuals from seeking needed medical treatment by promoting faith over traditional medical care.[6] Some religious communities oppose birth control, abortion, or the death with dignity movement. For example, whereas a majority of religious Americans support abortion in most or all cases, only 27% of White Evangelicals, 27% of Jehovah's Witnesses, and 32% of Latter-day Saints do.[7]

Of course, whether opposition to birth control, abortion, and assisted suicide is a positive or negative feature of religion depends on one's worldview or values. Most of us, however, likely view prejudice, intolerance, and violence as negative social behaviors. These are also the harmful behaviors that have been investigated most frequently by psychologists and social scientists in relation to religion.

RELIGION AND PREJUDICE

The role of religion is paradoxical. It makes prejudice and it unmakes prejudice.

— Gordon Allport[8]

[T]he association between fundamentalism and prejudice is rather unexpected, as it conflicts with the explicit tenets of many of the world's religions.

— Mark Brandt & Daryl Van Tongeren[9]

On the one hand, most religious communities explicitly discourage some forms of prejudice. They also promote acceptance and outreach towards disadvantaged groups such as refugees, immigrants, and the poor.

On the other hand, religious scriptures contain passages in which condemnation of particular individuals or groups can be seen as tolerated, encouraged, or even mandated. For example, the Bible describes same-sex relations as "an abomination" (Leviticus 18:22). The Muslim Quran proscribes against taking Jews and Christians as friends, protectors, or helpers (Quran 5:51). Many if not most religious people ignore or downplay such passages. However, for those who adopt a more selective and literal interpretation of religious scriptures—for example, religious fundamentalists and a majority of evangelicals[10]—such passages provide justification for a variety of prejudices.

Given this context, what can psychological research tell us about the relationship between religion and prejudice?

Psychological research on religion and prejudice dates back to at least the late 1940s. American psychologist C. Daniel Batson and colleagues reviewed much of the early work up to 1990 and found that the vast majority of studies linked religiosity to greater prejudice.[11] Some scholars found that mere identification with a group—whether based on religion, ethnicity, race, politics, or any other social category—is sufficient to trigger prejudice and discrimination towards other groups. Apparently, we all seek to maintain or enhance our self-esteem by evaluating our own group more favorably than relevant outgroups.[12]

Recent studies continue to find a relationship between religious involvement and prejudice towards people of different racial or ethnic backgrounds, sexual orientations, or religious or nonreligious affiliations. However, beginning in the 1960s researchers noted the importance of distinguishing different religious orientations in the study of prejudice.

Religious Orientation Makes a Difference

Four religious orientations are most frequently examined in the context of research on prejudice: fundamentalist, intrinsic, extrinsic, and quest. The latter three orientations were defined in Chapter 4. The first, religious fundamentalism, has been defined by psychologists as:

[T]he belief that there is one set of religious teachings that clearly contains the fundamental, basic, intrinsic, essential, inerrant truth about humanity and deity; that this essential truth is fundamentally opposed by forces of evil which must be vigorously fought; that this truth must be followed today according to the fundamental, unchangeable practices of the past; and that those who believe and follow these fundamental teachings have a special relationship with the deity.[13]

Consider, for example, the following three statements:

- God has given humanity a complete, unfailing guide to happiness and salvation, which must be totally followed.
- Whenever science and sacred scripture conflict, science must be wrong.
- Scriptures may contain general truths, but they should NOT be considered completely literally true from beginning to end.

If you are inclined to agree with the first two statements, and disagree with the third, you would be endorsing beliefs psychologists associate with religious fundamentalism.[14]

Numerous studies have found that religious fundamentalism tends to be associated with greater prejudice towards gays, lesbians, and transgender individuals; various racial groups; immigrants and refugees; religious outgroups, including atheists and the nonreligious; political radicals; and feminists.[15] Next most definitive are findings indicating that people with a *quest* orientation—characterized by a more open, flexible, and questioning approach to religion—tend *not* to exhibit prejudice towards gays and lesbians, other racial groups, or religious outgroups. Rather, people with a quest orientation show tolerance and interest in the diverse perspectives offered by these groups. The findings relating intrinsic and extrinsic religious orientations to prejudice have been less consistent or definitive.[16]

In the following sections, I elaborate on the nature of religious prejudice towards a number of specific groups.

Gay, Lesbian, and Transgender Individuals

Studies have consistently found a strong relationship between general religiosity and prejudice towards gay men and women, as well as transgender individuals. Indeed, this finding is robust across cultures.[17] For example, an analysis of 79 countries using data from the World Values Survey led to an unambiguous conclusion: Negative attitudes towards gay individuals are wide-spread across the globe and that within countries, people who describe themselves as more religious have the most negative attitudes.[18] Around the world, at least 67 countries—mostly religious countries in Africa and the Middle East—have anti-gay criminal laws, although Pope Francis and some other Christian leaders have denounced such laws as unjust.[19]

Similarly, sexism and sexual prejudice are associated with various aspects of religion in all of the major world religions, although the strength of the relationship varies.[20] In Afghanistan, the renewed Taliban crackdown on women's and girls' education, employment, wearing of the hijab, and access to public spaces offers a tragic example. The Catholic Church and the Southern Baptist Convention discriminate on the basis of gender by disallowing women priests or pastors. The belief in some religious communities that men and women have distinct but complementary roles in marriage, family, and religious leadership (i.e., *complementarianism*) can also be viewed as a form of sexism.

In contrast, countries with larger secular or nonreligious populations tend to be more equitable across genders and less prejudiced towards the LGBTQ+ community.

Studies that have looked specifically at attitudes towards transgender individuals have found that a majority of transgender individuals report having experienced rejection or feelings of being unwelcome in their religious communities. As a result, large percentages of transgender individuals have left the religions in which they were raised and a large majority now describe themselves as nonreligious.[21] Some Jewish and Christian clergy have pushed back, however, against anti-transgender laws that seek to deny gender-affirming care or sports participation.[22]

LGBTQ+ issues have also played out in individual religious communities. For example, thousands of congregations have disaffiliated from the Episcopal, Presbyterian, and United Methodist churches over the issues of same-sex marriage and ordination of gay bishops.[23] African church leaders within the world-wide Anglican Community have vociferously opposed the Church of England's recent decision to bless civil marriages of same-sex couples. Pope Francis's recent declaration allowing the blessing of same-sex couples has been similarly controversial, with the Catholic church hierarchy in Africa recently declaring their dissent. At many Christian colleges and universities, LGBTQ+ rights continue to be a source of tension, and claims of discrimination against LGBTQ+ students and in faculty and staff hiring are not uncommon.[24]

Not surprisingly then, large majorities of LGBTQ+ adults in the United States view many religious institutions as unwelcoming, including those associated with the Muslim religion, the Mormon Church, the Catholic Church, and evangelical churches. Somewhat more encouraging is the finding that fewer than half of respondents described the Jewish religion and mainline Protestant churches as unfriendly towards LGBTQ+ individuals and about 10% viewed then as friendly towards them.[25] Not surprisingly, when religious congregations and their leaders adopt more affirmative and supportive policies and practices towards the LGBTQ+ community, their congregants exhibit more positive attitudes towards LGBTQ+ individuals.[26]

Again, one's religious orientation is important. Anti-gay prejudice is strongest among religious conservatives or fundamentalists, while people with a quest orientation tend to show tolerance and respect for the LGBTQ+ community.[27] Indeed, extensive evidence shows that social conservativism, and its associated elements of authoritarianism and fundamentalism, is the best predictor of sexism and LGBTQ+ prejudice.[28]

Of course, religious conservatives are not likely to view their attitudes towards the LGBTQ+ community as prejudicial. Rather, they are likely to cite their religious beliefs about what is morally unacceptable or sinful behavior. Indeed, people sometimes justify their anti-gay attitudes by drawing on church teachings that one should "love the sinner, but hate the sin."[29] Similarly, evangelical elites writing in *Christianity Today*, the flagship magazine of the evangelical movement, have provided several narratives that enable rank-and-file members to justify anti-gay attitudes and the view that same-sex sexual behavior is morally unacceptable—regardless of whether gay identity is attributed to genetics, prenatal hormones, environmental development, or individual choice.[30]

Fortunately, attitudes may be changing. Even among White Evangelicals, about half of those under 50 years of age support same-sex marriage, while only 34% of those over 50 do.[31]

Racial or Ethnic Groups

Historically, psychological studies have shown an association between aspects of religiosity and prejudice towards racial or ethnic minorities. Most studies have examined prejudice towards African Americans.[32]

Indeed, African-American historian Jemar Tisby has described how the Christian church has often been complicit in support of racism in the United States. For example, the church offered a biblical defense of slavery and the idea that non-Whites are morally and intellectually inferior to European Americans. Some Christians were involved in the Ku Klux Klan. Many Christians were passive, indifferent, or outright opposed to desegregation. Conservative White Christians have supported movements and candidates that have resisted Black civil rights. Most recently, this has included the Black Lives Matter movement. Many White Evangelicals fail to acknowledge the structural features in U.S. society that have disadvantaged racial and ethnic minorities.[33]

As in studies of prejudice more generally, the most consistent evidence has involved the fundamentalist versus quest orientations, with the former being associated with increased racial prejudice and the latter being associated with reduced prejudice.[34] There is also some evidence that individuals with stronger intrinsic orientations to religion show less racial prejudice. However, the strength of the relationship appears to be modest and may depend on whether more overt or subtle racism is involved.[35]

Issues of religion and race continue to roil American society, as revealed, for example, in evangelicals' recent war on so-called "wokeness," critical race theory, and social justice.[36] Recent survey data also reveal that a majority of White Christians in the United States, especially White Evangelicals, may be oblivious to or in denial about racism in the country. Indeed, majorities of White Evangelicals (72%), White Catholics (60%) and White Mainline Protestants (54%) say that people seeing discrimination where it does *not* exist is a bigger problem than people not seeing discrimination where it *does* exist.[37]

The issue of racial bias has taken on renewed salience in recent years, as many countries have experienced a significant influx of immigrants and refugees. Several studies have found that merely being affiliated with a religious denomination has at least a small association with greater prejudice towards immigrants and refugees, although the findings are not always consistent.[38]

Again, in both Europe and the United States, fundamentalism or conservatism may be the best religious predictor of prejudice towards immigrants or refugees.[39] For example, in a Pew Research Center survey of Americans, the percentages of respondents stating that the United States does *not* have a responsibility to accept refugees were 68% for White Evangelical Protestants, 50% for White Mainline Protestants, 45% for Catholics, 31% for religiously unaffiliated, and 28% for Black Protestants.[40] In 2020 and 2021, 60-72% of White Evangelicals in the United States supported a temporary ban on travelers from Muslim countries, viewed newcomers as "invaders," supported a wall on the Mexican border, and believed that new immigrants increase crime.[41]

Additional factors, including having a conservative political ideology, can partially account for the relationship between religiosity and prejudice towards immigrants. For example, a meta-analysis of 70 studies found that greater prejudice toward refugees and asylum seekers was associated with being religiously affiliated, politically conservative, highly nationally identified, less educated, having authoritarian tendencies, and perceiving refugees as symbolic and realistic threats.[42] Many of the perceived threats associated with refugees are probably exaggerated or inaccurate but are nonetheless put forth by the media and some politicians.

On a more positive note, some religious leaders have pointed out that endorsement of White supremacist beliefs is a heresy and a sin, because Christian scriptures specify that all humans are made in God's image and are thus of equal worth (Genesis 1:26-27).[43] The National Association of Evangelicals helped settle Afghan immigrants after the Taliban take-over and called for the settlement of refugees from the war in Syria.[44] Many religious leaders have called for greater multicultural outreach and some increases in racial integration of churches has been observed. Nonetheless, racial diversity is still limited in most American congregations.[45]

Other Religious Groups

If you are religious, how do you feel about other religious groups? Some studies have found that greater religiosity, and perhaps especially religious fundamentalism, is associated with prejudice towards other religious groups.[46] In addition, exposing or priming people with concepts associated with their own religion can increase intolerance towards other religious groups, presumably by temporarily activating religious ingroup identities.[47] For example, in a study of adults in the Netherlands and England, Christian participants expressed more negative attitudes towards Jews and Muslims when passing in front of a Christian church than when passing in front of civic buildings.[48]

Negative attitudes towards Muslims may be the result of inaccurate stereotypes linking all Muslims to extreme religious views, perceptions that

Muslims represent a threat, and exposure to media coverage about religious extremism.[49] Overall, however, people with a quest orientation to religion, or with a more open stance towards existential questions, are more tolerant of religions other than their own. This is presumably because they are more curious about, and open to, alternative belief systems and sources of meaning.[50]

Also important is the extent to which religion permeates a religious group's private and public life, including its political deliberations—sometimes referred to as *religious infusion*. Indeed, greater religious infusion is associated with greater prejudice and discrimination towards other religious groups.[51] For example, in a study of 194 groups at 97 sites around the world, researchers found that prejudice and discrimination were greatest between competing religious groups, and between secular and religious groups, when religious infusion in the society was high.[52] Such findings provide a cogent case for the separation of church and state in public life.

Atheists and the Nonreligious

Around the world, atheists are one of the most negatively viewed groups, and greater religiosity is associated with greater prejudice towards atheists and the nonreligious.[53] According to the *2022 Freedom of Thought Report*, published by Humanists International, over 70% of people in the world live in countries that severely discriminate against nonreligious individuals. In more than 80 countries, religious blasphemy or apostasy is criminalized, with punishments including fines or imprisonment, or in 13 countries, death.[54] Prejudice against atheists tends to be reduced if not eliminated, however, in countries in which atheism is more common, such as Sweden and Denmark. Indeed, informing people of the prevalence of atheists, or that atheists have a coherent moral belief system, can reduce distrust of them and increase how positively they are viewed.[55]

In the United States, anti-atheist attitudes are strong and persistent.[56] A majority of Americans view atheism as incompatible with their vision for the country and would not vote for an otherwise qualified atheist for President. However, there are differences between political parties in this regard. About a third of Democrats and 60% of Republicans are unwilling to vote for an atheist for President.[57]

Why is disapproval of atheists so widespread, at least in relatively religious countries? One likely reason is the common view that moral behavior depends on belief in God.[58] For example, in recent survey data in 34 countries, a median of 45% of respondents said that belief in God is necessary to be moral and have good values. The percentage of people responding that religion is necessary for morality was substantially lower, however, in the eight Western European (22%) and six Eastern European (33%) countries surveyed.[59]

In short, a key factor in prejudice towards atheists is distrust that atheists can be counted on to follow religion-based moral norms.[60] Of course, this makes the dubious assumption that people cannot behave morally for nonreligious reasons. There are additional negative stereotypes about atheists. In comparison to religious people and people in general, atheists are perceived as more narcissistic and lower in empathy, warmth, competence, likability, and happiness.[61] Of course, many atheists would disagree with these stereotypes.

Given these negative attitudes and stereotypes about atheists, it is not surprising that many atheists see themselves as discriminated against. Indeed, 80-90% of self-identified atheists in the United States report experiencing discrimination, with intense narratives of stigma more often reported by atheists living in the South and Midwest.[62] In turn, perceived discrimination can negatively impact well-being. In an international study of members of an atheist association, perceptions of discrimination predicted lower self-reported psychological and physical well-being. At the same time, being more strongly identified as an atheist can provide some protection against the negative effects of stigma and discrimination, perhaps by promoting a sense of support, belonging, or purpose.[63]

Some atheists cope with the negative perceptions of atheists by conceal-ing their atheism.[64] They are most likely to do so in contexts where they represent a clear minority. For example, in the United States, higher levels of concealment are seen among women, among Republicans, those living in the South, and those who were raised in a religion or continue to attend religious services.[65] Indeed, the extent to which nonreligious people experi-ence discrimination may depend on the extent to which they "come out" as nonbelievers. In a nationally representative survey in the United States, participants who self-identified as atheist or agnostic reported experiencing much more discrimination than did participants who merely identified as being unaffiliated with any religion (sometimes referred to as "religious nones").[66]

How Can Religion Lead to Prejudice?

What is it about religion that can lead to prejudice? A number of proposed mechanisms or processes have been supported in research studies. As noted previously, religiosity is frequently associated with more traditional, con-servative, or conventional values, contributing to prejudice towards those perceived as violating these values, such as gay individuals and atheists. Certain groups may be viewed as threats to one's values or to the economic resources, political status, or survival of one's own religious or cultural group. Such perceived threats can induce feelings of uncertainty and anxie-ty, leading to defense of one's own worldview and derogatory attitudes and negative emotions towards those who hold opposing worldviews.[67]

Some research has also linked religiosity, particularly in its more fun-damentalist forms, to cognitive styles that promote prejudice. Researchers have described a "fundamentalist mindset" characterized by dogmatism, authoritarianism, intolerance of ambiguity, needs for closure, preference for consistency, and reduced integrative complexity or flexibility in thought regarding moral and existential issues.[68] Indeed, there is evidence that the relationship between religious fundamentalism and prejudice can be accounted for, in part, by such a mindset.[69]

Similarly, studies have shown that the link between religious fundamentalism and prejudice can be at least partially accounted for by the greater *right-wing authoritarianism* of religious fundamentalists.[70] Rightwing authoritarianism encompasses the strong belief that people should follow social conventions and submit to authority, even condoning the use of aggression towards those who fail to do so.

Finally, while psychologists have most often investigated religious fundamentalism as a mechanism underlying prejudice, sociologists in particular have investigated the link between *Christian nationalism* and prejudice. For example, consider your level of agreement with the following opinion statements:

- The United States was founded as a Christian nation with a special place in God's plan.

- The federal government should declare the United States a Christian nation, promote Christian values, and privilege Christianity over other religions in the public sphere.

- The success or prosperity of the United States depends on the nation's obedience to God's commandments as specified in the Bible.

- True Americans are those who were born in the United States and have American ancestry.

If you are inclined to agree with these statements, then you are endorsing the ideology of Christian nationalism.[71]

Sociologists Andrew Whitehead and Samuel Perry argue that Christian nationalism is as much about political power as it is about religion. Proponents seek to preserve traditional hierarchical structures involving race—that is, White supremacy—and gender, while fending off the growing challenge from secular and liberal culture.[72] Estimates of the percentage of Americans that endorse Christian nationalist ideology vary. One recent survey reported that 10% of Americans are avowed or hard-core Christian nationalists, while an additional 19% are sympathetic to Christian nationalist ideas. Among White Evangelical Protestants, however, nearly two-thirds are hard-core adherents or sympathizers.[73]

Christian nationalism and religious fundamentalism are not synonymous. However, research suggests that they share a number of features, including literal interpretation of the Bible, desires for order and structure, authoritarian tendencies, political conservatism, and perceived threat from secular and liberal culture.[74] Not surprisingly, then, Whitehead and Perry found that greater endorsement of Christian nationalist ideology is associated with greater prejudice towards refugees and immigrants; reduced support for interracial marriage and transracial adoption; greater opposition to same-sex marriage and transgender rights; and greater likelihood of judging Muslims and atheists to be morally inferior to Christians.[75]

Are Nonreligious People Also Prejudiced?

The evidence reviewed so far might give the impression that prejudice is unique to religious people. However, research has shown that nonreligious people also tend to exhibit prejudice or bias towards those who violate their values or ideologies. Here are some examples:

- In a study of primarily Catholic Polish adults, religiously orthodox individuals were prejudiced against atheists and gay people, whereas dogmatic atheists were prejudiced against Catholics and pro-life supporters.[76]
- In the United Kingdom, France, and Spain, atheists and agnostics, as compared to Christian respondents, showed more prejudice towards anti-gay individuals, religious fundamentalists, and Catholics, but not Muslims or Buddhists.[77]
- Members of the secular American Humanist Association tend to have favorable views of organizations closely affiliated with the Democratic Party, such as the National Organization of Women and AFL-CIO, as well as organizations that advocate for separation of church and state, but negative views of groups closely affil-

iated with the Republican Party, such as the Chamber of Commerce, National Rifle Association, and evangelicals.[78]

In sum, studies such as these reveal that both religious and nonreligious people tend to show bias against members of groups with opposing ideologies or values, particularly if their beliefs are strongly held.

Summing Up

We are all inclined to exhibit prejudice or bias towards individuals or groups that violate our important values or that we perceive as symbolic or realistic threats. Religious people are not exempt from such prejudice, despite religious proscriptions against some types of bias or discrimination. To some extent, religion-based prejudice may reflect adherence to traditional or conservative cultural values regarding sex, marriage, and family, or cognitive needs for clear and definitive answers in an ambiguous, complex, and changing world. As long as religious (and nonreligious) prejudices are limited to peaceful disagreements in values and policies they may not be unduly harmful. However, when such prejudices or disagreements become severe or uncompromising, extremism or violence may become a reality, as discussed in the next section.

RELIGION AND VIOLENCE

[W]e cannot simply ignore that religion is an important aspect of some violent conflicts in the world, not least because stakeholders in such conflicts say and believe it is so.

– Ziya Meral[79]

How much blame for the history of human violence can we ascribe to religion itself? The answer is not as simple as much of our popular discourse would suggest.

– Karen Armstrong[80]

Throughout history, religious differences have accompanied, and in some cases motivated, violence. Prominent historical examples include the Christian Crusades against Muslims during the 11th to 13th centuries; the Medieval Inquisition, implemented by the Catholic Church to combat perceived religious heresies; the European Wars of Religion in the 16th and 17th centuries; recurrent pogroms against Jews, culminating in the Holocaust; and, more recently, Islamic terrorism in the Middle East and beyond.

Religious hostilities continue. For example, according to a 2014 Pew Research Center report, one-third of the 198 countries and territories investigated had high levels of religious hostilities in 2012, with the largest recent increases occurring in the Middle East and North Africa.[81] From 1980 to 2003, about half of the 315 total suicide bombing attacks in the world were linked to Islamic fundamentalism.[82] Since then, the rate of suicide attacks has increased dramatically, with Islamic jihad the motivation behind many such attacks.[83]

The religious liberty organization Open Doors, in its 2023 World Watch List, listed the following countries in which Christians faced the greatest amount of religiously motivated violence in 2022: North Korea, Somalia, Yemen, Eritrea, Libya, Nigeria, Pakistan, Iran, Afghanistan, and Sudan. For example, in Nigeria alone, the organization reported 5,014 religiously motivated killings in 2022.[84] During the latter stages of my work on this book, the latest violent conflict between Muslims and Jews broke out, with the Palestinian group Hamas attacking Israeli civilians and taking hostages and Israel's military response resulting in massive Palestinian casualties.

Commentators and scholars disagree, however, about the extent to which religion should be blamed for violence—as compared to intertwining political, socio-economic, and psychological factors. The so-called New Atheists are among the most inclined to place primary blame on religion for much of the violence in the world. For example, philosopher and neuroscientist Sam Harris described religion as "the most prolific source of

154

violence in our history," linking it to millions of deaths.[85] English-American author and journalist Christopher Hitchens, described the "religiously inspired cruelty" he personally witnessed around the world and portrayed religion as "a menace to civilization" and "a threat to human survival."[86] English biologist Richard Dawkins has highlighted the divisive nature of religion, which—as a potent label for ingroup/outgroup hostility—amplifies and exacerbates group differences.[87]

Both the Bible and Islamic Quran offer messages of compassion and mercy. Yet one can also find a multitude of Bible verses or Quran *suras* that—if interpreted literally— would seem to justify violence. Some justify violence against believers in other faiths, nonbelievers, apostates, and heretics. Others mandate punishment by death for homosexuality, adultery, taking the Lord's name in vain, working on the Sabbath, or cursing one's parents. Some condone slavery, violence against women, and martyrdom for violent acts. Others present a violent image of God.[88] Christian theologians warn against interpreting such verses in isolation, while missing the overall moral core of the Bible, with its emphasis on justice and concern for the poor and disadvantaged. Nonetheless, the view that religion is the primary cause of many of the world's violent conflicts and terrorist acts is not limited to the New Atheists.

Indeed, American theologian William T. Cavanaugh—although himself critical of what he terms the "myth of religious violence"—observed that the idea of religion as the prominent cause of violent conflicts was prevalent during the 17th and 18th centuries in the work of Enlightenment philosophers such as Baruch Spinoza, Thomas Hobbes, John Locke, Voltaire, and Baron d'Holbach, and more recently in the work of philosophers John Rawls and Francis Fukuyama. Many of these philosophers attributed the many European Wars of Religion in the 16th and 17th centuries to fruitless debates over dubious religious doctrines.[89]

Cavanaugh also reviews the arguments of prominent scholars in religious studies, sociology, history, political science, and theology—arguments put forth in books with such compelling titles as *When Religion*

Becomes Evil by Charles Kimball, *Why People Do Bad Things in the Name of Religion* by Richard E. Wentz, *Terror in the Mind of God: The Global Rise of Religious Violence* by Mark Juergensmeyer, and *Sacred Fury: Understanding Religious Violence* by Charles Selengut. None of these scholars proposed that religion inevitably leads to violence. However, they view religion as especially conducive to violence or as a particularly important factor among others in exacerbating violence. They see religion as prone to violence because it is absolutist, divisive, and insufficiently rational.[90]

American political scientist Samuel P. Huntington offered a "clash of civilizations" thesis, which is often cited as a prominent example of the religion-causes-violence perspective. Huntington identified eight major civilizations: Western, Islamic, Orthodox, Sinic, Japanese, Hindu, Latin American, and African. These civilizations are defined by history, culture, and tradition, but with religion as a central defining characteristic. Huntington predicted that in the post-Cold War era, the most pervasive and dangerous conflicts would occur on the "fault-lines" between these major civilizations. In particular, he predicted that conflicts between Islam and Christianity (upon which Western civilization is based) would be most common. He attributed this potential for violence to the nature of the two religions themselves—for example, their dualistic "us-versus-them" nature, their claims to represent the one true faith, and their differing views on the relationship between religion and politics.[91] Although widely cited, Huntington's thesis has not escaped criticism.[92] For example, many scholars question how well religious factors can be distinguished from other intertwining factors in accounting for violent conflicts and terrorism.

As one prominent example, historian of religion Karen Armstrong, in her book titled *Fields of Blood: Religion and the History of Violence*, argues that even some of the most frequently cited historical instances of religion-inspired violence must be interpreted within relevant political contexts.

The Crusades were inspired by religious passion but were also deeply political: Pope Urban II let the knights of Christendom loose on the Muslim world to extend the power of the Church eastward, and create a papal monarchy that would control Christian Europe. The Inquisition was a deeply flawed attempt to secure the internal order of Spain after a divisive civil war. The Wars of Religion and the Thirty Years' War may have been pervaded by the sectarian quarrels of the Reformation, but they were also the birth pangs of the modern nation-state.[93]

Armstrong contends that even the recent history of Islamic terrorism and jihad needs to be understood—although not condoned—within a historical and political context of Western intervention in the Middle East and perceived threats associated with modernity. These threats arrived abruptly in the form of colonial subjugation and continued to be imposed on religious nations by secular rulers. Indeed, Islamic terrorism has often drawn on a "culture of grievance" associated with perceived historical aggression and injustice by the West and Israel.[94]

As another example, Turkish-British researcher and writer Ziya Meral provides a detailed account of the incessant violence between Muslims and Christians in Nigeria and Egypt, particularly since the late 1970s.[95] It is difficult to read about the multitude of instances of violence and mutual retaliation in the two countries without concluding that differences in religious identification have been a major factor in the violence. At the same time, however, Meral links the violence in both countries to a number of intertwining political and economic factors, including a heritage of colonial rule, the use of religion by political elites for mobilization and legitimation, poor governance and political instability, weak rule of law in which perpetrators are rarely punished, economic deprivation and fierce competition for limited opportunities, high levels of violence by both state and non-state actors, disputes over attempts to impose Sharia law and an Islamic state, and an increasing tendency to view the conflict in terms of the global battle between Islam and Christianity.[96]

In summary, some scholars see all instances of violence and terrorism as fundamentally political in nature—even in cases where religious motives might also be involved. Others, however, believe that religious factors should not be discounted as a prime motivator of radicalization and violence.[97] They point to the ways in which religion can promote or exacerbate violence.

How Does Religion Promote Violence?

Social scientists have pointed to numerous ways in which religion can motivate, justify, or exacerbate violence, even when other factors may be involved. Religion can inspire the level of commitment needed to carry out violent acts and provide the ideological glue that retains support for such acts in the broader religious community. Religion-inspired terrorism can provide a sense of power, identity, spiritual renewal, and purpose in response to perceived intrusions or humiliations from an outside world seen as immoral and materialistic (e.g., the West). Indeed, religious violence can be perceived as an effort to purify the world.[98]

When cast in cosmic, apocalyptic, or millennialist terms, believers can view religion-inspired wars or terrorist acts as hastening the Apocalypse or End of Days in which the battle of Good versus Evil will be won.[99] A salient example is the 1995 sarin gas attacks in the Tokyo subway by the Aum Shinrikyo movement. The group sought to spark World War III with the goal of repopulating a purified world. Some Islamic discourse about a battle between Muslims and the rest of the world also shows signs of apocalyptic thinking.[100]

The desire to organize the state around religion, or to counter such moves, has also motivated much religious violence. Examples include Islamic State (ISIS) efforts to form an Islamic state, the Taliban insurgency and takeover in Afghanistan, and fears among Christians in Egypt and Nigeria that Muslim majorities seek to install an Islamic state or Sharia law.

Religious motives can facilitate recruitment by religious or political leaders of combatants or terrorists. Combatants may be more motivated to fight for eternal spiritual values, even if material or political goals are primarily at issue.[101] For example, the Muslim Laskar Jihad group was formed to counter Christian militias during the violence that broke out in early 1999 in Maluku, Indonesia after the government encouraged Muslim migration to the formerly Christian region. Once the conflict was cast in terms of a holy war, both Muslim and Christian militants flocked to the region to fight.[102] A similar recruitment phenomena on an even grander scale occurred when Muslims from around the world flocked to Syria and Iraq to fight on behalf of the Islamic State group.

In addition to motivating violence, religion can be used to legitimize or justify it.[103] Violence or social injustice cast in terms of sacred values or a transcendent cause is more likely to be seen as morally justified or even mandated by God. For example, Alec Ryrie, a British historian of Protestant Christianity, has described how some people used Protestant Christianity to justify or provide an "idealistic veneer" for racial prejudice and apartheid in South Africa; slavery in the American South; and, during the 15th to 17th centuries, the execution of thousands of heretics, martyrs, and witches.[104] More recently, American-French anthropologist Scott Atran and colleagues have emphasized the important role of sacred, transcendent values in motivating militant jihadists in Syria, Israelis versus Palestinians, and Iran versus the West.[105]

Indeed, in summarizing the mind-set of religious terrorists, terrorism scholar Jessica Stern notes the following:

> They see themselves as defending sacred territory or protecting the rights of their coreligionists. They view people who practice other versions of their faith, or other faiths, as infidels or sinners. Because the true faith is purportedly in jeopardy, emergency conditions prevail, and the killing of innocents becomes in their view, religiously and morally permissible. The point of religious terrorism is to purify the world of these corrupting influences.[106]

Similarly, author and psychoanalyst Jerry Piven highlights the role of theological language in providing divine justification for terrorist acts.

The very discourse of terrorism, its *fatwas* and proclamations as well as the wills and final letters of suicide bombers, is steeped in a theological language of martyrdom, *jihad*, and immortality—divine sanction for slaughter.[107]

Piven argues that explanations of suicide bombings that focus on secular or strategic factors fail to sufficiently consider the theological language that permeates many terrorist organizations.[108]

Religious violence is also justified by the use of language that demonizes and dehumanizes members of other religious groups. This enables violent actors to suspend normal theological principles regarding the dignity and value of human life.[109] Religious identities—and their tendency to promote distinctions between "us" and "them"—play an important role in these processes. For example, American historian and religious scholar Michael Sells argued that violence in the former Yugoslavia was predominantly based on distinctions of religious identity, and motivated and justified through a robust use of religious symbols and power.[110]

Indeed, several researchers have linked acts of terrorism or extreme self-sacrifice for a group to the phenomenon of *identity fusion*.[111] Because the personal identities of highly fused individuals are closely tied to their group identity, some are willing to fight and die for the group when they perceive it to be under threat.[112]

The absolutist or exclusive truth claims frequently associated with religion can also promote conflict.[113] Indeed, Jessica Stern has observed that a distinguishing feature of religious terrorists is that "they know with absolute certainty that they're doing good" and are "less susceptible to self-doubt than most other people."[114] Once absolutist claims are made—for example, when positions are viewed as the will of God—it becomes more difficult for antagonists to compromise or negotiate. The long-standing Israeli-Palestinian conflict over the status of Jerusalem, West Bank settlements, and the Palestinian right of return provides a cogent and discouraging example of this phenomenon.

Finally, holocaust and genocide scholar James Waller, in discussing the role of religion in genocide, has made a useful distinction between *sins of omission* and *sins of commission*. For example, Waller describes the Christian Church's inadequate response during the Holocaust as a sin of omission. In contrast, sins of commission were evident in the Rwanda genocide of Tutsis by Hutus in 1994. Historically, both Catholic and Protestant churches in Rwanda had encouraged and reinforced "us" versus "them" thinking, as they sought to align with the Hutu government in power. During the genocide itself, some church leaders and nuns were found to have encouraged or abetted massacres, and in some cases joined in the killing.[115]

The discussion so far has been based largely on historical and case study analyses of violent conflicts and terrorism, and in some cases interviews with perpetrators of violence. We can also ask what quantitative surveys and laboratory studies can tell us about the relationship between religion and violence.

What Do Survey and Laboratory Studies Tell Us?

Quantitative surveys and laboratory-based studies of religion and violence are still relatively uncommon, which makes definitive conclusions more difficult. In this section, I address the questions most frequently asked, drawing on sample studies.

Are religious people more supportive of terrorism and violence? Apparently, yes. Several studies have found that religious people, as compared to secular or nonreligious people, are more supportive of terrorism, torture, or political violence.[116] For example, using survey data from 31 countries in 2006 and 2008, including participants from all major religions, researchers found that nonreligious individuals were the most opposed to the torture of terrorists. Among people of religious faith, Muslims were the most opposed to torturing terrorists, perhaps because in the Global War on Terror, Muslims are more likely to be perceived as terrorists.[117]

Importantly, some research suggests that support for violence derives from religion's capacity to promote commitment to coalitional or group identities rather than its more personal devotional aspects.[118] For example, in the United States, endorsement of a Christian nationalist identity—or at least its ideology—is associated with greater support for political violence, including the January 6, 2021 attack on the U.S. Capital. This is especially the case for individuals who also endorse White identity beliefs, perceive themselves as victims in society, and endorse QAnon conspiracy beliefs. The researchers described Christian nationalism, White identity beliefs, perceived victimhood, and QAnon conspiracy beliefs as a "toxic blend" associated with support for political violence.[119]

Are religious people more worried about violence? Perhaps. In a representative sample of American adults, more religious Americans exhibited greater concern about terror attacks in several ways. They perceived terror attacks as more likely and thought more about them. They reported doing something differently because of possible attacks. And they reported greater willingness to report potential terrorist activity and meet with security officials about terrorism. These findings might be due to more religious Americans' greater conservatism, on average, which tends to be associated with greater concerns about security threats.[120]

Does exposure to conflict or war increase religiosity? Yes, it can. For example, in three countries that had experienced brutal conflicts 5 to 13 years earlier—Uganda, Sierra Leone, and Tajikistan—people who had been more exposed to this past war violence were more likely to be current members of a religious group and active in religious rituals. The researchers inferred that religion helped people deal with the trauma, uncertainty, and thoughts of death associated with their past war experiences.[121] In an even larger study—conducted in countries across the world—countries with a history of intense and sustained armed conflict showed gradual and enduring increases in their proportion of religious adherents.[122]

What religious conditions contribute to violence? Large-scale surveys conducted across many countries reveal some of the conditions that contribute to religious violence. Here are some sample findings:

- Armed conflicts within countries are more likely when one religion is dominant over others, perceived discrimination of religious subgroups is present, religious leaders call for violence, and religious identities overlap with ethnic identities.[123]
- Violence is more likely among individuals and groups within a society when *religious infusion* is high—that is, when religion plays a dominant role in the everyday lives of the people.[124]
- Islamist terrorist attacks are more likely in those Muslim countries that enforce blasphemy laws. Although these laws are intended to defend the faith against heresy, they apparently induce a culture of vigilantism that encourages terrorism.[125]

In summary, the results of survey and laboratory studies suggest that religion is most likely to contribute to violence when the communal or coalitional aspects of religion are strong, religious and ethnic identities overlap, dominant-subordinate and discriminatory relations are present between competing religious groups, and religion is strongly infused in the public sphere. Conversely, exposure to conflict or violence can lead to greater religiosity. These results are largely consistent with conclusions based on the historical and case study analyses I reviewed earlier.

WHAT ABOUT SECULAR VIOLENCE?

Any balanced account of the role of religion in violence needs to also acknowledge the violence perpetrated by secular actors. Indeed, violence has been linked to a variety of secular political agendas—including, the "isms" of nationalism, Marxism, and fascism. Historically, possible examples include the American, French, and Russian Revolutions; Otto von Bismarck's wars to unite Germany; two major World Wars in the twentieth century; the Korean War; the Vietnam War; the Khmer Rouge "killing fields" of Cambodia, and the recent war in Ukraine instigated by Russia (but also legitimized by the Patriarch of the Russian Orthodox Church). Some scholars have argued cogently, however, that religion also played a role in some of these purported cases of "secular" violence.[126]

In many cases, secular violence has involved nation-state persecution or repression of religious communities, including, among others, early Christians in the Roman Empire, Armenian Christians in Turkey during World War I, the Rohingya in Myanmar, Christian Copts and the Muslim Brotherhood in Egypt, Muslim Uyghurs in China, religious believers in North Korea, religious minorities in India, Catholics in Nicaragua, and the historical and ongoing persecution of Jews. Secular violence against religion was a focus of the Reign of Terror during the French Revolution and many communist countries have attempted to violently repress religion and enforce atheism.

Currently, about 350 million Christians live in countries in which Christians experience some form of persecution, including discrimination, false imprisonment, and in some cases death.[127] In some countries—for example, in India, Afghanistan, and Pakistan—this involves persecution by religious majorities. In other countries—for example, in China and North Korea—secular, nonreligious governments are responsible for the persecution. A recent survey by the Pew Research Center identified "high" or "very high" levels of government restrictions on religion in 55 (28%) of the 198 countries surveyed, including laws, policies and actions that limit religious beliefs and practices.[128]

A number of analysts have differentiated various types of radical or terrorist groups responsible for violence. Unlike religious extremist groups such as Hezbollah, al-Qaeda, Hamas, and Islamic State, many groups are not motivated primarily by religion. These include groups classified as nationalist-separatist (e.g., ETA in Spain), social revolutionary (e.g., Shining Path in Peru), extreme right-wing (e.g., White supremacist groups), extreme left-wing (e.g., FARC in Columbia), and single-issue groups (e.g., animal rights).[129] Indeed, an analysis of all severe internal state conflicts from 1950 to 1996 found that nonreligious conflicts were more frequent than conflicts involving religion, although religious conflicts were generally more intense.[130]

Taking a more historical approach, some experts refer to four waves of terrorism during the modern era. A first wave in eastern Europe and Central Asia involved Marxist and anarchist attacks on capitalist exploitation and the increasing power of nation-states. A second wave during the early to mid-20th century sought to force the withdrawal of imperial powers from colonized territories. In a third wave during the Cold War, state-sponsored terrorist organizations saw their attacks against the major powers as a struggle for liberation. Finally, a fourth wave involved violence by groups such as the Taliban, Al-Qaeda, and ISIS. Only the fourth wave strongly embraced religion as a means to frame and justify violent conflicts as sacred cosmic struggles.[131]

Presently, the primary source of terrorist attacks is again changing, at least in the United States. The U.S. Department of Homeland Security recently declared that White supremacy is the primary domestic terrorism threat. White supremacists are primarily motivated by grievances associated with race or ethnicity. However, to the extent that White supremacy attitudes overlap with the views of Christian nationalists, religion might also be playing a role.

To sum up:

Violence and terrorism have been associated historically with a variety of predominantly secular groups and causes. Thus, although religion often contributes to violence, eliminating religion would not eliminate violence. Secular political, economic, and racial/ethnic concerns are more than sufficient to motivate and legitimize violence.

Religion in Peace-Making, Reconciliation, and Transitional Justice

A balanced assessment of the role of religion in violence should also take into account the historical role of religion in peace-making and reconciliation efforts.

For example, in his account of religious violence between Muslims and Christians in Nigeria and Egypt, Ziya Meral noted the existence of numerous faith-based initiatives towards peace building and reconciliation at the grassroots level, as well as high-level clerical efforts to reduce tensions and stop the violence.[132]

Religious actors have also played important roles in post-genocidal reconciliation efforts, for example, in Rwanda and Bosnia,[133] and in efforts to obtain transitional justice during the movement away from authoritarian or violent regimes in countries such as Guatemala, Chile, Brazil, South Africa, Peru, Sierra Leone, East Germany, and East Timor.[134]

Historically, religion has also shaped a number of non-violent social movements. Examples include Mahatma Gandhi's efforts to win Indian independence from Great Britain, Martin Luther King, Jr.'s leadership during the U.S. civil rights movement, Bishop Desmond Tutu's call for a non-violent end of apartheid in South Africa, Poland's Solidarity Movement, and the Dalai Lama's protest against Chinese occupation of Tibet.

We can also note the role of interfaith dialogue among religious leaders seeking to promote world peace and conflict resolution. For example, a Millennium World Peace Summit at the United Nations in August 2000 brought together 2000 preeminent religious and spiritual leaders to discuss and commit themselves to world peace. In December 2001, after the September 11 attacks in the United States, more than 80 Christian, Muslim, and Jewish leaders met in Brussels to discuss means to curb religious conflicts, stress the importance of religious tolerance, and condemn the use of religion to justify violence.[135]

A number of faith-related groups are also involved in peace-making efforts. For example, Religions for Peace, an international interfaith coalition founded in 1970, advocates for nonviolent solutions to the world's conflicts.[136] The International Network of Engaged Buddhists has been promoting Buddhist-Muslim dialogue across the 10 ASEAN nations and working to counter the growing nationalism being instigated in temples across Southeast Asia.[137] In the United States, the Multifaith Neighbors Network, a network of Muslim, Christian, and Jewish leaders, promotes relationships, dialogue, civic engagement, and peace-making efforts with the goal of helping communities be more resilient against hate, violence, and polarization.[138] In Israel, the Abraham Fund and the Interreligious Coordinating Council have drawn on the shared Abrahamic roots of Jews, Muslims, and Christians in their peace-making efforts in the region.[139]

Recently, representatives of Protestant denominations that comprise the organization Churches Uniting in Christ met in Philadelphia to combat racism, promote unity, and continue theological dialogue.[140] In August, 2023, more than 6,500 faith leaders from 95 countries gathered in Chicago as the World Parliament of Religion to consider common action addressing climate change, human rights, and religious freedom.[141] On March 26, 2024, more than 140 global Christian leaders send a letter to U.S. President Joe Biden and other politicians calling for a permanent cease-fire and an end to foreign military support for Israel in its war with Hamas.[142]

On a smaller scale, the National Council of Churches and the Religious Action Center of Reform Judaism have been working with the Harvard Kennedy School to develop a faith-based blueprint to address possible reparations for African Americans. This interfaith effort hopes to develop resources for congregations and proposed legislation for Congress.[143]

The above examples provide a mere sampling of religious efforts to promote peace, reconciliation, dialogue, and justice. The bottom line: Religion does not always contribute to violence and can be a source of prevention, peacemaking, and reconciliation in the face of violence.[144]

RELIGION AND THE COVID-19 PANDEMIC

During my work on this book, the world was overcome by the COVID-19 pandemic. The pandemic presented religious communities with a dilemma. On the one hand, research suggests that participation in religious services can enhance physical and mental health—of particular importance during a pandemic. On the other hand, religious prescriptions to love thy neighbor—for example, by preventing virus spread—supported foregoing in-person religious services.[145] Indeed, studies and reports point to the mixed impact of religion on responses to the pandemic.

On the positive side, many religious organizations took pragmatic steps to mitigate the transmission of the coronavirus such as replacing in-person religious services with online or drive-in services, asking adherents to delay religious pilgrimages, and supporting virus mitigation measures. Some religious organizations provided assistance and materials to affected areas such as personal protective equipment, food, and student laptops. Some evangelical leaders urged evangelicals to eschew anti-vaccination conspiracy theories.[146]

In addition, religious faith likely helped many believers cope with the pandemic. Indeed, there is evidence, although not entirely consistent across countries, that faith and prayer intensified during the pandemic, that highly religious people and evangelicals reported less distress and perceived threat from the coronavirus, and that the positive emotions associated with religion could strengthen the immune system used to fight infection.[147] However, it is unclear whether these pandemic-related increases in religiosity will be sustained.

In contrast to these positive effects of religion, some conservative religious leaders and believers promoted interpretations of the pandemic that many believers and nonbelievers alike found distasteful. For example, some interpreted the pandemic as punishment for sins such as gay marriage, abortion, blasphemy, insufficient religious observance, working women outside the home, and turning one's back on God. Some portrayed the pandemic as a harbinger of the End Times and return of Jesus predicted in the Bible.[148] Indeed, a Pew Research Center survey found that 35% of Americans believed that the pandemic was sending a lesson from God.[149]

In addition, proactive coronavirus mitigation efforts were inhibited by the belief among some religious people—in some cases promoted by their leaders—that faith or obedience to God would protect them against the virus or that their fate should be left in God's hands. For example, in protests against vaccination we saw protest posters declaring that "Jesus is my vaccine" or "My vaccine is the Holy Spirit." As of late February 2021, 45% of White Evangelicals in the United States had said they would not get vaccinated, citing their religious faith or distrust of science. Such concerns were further aggravated by general distrust of institutions and by online conspiracy theories.[150] Some of these conspiracies involved religious themes—for example, the belief that the pandemic was a punishment for Jewish denial of the divinity of Jesus, or that COVID-19 was a Western plot to sterilize Muslim women.[151]

Some religious groups were the source of super-spreader events. For example, at one point in South Korea, an estimated 60% of the coronavirus infections were attributed to the Shincheonji Church, whose adherents declined preventative measures and inhibited contact tracing. Sixteen thousand Muslims participated in a pilgrimage to Malaysia, then spread the virus to several other countries when they returned home.[152] In India, millions of Hindu pilgrims converged on the Ganges River for the festival of Kumbh Mela. Although authorities promoted COVID-19 precautions, the event coincided with a devastating second wave of infections and deaths in India.[153]

Available research studies confirm many of these negative effects of religion on the pandemic. Here are some sample findings:

- In an online international survey, higher religiosity predicted less trust in science, which, in turn, predicted less compliance with government recommended COVID-19 prevention guidelines.[154]

- In studies with Americans, greater religiosity was associated with lower vaccine uptake and intentions, as well as unreasonable coping behaviors (e.g., avoiding 5G networks), but not with reasonable coping behaviors such as washing hands more or avoiding crowded spaces. Vaccine hesitancy was partially accounted for by religious people's greater belief that a person's health depends on external factors such as God, chance, or powerful others.[155]

- In a study in England, greater religiosity was associated with endorsement of coronavirus conspiracy beliefs, which in turn were associated with less compliance with virus mitigation efforts such as willingness to accept diagnostic tests and vaccinations.[156]

- Several studies of Americans, including large representative surveys, showed that skepticism about science and the pandemic, distrust of media coverage, vaccine hesitancy, and resistance to COVID-19 mitigation measures could all be predicted by the conservatism of one's religious and political beliefs, one's endorsement of Christian nationalist ideology, and one's support for former President Donald Trump.[157]

Regarding this last finding, a number of researchers pointed to the early politicization of the pandemic in the United States and the entanglement of conservative religion and politics in perceptions of the pandemic and the need for mitigation measures.

Overall, the evidence indicates that greater religiosity—at least in its more conservative forms—has been associated with reduced trust in science, greater endorsement of COVID-19 conspiracy beliefs, and reduced adherence to pandemic mitigation measures. All of these effects likely inhibited containment of the coronavirus and, unless successfully countered, could undermine responses to future pandemics.

TAKEAWAYS

This chapter, and the previous one on the psychosocial benefits of religion, are particularly important in addressing the relative merits and viability of religion versus secular humanism. The most significant—but not unexpected—takeaway from these two chapters is that the outcomes of religion are both positive and negative. On the one hand, religious commitment can positively impact physical and psychological well-being and promote prosocial behavior. On the other hand, religion can contribute to religious struggle or guilt; prejudice and intolerance; and violent conflict and terrorism. Even when political factors are the primary cause of conflicts, once "religionized," religious identities become salient and conflicts can take on a sacred aura, further exacerbating or prolonging the conflicts.

Even the positive outcomes of religion need to be qualified. As we saw in the previous chapter, the impact of religious commitment on well-being is, on average, generally modest. Religion's impact on prosocial behavior is frequently situation-specific; limited to members of ingroups such as family, friends, and co-religionists; and motivated, at least in part, by the desire to view oneself as altruistic and to maintain a positive image. In addition, the impact of religion on prejudice and violence is double-edged. Religion can facilitate tolerance, peace, reconciliation, and transitional justice. But it often contributes to prejudice, violent conflict, and terrorism.

The complex relationship between religion and social behavior was captured in an interesting way in a recent review article, in which the authors suggested that existing findings support a "new trinity of religious moral character."[158] *The Cooperator* is motivated by religious reverence to sacrifice self-interest and behave in a prosocial manner, at least towards ingroup members and perhaps even towards people outside one's religious or social group. *The Crusader* is motivated by religious tribalism and exhibits prejudice, intolerance, and aggression towards members of outgroups. Finally, *the Complicit* use their belief in religious absolution and a forgiving God to excuse their immoral or unethical transgressions. The authors pointed to

171

the sexual indiscretions of Jimmy Swaggart and other televangelists as illustrative of the Complicit type.[159] The Cooperator and Crusader types, respectively, recall the positive and negative outcomes of religion reviewed in the previous and current chapters, whereas research on the Complicit type is much less extensive.

In any case, it is disappointing that religious prosociality appears to be more a function of the situational context than a person's general level of religiosity or religious disposition. If religion is a potent motivator of prosocial behavior, why should religious people have to be "primed" or reminded with religious cues in order to behave in a more prosocial manner than less religious people? Furthermore, the impact of religious cues appears to be rather transient or ephemeral, suggesting that such cues need to be presented frequently in order to sustain religiously motivated prosocial behavior.

Sociologist Mark Chaves speculated that for religion to translate confidently into prosocial behavior it may need to be deeply internalized, becoming automatic and unconscious, so that religious schemas spring automatically to mind in relevant situations.[160] A reliable link between religiosity and prosocial behavior is more possible, Chaves argues, when people are deeply embedded in networks of similarly thinking friends, family, and authorities—which may themselves serve as religious reminders or cues. One implication of these findings is that prosocial behavior may be more reliably promoted by religions, denominations, or practices that make religious cues ubiquitous, for example, through regular calls to prayer, more frequent religious services, and regular interactions with fellow members of one's religious community.

The Relevance of Religious and Political Orientations

One consistent theme in the scientific literature is that the outcomes of religion depend on one's religious orientation. For example, individuals with an intrinsic, as compared to an extrinsic, orientation show more positive outcomes for psychological well-being and prosociality. The most definitive contrast, however, involves the distinction between fundamentalist and quest orientations. On the one hand, a more fundamentalist orientation may be adaptive in facilitating a sense of coherence, control, and certainty. On the other hand, fundamentalists' greater doctrinal certainty, literalism, and need to protect their absolute truth claims makes them more prone to prejudice against a variety of outgroups and more likely to support religious violence.

In contrast, individuals high in the quest orientation—with their more open and questioning approach to religion—may experience less existential security. However, their greater open-mindedness and flexibility may promote greater self-actualization, more universal prosociality, and greater tolerance and acceptance of diverse values and perspectives. As Belgian sociologist Filip Van Droogenbroeck and colleagues have noted:

> A religious quest orientation gives hope for the development of tolerance from within the religion that does not require the abolishment of the religious identity to be in congruence with secular values.[161]

Another consistent theme in the research literature links some forms of bias—for example, against gay people, migrants, and federal social welfare programs—to the conservative cultural and political values held by some religious people. This suggests that it might be possible to reduce prejudice in such cases by weakening the link between religiosity and conservative identities or by encouraging forms of religiosity that are associated with more liberal values.

Religious Versus Secular Perspectives

Again, we can ask whether religious or secular perspectives are preferable based on the findings reviewed in this chapter. A secular humanistic perspective appears to have a clear advantage when it comes to tolerance and lack of prejudice towards certain marginalized groups in society—for example, members of the LGBTQ+ community, atheists, migrants, and religious minorities—particularly if the religious perspective is relatively fundamentalist or conservative. Similarly, however, along the spectrum of nonbelievers, we should also aim for a less dogmatic approach towards groups that are perceived to violate their values. In short, we should strive to reduce or eliminate dogmatic, unquestioning attitudes on both sides of the religious-secular divide.

Both religious and secular perspectives are capable of contributing to violence, but also peace and reconciliation. Nonetheless, there is evidence that when religious identities become salient, conflicts can be exacerbated, prolonged, and cast more broadly as cosmic or global war. Eliminating religion would not end violence. However, it might reduce its intensity, persistence, and potential for global impact, while increasing opportunities for negotiation and compromise. In addition, as Azim Shariff has noted, with the increasing power of secular institutions in some societies, the role of religion in reducing violence "may be in the process of being obviated, at least in many parts of the world."[162]

Of course, these inferences refer to average trends and do not fully account for differences among people. For example, for some people, the benefits of religious involvement for well-being and prosociality may be greater than typical. Similarly, for some people, strong religious beliefs or commitments might reduce prejudice. And, of course, the vast majority of religious people, even among fundamentalists, do not participate in violent acts.

Some Practical Implications

Finally, the findings reviewed in this chapter suggest a number of practical implications regarding religion-based prejudice or violence. For example, although challenging, it might be possible to reduce religion-based prejudice and violence by exploring ways to transform more fundamentalist or conservative religious orientations to more "open and affirming" approaches or to a quest religious orientation.

One approach might be to promote information, dialogue, and experiences aimed at reducing the perception of symbolic or realistic threats associated with particular marginalized groups. For example, we could start by challenging questionable beliefs about these groups. Do gays and lesbians really put the morality and safety of others at risk? Are atheists really unable to behave morally? Does my religion actually have a monopoly on the most central religious truths? Do migrants actually constitute a threat to one's economic well-being or political power?

Religious institutions could also take a more active role in unmaking prejudice. For example, in the United States, racial prejudice is increasingly proscribed, but many religious institutions still portray same-sex sexual relations as sinful. In many Islamic countries, such behavior can warrant a death sentence, as can abandonment of one's Islamic faith.

Drawing on the scientific literature on prejudice reduction, Joanna Burch-Brown and William Baker proposed a number of ways in which religious communities can help to reduce prejudice. For example, they can promote the idea that differences between groups are often the result of circumstances, rather than inherent, unchanging attributes. They can teach that all people, regardless of their religion or lack thereof, share a common humanity, while also contributing something valuable and distinctive. They can encourage more open and questioning approaches to religion, for example, by giving young people practice in exploring diverse perspectives and thinking flexibly, thus reducing needs for closure and certainty. They can challenge ideologies or worldviews—such as right-wing authoritarianism and religious fundamentalism—that legitimize social hierarchies and divisions between groups. Finally, they can promote intergroup contact, cooperation, and friendship under conditions that tend to reduce prejudice—for example, by promoting intergroup activities that involve cooperation towards shared goals, with each group treated as equal in status.[163]

Beyond the role of religious institutions in reducing prejudice, both religious and secular individuals should take personal responsibility for recognizing and trying to reduce their own biases. At least in the United

States, the Millennial generation, as compared to older generations, has been found to be less religious, more uncomfortable with dogmatism, and more tolerant of diversity, which may bode well for decreasing prejudice in the future.[164]

Given the near universal stigmatization and discrimination experienced by atheists, efforts to increase tolerance and reduce prejudice towards these individuals are also worth considering. Some scholars have offered some suggestions on how to do so. For example, people can be provided information about the prevalence of atheists in society. Religious believers can be informed that atheists endorse moral concerns about caring and compassion. Religious fundamentalists can be asked to imagine having a relaxed, positive, and comfortable interaction with an atheist. Or, better yet, religious believers and nonbelievers can be encouraged to dialogue and interact with each other under non-threatening conditions or while pursuing worthwhile common causes.[165]

If religious people become more aware of how common atheism and agnosticism are in the world—and interact with a number of moral and prosocial nonbelievers—their attitudes towards atheism might change, in much the same way that acceptance of alternative sexual orientations has increased rapidly in some countries in recent years. This also implies that prejudice towards atheists and agnostics might decrease over time as more of them choose to disclose their belief systems. Of course, presently in the United States this could doom any high-level political ambitions, and in some countries, it would be dangerous to "come out" in this manner.

Finally, given cross-national findings linking violence to greater religious infusion in societies, religion's contribution to violence would likely be reduced by decreasing the role of religion in politics and the public sphere. Indeed, this goal was one of the rationales for the doctrine of church-state separation enshrined in the United States Constitution. Presumably, religion-inspired violence would also be decreased by reducing discrimination against various religious groups within and between countries. Nations and their political leaders should also be cognizant of, and avoid contributing to, the political and economic resentments that can motivate religious violence.

In Part I of this book, I have addressed the origins, functions, and outcomes of religion and made some initial inferences regarding the relative advantages and disadvantages of religion versus secular humanism from the perspective of psychological and social science research. In Part II, I focus more directly on the nature of secular humanism and its prospects by addressing (a) prominent individuals and themes in the history of humanism and religious skepticism (Chapter 7); (b) the extent to which secularization has taken place over recent centuries, and the factors that have contributed to it (Chapter 8); (c) the characteristics of secular individuals and secular living, including the diverse forms of personal secularity (Chapter 9); and (d) what psychological science can tell us about how to live meaningful and fulfilling lives with or without religion (Chapter 10). In the Conclusion, I revisit the religion versus secular humanism debate and offer some proposals expected to improve individual and societal well-being while reducing religious-secular conflict.

Part II

Secular Humanism as an Alternative Life Stance

Chapter 7
A Brief History of Humanism and Religious Skepticism

Throughout history, skeptics have expressed doubts about religious claims and offered significant critiques of institutional religion. In addition, a long humanist tradition has argued that moral and ethical lives with meaning and purpose are possible without religion and that the universe and all living things can be explained through natural means without recourse to a Creator or the supernatural. To the extent that the recurrent critiques of religion—and the proposed humanistic alternatives—resonate with individuals, it can impact perceptions of the relative cogency and viability of religious versus secular humanistic life stances. In this chapter, I provide a brief historical overview of prominent figures and themes in the emergence of religious skepticism and the humanistic tradition.

Humanism is a philosophical outlook, but in itself is a minimalist one, deliberately so because a key requirement of it is that individuals should think for themselves about what they are and how they should live.

— A. C. Grayling[1]

Great believers and great doubters seem like opposites, but they are more similar to each other than to the mass of relatively disinterested or acquiescent men and women.

— Jennifer Michael Hecht[2]

The word *humanism* was not widely used in its current sense until the late 19th and early 20th centuries. The expression *secular humanism* was first used in the 1940s and 1950s to contrast it with Christian or religious humanism.[3] Thus, earlier proponents of "humanistic" ideas would not have identified themselves as humanists, much less as secular humanists. Nonetheless, the themes that comprise humanistic thought can be traced from ancient and classical times through the medieval period, the Renaissance and Enlightenment, and subsequent centuries, where we continue to see a number of recurrent themes.

From the beginning, religious skepticism or doubt, and criticism of organized religion, were foundational in the emergence of the humanist tradition. This remains the case among many of today's secular humanists. However, beyond a critique of religion, we also see the emergence of more affirmative humanistic themes that emphasize the following:

- Personal responsibility in choosing one's own values, meaning, and purpose;
- An approach to ethics, morality, and the good life based—not on religious authority—but on human experience, reason, and social utility;
- Reason or rationality in the pursuit of truth and knowledge for its own sake;
- Social and political reforms aimed at improving the human condition;
- In more recent centuries, an increasingly naturalistic and scientific worldview.

In my overview, I draw extensively, but not exclusively, on the excellent histories of Jennifer Michael Hecht (*Doubt: A History*); Susan Jacoby (*Freethinkers: A History of American Secularism*); Kerry Walters (*Revolutionary Deists: Early America's Infidels*); Garry Wills (*Head and Heart: A History of Christianity in America*); S. T. Joshi (*The Unbelievers: The Evolution of Modern Atheism*); Callum Brown, David Nash, and Charlie Lynch (*The Humanist Movement in Modern Britain: A History of Ethicists, Rationalists, and Humanists*); and Mark Lilla (*The Stillborn God*).[4] I encourage readers to consider the cogency of the religious critiques and humanistic ideas put forth across the centuries by past and present humanists.

ANCIENT AND CLASSICAL HUMANISM

Although religious skepticism was plausibly present among some individuals since the emergence of the earliest forms of religion, historian Jennifer Michael Hecht locates the earliest historical record of religious skepticism at 2600 years ago, that is, about 600 BCE. In the West, this included the emergence of Greek philosophers and poets who questioned the existence of the Olympian gods or redefined them in non-anthropomorphic terms. For example, the pre-Socratic philosopher Anaxagoras (c. 510- 428 BCE) was the first known person to be indicted for atheism after he concluded that the sun and other stars were material in nature rather than deities. The pre-Socratic philosopher Protagoras presented an early agnostic view when, in his treatise *Concerning the Gods*, he observed that we have no way of knowing whether or not the gods exist.[5]

Neither the Greek Cynics, with their rejection of conventional rituals and striving, nor the Stoics, with their fatalistic acceptance of suffering in the world, needed to refer to gods in their approaches to life. Epicurean philosophers did not necessarily reject religious practice or the existence of the gods. Indeed, taking part in the religious conventions of one's society could promote the Epicurean goal of a trouble-free life. However, Epicurus himself rejected the idea that the gods watch us or concern themselves with human affairs. Rather, the Epicurean route to happiness was a life lived in moderation, with an appreciation of its modest pleasures. In contrast, the Skeptic philosopher Carneades attacked theistic beliefs by refuting the arguments of his time for the existence of gods.[6]

In the 7th century BCE in India, a naturalistic doctrine called Lokâyata, whose adherents were the Carvaka, rejected the idea of gods, the existence of a disembodied spirit or soul, and the reality of an afterlife. The Carvaka believed that our sense perceptions, rather than religious revelations, are the only source of knowledge. They refuted the Hindu ideas of *karma* and rebirth, and believed that the goals of life were this-worldly pleasure, love, and kindness to others.[7] The nontheistic religion of Buddhism—at least as originally put forth by Siddhartha Gautama around 566 BCE—rejected the supernaturalism associated with Hinduism, as did Jainism. For example, the way to enlightenment in Buddhism involved knowledge of the human condition, reduction of one's sense of separate self, yoga meditation, and an eightfold path that included "right views, right intent, right speech, right conduct, right livelihood, right effort, right mindfulness, and right concentration."[8]

In the ancient Hebrew tradition (e.g., 600 BCE – 1 CE) we see questions raised about divine justice, the afterlife, and the "vanity" in life in the Old Testament Books of Job and Ecclesiastes. In Ecclesiastes, we are offered the advice to find pleasure or contentment in the moment and in the mundane concerns of daily living.[9]

Early religious skepticism and humanistic thinking were also apparent in the ancient Roman world. For example, in his book *The Nature of the Gods*, Marcus Tullius Cicero (106–43 BCE) had three Romans—representing an Epicurean, a Stoic, and a Skeptic—debate the nature and existence of the Roman gods, and apparently concluded that "we cannot know if the gods exist—but it seems unlikely."[10] In his book-length poem, *On the Nature of Things*, Titus Lucretius celebrated the rationalism of Epicurus, rebutted the idea of a soul that outlasts the body, and presented a naturalistic view of the universe in which "all our world is made by nature, of her own, by chance, by the rush and collision of atoms."[11] In his *Meditations*, the Emperor Marcus Aurelius displayed an agnostic's uncertainty about the existence of God and meaning in the universe and questioned the existence of a soul that survives after death.[12]

MEDIEVAL HUMANISM

Although the Middle Ages have often been depicted by critics of religion as "hopelessly entrenched in the fables of faith," Hecht describes the views of many Muslim, Jewish, and Christian rationalists and religious skeptics during this period.[13] Similarly, humanist chaplain Greg Epstein—while observing that humanism and atheism "went nearly underground" during this time—notes the contributions of a number of "proto-humanists."[14]

Among Muslim skeptics were Ibn Al-Rawandi (827-911), who adopted Aristotle's contention that the universe was eternal rather than created by God, pointed to inconsistencies in the Quran, disputed the reality of miracles, and questioned the benevolence of God given the extent of evil in the world.[15] Abu Bakr al-Razi (854-925), in books such as *The Prophet's Fraudulent Tricks, The Stratagems of Those Who Claim to Be Prophets*, and *On the Refutation of Revealed Religion*, questioned why God would communicate knowledge only to prophets rather than to everyone, lamented the violence engendered by religion, and argued that the variety of religions proved the erroneousness of them all.[16]

Perhaps the best-known Muslim skeptic was Abu al-Walid Muhammad ibn Ahmad ibn Rushd (1126-1198), referred to as Averroës in the West. He lived in Spain and North Africa during the 12th century and was skeptical about the supernatural elements in Islam. Averroës defended a rational approach to truth and argued that inconsistencies between reason and scripture called for allegorical interpretation of the scriptures. Averroës was also "a major early voice" in whether philosophers should share their doubt with the masses, for which a literal interpretation of the scriptures might be best.

Among Jewish skeptics during the Middle Ages was the philosopher Saadia ben Joseph (or ibn Joseph, 882-942), who believed in God's existence, but understood that all philosophies and revealed religions were based on uncertain knowledge. He viewed the search for philosophical truth as a religious obligation.[17] Most famous was the Jewish scholar Moses ben Maimon, known as Maimonides (1135-1205). Maimonides believed in God, but not a God that is involved in human affairs. In his *Guide for the Perplexed*, he argued that we cannot know what God wants and that keeping the laws is a human responsibility. Even so, belief in God and the

185

scriptures is necessary for regulating social relations, and people need religion for political and emotional reasons. Hecht describes Maimonides as the "first Jew we have on record as giving this kind of secular, political, and psychological explanation for the Jewish way of being"[18] and as offering "brilliant beginnings to the philosophy of secular Judaism."[19]

In medieval Christian Europe, the discovery of the classical works of Aristotle was central in a turn towards the more rationalistic and philosophical approach to religion that characterized Christian Scholasticism. For example, it was in this context that Anselm of Canterbury (1033-1109) devised his ontological proof of God.[20] In Paris, the French theologian Siger de Brabant (died ca. 1284) refuted the immortality of the soul and argued that the world was external rather than created. Evidence that a more rationalistic approach to Christianity was taking hold during this period could be found in the Catholic Church's condemnation of 291 propositions that reflected the new rationalist thinking.[21] Hecht notes that the Condemnation spurred Scholastic rationalism in new intellectual directions in which God was not a central issue and "[t]heology was becoming a mix of logic and natural science that left very little room for anything spiritual."[22]

RENAISSANCE HUMANISM

The Renaissance in Europe involved a "re-birth" or rediscovery of classical literature, art, history, and philosophy. Taking place during the 14th to 17th centuries, the Renaissance reflected a transition from the Middle Ages to the modern era, during which humanism was "rescued…from its subordination to Christian theology."[23] Dutch philosopher and Catholic theologian Erasmus of Rotterdam (1469?-1536) was an outstanding example of a Christian humanist who sought to reform the Church. He ridiculed the intellectualism of the Scholastics and advocated for religious tolerance and moderation, while calling for a simplified Christian life. His widely distributed works helped create the atmosphere for the Protestant Reformation.[24]

186

Hecht cites a number of prominent Renaissance skeptics with humanist ideas. For example, the Italian philosopher Pietro Pompanazzi (1462–1525) published books in which he concluded that the soul is mortal and that people can be moral without the threats of heaven and hell. Italian philosopher Giordano Bruno (1548–1600) accepted the Copernican heliocentric (sun-centered), rather than Earth-centered, system of the universe; adopted a pantheistic view of God as one with nature; and rejected the divinity of Jesus, the virgin birth, and the resurrection. The Italian freethinker Lucilio Vanini (1585–1619) wrote that all religions are invented by humans and used by kings and clergy to maintain power. The latter two religious skeptics were burned to death for their heretical beliefs.[25]

Prominent humanist thinkers in the 17th century included philosophers Baruch Spinoza (1632-1677), Thomas Hobbes (1588-1679), and Pierre Bayle (1647-1706). The Dutch philosopher Spinoza, of Portuguese ancestry, equated God with nature, ruling out an anthropomorphic or consoling God with intentions or goals.[26] Spinoza rejected divine authorship of the Bible, arguing that the scriptures—although morally valuable—are works of human literature. He discounted the validity of miracles as inconsistent with natural science and promoted virtue, reason, and the pursuit of knowledge for their own sake. He distinguished organized religion from true piety, which involved moral behavior and simple love for God and others. For Spinoza: "Religion stands in no need of the trappings of superstition. On the contrary, its glory is diminished when it is embellished with such fancies."[27]

Spinoza lamented the divisive sectarian loyalties associated with religion and sought to liberate citizens from ecclesiastical authority. Like some other philosophers of his time, Spinoza did not intend his ideas for the masses, however. He believed that common people would not be able to relinquish their superstitions, fears, and passions or pursue a more intellectual or philosophical approach to human flourishing. Summarizing the impact of Spinoza's *Theological-Political Treatise*, American philosopher Steven

Nadler concluded that "[m]ore than any other work, it laid the foundation for modern critical and historical approaches to the Bible."[28]

The English philosopher Thomas Hobbes (1588-1679), in his influential book *Leviathan*, turned religion on its head, presenting it as a human rather than divine phenomenon—originating in the fears and ignorance of people in the face of life's uncertainties.[29] Thus, as observed by humanities scholar Mark Lilla, Hobbes changed the traditional focus of theology from "God and his nature" to "man and his religious nature."[30] Hobbes sought to get people to distrust their religious leaders and their interpretations of scripture, and linked religious passion to political violence. He ruled out the idea of an incorporeal soul. He also expressed skepticism that the Bible is the Word of God, given human involvement in writing the scriptures much later than the reported events.

Lilla describes Hobbes' *Leviathan* as "the most devastating attack on Christian political theology ever undertaken."[31] Hobbes' unfortunate solution to the theological-political problem, however, was to empower a single absolute sovereign ("an earthly god"), who would protect his subjects and control all ecclesiastical matters—a solution that is anathema to the more democratic perspectives of later Enlightenment figures.

The French skeptic Pierre Bayle (1647-1706) offered the first vigorous defense of the morality of atheists. He argued that people could be moral without a belief in divine punishment and thus "a nation of atheists could exist without descending into chaos."[32]

Enlightenment Humanism

During the 18th century Enlightenment—with its emphasis on reason, experience, and natural philosophy as the bases for knowledge—major Enlightenment figures opened people's minds to the emerging secularism. Voltaire (1694-1778), the French writer and philosopher, questioned religious morality and myth and argued against religious intolerance. The Scottish philosopher David Hume (1711-1776), in his influential *Dialogue Concerning Natural Religion*, had characters rebut various arguments for the existence of God. French-German philosopher Baron D'Holbach (1723-1789), a confirmed atheist, referred to gods as imaginary beings, and religion as an invisible crutch for some people.[33]

An important alternative to the traditional Christian worldview sprang from the Enlightenment, as reason and new developments in science seemed to require a new conception of God. This new conception—referred to as Deism—was often denigrated as atheistic by more orthodox Christians.[34] Deists generally retained a belief in a rational and benevolent deity. However, they rejected most of the orthodox doctrines of Christianity such as the divinity of Jesus, the divine authorship of the scriptures, the resurrection, predestination, and original sin. These doctrines were viewed as incompatible with reason and experience.

Deists conceived of God as a First Cause, Creator, or Supreme Architect of a universe that conforms to the kinds of universal and immutable laws of nature identified by Enlightenment scientists such as Isaac Newton. The rationality and benevolence of the Deist God was viewed as observable in the order and design of nature. However, this God was also seen as distant and impersonal, interacting little, if at all, with its creation. From this perspective, the best way to attain knowledge of God was through the rational and empirical study of nature, rather than through scripture or revealed religion.

There were differences among Deists in the extent to which they tolerated or disparaged orthodox religion, their willingness to reveal their Deistic beliefs, and their acceptance of some religious doctrines. However, all advocated the primacy of reason and experience as the bases for evaluating religious ideas. Some proponents viewed Deism as a rational "third-way" between orthodox religion and atheism, while critics could understandably view it as "a half-way house" inevitably leading to atheism.[35] Deists were well represented among America's Founding Fathers. They promoted such humanistic causes as republican forms of government, free speech, separation of church and state, universal education, and pluralistic tolerance.[36] In addition, Deists were concerned with morality and ethics, which they saw as based on human reason, experience, and moral intuitions. Indeed, for Deists "the highest, most noble form of worship is the exercise of virtue."[37]

American Deism was influenced by Enlightenment ideas; British Deism; French radicalism's anticlericalism and focus on social, political, and humanistic concerns; and the gradual reduction of Calvinist dominance in the 18th century. Another important influence was the rise of Unitarianism, in part as a reaction to the religious fervor, emotional excess, and fanaticism of the First Great Awakening, an American religious revival during the 1730s-40s.[38]

Unitarians reject many orthodox Christian doctrines, in particular, belief in the Holy Trinity. American author and historian Garry Wills commented on the reaction against the First Great Awakening, observing that "[o]nce men recoiled from emotional excess, they looked more carefully at how reason could be used to guide religion into more acceptable paths."[39] This included abandonment of the doctrine of the Trinity because it was viewed as counter to reason. Wills notes that Unitarianism had been the "secret creed" of 17th century English intellectuals such as the poet John Milton, scientist Isaac Newton, and philosopher John Locke. However, these intellectuals "had to keep their views to themselves, since denial of the Trinity had been a heresy that led to execution between 1548 and 1612, and it was still condemned in the 1689 Act of Toleration."[40]

Deists in the American context included prominent figures of the American Revolutionary period. The "ambivalent Deist" Benjamin Franklin (1706-1790) struggled to accommodate both Deistic and Calvinistic elements in his religious philosophy.[41] The "frontier Deist" Ethan Allen (1738-1789), a controversial hero of the American Revolution, wrote a Deistic treatise titled *Reason the Only Oracle of Man*, which American author and philosopher Kerry Walters describes as "the first systematic defense of natural religion written by an American."[42] The "iconoclastic Deist" Thomas Paine (1737-1809) argued in *The Age of Reason* that the basic tenets of Christianity—unlike the Deistic religion of nature and reason—

are untenable from a rational perspective, even for the clerics that promulgate them.[43]

The "Deistic Christian" Thomas Jefferson (1743-1826) was a key advocate for the separation of church and state in the U.S. Constitution. He sought to demythologize the New Testament by editing out all aspects that were inconsistent with reason and experience. This left only Jesus' philosophical and ethical teachings and an account of his life.[44] Humanist chaplain Greg Epstein has suggested that Jefferson may have been the first truly humanist head of state.[45] Elihu Palmer (1764-1806), described by Walters as the "Crusader for Deism," wrote the book *The Principles of Nature,* which became the bible of American Deism. Palmer also founded a network of Deistic societies.[46]

By the early 19th century, however, the appeal of Deism largely dissipated. Its leading proponents died off and the movement came to be seen as too rational, mechanistic, and intellectual, with an aloof, detached, and impersonal God. Nonetheless, Deism's critique of the more dogmatic and supernatural elements of conventional theology did tend to reduce the influence of such elements. This is reflected, for example, in more liberal and rationalist denominations such as Unitarianism and Universalism, but also in more mainstream Protestant denominations.

In fact, American author Susan Jacoby observed that "[t]he connection among freethinkers, Unitarians, and Universalists was such that many religious conservatives considered the liberal Protestant sects just another species of infidelity."[47] As noted previously, Unitarians reject many orthodox Christian doctrines, in particular, the idea of the Holy Trinity. Universalists reject Calvinist predestination—the doctrine that God has predetermined who will be saved and go to heaven—believing that all human beings are saved. Jacoby noted that:

Between 1790 and 1830, approximately half of the tax-supported Congregationalist churches in Massachusetts were transformed into Unitarian congregations...[and that] [a]nother way of looking at Unitarianism is that it moved religion itself into the camp of Enlightenment rationalism...[A]t the core of their religion lay not an unquestioning faith but a deep reverence for the power of the human mind and the value of human doubt.[48]

Commenting on the American Deists of the Revolutionary period, Garry Wills opined that "[w]hatever their faults, the Deists delivered us from the horrors of pre-Enlightenment religion, title enough to honor. They also founded this country."[49] At the same time, however—and in part as a reaction to Deism—a more populist and conservative religious revival, the Second Great Awakening, had arisen. This revival emphasized personal piety, salvation, emotional fervor, and biblical fundamentalism. Garry Wills has described this contrast between "Enlightenment" and "revivalist" religion as representing the "head" and "heart" of religion, respectively.[50]

NINETEENTH CENTURY HUMANISM

In the view of Jennifer Michael Hecht, "[t]he nineteenth century was easily the best-documented moment of widespread doubt in human history."[51] Similarly, child psychiatrist Robert Coles, in *The Secular Mind*, highlighted the "decisive impact" of the latter years of the 19th century on the "secularist assumptions in the West."[52] Prominent nineteenth century humanists and religious skeptics included social reformers, philosophers, writers, poets, and scientists.

A new generation of humanist social reformers emerged. Hecht remarked that religious skeptics often take up social causes because, in the perceived absence of God, "humanity must design a better world for itself."[53] For example, Robert Dale Owen (1801-1877), a confirmed atheist, was the first American to openly advocate for birth control. Francis (Fanny) Wright (1795-1852) wrote and lectured against religion and promoted the idea of a Hall of Science in every American community. Ernestine L. Rose (1810-1892), a Jewish immigrant to the United States, gave public speeches on atheism, abolition, and women's rights. Karl Marx (1818-1883), the German philosopher and political economist, believed that religion and the "illusory happiness" it offered was the result of oppression and would wither away once people's economic situations were improved.

Elizabeth Cady Stanton (1815-1902) is best known for her efforts on behalf of women's rights and the abolition of slavery. However, she also critiqued religion and the Bible from a feminist perspective, spoke out for separation of church and state, and promoted reason over religion.[54] Other contributors to the anti-slavery movement, such as William Lloyd Garrison (1805-1879) and the Quaker sisters Angelina and Sarah Grimké, were religious believers, but were strongly anticlerical and critical of orthodox religion, which offered a scriptural justification for slavery.[55] Writer Susan Jacoby argued that the only consistent opponents of censorship from the 1870s to World War I—for example, in reaction to the Comstock laws—were also humanistic freethinkers.[56]

In America, the most prominent 19th century orator and advocate of a secular perspective was Robert Green Ingersoll (1833-1899). Susan Jacoby observes that Ingersoll "bridged the gap" between Enlightenment Deism and practical freethought as he advocated for the "freedom *not* to worship any god as well as to worship God in one's own way."[57] Ingersoll promoted a variety of social causes. For example, he spoke against corporal punishment, the death penalty, and laws requiring the return to owners of fugitive slaves, while supporting civil and women's rights. For Ingersoll, agnosticism was the most honest position regarding the existence of God.[58]

In 19th century Great Britain, nonbelievers were also active in social reform movements. For example, the British atheist Charles Bradlaugh (1833-1891) founded the National Secular Society and, as a member of Parliament, championed the working class, encouraged public vaccination, and promoted the right of atheists to affirm rather than swear when taking oaths in court cases. A close collaborator of Bradlaugh's, Annie Besant

(1847-1933), wrote *The Freethinker's Text Book* and *The Gospel of Atheism*; criticized religion as a barrier to civil and social progress; and was a leader of the Theosophical Society, which pursued a blending of Eastern and Western philosophies, religions, and spiritualism.[59]

The British freethinker George Jacob Holyoake (1817-1906) popularized use of the term "secularism" to distinguish his perspective from atheism, which he viewed as too combative towards religion and too definitive in its rejection of God's existence. Holyoake's stance was both ethical and *agnostic*—a term later introduced by Thomas Huxley. Holyoake defined secularism as:

> ...a code and duty pertaining to this life, founded on considerations purely human, and intended mainly for those who find theology indefinite or inadequate, unreliable or unbelievable. Its essential principles are three: 1. The improvement of this life by material means. 2. That science is the available Providence of man. 3. That it is good to do good.[60]

Among the most prominent skeptical or atheistic philosophers in the 19th century were Arthur Schopenhauer (1788-1860), Ludwig Feuerbach (1804-1872), Sören Kierkegaard (1813-1955), Friedrich Nietzsche (1844-1900), and John Stuart Mill (1806-1873).[61] In his *Dialogue on Religion*, German philosopher Arthur Schopenhauer's characters describe religion as "the metaphysics of the masses," providing comfort and guidance in life. Schopenhauer lamented that a sincere search for truth must struggle against this early and well indoctrinated metaphysics.

German philosopher Ludwig Feuerbach, in his books *Thoughts on Death and Immortality* and *The Essence of Christianity*, argued that Christianity involves a projection of human emotions and longings, that humans invented the idea of God as a means of consolation, and that the ideas of heaven and immortality trivialize death and divert attention from the joys and concerns of the one life we have.[62] Alister McGrath, a current Northern Irish theologian and Anglican priest, summarizes Feuerbach's view as follows:

> The human mind, without being aware of what it is doing, projects its longing for immortality and meaning onto an imaginary transcendent screen, and gives the name "God" to its own creation.[63]

Just as humans had created God in a misguided effort to find consolation and meaning, they could also reject their invention.

The Danish philosopher Sören Kierkegaard, although deeply religious and a preacher himself, was relentlessly critical of official Christianity as practiced in Europe. He viewed it as incompatible with Christianity as depicted in the New Testament, which called for greater renunciation of worldly possessions and attachments.[64]

German philosopher Friedrich Nietzsche, *in The Gay Science*, famously announced that "God is dead" and that "we have killed him." Nietzsche was scornful of Christianity because he believed it promoted meekness and humility. This was incompatible with his vision of a new morality based on the "super-" or "over-man" (*übermensch*), a person who transcends conventions and has the strength to pursue all that life has to offer.[65] Nietzsche viewed faith itself as an indicator of weakness and as inconsistent with vigor of mind and a desire to know the truth.[66]

English philosopher John Stuart Mill, in posthumously published essays, refuted some of the usual arguments for God's existence. He questioned the omnipotence and benevolence of God in the face of so much evil in the world. He argued that moral truths stand on their own evidence without the imprimatur of religion. And, he proposed a "Religion of Humanity" that excluded the supernatural.[67]

Many 19th century humanists and religious skeptics were prominent poets and writers. For example, the English poet Percy Bysshe Shelley (1792-1822) promoted free thought and tolerance, believed that the universe is eternal rather than created, and rejected the Deistic view of God. The English novelist George Elliott (Mary Ann Evans, 1819-1880) translated German theologian David Friedrich Strauss's controversial *Life of Jesus Critically Examined*. Strauss's book described the Gospels as historical myths, calling into question the literal truth of the Bible. Strauss's work was an example of the so-called Higher Criticism movement that emerged, particularly in Germany, during the late 18th century, and examined the Bible from a historical, literary, and often secular perspective.

In the United States, philosopher, essayist, and poet Ralph Waldo Emerson (1803-1882) initiated the Transcendentalist movement. The movement rejected formal Christianity, even in its more liberal forms, and adopted a spiritual perspective on the natural world (i.e., nature as a divine force).[68] Garry Wills describes Transcendentalism, which split off from Unitarianism, as a reaction in the Romantic era against the cool rationalism of the Enlightenment. Many Transcendentalists were also social reformers. They opposed slavery, advocated for labor, and brought the German Kindergarten Movement to the United States.[69]

The American poet Walt Whitman (1819-1892) predicted—in the preface to his controversial collection of poems *Leaves of Grass*—that "There will soon be no more priests...[that] every man shall be his own priest...and [that] the new breed of poets shall find their inspiration in real objects today" [rather than] "deign to defend immortality or God...".[70]

Mark Twain (Samuel Langhorne Clemens, 1835-1910) was apparently a believer, but rejected divine inspiration of the Bible, the idea that God intervenes in human affairs, and the idea of eternal punishment. Twain mocked the large gap between religious ethics and actual practice, for example, pointing to such immoral practices of the Christian church as ownership of slaves and persecution of "witches."[71]

Leslie Stephen (1832-1904), a British intellectual and agnostic—and father of writer Virginia Wolfe—published a series of essays in which he criticized religious orthodoxy. He questioned the persuasiveness of religious beliefs. He noted the incompatibility between theology and scientific evidence. And, he argued that morality stands independent of religious authority. American writer and scholar S. T. Joshi has suggested that Stephen's writings "paved the way" for a transition from Thomas Huxley's 19th century agnosticism to the more open rejection of religion by 20th century figures such as Bertrand Russell and H. L. Mencken.[72]

The British scientist Thomas Henry Huxley (1825-1895) had coined the term *agnosticism* in 1869 at a meeting of the Metaphysical Society convened to consider the very question of God's existence.[73] An avid promoter of Charles Darwin's theory of evolution, Huxley argued that evolution "excludes creation and all other kinds of supernatural intervention."[74] In S. T. Joshi's view, Huxley's debates and writings on religion "perhaps had more influence than those of anyone else in his generation on the demise of biblical inerrancy, the fashioning of a secular view of life, and the establishment of science as the chief arbiter of empirical truth."[75]

Finally, in the late 19th century, German-American professor Felix Adler (1851-1933) founded the Ethical Culture movement in New York city. Parallel developments soon followed in the United Kingdom, with significant early contributions from American Stanton Coit (1857-1944), an associate of Adler.[76] The movement emphasized the importance of ethical behavior, moral development, and social welfare through community engagement. It did so while contending that ethical and moral behavior need not depend on religious doctrine.[77] The spirit of the movement is captured by a passage from one of Adler's lectures:

> The Ethical Movement is religious to those who are religiously-minded and to those who interpret its work religiously, and it is simply ethical to those who are not so minded.[78]

Or, as described in 1896 by the Union of Ethical Societies (later the Ethical Union) in the United Kingdom, the aim was to assist, "by purely natural and human means" individual and social efforts towards "right living," adding in 1906 that "[t]he moral life involves neither acceptance nor rejection of belief in any deity, personal or impersonal or in a life after death."[79]

In his lifetime, Adler sought to distinguish the Ethical Culture movement from the organized humanism that developed in the 20th century, which he viewed as too naturalistic. Even so, in both the United States and United Kingdom, the Ethical Culture movement was an influential forerunner of 20th century humanism.[80]

TWENTIETH CENTURY HUMANISM

By the 1910s and 1920s, organized *religious humanism* was emerging. Important figures in the United States included the clergymen John H. Dietrich (1878–1957), Charles Francis Potter (1885-1962), and Curtis W. Reese (1887-1961). Dietrich, a Unitarian minister, conceived a "Religion without God." It was not explicitly atheistic in today's sense, but downplayed the importance of belief in God in favor of principles and rituals that celebrated nature and humanity.[81] As the first to outline the idea of an American church without religion, Dietrich is often referred to as the "Father of Religious Humanism."[82] However, Reese and Potter did more to develop and promote the idea nationally. Potter left the Unitarians and formed the First Humanist Society in New York, the first independent humanist institution. Reese edited the first Humanist Manifesto in 1933— a religious humanist document that calls for moving beyond theism and a supernatural basis for human values. He also helped found the American Humanist Association (AHA) in 1941.

It was not until 1980 that American philosophy professor Paul Kurtz (1925-2012) founded the Council for Democratic and Secular Humanism (currently the Council for Secular Humanism under the Center for Inquiry umbrella). This new organization provided a definitively secular humanist home for individuals who might otherwise join the AHA or American Ethical Union, with their traditions of religious (albeit nontheistic) humanism. Professor of Religious Studies Joseph Blankholm, referring to "generations of nuanced debate over terms and ideologies," observed that:

The divide between religious and secular humanism grew out of an older tradition of expressly religious humanism, which in turn sprang from nineteenth-century movements like Holyoake's Secularism, the Freethought movement, Comte's Religion of Humanity, and the Unitarian Church.[83]

As in the 19th century, many 20th century humanists and atheists were social reformers. In the United States, prominent examples included Margaret Sanger (1879-1966) and Madalyn Murray O'Hair (1919-1995). Sanger adopted the motto "No Gods, No Masters" for her journal, opened the first birth control clinic in 1916, and established the American Birth Control League, which later became the Planned Parenthood Federation of America.[84] O'Hair was a brash and controversial atheist whose most significant accomplishments were her successful efforts to (a) have officially sanctioned prayers banned from the public schools and (b) eliminate state requirements that elected officials acknowledge the existence of a Supreme Being in their oaths of office.[85] During the 1960s, the civil rights movement in the United States involved social activism by both religious and secular individuals. However, the renewed struggle for women's rights was definitively a secular feminist movement.[86]

Two 20th century American humanists achieved fame, in part, through their participation in the Scopes "Monkey" trial in Dayton, Tennessee in 1925. John Thomas Scopes was put on trial for breaking the state's law prohibiting the teaching of evolution in the public schools. Clarence Darrow (1857-1938) was the defense lawyer in the case. He also participated in public debates with religious figures, in which he argued against the existence of God and an immortal soul, questioned the religious basis for morality, and advocated for separation of church and state. H. L. Mencken (1880-1956) was a journalist and cultural critic who covered the Scopes trial. He ridiculed Tennesseans for passing such a law and putting Scopes on trial. Mencken was critical of atheism. However, he believed that the impact of religion on ethics was modest, particularly in comparison to the negative impact of religion on clear and honest thinking. He also doubted the immortality of the soul, believed that science had overtaken many of the tenets of Christianity, and pointed to the many inconsistencies in the Bible.[87]

Throughout the 20th century, social reform was also a primary focus of humanists in the United Kingdom. Prominent figures such as Harold Blackham (1903-2009)—viewed by some as the father of British humanism—Hypatia Bradlaugh Bonner (1858-1935), Barbara Smoker (1923-2020), and David Pollock (b. 1942), among many others, advocated for a number of social causes. Prominent causes included support for moral education and sex education in the schools; inclusion of humanism as an alternative life stance in religious education curricula; penal reform and the abolition of capital punishment; freedom of speech and the repeal of blasphemy laws; contraception, abortion, and family planning; same-sex marriage and decriminalization of homosexuality; marriage and divorce law reform; voluntary euthanasia; nuclear disarmament; anti-war, anti-apartheid, and anti-imperialism movements; and human rights generally. In recent years, UK humanists have sought to provide support for nonreligious asylum seekers and for people leaving their religion, especially high control religions.[88]

A number of prominent 20th century philosophers were explicit atheists. For example, Bertrand Russell (1872-1970) refuted purported proofs of God's existence in his influential essay *Why I Am Not a Christian*. He believed that life could have emerged through natural laws without a Creator. And, he argued that morality derives not from religion but from social utility. Indeed, he contended that organized Christianity has been the chief enemy of moral progress in the world. Russell conceded that he could not prove that gods do not exist. However, he viewed the possibility that gods exist as too improbable to warrant serious consideration.[89]

Existentialist philosophers, some of whom, such as Jean-Paul Sartre (1905-1980) and Albert Camus (1913-1960), were atheists, pointed to the "absurdity" and lack of intrinsic meaning in our lives. This requires individuals to take personal responsibility for defining their own "essence" and sense of meaning through their free choices and actions. In a 1946 lecture, Sartre argued explicitly that existentialism—with its emphasis on free choice, independent of religion and society—is a form of humanism.[90]

Among the prominent atheist writers in the 20th century were H.P. Lovecraft (1890-1937), the science fiction writer, and Gore Vidal, novelist, essayist, and public intellectual. Lovecraft, in posthumously published letters of correspondence, drew on his knowledge of science, including evolutionary theory, to refute the immortality of the soul and predict that life might eventually be generated in the laboratory. Like Bertrand Russell, Lovecraft viewed the existence of a God or spirit world as very unlikely. Thus, although an agnostic in theory, he considered himself "practically and provisionally, as an atheist."[91] Gore Vidal (1925-2012) satirized and attacked monotheism and Christian doctrine; religious bias towards women, gays, and other groups; and the undesirable intrusion of religion into the secular domain.[92]

Atheism—or at least disbelief in a *personal* God—was common among 20th century scientists. I note just two prominent examples. The famous astronomer Carl Sagan (1934-1996) pointed to the thousands of mutually contradictory religions in the world as evidence that they reflect local culture rather than valid universal truths. He also found many of the proposed proofs of God's existence less than compelling. Sagan wondered why an all-knowing God did not include some accurate future knowledge or predictions in the scriptures (e.g., the structure of DNA), which would have provided impressive evidence for His understanding of the world He had created.[93]

Steven Weinberg (1933-2021), a theoretical physicist and Nobel Laureate, noted that we can go very far in explaining life and the universe by drawing on available evidence from the sciences, without appealing to divine intervention. For example, he was not persuaded by arguments for God based on the so-called fine-tuning of the universe. He also opined that any attribution to God of the beauty of nature would also have to consider God's role in such evils or misfortunes as birth defects and cancer.

For Weinberg, religious beliefs reflect wishful thinking. Nonetheless, he expressed some nostalgia and sense of loss that the laws of nature are not likely to reveal the plans of a "concerned Creator."[94]

Weinberg's sense of nostalgia or loss in turning away from religion has also been experienced by some philosophers and writers, who find themselves nonetheless unable to accept the beliefs associated with their former faiths.[95] Weinberg understood people's need to seek consolation in religion, but considered it a moral "point of honor" to resist this temptation. In his view, "[t]he honor of resisting this temptation is only a thin substitute for the consolations of religion, but it is not entirely without satisfactions of its own."[96]

TWENTY-FIRST CENTURY HUMANISM

In the first decade of the 21st century, a series of books by the so-called New Atheists achieved an elevated but contentious public profile. These books included Richard Dawkins' *The God Delusion*; Sam Harris' *The End of Faith: Religion, Terror, and the Future of Reason* and *Letter to a Christian Nation*; Christopher Hitchens' *God is Not Great: How Religion Poisons Everything*; and Daniel Dennett's *Breaking the Spell: Religion as a Natural Phenomenon*. Overlapping views were also offered by physicist Victor Stenger, for example, in *God: The Failed Hypothesis*. The New Atheists criticized religion with varying degrees of intensity and offered naturalistic accounts of religion, morality, and life. Given their prominence, I address here some of the dominant themes found in these works.[97]

The most consistent theme—which recalls the views of religious doubters and skeptics throughout human history—is the contention that morality does not derive from nor require religion. Rather, humans have naturally evolved moral sentiments such as empathy and gratitude, which are further elaborated through reason and a consideration of human and societal interests. These moral intuitions are reflected in, but do not originally derive from, religious scriptures or doctrine. For example, as argued by American physicist Victor Stenger:

In the scriptures and other teachings of the great monotheisms we find a repetition of common ideals that arose during the gradual evolution of human societies, as they became more civilized, developed rational thinking processes, and discovered how to live together in greater harmony. The evidence points to a source other than the revelations claimed in these scriptures.[98]

For Daniel Dennett, the proposition that people cannot be moral without religion presents "a demeaning view of human nature."[99]

A second theme is the contention that evolution via natural selection is sufficient to explain the origin and development of all life forms, including human beings. In addition, the science of cosmology can adequately account for the universe we live in without recourse to an intelligent designer or Creator God. For example, Stenger noted that prominent cosmologists have published a variety of scenarios "by which the universe could have come from nothing naturally."[100] The existence of a non-physical soul is also called into question. Brain imaging and stimulation studies suggest that neural activity in the brain is sufficient to account for the functions typically attributed to the soul by religion, such as consciousness, thinking, will, and conscience.[101] Indeed, several of the New Atheists have argued that religious propositions and phenomena can and should be investigated by science, despite the reluctance by many scientists and theologians to impinge on each other's domains.

Third, the New Atheists often highlight the evils of religion, particularly its role in violence and terrorism across history. Harris singled out Islam as particularly problematic today. In addition to religious violence, these critics lament that religion is sometimes used to oppose vaccination, condom use to prevent AIDS, humane assisted dying, and potentially life-saving medical care and research, while promoting genital mutilation and turning a blind eye to child abuse by clergy.[102]

Fourth, the New Atheists have criticized religious scriptures for their intellectual and moral shortcomings, inconsistencies, obvious borrowing from neighboring civilizations, and incompatibilities with science. These features suggest that the scriptures are human products of their historical eras.

Fifth, some of the New Atheists raised the contentious issue of whether religious moderates are part of the problem when it comes to countering more extreme forms of religion. Sam Harris and Daniel Dennett, in particular, take this position, arguing that the tolerance of religious moderates makes it difficult and politically incorrect to criticize religion and to oppose its more dangerous or extreme forms.[103] Dennett attributes this dilemma, in part, to the fact that many people—even some who do not believe in God—retain a *belief in belief* in God. This is the view that belief in God is sufficiently important for individuals or society to justify avoiding criticism or disconfirmation of religion. For Dennett, part of the solution lies in making religion "less of a 'sacred cow' and more of a 'worthy alternative'."[104]

Aside from the New Atheists, some prominent 21st century humanist writers have specifically addressed Islam. For example, in his classic book *Why I Am Not A Muslim*, Islamic scholar Ibn Warraq (b. 1946) criticized Islam and many of its doctrines. These include Islam's concept of predestination, which seems to dismiss the possibility of moral responsibility; the idea of jihad or Holy War; Islam's treatment of women as inferior; an ethical system based in fear and barbaric forms of divine punishment; and the rigid and irrational nature of much of Islamic or Sharia law. Warraq draws on historical scholarship on the Quran's emergence, its multiple variants, and its contradictory contents to conclude that it is human-made rather than the word of Allah as believed by its most faithful adherents. He cites numerous examples of violence committed in the name of Islam, and argues that Islam is totalitarian in nature and incompatible with democracy and human rights.[105] Warraq is critical of multicultural or relativistic attitudes that lead people in Western countries to turn a blind eye to acts that would be considered immoral or counter to Western values in order to avoid being critical of Islam.[106]

Similarly, activist and writer Ayann Hirsi Ali (b. 1969), among others in the Islamic world, has argued that we should not limit criticism of Islam by either moderate Muslims or Western intellectuals. She has called for a Muslim Reformation that will ensure that aspects of the faith that she views as problematic—such as sharia law and the call to jihad—will be open to interpretation and criticism.[107] Indeed, a number of additional Muslim intellectuals, writers, and activists have been advocating for a humanistic revolution in the Islamic world and a number of atheist, freethought, and ex-Muslim groups have sprung up in Britain, France, North America, and several Arab countries.[108] Paradoxically, Ali recently announced her conversion to Christianity, which she now sees as a more formidable foe than atheism against the perceived menace of Islam.[109]

Potent critics of religion persist. Take, for example, the prominent British philosopher and secular humanist A. C. Grayling (b. 1949). In his book *The God Argument: The Case against Religion and for Humanism,* Grayling describes religion as akin to astrology and magic, having originated in "the pre-scientific, rudimentary metaphysics of our ancestors."[110] Religion persists today, he argues, for several reasons. We indoctrinate children while they are too young to reason. Societies reinforce religious traditions and we experience social pressures to conform. Religion appeals to our emotions. And, people are uninformed regarding both science and the history of religions.[111] Grayling points to a number of evils that call into question the morality of religion such as denial of rights to gays, genital mutilation, suicide bombings, and the stoning of adulterers to death.[112] He also laments that almost all religions try to impose themselves on others and that religious apologists often resort to claims of ineffability for religious ideas that are vague, incoherent, or contrary to reason and experience.[113]

As an alternative to religion, Grayling advocates for a humanistic view on ethics and morality, which should be a matter of discussion based on human experience rather than divinely imposed. For the humanist, the "good life" is one of meaning, purpose, and activity; intimate relationships; honesty and authenticity; and personal responsibility and integrity.[114]

Given the outsized influence of the New Atheists on debates about religion in the early 21st century, some comments on their impact are warranted. On the one hand, their works and commentaries raised the international profile of the atheist movement and recruited additional people to the secular fold.[115] On the other hand, their efforts elicited significant push back, from theologians and religious commentators of course, but also from some prominent figures in the secular humanism movement.

In content, the New Atheists have been criticized for the following:

- Their predominant focus on monotheistic religions;
- Their simplistic and biased understanding of religion, even in its more moderate and tolerant forms;
- Their tendency to ignore the wisdom and insights found in religious scriptures;
- Their over-emphasis on the intellectual or cognitive aspects of religion (i.e., religious beliefs and doctrines), while giving short shrift to the emotional, ritualistic, and community aspects;
- Their contention that evil and violence are intrinsic and inevitable features of religion;
- Their overconfidence in reason's ability to discern the nature of reality and moral behavior;
- An uncritical "faith" and one-sided perspective on the importance and capabilities of science;
- Their over-emphasis on attacking religion, rather than promoting the positive values associated with secular humanism.[116]

In tone, the New Atheist books, in varying degrees, are perceived by many as strident, dogmatic, condescending, and one-sided. Indeed, some critics see the New Atheism—as well as evolutionary science specifically— as a "surrogate religion" or atheistic form of fundamentalism.[117] Indeed, some people's negative reactions to the New Atheist works have led to religious conversions.

As a result, even some secularists view the efforts of the New Atheists as detrimental to the secular humanist cause. For example, they may have further polarized relations between secular and religious communities and conflated in the public's eye all secularism with its more militant or confrontational forms. Emerging rifts and infighting within the atheist movement itself—for example, over issues associated with gender, feminism, LGBTQ+ rights, privilege, race, and controversial social media posts—also weakened the movement in popular culture.[118]

Indeed, by 2015 some commentators were asking "Is the New Atheism dead?" They pointed to a "new wave" of more "temperate" atheists who approach religion with less animosity, greater tolerance, and more circumspect rhetoric.[119] Reflecting this trend, a number of popular books by atheists have adopted a more conciliatory tone toward religion. Examples include Greg Epstein's *Good without God: What a Billion Nonreligious People Do Believe,* Chris Stedman's *Faitheist: How an Atheist Found Common Ground with the Religious,* Alain de Botton's *Religion for Atheists: A Nonbeliever's Guide to the Uses of Religion,* Thomas Sheridan's *Respectful Atheism: A Perspective on Belief in God and Each Other,* Philip Kitcher's *Life After Faith: The Case for Secular Humanism,* and Steven Pinker's *Enlightenment Now: The Case for Reason, Science, Humanism, and Progress.* Several of these books have made an explicit case for secular humanism as an alternative to religion.

For example, British philosopher Philip Kitcher offers a largely philosophical and rational analysis of whether secular humanism can provide a meaningful and satisfying substitute for religion. He discusses some of the issues that lead many secularists to experience legitimate doubts about religion, including the diversity of religions, changes and disputes involving religious doctrines, and the untestability of many religious claims. Nonetheless, Kitcher suggests that the proper secularist attitude may be one of openness and agnosticism and that fruitful discussions are possible between secular humanists and believers in more *refined religion*—that is, less doctrinal and more value-based versions of religion. In his view, secular humanists can find common cause with believers in refined religion, for example, in social justice endeavors.[120]

Humanist chaplain Greg Epstein, in his influential book, presents a secular humanist perspective on morality, meaning, and community. He refutes the idea that people cannot be moral without belief in God. Morality should be based on free inquiry and compassionate questioning rather than the purported objective and timeless values of religion. The Golden Rule offers a simple and widely endorsed guide to ethical behavior that does not require a God. In addition, people need to create and choose their own values and purposes in life and be passionate about worthy, this-worldly causes and ideals that transcend self-interest. The importance of community is at the heart of humanism. Epstein embraces a humanistic life stance he views as liberating. But he also promotes religious pluralism and literacy, interfaith dialogue (including with nonbelievers), and cooperation as allies between secular humanists and more progressive or liberal religious congregations, for example, in work on climate change.[121]

Cognitive scientist Steven Pinker also takes a more accommodating position towards religion than the New Atheists. Religious movements "should not be given a pass just because they are religious." However, the "art, rituals, iconography, and communal warmth that many people enjoy can continue to be provided by liberalized religions, without the supernatural dogma or Iron Age morality."[122] Regarding morality and the Bible today, Pinker observes that:

> ...enlightened believers cherry-pick the humane injunctions while allegorizing, spin-doctoring, or ignoring the vicious ones, and that's just the point: they read the Bible through the lens of Enlightenment humanism.[123]

TAKEAWAYS

My historical overview of humanism and religious skepticism has been necessarily selective. Many additional people could be mentioned.[124] Nonetheless, I can offer a number of summary observations that are relevant to a consideration of the relative cogency, merits, and viability of religion versus secular humanism.

First, the history of religious doubt or nonbelief is likely as long as the evolution of religion itself, and has certainly been evident since written records have existed. Religious skepticism and even atheism would likely have been even more visible in earlier centuries had it not been dangerous to express ideas considered heretical. Religious skeptics have questioned the nature of God, the immortality of the soul, the divinity of Jesus, God's responsibility in the face of evil, whether He is interested or involved in human affairs, and whether He even exists. Many have questioned central religious doctrines they view as inconsistent with reason, clear thinking, science, experience, and the search for truth. At the same time, many have offered a naturalistic view of the universe and a humanistic view of human evolution and behavior.

Second, many humanists and religious skeptics have observed that religious scriptures reflect the time and local historical contexts in which they were written and point to their many inconsistencies and errors, based on our current knowledge of history and science. Theologians take such inconsistencies in stride—for example, as invitations to deeper exploration of the sacred texts.[125] However, to many critics such discrepancies suggest that the scriptures are human products and not divinely inspired.

Third, many skeptics see the vast number of incompatible religions across human history—and still today—as raising serious questions about the validity or truth claims of any of them. Even the prominent Christian theologian-scientist John Polkinghorne has described this diversity of faiths as "the elephant in the room," requiring religious people to exhibit "persistent fortitude as they face the apparent incompatibilities between the faiths."[126] Other critics note that rulers and clergy, often in support of each other, have frequently used religion as a tool of political power. Since at least the 18th century, this has provided a powerful rationale for the separation of church and state.

A minimum implication of these observations is the following: Although today's religious skeptics and atheists may be denigrated or worse in some societies, they can take some comfort in knowing that their skepticism follows a long history in all religious traditions. Many of the criticisms of religion by humanists and religious skeptics have been repeated across history. This may enhance the persuasiveness and perceived cogency of these criticisms, at least for some readers.

Arguably, given our inability to validate these doubts about religion with certainty, agnosticism may be the most rational or sound position to take regarding God's nature and existence. Nonetheless, like many previous skeptics, some current doubters may decide that the likelihood of God's existence is sufficiently small to make an atheistic stance reasonable if not preferable in practice. At least since the 19th century, when explicit atheism became more common, we can observe a continuum among religious skeptics that ranges from highly combative and rejectionist towards religion to positions that are more accommodating and open to the possible merits or truth claims of religion. In general, we would expect agnostics to be more accommodating towards religion than declared atheists.

Fourth, throughout history, a consistent contention of humanists is that by drawing on reason, empathy, and a consideration of human and societal interests, people can lead ethical and moral lives without religion. Indeed, the vast majority of nonbelievers do so. For example, as we have seen, many humanists and nonbelievers have made major contributions in the promotion of social reforms. This social activism likely reflects their belief that in the absence of God humans become responsible for improving the human condition. In this sense, disbelief—particularly if expressed in humanistic terms—may be a powerful motivator of prosocial behavior.

In short, religion is not the only source of moral and ethical behavior, despite the persistence of this common and erroneous belief among many adherents of religion today.

But are there some people who are *unable* to be moral and ethical without religion? As noted earlier, some critics of religion have argued that religion should nonetheless be retained for the "masses," who may need religion to regulate their behavior. Religious faith has undoubtedly helped some people behave in a more prosocial manner. However, the idea that religion is needed to ensure ethical behavior from all representatives of the "masses" is probably elitist. Nonetheless, it may be an argument in favor of religion's persistence since the "prod" of religion likely plays a role in the prosocial behavior of some people.

Fifth, throughout history, humanists and critics of religion have offered alternative principles or guides for living meaningful lives without reference to gods or the supernatural. Humanists have also noted that it is possible to experience awe, wonder, and fulfillment in life through purely secular means. Some humanists have expressed feelings of nostalgia or regret at their loss of faith or inability to believe. At the same time, however, they point to a sense of personal honesty or integrity in resisting the temptation to turn back towards religion. Readers are invited to consider whether the alternative guides to living offered historically by humanists are sufficient to provide meaningful lives in the absence of religion—a question I will have more to say about in Chapter 9 on Secular Living.

Sixth, many humanists, atheists, and religious skeptics have denigrated the role that religion has played in violence and intolerance. Furthermore, some have suggested that religious liberals or moderates are part of the problem, because their tolerance or political correctness prevents them from adequately confronting more extreme elements in their respective religions. Although we often do see push back against religious extremism by more moderate religionists, it is worth reinforcing the importance of them doing so.

Importantly, the relative merits of liberal versus conservative forms of religion are likely to be central in any discussions about the future of religion. More conservative forms may inspire greater commitment and social cohesion, but also greater tendencies towards outgroup prejudice and violence. More liberal forms may inspire less commitment, but will likely accommodate and co-exist better with secular humanism.

Finally, in the present chapter, I traced the history of humanism and religious skepticism through the views and behaviors of prominent individuals. In the next chapter, I address the question of whether societies as a whole have become more secular and, if so, how this happened. The answers to these questions have direct relevance in assessing the likely long-term persistence and viability of religion.

Chapter 8
Is the World Becoming More Secular?

In this chapter I address the contentious issue of whether the world—or at least the Western or modern industrial world—is becoming more secular and, if so, how it happened. This question is central in assessing the viability and ultimate future of religion and secular humanism as alternative life stances. I also consider the likelihood that religion will persist in the near and long term.

The overwhelming trajectory for religion in most Western European nations over the past century has been that of unambiguous decline.
— Phil Zuckerman[1]

[R]ich societies are becoming more secular but the world as a whole is becoming more religious.
— Pippa Norris and Ronald Inglehart[2]

The glib and simplistic predictions of a secular or atheist society simply have not come about. Christianity turned out not to be a marginalized anachronism doomed to terminal decline, but instead a remarkably resilient and enduring part of the social and intellectual order.
— Alister McGrath[3]

Does modernization promote secularization and the decline of religion? Historically, this idea can be traced to the Enlightenment and subsequent thinkers—among them August Comte, Charles Darwin, Émile Durkheim, Sigmund Freud, G. W. F. Hegel, Karl Marx, Hebert Spencer, Ernst

Tröltsch, and Max Weber.[4] In the social sciences, the idea that modernization necessarily weakens the importance of religion is referred to as the *secularization thesis* or *paradigm*. Although generally endorsed by social scientists during much of the twentieth century, the thesis has been strongly challenged in recent decades. Today, the thesis remains controversial, with both strong advocates and opponents, and others calling for revision or more selective application of the thesis. In this chapter, I will try to make sense of the debate and draw some conclusions.

The answer to the secularization question could depend on how we define secularization. If we define secularization as the weakened authority or influence of religious institutions and symbols in the public sphere—for example, as reflected in their reduced impact on the arts, philosophy, science, and politics, and increasing separation of church and state—then it is clear that significant secularization has taken place over the past few centuries, at least in many developed countries.[5] More controversial is the extent to which individual piety, as reflected in religious beliefs, practices, and commitments, has also declined.[6]

Canadian philosopher Charles Taylor adds a third conception of secularization when he asks: "Why was it virtually impossible not to believe in God in, say, 1500 in our Western society, while in 2000 many of us find this not only easy, but even inescapable?"[7] Here, Taylor is referring to secularization as "a move from a society where belief in God is unchallenged and indeed, unproblematic, to one in which it is understood to be one option among others, and frequently not the easiest to embrace."[8]

As seen in the previous chapter, religious skepticism and doubt have existed among a minority of people throughout recorded history. However, religious disbelief as a viable, and perhaps preferable, option has emerged as a widespread alternative to religious belief relatively recently in human history. How did this come about?

214

THE REFORMATION PARADOX

Some scholars have proposed secularization influences that predated the 16th century Protestant Reformation. For example, in his monumental work on the cultural evolution of Western psychology and institutions, evolutionary biologist Joseph Henrich attributed the emergence of a number of Western psychological attributes—for example, individualism, analytic thinking, independence, nonconformity, and reduced devotion to tradition and authority—as well as the growth of various voluntary secular organizations, to the medieval Catholic Church's policies regarding marriage and family. These policies included prohibitions against marriage to blood relatives or affinal kin (i.e., in-laws), polygynous marriage (i.e., a man marrying multiple women), and arranged marriages.

Henrich and his colleagues have presented evidence that these policies had the effect of undermining the intensive kin-based institutions and authority structures associated with clans, lineages, and tribes that had previously existed in Europe. The result was the emergence of the aforementioned Western psychological attributes, which are often associated with increasing secularization.[9] Thus, we can infer that some of the psychological and cultural ingredients for secularization were already emerging gradually throughout the Middle Ages under the influence of the Catholic Church, but were boosted or accelerated by the Protestant Reformation. Indeed, Henrich contends that Protestantism served to "sacralize the psychological complex that had been percolating in Europe during the centuries leading up to the Reformation."[10]

In fact, a predominant view among historians and social scientists of religion is that the Protestant Reformation and its cascading effects played an unintended but pivotal role in the secularization of society and individual consciousness, at least in Western societies.[11] For example, in regards to secularization in the public sphere, one down-stream effect of the Protestant Reformation was concerns about the blending of church and state, which were brought to the forefront by the Wars of Religion during the 16th and 17th centuries. The separation of religion and politics is now a distinctive feature of most Western nations, although maintaining this separation is an ongoing challenge.

Scholars often refer to the "disenchantment of the world" brought about by the Protestant Reformation.[12] The medieval world of the Catholic Church was "enchanted" by mysteries, miracles, magic, spirits, demons, sacraments, saintly intercessions, sacred images, and Divine Providence. In contrast, Protestantism downplayed or divested itself of many of these sacred elements, leading to "an immense shrinkage in the scope of the sacred in reality" and a world that was no longer "penetrated by sacred beings and forces."[13] One result was a greater separation between the sacred and the secular and a turn towards greater naturalism. In a world "shorn of the sacred," Charles Taylor posits an "anthropocentric shift" in which humans feel freer to reorder society as they see fit, in accordance with human motives and reason.[14] In addition, the Protestant Reformation relinquished much of the imagery—such as majestic church architecture and religious art—that was important in elevating emotions and faith in medieval Christianity.[15]

I noted in the previous chapter how 18th century Deism served, in the view of its critics, as a halfway house between Protestantism and atheism. In addition, in the view of many scholars, the emergence of liberal Protestant theology during the 19th century, identified in particular with the German theologian Friedrich Schleiermacher, contributed further to secularization. In his major work *The Christian Faith* (1821), Schleiermacher downplayed the supernatural and God's revelation and emphasized the personal religious feelings and consciousness of individual Christians.[16] Liberal Protestantism in the 19th century was also associated with the application of historical methods in the study of the Bible. Most prominent was David Friedrich Strauss's two-volume work on the "historical Jesus" titled *The Life of Jesus Critically Examined* (1835-1836), in which Strauss rejected the divinity of Jesus.

In the view of intellectual historian Mark Lilla, liberal theology failed to animate religious commitment among nominal Christians and Jews, increasing the viability of more secular options. Although liberal theologians offered a set of values to live by, such as moral universalism and toleration, these values did not "provide divine hope or solace."[17]

Similarly, American sociologist Jerome Baggett has noted how Christian apologists (i.e., defenders) in the 19th century, in their efforts to combat atheism, actually made living without God more conceivable. They did so, for example, by adopting a this-worldly tone that deemphasized the transcendent otherness and ineffability of God. They also insisted on the reasonableness of Christianity and its compatibility with science, which enabled new scientific discoveries to undermine religion. And, they associated God's moral law with human moral values, which facilitated the abandonment of God in favor of a more secular version of humanism. In short, in their attempts to counter the challenge of modernity, Christian apologists "virtually surrendered to it."[18]

WHAT ARE THE ELEMENTS OF THE TRADITIONAL SECULARIZATION THESIS?

Proponents of the traditional secularization thesis have proposed a number of interrelated consequences of the Enlightenment and Protestant Reformation that contributed to increasing secularization and decreasing religiosity. I discuss those next.

Enlightenment Rationalism and Advances in Science and Technology

One effect of the Protestant Reformation was a "rationalization" of Christianity. Specifically, as sociologist Philip Gorski has argued, "the Reformation was largely an attempt to eradicate one kind of religiosity (magical, ritual, and communal) and replace it with another (ethical, intellectual, and individual)."[19] Similarly, the 18th century Enlightenment—with its

217

emphasis on reason, experience, and natural philosophy—was associated with the rise of a rational worldview based on empirical standards of evidence, scientific knowledge, and technological advances.[20] Indeed, so-called knowledge societies proliferated from 1600 to 1800, particularly those focused on science and technology after 1750.[21]

This increasingly rational worldview accelerated skepticism towards the supernatural and miraculous aspects of religion. In addition, the existence of immutable natural laws—distinct from any spirit world—raised the possibility of attaining inspiration from nature itself without reference to a divine Creator.[22] Specific religious doctrines about original sin, predestination, and Hell and damnation also came to be viewed by many people as objectionable and unreasonable, leading to their increasing rejection.[23]

In science, early astronomers, physicists, and geologists such as Galileo, Copernicus, Johannes Kepler, Isaac Newton, and Charles Lyell provided naturalistic explanations of the physical universe. Similarly, naturalist Charles Darwin's account of the evolution of species undermined the religious argument for the existence of God based on the argument from design. For many people, these developments seemed to throw God out of the universe and diminish the special status of humans among other animal species.

In addition, anthropological works such as Edward Burnett Tylor's *Primitive Culture* (1871) and Sir James George Frazer's *The Golden Bough* (1890-1915) documented the diversity of gods and other supernatural entities that primitive humans invariably created to account for natural phenomena they could not otherwise explain. This suggested that the gods of the monotheistic religions might also be human inventions.[24] Also, advances in biology and the medical sciences led to modern accounts of illness and medical treatment, eliminating the need for supernatural explanations such as spirit possession.[25]

Emeritus Professor of Religion Paul Gifford has argued that over the last few centuries the rise of science led to a change in consciousness that privileges this-worldly "useful knowledge" derived from observation, experiment, and measurement. The prioritization of this-worldly knowledge over the supernatural realm pushed religion to the periphery in the West. In Gifford's view, science has not disproved religion. However, it is difficult in the West today to take the supernatural for granted.[26] Similarly, sociologist Steve Bruce has argued that, "[s]cience and technology have not made us atheists, but the underlying rationality makes us less likely than our forebears to entertain the notion of the divine."[27]

Not all scholars have highlighted the role of science and reason in undermining religion. For example, historian of Christianity Alec Ryrie has acknowledged the role of the Protestant Reformation in promoting religious doubt. However, he has emphasized the role of two intermingling emotional streams—involving anger and anxiety—that contributed to the erosion of faith in the 17th century and beyond. Anger was elicited by the perceived use of religion by the clergy to exploit and oppress the people, leading to suspicion and defiance. In addition, many devout people were beset by anxiety, uncertainty, and obsessive self-examination over whether they would be among the saved—a frequent reaction to the Calvinist doctrine of predestination.[28] For some people, the resulting anger and despair led to a doubling-down on their faith. For others, however, it led to abandonment of their faith.

Industrial Capitalism and Economic Growth

In his influential book *The Protestant Ethic and the Spirit of Capitalism*, German sociologist Max Weber (1864-1920) argued that Protestantism and its associated beliefs were uniquely associated with the development of industrial capitalism and economic rationalism. In contrast to more "otherworldly" Catholicism, Calvinist Protestants viewed the worldly pursuit of wealth and business success through intense work, rational planning, and discipline as the expression of virtue and proficiency in a calling—and as signs of God's grace. The Protestant Reformation rejected the medieval idea that some vocations such as the monastic life were "higher" than others. Instead, in the Protestant view, any occupation performed well served to glorify God and sanctify the ordinary secular life of work and family.[29] In those countries most influenced by this "Protestant work ethic," economic success reduced the perceived indispensability of God's power and grace. In addition, the industrial process itself required a process of rational thinking that further promoted secularization. Economic prosperity itself can further reduce religiosity, as the need for religion as a source of comfort for the less advantaged became less imperative.[30]

Functional Differentiation of Societies

A dominant view among sociologists, particularly in the 1950s and 1960s, is that, during modernization, societal functions became more differentiated and dispersed among different institutions. One result was a reduction in the centrality of religious institutions, as secular institutions increasingly performed many of the functions that were once carried out by the church, such as education, healthcare, and social welfare.[31] In addition to reducing the power of the church, this reduced the amount of interaction people had with religious institutions in their daily lives.

Pluralism and Relativism

The Protestant Reformation and the subsequent proliferation of denominations and sects led to increasing pluralism or diversity of religious perspectives. This led to a number of consequences. For example, the proliferation of religious groups with different doctrines can erode the idea of universal truths and reduce the certainty that people have in the authority or credibility of their particular faith tradition. Also, to maintain harmony in diverse egalitarian societies, tolerance of other faiths is required, which introduces a sense of relativism. That is, if there are many paths to salvation or the good life, is there sufficient reason to favor one tradition over another? Greater pluralism also leads to more inter-faith marriage, which can motivate conversion to a partner's faith or greater secularity in the raising of one's children. Greater religious diversity in a population also leads to a greater likelihood of having one or more close friends of a different religion and thus exposure to different religious views.[32]

Where there is religious diversity, rather than one "true" or "universal" church, it becomes more typical for people to fashion their religion based on personal choice or preferences. They do so by drawing on the options available in the religious (or nonreligious) market place. As individual choice takes hold, further religious schisms and fragmentation are invited. Furthermore, as different religious groups compete for adherents, some groups may deemphasize more orthodox or supernatural elements to better cater to a more secular consciousness, leading to further secularization.

The perception that one's own faith tradition, or lack thereof, is not universally shared can also lead people to become more private about their religion. They become increasingly hesitant to disclose or discuss their belief systems outside their own religious or nonreligious community.[33] In the public sphere, the fragmentation of religion into diverse denominations and sects would also tend to accelerate the separation of church and state, as religious neutrality would become a prerequisite for a harmonious society.

Historian Brad S. Gregory, in his book *The Unintended Reformation: How a Religious Revolution Secularized Society*, traces in detail how "hyperpluralism" and doctrinal disagreements contributed to secularization by promoting the following:

- The post-Enlightenment "disenchantment" of the world;
- The understanding of religion as an individual and private matter;
- The perception of morality as subjective;
- The marginalization or "dethroning" of theology, particularly relative to science;
- The rise of secular research universities as the predominant source of knowledge and intellectual innovation;
- The relegation to science and reason alone the means to understand the natural world;

- The rise of liberal nation states that seek to protect freedom of religion (and nonreligion) among other individual rights;
- The "self-colonization" of the West by capitalism and consumerism, which—in the face of hyperpluralism—provide the "cultural glue" that holds together Western societies.

For Gregory, the primary origin of pluralism and doctrinal disagreements was the rejection of the authority of the Catholic Church and the Protestant turn toward scripture as the sole basis for Christian belief and practice. Rather than an interpretive consensus, this reliance on scripture alone (*sola scriptura*) generated a plethora of divergent understandings and conflicts.[34]

Individualism

In a number of ways, the Protestant Reformation led to a decrease in church authority over the individual believer. The Reformation replaced the Catholic doctrine of salvation through good works with Martin Luther's doctrine that faith alone was sufficient. Furthermore, the individual's relationship with God was no longer dependent on, or mediated by, the church. These phenomena left individuals with greater spiritual freedom but also greater responsibility in addressing life's questions and in securing the basis of their faith.[35]

In addition, the Calvinist doctrine of predestination—the idea that one's salvation has been predetermined rather than based on one's good works—must have led to "a feeling of unprecedented inner loneliness" for each believer, contributing further to the development of individualism.[36] Beginning in the early 17th century, the increasing rejection of Calvin's doctrines of predestination, original sin, and human depravity also coincided with a growing emphasis on individual choice and agency.[37]

As close-knit traditional communities became secondary to modern cities, states, and institutions—through industrialization, commerce, and social mobility—the more communal forms of living that sustain religion were weakened. Instead, people became more likely to conceive of themselves as pursuing their own goals and destiny.[38] Charles Taylor referred to this process of individuation—that is, viewing oneself as an individual first rather than as embedded in social roles and society—as the *Great Disembedding*.[39]

The Reformation also promoted literacy and education, as it required believers "to answer to God individually" and to assume greater personal responsibility for reading and interpreting scripture. This was facilitated by advancements in printing and by translations of the Bible into vernacular languages. In turn, the emergence of a more educated populace could support the rise of individual rights, egalitarianism, and liberal democracy—emerging secular values.[40]

German sociologist Ulrich Beck was not a supporter of secularization theory as typically presented. Nonetheless, his *individualization theory* is relevant here. Unlike secularization theory, which predicts a decline in religion with modernization, individualization theory predicts a change in the *form* of religion. From this perspective, it is crucial to distinguish between institutionalized religion, which is declining in the West, and personal faith, which increasingly takes on individualized forms.[41] Rather than automatically adopting the religious faith and organizations they were born into, individuals increasingly create individualized faith narratives that fit their own lives and experiences—"a God of one's own," to use Beck's descriptive phrase.[42]

EXISTENTIAL SECURITY ALSO IMPACTS SECULARIZATION

In contrast to secularization theories that focus on the downstream impact of the Enlightenment and Protestant Reformation, recent theories have emphasized the relationship between existential security and secularization. Political scientists Pippa Norris and Ronald Inglehart argued that it is premature to discount the secularization thesis, but proposed that it needs some updating. For example, they argue that the *human* development that comes from modernization is even more important than *economic* development. According to their *Existential Security Theory*:

> The modernization process reduces the threats to survival that are common in developing societies, especially among the poorest strata; and this enhanced sense of security lessens the need for the reassurance religion provides.[43]

From this perspective, secularization will take place to the extent that a sense of existential security is attained. Indeed, Norris and Inglehart report evidence that nations, and people within nations, that have greater existential security—as reflected in indicators of human development, economic equality, education and literacy, affluence and income, healthcare, and social welfare—tend to be less religious. Indeed, they concluded that:

> Analysis of data from societies around the world revealed that the extent to which people emphasize religion and engage in religious behavior could, indeed, be predicted with considerable accuracy from a society's level of economic development and other indicators of human development.[44]

Additional studies have been generally supportive of Existential Security Theory.[45] For example, in a recent analysis of 49 countries, several societal-level indicators of existential insecurity—especially lower scores on an overall human development index—were moderately to strongly associated with greater religiosity.[46] Similarly, a comparison of U.S. states found that more religious states tend to be more "dysfunctional," as assessed by indicators of crime, teen reproductive behavior, health, and mortality.[47] Also consistent with Existential Security Theory are studies showing that religiosity is reduced to the extent that governments spend more on social welfare.[48]

In his recent book *Religion's Sudden Decline*, Ronald Inglehart offered an *Evolutionary Modernization Theory* that augments Existential Security

Theory by also highlighting the importance of changes in fertility norms.[49] Whereas decreases in religiosity as a result of increased existential security has been going on for many years, the recent acceleration of secularization can be better accounted for in Inglehart's view by the increasing replacement of *pro-fertility norms* by *individual-choice norms*.

Historically, religions have promoted pro-fertility norms. These norms emphasize traditional gender roles and having many children, while stigmatizing behaviors not linked to sexual reproduction, such as divorce, abortion, contraception, and homosexuality. Pro-fertility norms were important for group survival during most of human history when infant mortality was high and life expectancy low. However, people in many societies today increasingly favor individual choice in how to live their lives, are more supportive of gender equality, and more tolerant of divorce, abortion, and homosexuality. As more people reject pro-fertility norms in favor of individual-choice norms, religion is necessarily weakened.[50] Indeed, a tipping point has been reached—particularly among younger and better-educated groups in high-income countries—that is sharply accelerating secularization trends, as more people shift from pro-fertility to individual-choice norms.[51]

Inglehart reports extensive support for this theory, drawing on international survey data covering the period from 1981 to 2020. For example, he reports a very strong relationship between lower country religiosity and greater support for individual-choice over pro-fertility norms. For example, Sweden, Denmark, Norway, and the Netherlands show both very low religiosity and strong support for individual-choice norms. In contrast, Muslim-majority countries and low-income countries in Africa and Latin America report both high levels of religiosity and support for pro-fertility norms.[52]

ARE THERE ADDITIONAL FACTORS THAT CAN INCREASE SECULARIZATION?

Indeed, some additional factors can be mentioned, in some cases in relation to specific countries. A few examples illustrate the point.

Based on extensive interviews, sociologist Phil Zuckerman attributed the decline in religiosity in Denmark and Sweden to several factors, not all of which are directly related to the general secularization factors discussed thus far. Specifically, Zuckerman pointed to:

- The dominance of a "lazy" state-supported Lutheran monopoly that obviates the need for the church to "market" or compete for parishioners;
- The high degree of societal and individual security, leading to erosion of the need for religion as a source of comfort and security;[53]
- The increasing workforce presence since the 1960s of women, who tend to be more central than men in setting the religious tone of the family;[54]
- The relatively high levels of education in these countries, given that more religious people tend to be less educated, on average;
- The reduced need in Scandinavian countries to use religion as a source of cultural defense or national and ethnic identity;
- The political influence of the Social Democratic party, which has on occasion sought to reduce the influence of religion on society.

Others have noted additional factors that have contributed to the decline of religion in the United States and beyond, including the following:

- Reactions against the rise of Islamic terrorism;
- Popular books by the New Atheists and other critics of religion;
- The mockery of religion by television comedians such as Bill Maher, Jon Stewart, and Stephen Colbert;
- Negative reactions to the political agenda of the Religious Right;
- American evangelical's support for politicians with serious ethical and moral short-comings;

- The perceived harm done to LGBTQ individuals and families by some religious communities;
- The patriarchal stance and teachings of some religious communities;
- White supremacist attitudes and racism in some religious communities;
- The Catholic Church's cover up of rampant child abuse;
- Push-back against the Intelligent Design movement in the public schools;
- A general loss of trust in societal institutions;
- Changes in the structure of families;
- The use of the Internet to connect with others who are experiencing religious doubts.[55]

These examples point to the limited ability of secularization theories—although generally applicable—to take into account the unique histories and processes associated with secularization in specific countries.

SO, IS THERE EVIDENCE SUPPORTING THE SECULARIZATION THESIS?

Yes.

Some of the best support comes from recent large-scale surveys. Indeed, based on their results, we can conclude that significant secularization *has* taken place in most, if not all, advanced industrial and post-industrial societies.

Secularization is generally viewed as having proceeded furthest in Europe. Indeed, recent survey data for Western Europe reveals overall declines in traditional religious beliefs, affiliation, and participation, and concomitant increases in the percentages of religiously nonaffiliated individuals.[56] Across many European countries, as well as Canada and Australia, about 20-40 percent of people no longer believe in God or any sort of spirit or life force.[57] Recent levels of weekly church attendance are highest in Poland (48.3%), Ireland (37.4%), Portugal (26.9%) and Italy (24.5%), but range from about 3 to 16% in the remaining European countries.[58] Although declines in religiosity have been particularly evident since the 1960s, the data also reveal generally linear declines across the 20th century, with younger generations increasingly less religious than older generations.[59]

We can also point to specific indicators of institutional decline, such as difficulties in recruiting clergy; significant declines in the numbers of monks, nuns, and seminarians; and the closure of religious facilities. For example, between 1970 and 2005 the Church of England alone closed about 1,700 religious structures.[60] Not surprisingly, then, we also observe a dramatic drop in knowledge of basic Christian teachings throughout Europe.[61] Within these broad generational shifts, there are, of course, some differences between countries in secularizing trends.[62]

Sociologist of religion David Voas proposed a *secular transition model*, which captures well how secularization took place in most European countries. Voas observed that most people in European countries are neither religious nor wholly secular. Rather, they exhibit what he calls a "fuzzy fidelity" to Christianity. They do not attend church regularly, but may participate in church weddings, funerals, and Christmas services. They may express belief in "something out there," but religion does not play an important role in their lives. Importantly, Voas has demonstrated a similar trajectory of religious decline in many European countries.

That is, with modernization, people increasingly transition from religiosity to a fuzzy fidelity to religion, setting the stage for subsequent generations to abandon religion entirely. The secularization process is thus a gradual one with fuzzy fidelity representing a transitional phase or "staging post" between religion and secularity. In Voas' data, European countries differed primarily in how early they began this process.[63] Subsequent research in the United States and Germany has provided some additional support for Voas' secular transition model, while also suggesting that culture-specific external shocks may impact the secularization trajectory.[64]

228

Is there evidence of secularization more broadly around the world? Indeed, global survey data shows that secularization trends now extend well beyond Western Europe, although they are not universal.[65] For example, in one analysis, 52 of 86 countries examined showed declines in religiosity, including 26 of 28 high-income countries.[66] Another analysis used data from the World Values Survey and European Values Study to track changes in religiosity from 1981 to 2020 in 103 countries. Countries in Latin America, Central Europe and the Baltics, and (recently) the Middle East and North Africa all became less religious during this period, although the rates of decline were smaller than in Western countries. Countries in the Middle East and North Africa remain highly religious, however, and their recent modest declines may reflect negative reactions to the Islamist political and military successes following the Arab Spring of the early 2010s.

In contrast, religiosity increased in countries in Eastern Europe and the former Yugoslavia until about 2010 before stabilizing. Religiosity increased in the Caucasus and Central Asia, with the exception of Azerbaijan. Religiosity was mostly high and stable in sub-Saharan African countries and was relatively stable in South Asia. In Southeast Asia, religiosity declined in Thailand, Singapore, and Malaysia; was stable in Indonesia and the Philippines; and increased moderately in Vietnam, where state restrictions on religion have been eased recently. In East Asia, religiosity decreased in South Korea and increased in China (again likely due to an easing of restrictions). Trends in Japan, Taiwan, and Hong Kong were difficult to interpret because different measures of religiosity showed variable results.[67] Nonetheless, other research indicates that Japan and Hong Kong are among many countries outside Western Europe that have shown meaningful declines in the percentages of people who belief in God.[68]

Overall, some of these results might argue against a strong or unqualified version of the secularization thesis linking modernization to reduced religiosity. Alternatively, they may suggest that country-specific countervailing factors can offset general secularization trends, at least in the short-run. Or, some societies may not have yet reached a tipping point signaling the beginning of a gradual, generational process of religious decline, as described in Voas's secular transition model.[69] The extent to which this secular transition model will apply more generally around the world is yet to be determined. However, it *is* clear that secularization has already taken place in most, if not all, advanced industrial and post-industrial societies. Indeed, although about 50-60% of people worldwide still identify themselves as "religious," 20-35% describe themselves as "nonreligious" and another 10-15% as "atheist."[70] In numeric terms, estimates of the total number of atheists, agnostics, or nonbelievers globally vary, but are typically in the 450-750 million range. This would make nonbelievers in God the fourth largest belief system in the world behind Christianity (2 billion), Islam (1.2 billion), and Hinduism (900 million).[71]

Is the United States an Exceptional Case?

Until recently, opponents of the secularization thesis pointed to the relatively high level of religiosity in the United States—a modern, economically prosperous country—as evidence against the thesis. Scholars offered a variety of explanations for this so-called "American exception." Various scholars attributed it to the greater number of religious options available to Americans,[72] the greater income inequality and personal insecurity of people in the United States,[73] and immigration patterns that bring religious immigrants to the country,[74] among other explanations.[75] In short, the United States was, until quite recently, somewhat of an outlier in its greater religiosity relative to other advanced industrial and post-industrial countries. Indeed, it is still somewhat of an outlier in relation to its per capita Gross Domestic Product.[76]

Importantly, however, the United States now appears to be following the pattern seen decades earlier in Western Europe.[77] For example, generational declines in church attendance are evident in the United States, with Gen-Xers and Millennials attending religious services less frequently, on average, than older generations.[78] Overall, 56% of Americans now report that they never or rarely attend religious services, double the percentage in the 1990s.[79] The percentage of Americans reporting no religious affiliation or "none" when asked about their religion, has increased from less than 10% in 1990 to almost 30% today.[80] These so-called "religious nones" are now the fastest growing "religious" orientation in the United States. They now comprise between 38 to 45 million American adults—one-third to one-half of which are atheists or agnostics. Importantly, nearly 90 percent of these religious nones express no interest in seeking out a religion that might be right for them. Not surprisingly, then, an estimated 6,000 to 10,000 churches in the United States are closing down each year with a much smaller number of new churches opening.[81] However, some religious groups have declined more than others in recent decades.[82]

Some of the most remarkable evidence for the recent decline of religiosity in the United States comes from comparisons of survey data from 1982 to 2017 by Ronald Inglehart. These data show significant changes over this time period in the percentage of American adults saying that God is very important in their lives (from 52% to 23%); that they are a religious person (from 85% to 55%); that they have a great deal of confidence in their country's religious institutions (from 26% to 12%); that they never or practically never attend religious services (from 16% to 35%); and that they do not believe in God (from 2% to 22%). From 1990 to 2017, the percentage of Americans saying that religion is very important in their lives fell from 53% to 38%, while the percentage saying that religion is not at all important in their lives rose from 5% to 17%. In comparisons involving 108 countries, the United States now ranks as the 12th least religious country in terms of the rated importance of God in their lives and the 45th least religious in terms of the rated importance of religion is their lives. For Inglehart, this represents "a massive collapse of religious belief."[83]

Indeed, the Pew Research Center recently predicted that by 2070, the percentages of Americans of all ages who are Christian will decrease from 64% in 2020 to about one-third to one-half of Americans by 2070.[84] Similarly, Robert Jones, CEO of the Public Religion Research Institute, has recently observed that:

The American religious landscape is being remade, most notably by the decline of the White Protestant majority and the rise of the religiously unaffiliated. These religious transformations have been swift and dramatic, occurring largely within the last four decades.[85]

Jones argues that by 2051, assuming that current trends continue, "religiously unaffiliated Americans could comprise as large a percentage of the population as Protestants."[86]

In short, the evidence reveals considerable support for the secularization thesis—at least when applied to most advanced industrial or post-industrial countries. In addition, the United States is no longer an exception to this secularization trend. Before drawing final conclusions, however, we should take a look at the arguments and evidence being put forth *against* the secularization thesis.

WHAT ARE THE ARGUMENTS AND EVIDENCE AGAINST THE SECULARIZATION THESIS?

Critics of the secularization thesis have pointed to several types of contrary evidence, including (a) examples of religious stability and growth around the world; (b) religious reactions against modernization and secularization; (c) the waxing and waning of religion over time; (d) religious conversions; (e) the changing forms of religion; and (f) the fertility gap between religious and secular societies and individuals.

I consider each phenomenon in turn. To foreshadow my overall conclusion, the fertility gap offers the biggest potential obstacle to the secularization process worldwide.

Examples of Religious Stability and Growth

As noted earlier, religion continues to thrive and even grow in some parts of the world. Indeed, in survey data from about 2017, the percentage of adults stating that religion is very important in their lives was 99% in Muslim-majority countries, 75% in sub-Saharan Africa, and 54% in South Asia and Latin America, but much lower in Catholic Europe (21%), Protestant Europe (11%), Baltic countries (10%), and Confucian-influenced countries (8%).[87]

Current and former communist countries represent a special case. Not surprisingly, increases in religious involvement were seen in many ex-communist countries after the fall of the Soviet Union, where religion had been actively suppressed. Still, the perceived importance of religion has since declined in four of the most secure ex-communist countries—Poland, Slovenia, the Czech Republic, and former East Germany—which are now part of the European Union.[88] As noted previously, religiosity has also increased recently in communist Vietnam and China, probably due to the easing of some restrictions on religion.

Critics of the secularization thesis also point to the remarkable growth of Pentecostalism in recent years, particularly in Africa and Latin America.[89] The Pentecostal movement, which emerged in the United States in the early 20th century, endorses a literal interpretation of the Bible, direct experience of the Holy Spirit, more ecstatic forms of worship such as speaking in tongues, and spiritual healing. Pentecostal ideas and experiences have also influenced the emergence of charismatic movements within some mainline Protestant and Catholic churches. Estimates of the number of Pentecostals, including charismatics, around the world now exceed 500 million.[90] Indeed, British historian of religion Alec Ryrie describes Pentecostalism as "the most dramatic religious success story of modern times," and as "global Protestantism's main engine."[91]

Even in Europe and the United States, there are some countervailing trends offsetting the overall picture of religious decline. In both places, religiosity is being augmented by the arrival of religious immigrants. For example, in 2010 over 160 mosques were being constructed or planned in Germany alone.[92] In the United States, there has been significant recent growth in Hispanic Protestant churches, with the majority of participants being immigrants to the country.[93]

Also in the United States, the number of megachurches (i.e., churches with more than 2000 members) has grown exponentially, from about 350 in 1990 to about 1750 in 2020. Membership in about three-fourths of these megachurches continues to grow, although a 20-year trend of decreasing weekly attendance has also been observed.[94] The growth of megachurches—coupled with the overall decline in religious affiliation in the United States—suggests that significant consolidation into larger religious congregations is taking place.[95]

Religious Reactions Against Modernization and Secularization

In some cases, reactions against modernization and secularization can strengthen religion. For example, in parts of the developing world with colonial histories, secular ideas have been viewed as foreign and lacking in legitimacy. In addition, when secular governments are imposed in religious countries—for example, with the Shah in Iran or military leaders in Egypt—religious backlash against secular ideologies has occurred.

Cultural transitions or the need to defend one's cultural identity can also increase religiosity or retard secularization. For example, religion provides an important source of social identity and support for Muslim immigrants in Europe. The rise of religious fundamentalism has also been viewed as a reaction against modern secular perspectives, although it is not clear that fundamentalism is currently growing around the world.[96] It is also unclear that religious reactions against secularization will be strong and persistent enough to offset long-term secularization trends.

Waxing and Waning of Religion

Rather than a linear or straight-line process of secularization, we can point to historical and recent examples of how religion can wax and wane over time.[97] For example, after the shock of World War I, Swiss theologian Karl Barth's neo-orthodox theology pushed back against the 19th century liberal humanistic theology of Friedrich Schleiermacher. However, neo-orthodoxy itself subsequently experienced a rapid decline after World War II when economic success made secularizing trends more difficult to denigrate. Sociologist Peter Berger described the dominance, then retreat, of neo-orthodoxy as an accidental interruption in the longer-term secularization process.[98]

In the United States, the "enthusiastic" religious revivals of the First and Second Great Awakenings—from about 1730-1750 and 1800-1840, respectively—involved dramatic but relatively short-lived outpourings of religious fervor and activity. Conversely, economic collapse and internal rifts within mainline Protestantism led to a "religious depression" from 1925-1935.[99]

More recent examples include the short-lived post-WWII Christian revival in the West; religious increases in ex-communist countries after the fall of the Soviet Union; the "evangelical counterattack" in 1970s America against the social upheavals of the 1960s; the boost to secularism in the 1980s and 1990s in response to the political overreach of the Christian Right; and the recent decline of evangelicalism at the expense of an increasingly coalescing "post-evangelicalism."[100] Finally, initial survey results from 14 countries during the COVID-19 pandemic revealed that 28% of American adults, and 10-15% of adults in several other countries, said that their religious faith had been strengthened during the pandemic.[101] However, it is not clear how long this effect will persist.

The point I am making is this: Although a general trend of secularization appears to have taken place in most modern and economically secure countries, the process may show "bumps," continuing to wax and wane over time, and play out differently in various countries depending on specific historical and cultural circumstances.

Religious Conversions

If we look at individual people rather than societies, we also see that secularization is not a one-way street. Indeed, there is a long history of religious

235

conversions. In the past, many religious conversions were "voluntary" only in the sense that they were done largely for social and economic advancement or personal survival.[102] Other cases involved "switching" from one religion to another, rather than from nonbelief to belief.[103] However, numerous individuals in the past did experience sincere "born again" spiritual awakenings—for example, during the 18th and 19th century religious revivals in the United States. Even many prominent former atheists have described their conversion to traditional religion.[104]

Today, about half of Americans report having undergone one or more spiritual or religious change experiences in their lives. Of those, about 65 percent report having had a "born again" experience.[105] The early or classical view of such conversions among psychologists was that they involve sudden and dramatic transformations in response to personal problems or emotional distress. However, current research on spiritual transformations indicates that such conversions can also involve gradual but active spiritual seeking.[106]

Religious conversions, particularly if involving former nonbelievers, represent another trend operating against secularization. However, the number of such conversions has not been nearly sufficient to offset the secularization trends observed in most modern and existentially secure countries.

Changing Forms of Religion

Other critics of the secularization thesis have argued that religion is not so much declining, but rather changing its form. A prominent advocate of this position is Ulrich Beck, whose Individualization Theory was introduced earlier in this chapter. In this view, people are increasingly conceptualizing their own personal God, drawing on those aspects of religion they find persuasive.[107] Other scholars argue that Westerners are more "unchurched" than irreligious, as many retain belief in some form of God or transcendent force in nature.[108] The expression "spiritual-but-not-religious" has become a catch phrase for many who seek alternative, nonreligious means to attain personal fulfillment, a sense of meaning, or transcendent experience.[109] Alister McGrath points to the renewed interest in spirituality as one indication, in his view, of the "twilight" or demise of atheism.[110]

However, such spiritual activities can vary significantly in the extent to which they incorporate metaphysical or transcendent elements. Indeed, we can question whether interest in alternative spiritualities such as yoga, meditation, and mindfulness can be treated as evidence of religious revival. Many such activities are focused on earthly motives for health and well-being without reference to the supernatural.[111]

For some people, a religious perspective can be retained by redefining their conception of God. For example, liberal theologian Paul Tillich replaced the concept of a personal, anthropomorphic God by a transcendent focus on one's *ultimate concerns*.[112] For example, the pursuit of social justice or environmental protection could serve as ultimate concerns with self-transcendent qualities.[113] Others have suggested that secular humanism is a different form of religion, although people who define religion as necessarily involving supernatural beliefs reject this contention.

On the one hand, these examples illustrate the ways in which religion, or at least some forms of spirituality, may persist in new forms. On the other hand, a case can be made that such changes actually argue *for*, rather than *against*, secularization theory, because they reveal a decline in organized religion and its authority over individuals and society.[114]

The Fertility Gap

The so-called *fertility gap* between more religious and secular people is especially important in determining the long-term fate of religion versus secular humanism—at least in the world overall. For example, a rigorous analysis of global fertility rates from 2010-2015 estimated an average fertility rate of 2.59 children per woman for religiously affiliated individuals and 1.65 for religiously unaffiliated individuals.[115] Some of the highest fertility rates, many close to or exceeding 4.0, are found in Africa, which remains a "bastion" of religious faith.

In contrast, in the more secular countries of Europe, the average number of children expected per woman over a lifetime is close to, and in most cases lower than, the replacement level of about 2.0—that is, the number required to maintain population size.[116] The causal dynamics behind this strong religion-fertility correlation are complex. However, it can be explained, in part, by traditional religion's pro-fertility norms, which emphasize family, children, and traditional roles for women, as well as religious proscriptions against divorce, homosexuality, contraception, and abortion.[117]

In his 2010 book *Shall the Religious Inherit the Earth?* demographer Eric Kaufmann raised the possibility—given this fertility gap—that religion may overwhelm secularity in the future. He pointed out that everywhere in the world, fertility rates are greater, on average, among religious fundamentalists than among religious moderates, who in turn have higher fertility rates than secular people. Religious fundamentalists also have higher retention rates in their religious communities than religious moderates or liberals.[118]

Since 2010, the fertility rates of some religious countries in Asia and Latin America have dropped dramatically.[119] Nonetheless, by most projections, at least over the next several decades, the proportion of religious people in the world will continue to increase relative to the proportion of nonreligious people as a result of this fertility gap. The gap will more than offset the fact that more people are switching away from religion than turning towards it.[120] Thus, while the proportion of atheists, agnostics, and other religiously unaffiliated people will continue to increase in secular countries, they will make up a decreasing proportion of the world's population.[121]

Of course, a number of factors could change such projections—for example, changes in fertility or retention rates among seculars and the religious. Nonetheless, these projections point to the dramatic impact that demographic factors alone could have on the extent of future secularization around the world.

SO, IS FUTURE SECULARIZATION INEVITABLE OR NOT?

At this point, I belief I have made a persuasive case that secularization has taken place in much of the world, particularly among more modern and existentially secure countries. The remaining question is whether this secularization process is inevitable and what it means for the viability of religion in the long-term. Before giving my own take on this question, I will briefly illustrate the varied opinions offered historically and today by psychologists and social scientists.

Historically, some scholars—for example, Sigmund Freud, Karl Marx, and Auguste Comte—expected religion to eventually disappear. Others, such as Émile Durkheim and Max Weber, anticipated that religion would decline but still be needed, at least in some form for some people. Modern scholars are understandably reticent to make definitive predictions about the fate of religion. However, even some proponents of the secularization thesis acknowledge that religion might persist, at least in some parts of the world.

For example, sociologist Phil Zuckerman surmised that the loss of religion in particular societies could happen but is not inevitable.[122] Sociologist Steve Bruce agrees, but finds it difficult to envision a reversal of the secularization trend, given the increasing autonomy of individuals.[123] Historian of religion Alex Ryrie declared that "Western Christendom is not about to snap back into place" and that "[t]he contemporary humanist surge is not a blip or anomaly, but a continuation of moral forces that have been at work within the Christian world for centuries."[124] American researcher and author Gregory S. Paul points to the "ease and speed" by which millions of Westerners have left religion behind and infers that when environmental conditions improve sufficiently, religion will be "readily abandoned."[125]

In contrast, sociologist Peter Berger confidently predicted in 1999 that the world would be no less religious in the 21st century, pointing to our natural religious impulses and the ever-present possibility that new charismatic religious figures will emerge.[126] Similarly, theologian Alister McGrath points to the "twilight of atheism" and reminds us that many people like their faith and believe it to be true.[127] Professor of Religious Studies Robert Fuller concedes that secularism might undermine religion, but believes the secularization thesis underestimates the cultural and biological factors that predispose all humans to religion.[128]

Philosopher Charles Taylor offered an even stronger prediction that religion will continue to thrive, because the sense of the transcendent "will not easily be uprooted from the human heart."[129] In Taylor's view, the dominant secularization narrative will become *less* convincing over time as other societies fail to follow the lead of secular societies and future generations search for something beyond the perceived "waste land" of secular life.[130]

Like Taylor, others who anticipate the persistence or growth of religion frequently point to the "impoverished" nature of a secular life without some transcendent God or spiritual force, or the "imaginative failure" of atheism or exclusive humanism.[131] For example, historian of religion Brad Gregory contends that modern philosophy has failed to provide a persuasive replacement for religion and expresses openness to the idea that religious claims are true.[132] *I will counter the claim that the secular life is an impoverished one in the next chapter.*

While hardly a comprehensive tally of perceptions regarding the future of religion, these examples are representative of the continuum of views. A plausible middle-ground position is offered by Pippa Norris and Ronald Inglehart. They foresee an ongoing secularization trend in those countries that experience the greatest societal or personal security, with a simultaneous increase in overall religiosity around the world due to differential fertility patterns.[133]

Scholars have also pointed to differences in the *type* of religion that is most likely to persist or thrive. A common view is that the religious communities most likely to thrive are those that (a) are more conservative, orthodox, or traditional; (b) cater more directly to the emotions (e.g., Pentecostals); and (c) show greater resistance to secularizing trends. Conversely, greater decline is expected for those religious communities that are most influenced by Enlightenment rationality and liberalism, and that adapt or "water down" their beliefs or practices to better conform to perceived modernity.[134]

Given these trends, scholars have predicted a growing gap between existentially secure (and predominantly secular) societies and existentially insecure (and predominantly religious) societies—as well as between secular and religious people within societies—as religion increasingly takes on more conservative or orthodox forms.[135] However, as I will note in the Conclusion to this book, the liberal Unitarian-Universalist Association may represent an exception to the anticipated decline of more moderate or liberal forms of religion.

TAKEAWAYS

So, is the world becoming less religious and more secular? This question is central in assessing the viability and ultimate future of religion and secular humanism as alternative life stances.

In this chapter I discussed the factors that have tended to undermine traditional religion in the past few centuries, at least in most modern industrial societies. Disagreement remains about the eventual fate or persistence of individual piety and institutionalized religion more broadly around the world. Nonetheless, it seems clear that—unlike several centuries ago—*we now live in a world in which many people, including a majority in some countries, see a life devoid of religious belief and practice as a viable if not preferable option.* The irony is that developments in theology and religion itself—including the Protestant Reformation—promoted the secularization process.

241

Scholars differ in the extent to which they see religion as declining, persisting, or growing. Nonetheless, they all describe the secularization process in terms of the social, intellectual, economic, and political changes that have impacted societies, starting especially in Western Europe. Thus, they attribute the growing prevalence of a secular, even atheistic, perspective in recent centuries to a natural—although not necessarily inevitable—process of cultural change.

This cultural evolutionary perspective can be contrasted with the contention of many cognitive scientists of religion (CSR) that religion comes naturally to us, but atheism does not. Recall that CSR proponents argue that all humans have certain innate or maturationally natural cognitive mechanisms that prepare them to believe in supernatural beings, a soul, and an afterlife. At least at first glance, this religion-is-natural view would seem to imply the inevitable persistence of religion because of the innate cognitive architecture of the human brain. CSR proponents have also suggested the implied corollary—that atheism or disbelief is *unnatural*, in the sense that deliberate and reflective thinking is required to overcome our intuitive capacity for religion.[136]

However, the long history of religious skepticism described in the previous chapter suggests that disbelief or atheism has existed as long as religion and thus may not be unnatural. The same conclusion can be drawn from the increasing secularization of many modern societies, and the increasing prevalence of nonbelievers. Although speculative at this point, several scholars have proposed ways in which religion and atheism could *both* have evolved through natural selection simultaneously. Thus, religion and atheism might represent equally natural, adaptive, and persistent worldviews, even if their relative prevalence might differ across time and environmental contexts.[137]

In any case, the material in this chapter is most relevant to the question of whether the world is secularizing and will continue to do so, and thus the ultimate viability and future of religion. As noted previously, I believe there is good support for the secularization thesis, at least as applied to much of the modern industrial world. At the same time, many of the downstream effects of the Protestant Reformation and Enlightenment may have already had their major impacts on reducing religiosity in selected societies. This would include the "disenchantment" of the world; the rise of rationality, science, and technology; individualism; religious pluralism; and the functional differentiation of societies. Going forward, the most salient factors in increasing secularization may be increasing existential security and continuing shifts towards individual-choice norms over the pro-fertility norms associated with traditional religion.

At least in the *near term*, these secularizing trends seem likely to continue. Younger generations in most countries exhibit less religious involvement. This should accelerate secularization in these societies—at least in the near future and barring significant unanticipated changes in social and economic security. At the same time, the fertility gap is likely to increase the overall proportion of religious people around the world, at least for the next several decades. Judging from past history, religiosity is also likely to continue to exhibit short-term ups and downs in the overall secularization trend based on social, economic, and political events, some of which will be specific to particular countries. "Fuzzy fidelity" to the major religious traditions is likely to remain a way station in the transition from religion to secularity. Individualizing trends are also likely to continue.

Long-term predictions are much more precarious. On the one hand, where governments are able and willing to provide social services that improve human development and existential security, religion will likely decline in importance. For example, it is a reasonable hypothesis that if the social safety net is strengthened in the United States and in other countries with less existential security, levels of religiosity will decrease over time. On the other hand, significant crises could substantially decrease societal and personal security and thus the longer-term drawing power of religion. Such crises might include, for example, the deleterious effects of climate change, deadly pandemics, major economic disruptions, significant wars, and ongoing immigration or refugee crises. Longer-term changes in fertility patterns that significantly impact population sizes in secular and religious countries are also possible and appear to have already begun.

In sum, continuing secularization seems likely, at least in the near term and in more existentially secure societies. At the same time, given current fertility patterns, the prevalence of existential insecurity around the world, and the functions religion fulfills, religion is likely to persist in much of the world well into the future, and probably forever. I will take up the question of whether religion *should* persist in the Conclusion chapter after further consideration of the merits and viability of secular living as an alternative life stance, which I address in the next chapter.

Chapter 9
Secular Living

In further evaluating the relative merits and viability of the religious and secular humanist life stances, we need to address two questions. How do fully secular or nonreligious individuals differ from their religious counterparts? And how do fully secular people address questions of morality and ethics; meaning and purpose; coping with life's difficulties, including death; and belonging and community. On the one hand, if the secular life is impoverished or incomplete in some way, its relative merits and long-term viability would be called into question. On the other hand, if a fully secular life of morality, meaning, well-being, and belonging is possible, then the need for religion would be less clear.

The glaring truth is that millions of people live their lives without religion—and they do so quite well. They aren't living aimlessly, adrift in a vacuum of nihilistic nothingness.

– Phil Zuckerman[1]

If humans are on their own in a universe that is either mismanaged or not managed at all, isn't it better, at least for some of us, to have the integrity to admit that fact and begin attempting to manage our own lives and societies as best we can?

– Greg Epstein[2]

We saw in the previous chapter that significant secularization has taken place in the past few centuries, at least in some parts of the world. Many people now see themselves as living without religion. Most secular humanists—rather than lamenting the perceived absence of God—view their secular stance as fully capable of leading to moral and ethical, and rich and meaningful, lives. Indeed, as English philosopher A. C. Grayling has observed in describing (secular) humanism:

[T]here is a beautiful and life-enhancing alternative outlook that offers insight, consolation, inspiration and meaning, which has nothing to do with religion, and everything to do with the best, most generous, most sympathetic understanding of human reality.[3]

Other scholars, however, generally writing from a religious perspective, have argued that the secular life is necessarily an impoverished one, lacking the transcendent "fullness" made possible by religion. In this chapter, I take a closer look at what psychologists and social scientists have learned about the characteristics of secular or nonreligious individuals and the nature of secular living. After reading this chapter, I am hopeful that readers can make their own judgments regarding the potential richness and meaningfulness of a fully secular life.

I should acknowledge some limitations of the research on secular living. For example, most of the relevant research has been conducted in the United States and Western Europe. Thus, it may be risky to generalize the findings reported here to less Westernized (and generally more religious) societies, unless otherwise noted. In addition, in many studies, people with diverse secular perspectives have been lumped together into a mixed group of nonreligious or religiously unaffiliated individuals—so-called "religious nones." We know from surveys in the United States, that self-identified atheists and agnostics differ in some ways from people identifying their religion as "nothing in particular." For example, atheists and agnostics, as compared to other "religious nones," tend to be more civically engaged, more educated, and less likely to believe in any kind of God or spiritual force in the universe.[4] In many studies, however, it is not possible to differentiate participants who identify as atheist, agnostic, secular humanist, spiritual-but-not-religious, indifferent, or some other form of nonreligious identity.

Nonetheless, studies in the relatively new academic field of *secular studies* reasonably presume that these diverse secular individuals or groups—despite some variability among them—differ in some shared and meaningful ways from those with a more religious orientation. Later in this chapter, I will say more about different "types" of personal secularity and some of the differences among them.

DEMOGRAPHICS: WHO ARE THE NONBELIEVERS?

We find nonbelievers among people of all genders, ethnicities, education levels, and occupations. However, at least in the United States they are more likely to be male, from younger generations, European American, and relatively highly educated, with a substantial minority holding graduate or professional degrees.[5] They are overrepresented in White-collar occupations and among scholars and scientists, particularly in the social and biological sciences and among those who are more research-oriented. They are more likely to be living in urban areas and outside the southern states.

In regards to race or ethnicity, it may be particularly difficult for African Americans to reject religious belief or participation because of the Black Church's central role in the civil rights movement, in resistance to White supremacy, and as a historical source of Black identity in the face of slavery, oppression, and discrimination.[6] For Latinos, adopting an atheistic stance is made more difficult by the deep intertwining of culture, family, and religion.[7]

A plausible explanation for these demographic trends, at least in some countries, is that people who occupy more privileged positions in society are more likely to feel they have personal control over their lives without relying on religion for security and consolation.

Atheism may be less common among women than men for a few additional reasons. Religion has traditionally been a domain of life in which women play a greater role in the family. Women may place greater value on the social and communal benefits of religion, perhaps due to socialization or personality differences. Men average modestly higher in analytic thinking, which has been linked to atheism. Conversely, women, on average, show greater intuitive thinking and mind perception, which have been linked to greater religiosity.[8] It is also noteworthy that women express greater religious commitment than men only towards the powerful and morally concerned gods of the major world religions, and not towards the more local ancestral or spirit gods of some cultural groups.[9]

The greater prevalence of atheism among younger people probably reflects generational differences in secularization and young people's desire for independence from established authorities. Indeed, as noted in the previous chapter, increasing secularization owes much to the replacement of more religious older generations with more secular younger generations.[10]

The greater prevalence of atheism among more highly educated individuals, and academics and scientists in particular, is probably not surprising. Increasing levels of education tend to be associated with lower levels of religiosity, at least in Western countries.[11] In addition, science is an important aspect of the worldview of many secular humanists and atheists, and the inquisitive nature of science and its demands for evidence can be seen as undermining religion.[12]

It is important to note, however, that a lack of religious affiliation is not necessarily limited to privileged elites. Indeed, in a number of countries, a *majority* of people are unaffiliated with any religion, including Australia, China, the Czech Republic, Estonia, France, Great Britain, Hong Kong, Hungary, Japan, Macau, the Netherlands, South Korea, Uruguay, and Vietnam.[13]

INTELLECT AND COGNITION

Of course, the full range of intelligence levels is evident among *both* religious and nonreligious people. Nonetheless, researchers have found a modest association between higher intelligence and reduced religiosity.[14] Nonreligious individuals also tend to have intellectual interests and values. In comparison to Western Christians, they place greater importance on rationality and have greater trust and literacy in science.[15] There is some evidence of racial differences in the relationship between religiosity and cognitive ability. However, on average, fundamentalist religious beliefs are associated with reduced verbal ability in all racial groups, at least in the United States.[16]

Scholars have offered several plausible explanations for these modest relationships. On average, more intelligent people may be more self-sufficient in obtaining resources and thus in satisfying the needs for security and personal control frequently met by religion. They may be more independent and thus less likely to conform to societal conventions such as religion. Finally, more intelligent people tend to engage in more analytic, cognitively complex, and divergent or creative thinking, all of which tend to undermine religious beliefs.[17]

Indeed, in recent years, a number of studies have focused on the relationship between religiosity and *analytic cognitive style*—that is, a style of cognition or thinking that is more deliberate, reflective, and systematic. A meta-analysis of 31 studies found a modest tendency for people with a more analytic cognitive style to report weaker religious beliefs. In studies with university students in England, researchers found that self-identified atheists scored 18.7% higher than religiously affiliated individuals on a measure of analytic thinking.[18] There is some evidence that the relationship between religiosity and lower analytic thinking is stronger than the relationship between religiosity and lower intelligence.[19] In addition, the relationship between intelligence and lower religiosity may be partially accounted for by the greater analytic thinking tendencies of more intelligent individuals.[20]

Greater religiosity has been associated with additional aspects of cognitive style. On average, religious people have stronger preferences for definitive answers (i.e., needs for closure), experience less enjoyment and engagement in effortful thinking (i.e., lower needs for cognition), and exhibit less open-minded and flexible thinking.[21] However, there is some evidence that Eastern forms of religion such as Buddhism are not associated with greater needs for closure or authoritarianism.[22]

It is less definitive whether the modest relationship between analytic thinking and reduced religiosity will hold up in a variety of cultures.[23] However, some studies have replicated the relationship in Turkey and India.[24] There is also some evidence that analytic cognitive style is related differently to various religious orientations. That is, people with greater intrinsic and extrinsic religious orientations tend to show less analytic thinking than nonreligious people, on average. However, people with a quest orientation tend to show greater analytic thinking, on average.[25]

In any case, the strength of the relationship between greater analytic thinking and reduced religiosity is relatively modest. This indicates that many people who adopt an atheistic perspective do so for reasons other than a tendency towards analytic thinking.

PERSONALITY

Are there any personality differences between religious and secular people? Indeed, research presents a fairly consistent picture.[26] Fully secular or non-religious people tend, on average, to be relatively individualistic, nonconforming, and antiauthoritarian. They value autonomy and independence, both as adults and in their children.[27] They believe they are capable of personal control over their lives. Because of their individualism, they may also be lower in sociality, with fewer social obligations and less social support.

Of the "Big Five" personality traits, Openness to Experience best distinguishes nonbelievers from believers. Nonbelievers, on average, are more open to new ideas and values, and more intellectually curious and engaged. At least in relatively religious countries, it probably requires a degree of nonconformity to be nonreligious.

Again, however, I offer a reminder: The impact of personality on one's orientation towards religiosity or secularity is modest, with socialization being much more important.

MORALITY AND ETHICS

Can we be moral and ethical without religion?

Many people around the world still believe that one must be religious to be moral. For example, in the United States, majorities of White Evangelicals and Black Protestants retain that belief, but only 11% of religiously unaffiliated individuals do so. However, recent survey data indicates that in most countries, majorities now say that belief in God is *not* necessary to be moral.[28] Indeed, the contention that morality depends on religion is refuted by the existence of many moral humanists, atheists, and agnostics, and the fact that many of the most peaceful, healthy, and functional societies in the world are among the most secular.[29]

For secular humanists, one bedrock of morality and ethics is—at least implicitly—the Golden Rule. Humanist Greg Epstein observes that while virtually all religions endorse some version of the Golden Rule, none of these versions requires a God. Indeed, for Epstein, being "good without God" is the very essence of a humanist worldview.[30] For the secular humanist, moral and ethical judgments rely on the empathy that most people develop by living among others; consideration of human interests, needs, and relationships; and reason and compassion in applying these considerations in particular situations.[31] This requires us to take personal responsibility for our moral decision-making, rather than being motivated by thoughts or fears of divine reward or punishment.

Indeed, some secular humanists contend that relinquishing this responsibility to God or religion can be viewed as a kind of "moral outsourcing" that is less admirable than making the difficult and thoughtful choices on our own. As humanist A. C. Grayling observes:

> If I see two men do good, one because he takes himself to be commanded to it by a supernatural agency and the other solely because he cares about his fellow man, I honour the latter infinitely more.[32]

Thus, from a philosophical perspective, secular humanists tend to be *consequentialists*. That is, their moral reasoning is grounded in the social and human consequences or utility of behavior.[33] However, as noted in Chapter 2, this moral reasoning, which tends to be deliberate and reflective, serves to supplement more automatic moral intuitions.

Some humanists argue that our personal responsibility for moral and ethical behavior should extend beyond our family, friends, and country to include human rights, social justice, and the environment more broadly.[34] Indeed, we saw in Chapter 7 that many humanists throughout history have been immersed in such efforts. At the same time, a case can be made for a "morality writ small" that is more modest and realistic in its ambitions. Indeed, in his interviews with American atheists, sociologist Jerome Baggett observed that the moral or ethical convictions of many of them could be described in this more modest way—emphasizing obligations to others that are actually achievable by ordinary people.[35] This idea of morality writ small among atheists recalls the "minimal prosociality" discussed in relation to religious people in Chapter 5.

At the societal level, secular humanists view morality and ethics as a matter for discussion, with the hope of some degree of consensus, rather than being based on divinely imposed or permanent moral truths.[36] For example, whereas slavery was once defended as consistent with the Christian Bible, by consensus it is now considered immoral in most societies. Indeed, there is evidence of some cross-cultural universality in the behaviors viewed as moral.

For example, researchers in one study identified seven moral or cooperative behaviors that were viewed positively in the ethnographic records of 60 diverse societies, and thus comprised possible universal moral rules.[37] These seven behaviors included helping kin, helping your group, reciprocating, being brave, deferring to superiors, dividing disputed resources, and respecting prior possession. Other near-consensus moral rules can likely be identified, for example, proscriptions against murder, genocide, or kidnapping. The United Nations Declaration of Human Rights delineates a number of fundamental rights considered universally applicable as a basis for moral, ethical, and legal behavior around the world.[38]

I should acknowledge some limits to moral consensus, as revealed, for example, by contentious debates over issues such as abortion, stem-cell research, gay rights, same-sex marriage, the death penalty, and assisted suicide. Some critics argue that, in the absence of God, moral codes reflect nothing more than subjective opinions. At the same time, however, there are also limits to the moral consensus that can be derived from religion. Major religions or religious denominations offer conflicting views on many of these same contentious moral issues.[39]

SOCIAL AND POLITICAL VALUES

Although there are both historical and modern exceptions, the social and political attitudes of secular humanists tend to be relatively progressive or liberal, at least in Western societies.[40] This phenomenon likely reflects a number of factors.

First, secular humanists have a this-worldly focus, which implies the need to work for the improvement of the human condition in the here-and-now, rather than hoping for an eternal afterlife. Second, because of their consequentialist moral philosophy, behaviors and attitudes are evaluated, not in terms of existing conventions, but in terms of how well they are perceived to promote the well-being of individuals and society.[41] Third, secular humanists tend to be relatively open to experience, inquisitive, and nonconforming and less influenced by traditional or conservative religious doctrines or prescriptions. Finally, secularists tend to take into account situational factors such as poverty, racism, and differential opportunity in accounting for social problems and personal misfortune, rather than viewing such misfortune as entirely due to individual culpability.

Among the progressive social positions supported by many secular humanists, particularly in comparison to more conservative religious groups, are the following: civil rights and racial equality; gender equality and women's rights; gay rights; immigrant rights; physician-assisted suicide; less punitive penalties for criminals, including opposition to the death penalty; animal rights; environmental protection and action to ameliorate climate change; separation of church and state; advocacy in support of science; support for stem cell research; and access to birth control and safe abortion.[42]

Conversely, American secular humanists tend to be less supportive of exclusive patriotism and the idea of American exceptionalism. Indeed, sociologist Phil Zuckerman cites research supporting the greater average cosmopolitanism and reduced nationalism, patriotism, or ethnocentrism of secular people as compared to religious people in a variety of countries. Cosmopolitanism emphasizes the unity of humanity or the idea that we are all part of one global community.[43]

Given their generally progressive socio-political attitudes, it is not surprising that secularists in the United States are much more likely to identify as Independents or Democrats than as Republicans. For example, a national survey in the United States found that the most frequent political affiliation of atheists and agnostics is Independent. Of those who did join one of the two major political parties, only 11-12% selected the Republican Party. Americans with an affirmative secular humanist worldview and identity—for example, members of the American Humanist Association—are even more likely to be associated with the Democratic Party than are the merely nonreligious.[44] Secularists, on average, are also more likely than religious individuals to be interested in politics and public affairs.[45]

I should point out that the largest average differences in the social and political attitudes mentioned here are between secular people and more conservative or fundamentalist religious people. Indeed, in their relatively liberal social and political attitudes, secular humanists are actually similar to many religious progressives, indicating the potential for cooperation in pursuing progressive causes. The civil rights movement in the United States, which was largely driven by seculars and liberal religious denominations, provides a historical example of such cooperation.

MEANING, PURPOSE, AND TRANSCENDENCE

Can we find meaning and purpose in life without religion?

Critics of secular humanism sometimes portray the secular worldview as nihilistic—without meaning or purpose. Without God's plan for us and His creation, what basis exists for meaning or purpose in society and in our individual lives? Secular humanists reply that it is up to each of us to create and discern our meaning or purpose in life. That is, rather than discerning the "ultimate" meaning of the universe or existence, they seek meaning in a more personal sense. Again, personal responsibility plays a central role. Instead of asking "what's the meaning of life, we should ask what makes our own lives meaningful."[46]

As in the case of morality, some secularists view the adoption of a purpose in life based on religion—such as personal salvation or living in accordance with God's will—as a form of outsourcing of responsibility. From a secular humanist perspective, "true nobility" involves being honest about the fact that the universe has no ultimate purpose for us, other than what we create and choose.[47] At the same time, although we are free to choose our sources of meaning and purpose, we should not, argues philosopher Michael Ruse, ignore our evolved human nature. As a result of natural selection, humans have evolved to be a highly social species with moral sentiments or intuitions and a creative mind. From this perspective, a meaningful life is one lived in accordance with our human nature, that is, as a social being with family and friends, a sense of duty and generosity to others and society, and a life of the mind or creative imagination.[48]

What other sources of meaning and purpose are available to secular or nonreligious people? In a book titled *The Age of Nothing: How We Have Sought to Live Since the Death of God*, British historian Peter Watson provides a wide-ranging historical review of secular efforts to find replacement sources of meaning, or ways to live, since Nietzsche declared "the death of God."[49] Many of these efforts have involved the creative arts. For example, Watson observes that in the period leading up to and during World War I, the arts were viewed as far more important than they are today. This was especially the case for poetry, which some viewed as having spiritual qualities and as "the natural heir to religion."[50]

Similarly, Watson quotes the American philosopher Richard Rorty, who cites "the hope for a religion of literature, in which works of secular imagination replace Scripture as the principal source of inspiration and hope for each new generation."[51] American philosophers Hubert Dreyfus and Sean Dorrance Kelly also see art as a source of meaning and purpose in a secular age:

> The job of a work of art is to disclose a world, give meaning, and reveal truth. In this sense, works of art working can be thought of as sacred. They give meaning to people's lives and people guide their lives by them, so people treat them as divine...In this way artworks can play the traditional role of a God. They are a nonhuman authority that gives meaning and purpose to those whose lives are illuminated by them.[52]

Beyond the arts, Watson reviews other historical attempts to find secular meaning in the form of "ways to live" in the absence of God. In many instances, these ways to live were explicitly presented as alternatives to religion by their proponents. Examples include appreciating simple pleasures and moments of wonder, joy, or being; living life with intensity, passion, or playfulness; having a practical impact on the world, living a life of action or doing; perceiving and accepting life as it is, including its struggles and horrors; striving for an exemplary life of dignity and self-respect; discovering and actualizing one's self, expressing one's individuality; finding intimacy, love, and communion with others; performing work as a duty or calling; pursuing ideals; maintaining a humble perspective amidst an expansive and awe-inspiring universe; making a commitment to the environment; pursuing scientific knowledge, inquiry for its own sake; and pursuing activities that are intrinsically enjoyable.[53]

Watson also notes how psychologists such as Carl Jung, Carl Rogers, and Abraham Maslow viewed the psychological concepts of personal insight, flourishing, and well-being as alternatives to the religious concept of salvation, and psychotherapy as a substitute for religious confession. For still others, political and economic "isms" such as nationalism, patriotism, socialism, Nazism, communism, consumerism—and even "redemptive" war—have been seen as substitutes for religion. Watson also points to the mix of spiritual, mystical, and occult traditions that have emerged over time as replacements for traditional religion. Finally, science has been included among these proposed replacements for religion. However, many observers have acknowledged that reason and science alone, despite their successes, fall short of the sense of meaning, wholeness, and transcendence offered by religion.

Watson acknowledges that most, if not all, of these proposed "ways to live" fail to provide the comprehensive worldview offered by religion. Indeed, he observes that in the 20th century we saw a retreat from the idea of an all-encompassing source of meaning. Rather, secularization has taught us "how to look out upon the world, appreciating it detail by detail."[54] There are many sources of meaning and we each need to find meaning and purpose for ourselves.

Watson adopted a historical perspective. However, in the writings of today's secular proponents—some of whom have drawn on interviews with nonbelievers— we see many of the same proposed secular means to attain a sense of meaning or purpose. These include appreciation of the arts or nature; passionate pursuit of valued goals or worthwhile ideals; pursuing meaningful work or a calling; mutual concern and connection to others; making a positive difference in the world; community involvement, service, or leadership; maintaining a sense of dignity, grace, and integrity; fully engaging in life and its challenges; continuing to grow, seeking the best in ourselves and others; being active in doing, creating, or learning; awareness and appreciation of the moment; and appreciating the time, health, and one life that we have.[55]

Both religious and nonreligious readers may wish to consider which of these proposed "ways to live" provide meaning and purpose in their own lives.

Importantly, secular humanists argue that none of these sources of meaning necessarily requires a God or religion. Nor does the meaning associated with the major transitions in our lives—birth, growth, love, family, work, and death. As atheist philosopher A. C. Grayling has noted:

[I]t is a failure of imagination not to see that when people go to concerts or exhibitions, enjoy country walks, gardening, gathering with friends round a dinner table, reading, creating something, learning, working at something absorbing and worthwhile—whatever refreshes and lifts the heart, and brings fulfillment—they are in different ways satisfying the needs for creativity, recreation, community and friendship which are vital to lives well lived.[56]

In Chapter 10, I will have more to say about sources of secular meaning and fulfillment, as investigated by psychologists.

But do fully secular people, in fact, experience as much meaning and purpose as religious people? On the one hand, research shows that atheists as a group *do* show a modest tendency to report lower meaning in life than religious believers. On the other hand, atheists report less *need* for ultimate meaning. They share most of the same sources of meaning as religious believers. And, they do not differ from religious believers in self-reported fatalistic or nihilistic attitudes.[57]

Indeed, there is evidence that the majority of atheists experience life as meaningful and do not differ from religious people in the frequency in which they experience crises of meaning.[58] The authors of a recent review concluded that the available evidence "challenges the idea that nonreligiosity entails a 'meaning gap' or that the meaning in life experienced by nonbelievers qualitatively differs from that experienced by believers."[59]

But can the meaning experienced by nonreligious individuals, with their this-worldly focus, provide the type of transcendent experiences attributed to religion? Is the secular life necessarily impoverished or incomplete, as argued by some critics?

Secular humanists argue that this-worldly sources can indeed provide a sense of transcendence, although not in a supernatural sense. Secular humanists *do* encounter profound, memorable, or transformative experiences, as well as feelings of awe, wonder, unity, or gratitude. For example, such experiences and feelings can arise in response to a beautiful piece of music, a spectacular view in nature, the humbling mystery of the vast universe, or through more mundane moments of joy and gratitude with someone we love or while deeply engaged in a meaningful task. Secularist scholars use a variety of terms to refer to such experiences, such as awe, wonder, self-transcendent experiences, peak experiences, gratitude, flow, or fullness.[60] Indeed, one recent national survey of Americans found that 65% of agnostics and 53% of atheists report feeling "a deep sense of wonder" at least once a month.[61]

SECULAR COPING AND WELL-BEING

How do secular individuals cope with life's difficulties and achieve a sense of well-being without religion?

All of the methods of coping with stress, problems, and trauma that are available to religious people are also available to secular humanists—with the exception of drawing on God and religion for guidance, consolation, and support. These include cognitive restructuring—for example, taking a different perspective on a situation or challenging dysfunctional beliefs; social support from family and friends; taking personal control over what we can; and, when needed, seeking counseling or therapy. Meditation, relaxation techniques, and physical exercise are also effective methods for dealing with stress and improving physical and mental health.

Leaving behind one's religion can be difficult and painful for some people. However, many atheists and secular humanists observe that once they have done so they feel liberated and more consistent with their authentic self. For example, they no longer have to struggle with religious doctrines they no longer find credible.[62]

Indeed, in-depth interviews with American *apostates*—that is, people who have left their former religion—reveal that people leave their religion for a number of reasons. These include, among others, educational attainments that lead them to question religion and their own beliefs and values; personal misfortunes that cause them to question God's existence; and the awareness of tragedy, suffering, and evil in the world, leading them to question God's goodness.[63] Even in the face of life's difficulties, it is possible for secular humanists to experience hope through meaningful relationships with others and through the modest contributions they can make to improving society or the world.

The absence of a religious community in times of tragedy can be a disadvantage for secular individuals. This might be especially the case in dealing with death. For believers, it can be consoling to believe that their loved ones are now in a better place or that they will eventually be reunited with them in heaven. Nonbelievers might instead focus on the good memories associated with the loved one or the good they accomplished in life. For secular humanists, the focus is not on an afterlife, but on making the best of the one life we have.[64] In this sense, secular humanists "believe in life *before* death."[65]

Indeed, as writer Lesley Hazleton argued: "The awareness of mortality is part of what gives life meaning; it sharpens our appreciation of being alive."[66] Based on interviews with 518 American atheists, sociologist Jerome Baggett observed that atheists focus on making the most of the one life they have, and that this focus elicits feelings of both personal responsibility and gratitude.[67] It is perhaps for these reasons that secular Americans have been more involved than their religious counterparts in advocating against prolonged end-of-life suffering and in supporting the death with dignity movement.[68]

Of course, the key question is whether secular individuals, using secular coping methods, are able to experience levels of well-being comparable to religious individuals. In Chapter 5, I cited evidence that only the most fervent believers and those who actually practice their religion experience modestly greater well-being or meaning than nonreligious individuals. Indeed, a growing number of studies suggest that the relationship between religion and well-being is curvilinear. That is, well-being is highest among both highly religious *and* affirmatively nonreligious individuals (e.g., atheists), with lower well-being or greater mental distress found among people who are only weakly or nominally religious.[69] Here are some example findings from national surveys:

- Actively religious Americans were more likely to report greater happiness and personal satisfaction with their lives than religiously unaffiliated believers and people who see their religion mainly as a cultural identity. However, the differences in happiness and satisfaction between actively religious individuals and atheists or agnostics were trivial after controlling for social and demographic variables.[70]

- American atheists reported better physical and mental health outcomes than members of many organized religious traditions, whereas the worst physical and mental health outcomes were reported by religious believers who were unaffiliated with any religious tradition.[71]

- In Canada, atheists did not differ meaningfully from various religious groups in self-rated health, emotional well-being, or psychological well-being. However, they did report lower social contributions or feelings of community belonging.[72]

A plausible interpretation of these findings is that people who have a more affirmative or definitive belief system—whether religious or nonreligious—experience a greater sense of comfort and emotional stability than those who are more confused, noncommittal, or ambivalent about their belief system. As Phil Zuckerman and colleagues concluded:

There is emerging evidence that atheists and agnostics, particularly those involved with organized secular groups and who are embedded within their community are not different than engaged religious believers with regard to mental or physical health.[73]

BELONGING AND COMMUNITY

How do secular individuals experience a sense of belonging or community? Humanists and atheists can draw on many of the same sources of belonging and community as religious individuals, such as family, friends, and various secular groups and activities in their local communities. For the minority who wish to engage more formally with their nonreligious identity, there are also a number of international and national organizations available to humanists and atheists,[74] as well as humanist or secular holidays.[75] Secular versions of various lifecycle rituals—for example, baby naming ceremonies, marriages, and memorial services—can also provide a sense of community or identity. In the United States, Camp Quest is a summer camp catering to secular families.

For those who wish a more "congregational" experience, there are now a number of secular Sunday Assemblies around the world, mostly in Europe and North America.[76] In addition, Unitarian Universalist, Humanistic Judaism, and Ethical Culture communities provide a home for both religious and nonreligious humanists. Many local communities have secular humanist groups that gather regularly to socialize or participate in community service activities.[77] In response to the growing presence of secular humanism on college campuses, the number of humanist campus chaplains, although still small, has been growing.[78] In addition, the Internet is a vibrant source of interaction, identity, and activism for humanists and atheists in many countries.[79]

Members of the secular humanist community acknowledge the limitations of these organizational or community efforts. For example, most secular humanists and atheists are not interested in joining such groups, perhaps reflecting, in part, their individualistic orientation. For most, being

262

atheist or agnostic is not an important part of their identity. For example, data from the 2017 Secular America Study reveals that seculars in the general population have a weaker sense of group identity than members of the American Humanist Association, which, in turn, have a weaker sense of identity than evangelicals.[80] Similarly, American Professor of Religious Studies Joseph Blankholm observed that nearly a third of the local nonbeliever groups he identified in 2012 were no longer active in 2017, while many new groups had formed.[81] This degree of turnover raises questions about the sustainability of such groups.

Indeed, Humanist chaplain Greg Epstein has described the idea of organized secularism as an oxymoron, because many seculars resist the idea of anything that appears "too churchy."[82] According to U.S. and international survey data, strongly religious individuals are more likely to be involved with religious and service groups, whereas nonreligious individuals are more likely to be involved in professional societies and in literary, arts, or political organizations related to their careers and personal interests.[83] In general, humanism has historically done a better job of responding to the "head" of religion, for example, through criticism of religion, critical thinking, and advocacy of science and church-state separation. It has done less well responding to the "heart" of religion, which would require affective replacements for the rituals and communities associated with religion.[84]

Another limitation of the secular community can be acknowledged. Whereas religious communities can readily mobilize their members through their local, state, and national churches, the secular community is more diffuse, dispersed, and bottom-up. As a result, the ties among members of the secular community tend to be looser and weaker than those in religious communities.[85] There is growing evidence, however, that participants in secular Sunday Assemblies report feeling as connected to their congregations as do participants in traditional religious congregations. Participation in Sunday Assemblies and the associated social activities also contributes to feelings of well-being.[86]

In short, although secular humanists may be less likely to join such groups, participating members of secular and church groups with comparable levels of attendance may receive similar social benefits. This suggests that these social benefits come from group participation—whether religious or secular—rather than religion per se.[87]

SECULAR DIVERSITY

So far in this chapter, I have reviewed some differences between religious and secular or nonreligious people. But are there important differences among various *secular* people? If so, it would mean that people with various secular identities do not constitute a homogeneous group. They might vary in personality, motives, well-being, and perspectives, including their attitudes towards religion.

First, a couple of caveats. Any attempt to delineate the varieties of personal secularity will have shortcomings. In addition, some scholars have cautioned against generating too many categories or "types" of nonbelievers, in part, because the major differences in worldview appear to be between believers and nonbelievers.[88] Nonetheless, a number of scholars have attempted to delineate the multiple paths or trajectories taken by nonreligious individuals. Unfortunately, different classification schemes often reflect independent efforts with limited overlap. Therefore, rather than reviewing all such efforts, I instead try to capture the primary varieties of personal secularity that have been observed and labeled by scholars.

Varieties or "Types" of Personal Secularity

The following categories or identities are not all mutually exclusive—that is, a person could identify with more than one category. Nonetheless, they provide some indication of the scope and variety of personal secularity. Secular readers could try to locate their own secular or nonreligious identity among one or more of these "types."

- Ritualists—individuals who do not believe in God or who reject many religious doctrines, but participate and find community in the rituals, celebrations, and services associated with church life; sometimes referred to as "belonging without believing;" might also encompass "congregational humanists" and participants in Sunday Assemblies.

- Nonaffiliated believers—individuals who retain traditional religious beliefs but choose not to be affiliated with a religious community; sometimes referred to as "believing without belonging."

- Nonaffiliated spiritualists, or spiritual-but-not-religious—individuals who are not affiliated with traditional religion, but maintain belief in spiritual or transcendent forces or energies in nature and the universe.

- Culturally religious—individuals who retain the cultural identity of a religious group, for example, as Catholic, Jewish, Lutheran, and so forth, regardless of whether they are believers or regularly attend religious services.

- Religiously indifferent—individuals who are indifferent or apathetic about religion, but not antagonistic towards it. Variants are referred to by various authors as *apatheism* (i.e., apathy towards the existence or non-existence of God), benign indifference, reluctance/reticence, or inCREDulous atheism (i.e., atheist because of lack of exposure to credibility-enhancing religious experiences).

- Transitionals—individuals who are "betwixt and between" a religious and secular identity, personally unresolved, and possibly confused or conflicted. Sometimes referred to as "liminals" or "perplexed" and may also describe some "fuzzy fidelists."

- Atheists—individuals who affirm disbelief in God. A number of non-mutually exclusive variants have been described, including (a) intellectual atheists, who educate themselves on topics related to science, philosophy, theology, and politics as they relate to religion, and tend to be associated with rationalist and free-thinking groups; (b) analytic or reflective atheists, whose strong analytic thinking leads them to disbelief in God; (c) confrontational atheists—sometimes referred to as anti-theists, militant atheists, argumentative atheists, or hard atheists—who believe that religion should be actively confronted as irrational or dangerous; (d) accommodationist or respectful atheists, who view direct confrontation with religion as counterproductive and may seek common cause with religious communities to achieve shared goals; and (e) pragmatic or ethical atheists, who believe that God's existence is essentially irrelevant since it is not required for moral and ethical behavior.

- Agnostics—individuals who believe that God's existence cannot be proved or disproved, although some agnostics consider the likelihood of God's existence to be sufficiently low to warrant atheism in practice.

- Religious humanists—individuals who retain some religious structures or community while emphasizing a humanistic ethical philosophy centered on human needs, interests, and values. Prototypical examples include Unitarian Universalist Humanism, Humanistic Judaism, and the Ethical Culture movement.

- Secular humanists—individuals who reject belief in the supernatural, while adopting a humanistic stance on morality, meaning, and community as described in this book.[89]

A handful of studies have examined how people with some of these secular identities differ.[90] Most of the findings involve atheists, some of which are not surprising. For example, compared to some of the other secular identities, atheists tend to be less accepting of religion and view it as less important in their lives; are more invested in their philosophical views; perceive a greater conflict between science and religion; and are seen as more narcissistic and dogmatic, and less agreeable.

Relatively few of these studies have specifically examined people who identify as humanists. The available findings suggest that humanists have a more accepting attitude towards religion than do atheists. They are more invested in their philosophical views than are agnostics and spiritualists. They report greater emotional well-being than agnostics and spiritualists. And they report being more agreeable than agnostics and atheists. While limited, these findings suggest that the affirmative worldview of self-identified humanists is associated with some positive outcomes, including emotional well-being, agreeableness, and tolerance of religion—at least when compared with some of the other secular identities.[91]

Further systematic research on the differences between various secular identities or "types" is needed. It would be helpful if researchers could agree on a set of consensus categories or types so that findings could be more readily integrated across studies.

I discuss the similarities and differences between atheists and agnostics more fully in the next section. After that, I discuss secular spirituality and the characteristics of spiritual-but-not-religious individuals, as well as confrontational versus accommodationist strategies towards religion.

Agnosticism Versus Atheism

Some critics—including some committed atheists—view agnostics disparagingly as wishy-washy, passive, and uncourageous "fence-sitters" who are unwilling to take a committed stand regarding the existence or nonexistence of God. Indeed, adopting the agnostic rather than atheistic label can be perceived as "a polite and cautious way to signal nonbelief" and reduce "the risk of social stigma."[92] For other critics, the term agnosticism sounds too intellectual and fails to capture the more emotional or self-transcendent, albeit this-worldly, aspects of secular humanism such as awe and wonder.

Other secularists, however, see the agnostic life stance as a principled one. They argue that it takes more courage and honesty to acknowledge that we simply don't know whether or not God exists. Some things may be unknowable or lack definitive answers.[93] In this sense, the agnostic stance can be seen as a "humanism of humility" that contrasts with the perceived

267

hubris of some atheists who believe that science can or will eventually explain everything.[94]

Some agnostics feel it is appropriate or even important to remain open to the possibility of future evidence for the existence of God. Philosopher Philip Kitcher refers to such a position as "soft atheism."[95] Indeed, the agnostic's doubt or uncertainty can open up further inquiry into life's "big questions."[96] In this regard, agnostics show some resemblance to the quest religious orientation. In contrast, many religious conservatives and confirmed atheists alike may desire certainty or closure in a domain of existence where certainty is unlikely to be found.

In sum, as philosopher and former Anglican priest Mark Vernon has argued, the "radical unknowability of God" warrants a "passionate agnosticism." "Rather than debunking reason, [agnosticism] is an approach that focusses on reason's limits."[97]

Whatever the relative merits of atheism versus agnosticism, research has shown that atheists and agnostics do differ in meaningful ways. For example, in two recent studies in Europe, atheists, as compared to agnostics, were higher in dogmatism, need for closure, endorsement of scientism, openness about their worldview, and emotional stability. Agnostics were higher than atheists in openness to spirituality, extent of past religious upbringing, and self-reported agreeableness and social curiosity. The authors of one of these studies concluded that agnostics were similar to atheists in reasoning and curiosity, but tended to be more prosocial and spiritual, less dogmatic, and less emotionally stable than atheists.[98]

Spirituality and the Secular Life

We also observe diversity in how different secularists view the concept of *spirituality* and whether it has a role to play in secular humanism. Philosopher of religion Peter H. Van Ness defined *secular spirituality* as "an attempt to locate optimal human experience within a nonreligious context of existential and cosmic meaning."[99] In more common parlance, the phrase "spiritual but not religious" (SBNR) is often used to describe individuals who have abandoned organized religion, but still seek some form of spiritual or transcendent experience.

Estimates of the prevalence of the SBNR phenomenon are quite variable. In the United States, most survey estimates range from about 18% to 27% of adults, although some researchers suggest that the prevalence of SBNR individuals is actually much smaller.[100] Estimates for Western European countries tend to be lower, ranging in a 2018 survey from 4% in Austria to 17% in Belgium and Spain, with an overall median across countries of 11%.[101]

In some ways, individuals who identify as SBNR differ from *both* conventionally religious and wholly secular individuals. SBNR individuals are more likely to report (a) paranormal beliefs in extrasensory perception, out-of-body experiences, reincarnation, karma, and psychic powers; (b) mystical experiences and a connection with everything around them; (c) greater proneness to fantasy, dissociation, self-forgetfulness, and hallucinations; (d) strong reliance on personal intuitions and subjective experience; and (e) a questioning, open-ended, and eclectic approach to religion and spirituality that resists definitive answers. Many SBNR individuals use psychological concepts such as self-fulfillment, self-realization, individuation, and peak experiences to describe their spiritual paths.[102]

In some ways, however, SBNR and traditionally religious individuals do *not* differ. For example, both groups are higher, on average, than fully secular individuals in cognitive tendencies to anthropomorphize—that is, attribute human-like characteristics to non-human entities; perceive the mind and body as distinct; and mentalize about others' feelings and motives (i.e., mind perception).[103]

Similarly, in some ways, SBNR and wholly secular individuals do not differ. For example, both groups, in comparison to traditionally religious individuals, average higher in Openness to Experience and lower in traditionalism, conventionality, and authoritarianism. Indeed, Professor of Religious Studies Robert Fuller asks why—given their shared Openness to Experience and relatively high average levels of education—fully secular individuals reject the supernatural while SBNR individuals adopt metaphysical ideas. Fuller concludes that this difference reflects SBNR individuals' greater tendency to be guided by their personal intuitions and subjective experiences rather than by analytic thinking.[104]

In sum, there is clear evidence that individuals identifying as SBNR can be distinguished in some ways from both traditionally religious and fully secular individuals. Thus, the SBNR worldview warrants attention as a possible intermediate life stance between traditional religion and secular humanism.

That said, a number of scholars and secularists have offered disparaging assessments of secular spirituality, or the SBNR life stance, as a replacement for *either* traditional religion or secular humanism. Various critics have described the term spirituality as "squishy," "vague," "nebulous," a "watered-down" version of traditional religion, or indicative of an unwillingness to take a stand.[105] Some critics lament the absence of a less-loaded term than spirituality to describe essentially humanistic values such as the search for meaning.[106] Other critics point to the "subjective anarchy" associated with the diverse individualized forms of spirituality and argue that "no amount of vague spiritual yearning will generate a shared belief system."[107]

Take, for example, Linda Mercadante—a Professor of Theology, ordained Presbyterian minister, and former self-identified SBNR individual. She has observed that the SBNR phenomenon frequently involves an eclectic and internally inconsistent blend of elements. However, many of her interviewees were unaware or unbothered by this fact. Indeed, she observes that the freedom to select from a diverse and idiosyncratic cafeteria of options is one hallmark of this new spirituality.[108] Mercadante acknowledges that the SBNR phenomenon may not coalesce into a new theology or spirituality that achieves culture-wide acceptance. She also observes that "the longer [religious] nones stay away from organized religious practices, the less spiritual they become."[109]

270

Atheist philosopher Daniel Dennett is similarly skeptical about the SBNR phenomenon:

> What fascinates me about this delightfully versatile craving for "spirituality" is that people think they know what they are talking about, even though—or perhaps because—nobody bothers to explain just what they mean…. When I've asked people to explain themselves, they typically beg off…[110]

Finally, even Robert Fuller—who adopts a neutral if not appreciative stance towards the SBNR phenomenon—thinks that secular spiritualities may in time be undermined by neurophysiology and secular reasoning processes in much the same way these processes have undermined traditional religion. If so, "[s]ecular spiritualities might appear to future historians as little more than last-ditch efforts to forestall the inevitable progress of nonreligious secularism."[111]

In any case, it is important to distinguish "spiritual" phenomena that are strictly this-worldly from those that claim supernatural, metaphysical, or mystical elements. Many of us encounter or seek out experiences that elicit feelings of awe, depth, harmony, or peace that "transcend" the self and everyday concerns—yet are entirely this-worldly in nature. Examples include the elevated feelings one experiences listening to a beautiful piece of music; viewing magnificent architecture; communing with nature; or engaging in a meaningful task, calling, or relationship. Such experiences transcend or elevate everyday experience, but do not involve metaphysical elements such as perceived forces, energies, "higher powers," or dimensions beyond physical realities.

Similarly, many secularists practice meditation and yoga techniques that originated in Eastern religions to promote physical and mental health, or greater mindfulness and self-awareness, without superimposing supernatural elements.[112] There is some evidence that, for religious people, techniques or treatments that incorporate spiritual elements may be more effective and more consistent with their beliefs.[113] However, there is little evidence that spiritual methods are generally superior to comparable secular methods, particularly for more secular people.[114] Secular humanists encourage this-worldly experiences of awe and wonder as an important part of living a full secular life. Indeed, substantial numbers of secularists report having such experiences.[115] However, many prefer not to apply terms such as "spiritual" or "sacred" to these experiences given the religious or metaphysical connotations of such terms.

In contrast, some people—who otherwise live largely secular lives—seek out spiritual experiences that *do* incorporate metaphysical or mystical elements thought to impact psychological or physical well-being. These typically eclectic approaches go beyond the awe-inducing quality of the experiences themselves to make supernatural or nonmaterial claims about reality in an attempt to understand the self in a larger metaphysical context.[116] Secular humanists and atheists question these metaphysical claims and the viability of these approaches as alternatives to an exclusively secular philosophy or lifestyle.

In sum, the SBNR life stance can be distinguished from conventional religion and secular humanism, and may, in fact, represent a transitional stage between organized religion and this-worldly secularity. The SBNR life stance tends to be idiosyncratic, diffuse, and vague. Thus, it seems unlikely that it can compete as an alternative to secular humanism in the long term, at least as a coherent and consensus worldview.

Confrontation Versus Accommodation Strategies

Another important difference among secularists is their strategy or stance towards religion. The confrontational approach is more combative towards religion. It points to its perceived irrational or superstitious elements. It denigrates religion's contribution to violence and terrorism. It takes assertive action such as lawsuits in support of science education and separation of church and state. Confrontational atheists contend that more accommodating approaches might avoid "rocking the boat" for strategic purposes, but fail to adequately confront the perceived untruths and obstacles to critical thinking perpetuated by religion.

In some circumstances, the need for a confrontational approach may feel urgent. For example, it may be required when religion inhibits progress essential to our survival—for example, efforts to overcome global warming, overpopulation, epidemics, and poverty—or when religion poses a danger to democracy. The danger to democracy is more likely when religion becomes fused with nationalism. Many secular humanists seek to go beyond mere criticism of religion to emphasize a humanistic stance or philosophy. However, some confrontational or hardline atheists argue that this more "positive" approach may dilute the antitheist message or agenda.

In contrast, accommodationists view attacks on religion as alienating and counterproductive. For example, it can inhibit attempts to find common cause with religious communities in pursuit of shared goals such as social justice, climate action, church-state separation, and support for science education. Direct attacks on religion may also be counterproductive because people resist challenges to their existing worldviews. Rather than aggressively taking on religion, accommodationists—and many secular humanists—may seek to enhance acceptance and support for secularity through humanitarian action. For example, the humanist Foundation Beyond Belief, and many local humanist groups, promote secular volunteering and charitable giving. While such activities are motivated by genuine humanitarian impulses, they may also serve to demonstrate that people can be "good without God," contrary to the belief of some people.

To some extent, the differences between confrontational and accommodationist approaches may reflect differences in agendas, such as confronting the perceived evils and untruths of religion versus recruiting allies in support of shared goals, respectively.[117] These differences in approach can also play out at the organizational level. For example, UK humanist Callum Brown and his co-authors have described how in the UK, the National Secular Society has traditionally adopted a more confrontational approach towards religion and objected to the long-running efforts of the

British Humanist Association (now Humanists UK) to find common cause and accommodation with more liberal religious communities.[118]

At this point, we can ask: Is the cause of secularization and secular humanism better served by a confrontational or accommodating approach to religion? The answer is not entirely clear. It is possible that both approaches have a role to play. As already noted, confrontational approaches can generate resistance. They may also contribute to the perception of atheists as narcissistic, dogmatic, and "fundamentalist," which may turn off many potential converts to secularism. However, firm and definitive attacks on religion probably elicit more attention and exposure and may persuade some people to leave religion behind.

In fact, responses to the confrontational New Atheist books discussed in Chapter 7 reveal a dual impact. That is, these books induced some people to abandon religion, while other people reacted by converting to religion. For some people, however, more accommodating approaches that focus on the promotion of humanistic values and behavior may be more effective in communicating the appeal of a secular humanistic philosophy.

In any case, the need for a more confrontational approach will probably decrease, and perhaps be eliminated, once religion's impact in a society is sufficiently reduced—as in many of the most secular countries today. Indeed, some sociologists view atheist activism as indicative of early stages of secularization when religion is still influential in a society. After sufficient secularization has taken place, religious indifference becomes the norm, such that both "religion *and* irreligion become non-issues."[119]

Personally, I have found the more confrontational atheistic writings to be stimulating and frequently persuasive—albeit one-sided. Nonetheless, I believe that more accommodating approaches—such as those of Greg Epstein, Philip Kitcher, William Irwin, and Chris Stedman—are more likely to facilitate common cause and cooperation across the religious-secular divide.[120] Many secular humanists who adopt a more accommodating stance towards religion understand that many people—at least in the current state of the world—will find comfort, meaning, and a sense of com-

munity and identity through religious engagement. Most secular humanists merely ask that tolerance be reciprocated and that religion not be unduly imposed in the public sphere.

Indeed, it is worth noting that the distinction between confrontational
and accommodationist approaches can also be applied in describing the
different approaches of religious people toward secular humanists. For example, evangelical Christian theologian and pastor Russell Moore has lamented that many conservative evangelicals are so fearful of the secular left
that they see emergency conditions prevailing, thus justifying a "gloves-off
'fighting' evangelicalism."[121] In contrast, some interfaith efforts are more
accommodating, even including atheists and humanists in their discussions
and outreach activities.

IS THE SECULAR LIFE IMPOVERISHED?

As I described in this chapter, many scholars—and the secular people they
study—view secular living without religion as fully capable of nourishing
moral and ethical lives with meaning, purpose, and even awe and wonder.
In addition, it is certainly not the case that nonbelievers in religion believe
in nothing. For example, a recent study of secular worldviews in ten countries identified a number of belief or worldview categories that are frequently mentioned by secular people. These include, among others, endorsement of the essential equality and dignity of all humans; the idea that
humans are subject to the same laws as the rest of the natural world; the
importance of empathy and concern for others, caring for the earth, and
individual liberty; the value of science, critical thinking, and evidence; and
progressive political causes.[122]

Nonetheless, a number of critics of secularity—typically writing from a
religious perspective—have suggested that the secular life is necessarily an
impoverished one.[123] Although I don't agree, we should hear them out.

For example, Alister McGrath, a theologian, intellectual historian, and
former atheist, has referred to the "imaginative failure of atheism." He describes how as an atheist his "mental map" led him to see the universe as

cold and indifferent, and himself as of no consequence.[124] Atheism fails, in his view, to provide sufficient meaning and emotional appeal to "excite" people, leading them to seek out a spiritual dimension. Because human beings have been created to relate to God, they will naturally experience a sense of yearning in the absence of such a relationship.[125] McGrath concedes that secularists can experience awe and reverence for nature without believing in God. However, he argues that such feelings can be experienced all the more when nature is seen as reflecting "something still greater."[126]

Similarly, in his monumental book *The Secular Age*, philosopher Charles Taylor uses vivid terminology to describe the purported characteristics of the secular age. These characteristics include a "buffered self" that is insulated and isolated; a loss of sociality or communitarianism; a "lowering of the bar" for flourishing or a life well-lived; restlessness and fragility regarding the meaning of life; and a sense of emptiness, "malaise of immanence," or "felt flatness" in a "disenchanted" world.[127] In Taylor's view, people react to the perceived loss of a transcendent dimension to life in different ways. However, they all share a sense that their actions and achievements "have a lack of weight, gravity, thickness, substance" or the "deeper resonance" that they feel should be there.[128] As a result of this predicament, Taylor argues, we observe a "nova effect"—a proliferation of efforts to identify new modes of being in a secular world.[129]

Similarly, a number of scholars have pointed to the challenges that secularists experience trying to replace the sense of community associated with religious congregations. Outside religious communities, the secular world provides few opportunities for discussion of beliefs and doubts about existential questions. In addition, most secular groups or organizations seem less tailored to addressing emotional and psychological needs. As a consequence, some authors, among them writer Alain de Botton in his book *Religion for Atheists*, have advocated the creation of secular analogs of religious rituals and practices that meet these needs.[130]

For example, philosopher Philip Kitcher suggests that models for secular efforts might be found in some of the more liberal religious or ethical communities such as Unitarian churches, Ethical Culture societies, or Jewish Community Centers. Kitcher acknowledges that initial efforts may seem like "pallid imitations of the religious prototypes."[131] He also notes that such efforts may require time and perseverance to be successful, while reminding us that religious traditions have had centuries to practice.[132] Similarly, writer Catherine Ozment, after participating in many secular group gatherings around the United States, acknowledged that efforts to develop secular rituals from scratch can feel contrived.[133]

The above discussion points to what American Professor of Religious Studies Joseph Blankholm has referred to as the *secular paradox*, which he views as an inherent condition of being secular. In Blankholm's view, secularists cannot avoid the need to navigate—and in many cases, struggle with—their ambivalence towards religion. On the one hand, many secularists seek to avoid anything that feels too religious. On the other hand, they may struggle in deciding what is too religious and may even embrace some religion-like traditions.[134]

To sum up:

Secular or nonreligious readers can draw on their own life experience to assess whether they find the fully secular life to be impoverished, "flattened," or unfulfilling. There is apparently some variability in how secularists experience the secular life without religion. Some—likely a minority—acknowledge feelings of nostalgia, regret, or ambivalence, or a felt loss of depth, transcendence, or community. Conversely, others report feelings of regret for time they perceive as wasted on religion earlier in their lives.135 And importantly, many, if not most, secularists experience the secular life as meaningful, honest, and fulfilling and do not feel a need for secular substitutes for religious communities. I take up this last point more fully in my Takeaways section.

TAKEAWAYS

To further address the overarching question in this book, I focus my discussion here on a central question: Does a fully secular life—a life without religion—offer a means to a moral and ethical life with meaning and purpose, a sense of community, and ways to cope with life's difficulties? Or, is the secular life necessarily an impoverished one?

As I noted in this chapter, many secular humanists argue that it is indeed possible to live moral, meaningful, and fulfilling lives without religion. Guided by moral intuitions, empathy, and mutual human interests, they are able to behave in moral and ethical ways. They find meaning and purpose in their work, relationships, and leisure activities. They sometimes experience a sense of self-transcendent awe or wonder in the arts, nature, science, or other aspects of the world we live in. They use secular means such as social support and cognitive restructuring to cope with difficulties and stress, and, if needed, may seek out counseling or therapy. They may experience anxiety or sadness about their mortality. However, these emotions are more likely due to regret about the relationships, activities, and goals that will be cut short or left behind, or the pain and suffering associated with the dying process itself, rather than fears about their fate in an afterlife. Furthermore, their lack of belief in an afterlife provides a powerful incentive to make the most of the one finite life we have.

In short, the secular life—which requires individuals to take personal responsibility for morality and meaning—can be viewed as a life of courage and integrity. Nonetheless, some questions can be raised about the guidelines that have been proposed for secular living. I should address them.

First, regarding morality:

The Golden Rule could be an imperfect guide for moral and ethical behavior if people disagree about the behaviors that best serve human interests and needs. Philosophers can also point to complex moral dilemmas in which consequentialist or utilitarian approaches to maximizing well-being will likely be limited. Some critics of secularity express less optimism about people's ability to derive consensus on moral and ethical decisions based on human reason.[136] Certainly, there are limits to this consensus, as indicated by today's contentious debates over issues such as abortion, stem-cell research, gay rights, same-sex marriage, religious freedom, church-state relations, assisted suicide, and mask and vaccine mandates.

Nonetheless, there do seem to be a number of moral norms or ideals that nearly all people agree are desirable in most contexts and that are needed to maintain cooperation, peace, stability, and prosperity in all societies. For example, do not kill or inflict needless pain. Do not kidnap. Be trustworthy. Reciprocate kindness. This is certainly not a complete list and other potential moral universals were presented earlier in this chapter. Importantly, even if we rely on religion in hopes of discerning more definitive, objective, or permanent moral principles, we will not always achieve consensus. Different religious communities disagree in some of their prescriptions and proscriptions for behavior.

The consequentialist and this-worldly focus of secular morality probably underlies the progressive socio-political attitudes of many secular humanists, at least in Western cultural contexts. Unfortunately, increasing socio-political polarization between secularists and religionists—particularly religionists of a more conservative orientation—is likely to complicate attempts to achieve common ground, particularly as these disagreements become increasingly linked to entrenched political affiliations. These political affiliations—and associated media preferences and confirmation biases—are also likely to inhibit liberalization of conservative religious groups, and, conversely, conversions from a secular to religious belief system. Secular humanists are likely to find greater common ground on moral and socio-political issues with more liberal religious communities.

Second, regarding the search for meaning:

Many of the proposed secular sources of meaning or "ways to live" without religion fail to provide the comprehensive worldview offered by religion. Interestingly, artists, poets, scientists, philosophers, and others have shown a striking, if not surprising, tendency to see the meaning or purpose in life as best reflected in their own chosen fields of endeavor. On the one hand, this probably reveals a near-universal and self-serving need for each of us to justify the importance and meaningfulness of our own chosen paths. On the other hand, it also demonstrates that most people are adept at creating their own sources of meaning in the absence of religion.

Secular humanism, as described in this book, does provide a fairly comprehensive framework for living. And, it is fully capable of subsuming all of the proposed this-worldly "replacements" for religion cited in this chapter such as pursuing meaningful goals, expressing one's individuality, finding intimacy, enjoying simple pleasures, creating or appreciating art or science, and so forth. Secular humanism will probably not suffice, however, for people who still desire more "other-worldly," metaphysical forms of spirituality.

Third, regarding belonging and community:

Secular groups and communities probably do not typically provide the kinds of close ties or commitments of support that religious communities can provide. There may be exceptions among the growing number of secularists—but still a small minority—who participate in secular congregations such as Sunday Assemblies or in congregations that welcome both believers and nonbelievers such as Unitarian-Universalist and Ethical Culture communities. For example, as noted previously, there is growing evidence that participants in secular Sunday Assemblies report feeling as connected to their congregations as do participants in traditional religious congregations. More research is needed on this topic. In any case, many secularists are perfectly happy to leave religious communities behind, and feel no need to identify with or seek out community with other nonbelievers. In the United States, nearly 90% of those who report "none" as their religious affiliation express no desire to seek out a religious community.[137]

Finally, regarding coping and well-being:

It should be acknowledged that people with deep religious convictions have additional sources of coping that are not available to the nonbeliever. Secularists do not have the comfort of believing in God's guidance, assistance, and protective love, much less the possibility of miracles. In addition, secular communities do not typically provide the kinds of close ties or commitments of support in the face of tragedy that religious communities can provide. Many secularists may need to rely on a smaller community of family and friends, their own resilience, or, when needed, counseling or therapy to cope with life's traumas and difficulties. For some people these sources of support may not feel sufficient.

Nonetheless, growing evidence suggests that secular humanists who are confident in their belief system experience levels of well-being that are comparable to those of committed religious people, and greater well-being, on average, than people who have weaker or less certain religious or atheistic commitments. This implies that there are psychological advantages in coming to some resolution regarding one's religious, atheistic, or agnostic convictions. Research also indicates that whatever benefits religion has for well-being—which, in any case, are generally modest—are more likely to be attained in countries that are relatively religious and experiencing difficult circumstances (see Chapter 5). For example, in countries with blasphemy laws or where atheism is punishable by death, it will presumably be difficult for secular individuals to experience a sense of security and well-being that is comparable to that experienced by religious individuals.

The bottom line: Despite the potential limitations of secular morality, meaning, community, and coping, we cannot conclude that the secular life is necessarily an impoverished or "flattened" one, as argued by some critics. Rather, many of the findings reported in this chapter strongly suggest that most secular individuals are able to live moral, meaningful, and fulfilling lives without religion. They also encounter an abundance of inspiration and wonder from strictly secular sources.[138] Indeed, many secular individuals report feeling liberated after discarding religious doctrines they find unbelievable or religious proscriptions they find undesirable. In some secular countries, such as in Scandinavia, many people now give little, if any, thought to religion.[139]

In addition, secularists need not feel guilty or hypocritical for enjoying religious music, art, and architecture; appreciating religious myths and parables; or being interested in religious ideas and history. These are all part of our rich cultural heritage as human beings. Secular humanists can appreciate these religious aspects of our cultures without superimposing supernatural elements. Of course, religious faith, or some other form of spirituality, remains an option for those who find this-worldly sources of inspiration to be insufficient.

In the current chapter I discussed the nature of secular living from the perspective of its proponents and researchers who have specifically studied nonreligious individuals and societies. In the next chapter, I review what psychological science can tell us more generally about how to live a meaningful and fulfilling life—with or without religion.

Chapter 10
The Psychology of Well-being
(With or Without Religion)

Psychological science investigates how people can live happy, meaningful, and fulfilling lives. If the guidance offered by psychological science typically leads to happy and fulfilling lives—regardless of one's religious or secular worldview—then the worldview one adopts would be less crucial for one's psychological health or well-being. Psychological science has identified goals, motives, emotions, sources of meaning, character strengths, activities, and interventions that increase well-being and are available to both religious and secular individuals. In the Takeaways section, I consider the implications of this evidence for the viability of the secular humanist life stance and again refute claims that such a life stance is necessarily impoverished or unfulfilling.

If we were to ask the question: "What is human life's chief concern?" one of the answers we should receive would be: "It is happiness."
— William James[1]

Eudaimonic living requires thoughtful deliberation and choice of actions and life plans reflecting one's abiding values and beliefs.
— Richard Ryan, Randall Curren, & Edward Deci[2]

Can most of us live happy, meaningful, and fulfilling lives, regardless of whether we are religious or not? Probably. And psychological science tells us how to do so.

283

Much, but not all, of the relevant research on this question has been associated with a field of study referred to as *positive psychology*, which investigates the positive emotions, traits, and institutions that facilitate optimal functioning or "flourishing" in individuals and societies. The focus is on happiness and well-being, virtues and character strengths, and elements of a life well lived, rather than the traditional focus in clinical psychology on mental illness or psychopathology.[3] Although this research has not specifically addressed secular humanism, the findings are pertinent to anyone seeking a meaningful and fulfilling life, whether they are religious or not.

HOW DO PSYCHOLOGISTS DEFINE WELL-BEING?

Psychologists frequently differentiate two distinct but related aspects of well-being, *hedonic* and *eudaimonic*.[4] Hedonic well-being has been defined simply as the experience of pleasure and the avoidance of pain. This conception of well-being can be traced at least to the Greek philosophers Aristippus (435-356 BCE) and Epicurus (341-270 BCE) and was a foundation of the classical utilitarian philosophies of Jeremy Bentham (1748-1832) and John Stuart Mill (1806-1873).[5] In psychological science today, hedonic well-being is often referred to as "happiness" or *subjective well-being* (SWB). SWB refers to the perceived balance of positive versus negative emotions or affects, plus the cognitive evaluation of one's life as a whole. The three components of SWB—positive affect, negative affect, and life satisfaction—are moderately related. For example, people who experience more positive affect than negative affect also tend to be more satisfied with their lives.[6]

The concept of eudaimonic well-being is typically traced to Aristotle's *Nichomachean Ethics*, written in 350 BCE. Aristotle considered the pursuit of happiness in the hedonic sense—for example, through pleasure, amusement, wealth, or power—a vulgar or crass endeavor. Instead, he advocated living in accordance with reason and moderation; being reflective about one's actions and goals; and pursuing virtue, excellence, and the realization of one's true talents and potential. This conception of eudaimonic living is consistent with the ancient Greek imperatives to "know thyself" and "become what you are," as well as the admonition of existentialist philosophers such as Søren Kierkegaard and Jean-Paul Sartre to act in ways that reflect one's authentic or true self. When current scholars define the elements of eudaimonic well-being they refer to the discovery and expression of one's aptitudes and talents; living in accordance with one's most important values; engaging in activities that express who one really is; and experiencing a sense of meaning and purpose—in short, the realization of one's true nature or *daimon*.[7]

Which type of well-being—hedonic or eudaimonic—is more important in living a fulfilled life? On the one hand, feeling happy and satisfied with one's life—that is, experiencing hedonic or subjective well-being—is among the most basic goals of most people. On the other hand, critics of the hedonic approach, like Aristotle before them, view the pursuit of hedonic happiness as potentially superficial, less meaningful or growth oriented, and even, in some cases, counterproductive.[8] Indeed, while pleasurable activities might bring us short-term happiness, they might not always be good for our longer-term well-being or congruent with our true self or important values. In any case, the two types of well-being tend to co-occur in the same individuals. That is, people who report higher hedonic well-being also tend to report higher eudaimonic well-being and vice-versa.[9]

In the Christian tradition, the concept of well-being, flourishing, or the good life also incorporates such elements as the quality of one's relationship with God, the presence of God's grace, spiritual growth, and a virtuous life that ends in personal salvation.[10] Indeed, epidemiologist Tyler VanderWeele distinguishes *spiritual* and *temporal well-being*. Spiritual well-being refers to "a state in which all aspects of a person's life are good with respect to his or her final end in God." Temporal well-being incorporates the elements of hedonic and eudaimonic well-being described above.[11] For the religious or spiritual person, spiritual well-being addresses an additional element or source of overall well-being. However, spiritual well-being like-

285

ly contributes to, and should be largely reflected in, religious respondents' evaluations of their overall hedonic and eudaimonic well-being.

In the rest of this chapter, I address what psychologists have learned about the two general types of well-being, beginning with hedonic or subjective well-being. *I then consider the implications of this evidence for the viability of the secular humanist life stance.*

HEDONIC OR SUBJECTIVE WELL-BEING

Are Most People Happy?

If most people are reasonably happy, particularly in relatively secular societies, it would suggest that secular humanism is not typically an unhappy or impoverished life stance. Until recently, surveys suggested that most people around the world report being mildly to moderately happy overall and more satisfied than dissatisfied with their lives.[12]

However, an analysis of Gallup World Poll data for 2005 to 2015 involving 166 countries painted a more mixed picture.[13] On the one hand, researchers found that 74% of respondents worldwide reported more positive than negative feelings during the past day. On the other hand, life satisfaction ratings were less positive. Slightly less than half (47%) of respondents worldwide rated their life satisfaction in the positive direction (i.e., above the neutral point). In the happiest nations, 67% of people did so, while in the least happy nations, only 33% did so. Results were worse for respondents who had experienced certain adverse events during the past year and worse still if they also reported a lack of social support and feelings of not being respected. Among these least fortunate people, only 20% reported more positive than negative feelings and only 12% reported life satisfaction in the positive direction. Such results reveal—not surprisingly—that not everyone is happy or satisfied with their lives, particularly people who are subject to adverse living conditions.[14]

Can Our Levels of Happiness or Subjective Well-being Change?

Yes. On the one hand, a number of psychologists have argued that individuals experience a characteristic and relatively stable level of subjective well-being (SWB) and will typically return to this level over time as they adapt to various positive and negative events.[15] This expectation is typically attributed to two things. First, people have relatively stable personality traits, due in part to personality's partial genetic basis (i.e., heritability). Second, personality traits have a significant impact on our levels of happiness or subjective well-being. Indeed, both personality traits and levels of SWB are moderately heritable and personality traits are good predictors of SWB. In particular, people who are more extraverted and less neurotic tend to report greater subjective feelings of well-being.[16]

On the other hand, the moderate heritability of personality and SWB still leaves much room for life circumstances to impact SWB. Findings that link lower SWB to adverse living conditions demonstrate that life events and circumstances do affect well-being.[17] In addition, although research reveals that we adapt to some extent over time to both positive and negative life events, the impact on SWB of some major life events, such as disability, unemployment, and bereavement, can persist.[18] Yet another indication that SWB is malleable, at least in the short term, comes from findings in which various activities such as meditation, expressing gratitude in one's daily life, or writing about one's positive experiences have increased SWB for up to at least six months.[19] More intensive programs of psychological therapy can have longer-term effects.[20]

In short, despite the influence of heritable personality dispositions on our feelings of well-being, the SWB of both individuals and societies can change over time.

What Factors or Experiences Contribute to Subjective Well-being?

Virtually all of the factors or experiences that contribute to subjective well-being are available to both religious and fully secular individuals. Indeed, one of the most important determinants of happiness or subjective well-being is social relationships—having close relationships with friends, family members, or colleagues at work, church, or in the community. For example, surveys indicate that married people report, on average, greater SWB than those who are divorced, separated, or never married.[21]

Also important is satisfaction of important needs, commitment to valued goals, and perceived progress on goals.[22] However, not all needs and goals contribute equally to SWB. SWB is enhanced most by goals that are intrinsic rather than extrinsic, consistent with one's motives and needs, realistic, valued in one's culture, and not in conflict with other personal goals. Not surprisingly, participation in leisure activities is another antecedent of SWB. However, the diversity of one's leisure activities apparently has more impact on SWB than the mere amount of time spent in leisure, perhaps because different activities satisfy different needs.[23]

Does personal income or wealth contribute to SWB? The relationship between wealth and SWB has typically been interpreted as small to medium in size, although the relationship is stronger in poor countries. This has led some psychologists to conclude that once a person is reasonably comfortable financially and able to meet basic needs, additional wealth has only a modest effect on happiness or SWB.[24] However, an analysis of two large data sets, including World Value Survey data, showed that the modest relationship between personal income and SWB can translate into large average differences in the SWB of rich versus poor people, and even meaningful differences in SWB between the rich and those of average wealth.[25]

Some caveats should be noted, however. Over-pursuit of wealth and material goods can have detrimental effects on eudaimonic well-being by diverting effort away from more intrinsic or meaningful goals. In addition,

288

perceptions of one's relative wealth compared to others may be more important than one's absolute level of income. Also, allocation of one's discretionary resources to positive life experiences appears to contribute more to SWB than allocation of such resources to material goods.[26]

Lauren Kuykendall and colleagues provided a useful summary of the factors that can impact individuals' SWB. They summarized the results of 20 meta-analyses in which SWB was predicted from factors in various life domains, including work (e.g., occupational status, job satisfaction), health (e.g., self-rated health, number of health problems), finances (e.g., income), family and social relations (e.g., marital status, quality and quantity of social relations), and self (e.g., core self-evaluations, competence). The average effects of the factors in these domains on SWB were generally fairly strong.[27] Greater education is an additional predictor of SWB, although perhaps less so for minorities, due to racism and discrimination. Age also predicts SWB, with the lowest average levels of happiness in middle age, increasing again in one's 50s and 60s, but decreasing again after 75.[28]

But it is not just objective circumstances or events that can impact SWB. Happy and unhappy people also tend to differ in how they interpret events. For example, happier people tend to interpret current circumstances and future events in optimistic or positive ways. They perceive more control over life's outcomes. They have confidence in their abilities. And, they derive meaning from negative experiences rather than ruminating about them.[29]

Aspects of society as a whole also impact SWB or happiness. Countries with higher average happiness or SWB tend to have the following characteristics:

- Higher levels of economic development and wealth, and less income inequality;
- Governments that are effective, low in corruption, strong in the rule of law, and supportive of human rights and political freedoms;

- More generous income security, unemployment policies, health care coverage, and progressive taxation;
- Healthy and sustainable natural environments, including clean air and green space.[30]

Not surprisingly, then, when we examine the happiness of various countries based on average survey ratings, the ten most happy countries typically include the Nordic nations and other wealthy Western countries.[31]

In sum, research reveals that the SWB or happiness of both individuals and countries is subject to a variety of individual and societal factors.[32] Such findings provide a guide to how people can achieve subjective well-being, *with or without religion.*

What are the Consequences of Subjective Well-being?

It is typical to view happiness or SWB as an *outcome* of the factors just discussed. At the same time, there is considerable evidence that SWB, particularly the experience of positive emotions, can in turn have positive *effects* on a host of important outcomes.[33]

For example, a number of research reviews have concluded that people who frequently experience more positive affect subsequently exhibit a variety of indications of good physical health, as well as greater average life spans.[34]

The size of the impact of SWB on health and longevity is not trivial. For example, one review concluded that in economically developed nations a generally happy person might live 4-10 years longer than a generally unhappy person.[35] In a representative sample of American adults, people who described themselves as "very happy" were 6% less likely to die during a multiyear follow-up period than "pretty happy" people, and 14% less likely to die than "unhappy" people, even after controlling for demographic, socioeconomic, and lifestyle-related factors.[36]

Why might positive emotions impact health outcomes? Because positive emotions can lead to healthy behaviors such as exercise, participation in social activities and other restorative activities, better sleep quality, less smoking or alcohol abuse, stronger immune and cardiovascular systems, and lower levels of stress hormones.[37]

Beyond health outcomes, the experience of more frequent positive emotions is also linked to a variety of positive outcomes in the work and relationship domains. In the work domain, these outcomes include higher job satisfaction, higher incomes, lower unemployment, more positive evaluations by supervisors, and better organizational citizenship. In the relationship domain, these outcomes have included greater marital satisfaction, lower rates of divorce, greater satisfaction with friends, and perceptions of better support from friends and neighbors.[38]

American psychologist Barbara Fredrickson drew on such findings in proposing a *broaden-and-build theory*. The theory proposes that the experience of positive emotions momentarily broadens our scope of awareness and action-thought tendencies, leading us to accrue over time new cognitive, psychological, social, and physical resources. In turn, these resources set us up to experience *further* positive emotions, resulting in a dynamic spiral of increasing resource development and positive emotionality.[39] Recently, the theory has been extended to describe how religious and spiritual practices such as meditation, prayer, and collective worship provide opportunities to experience positive emotions, which in turn motivate continued adherence to these practices.[40]

Research support for broaden-and-build theory is fairly extensive.[41] As the researchers in one study concluded, "people judge their lives to be more satisfying and fulfilling, not because they feel more positive emotions per se, but because their greater positive emotions help them build resources for living successfully."[42]

Summing Up

Why are the findings presented so far important? First, they show that people around the world—whether religious or not—commonly experience mild to moderate levels of hedonic or subjective well-being, at least in the absence of significant personal or societal adversity. Second, they show that SWB can be changed and we have a good understanding of the factors and experiences that contribute to it. Again, these factors and experiences are potentially available to both religious and nonreligious people. Third, the findings show that hedonic well-being is not just about experiencing short-term happiness or pleasure. When positive emotions are experienced reliably over time, this can build personal resources that are also important for eudaimonic living and well-being—that is, a life of meaning, purpose, and fulfillment.

In short, psychological science shows that most people, *including secular humanists*, can experience happiness and life satisfaction, and provides guidance on how to do so.

EUDAIMONIC LIVING AND WELL-BEING

In the view of many psychologists and philosophers, a life of meaning, purpose, and authenticity is more important than mere happiness or positive emotions. That is, eudaimonic well-being is more important than hedonic or subjective well-being.

For my purposes here, the most relevant questions are the following: What constitutes eudaimonic living and well-being? Is eudaimonic well-being typically achieved? If so, what are its consequences? The pursuit of eudaimonic living and well-being is sensible for both religious individuals and secular humanists. However, the answers to these questions may be particularly salient for secular humanists and others who seek meaning, purpose, and fulfillment without religion.

Regarding what constitutes eudaimonic living, I start with the contributions of humanistic psychologists. Since the 1950s and 1960s, human-

292

istic psychologists have elaborated on what it takes for people to live authentic, fully human lives. Their rich ideas regarding human potential and fulfillment foreshadowed many of the conceptions of eudaimonic living and well-being investigated by psychologists today.

Contributions of Humanistic Psychology

Humanistic psychologists emphasize the following in their conception of an authentic, fully human life:

- Personal growth and self-actualization through the expression of one's inherent capabilities and potential;
- Autonomy and personal responsibility, and the inevitable need to make free choices;
- Self-awareness and authentic self-expression;
- Emotional expressiveness, empathy, and love;
- Values of mutual respect, integrity, and diversity;
- The need to discover one's own sense of meaning;
- Concerns for social welfare and an activist approach to improving the human condition;
- A counter-cultural and democratic perspective towards both society (e.g., anti-materialism; aversion to bureaucratic institutions) and science (e.g., pointing to the limits of science and technology).

Humanistic psychology is a holistic approach that seeks to integrate the whole person, including physical, mental, emotional, and spiritual aspects.[43]

The most prominent humanistic psychologists were Carl Rogers and Abraham Maslow. Rogers described the *fully functioning person* based on the characteristics of people who benefited most from person-centered therapy. For these individuals, the good life is a process rather than a state of being. It involves increasing openness to experience rather than defensiveness; the ability to live in the moment and adapt to the flow of experi-

293

ence (i.e., existential living); and increasing trust in one's organism as a basis for deciding the most satisfying behaviors—that is, doing what "feels right." As a result of these characteristics, Rogers argued, the fully functioning person is able to experience a greater sense of freedom; live creatively; behave in an authentic, constructive, and trustworthy manner; and fulfill his or her potentialities.[44]

Similarly, Abraham Maslow contended that all people have an inner core or nature that is good or neutral and that presses for actualization or expression. Maslow drew on case studies of extraordinary individuals— including historical figures such as Albert Einstein, Henry David Thoreau, and Eleanor Roosevelt—to describe characteristics of the rare individuals who, in his view, were self-actualized or "fully human." Among these characteristics were superior perceptions of reality; acceptance of self and others; autonomy and self-reliance; resistance to enculturation or dependency on others; motivation by growth rather than defensiveness; detachment and appreciation of privacy; spontaneity and expressiveness; creativity; a problem-solving focus; tolerance of ambiguity and the unknown; and a democratic value structure.[45]

Maslow also introduced the concept of *peak experiences*, which encompass not only the mystical or spiritual experiences traditionally associated with religion, but also the more naturalistic experiences of awe and wonder that even nonreligious people can experience. Maslow argued, however, that many reports of religious or mystical revelations probably represent naturalistic experiences that can be readily examined by science.[46]

Importantly, most of the characteristics associated with the self-actualized or "fully human" person by humanistic psychologists are compatible with the secular humanistic life stance described in this book. Thus, these characteristics can provide a useful guide to a fulfilling life as a secular humanist.

However, secular humanism can be sharply contrasted with humanistic psychology in two ways. First, secular humanism rejects supernatural elements and is skeptical of purported "transpersonal" aspects of life such as the paranormal, higher forms of consciousness, or energy transfer among individuals. In contrast, spiritual and transpersonal elements have flourished in humanistic (and especially transpersonal) psychology, despite humanistic psychology's general antagonism towards conventional religion. Second, secular humanists are typically strong advocates of science and its methods of inquiry. In contrast, humanistic psychologists frequently point to the limitations of science, particularly its emphasis on experiments, quantification, and statistics.

Some scholars have criticized humanistic psychology, for example, by questioning its scientific rigor, overreliance on qualitative research methods, and uncritical rejection of experimental and quantitative methods.[47] Fortunately, these criticisms need not overly concern us here, because many of the ideas and concepts of humanistic psychologists have been adopted and tested rigorously by mainstream and positive psychologists. Indeed, some psychologists have drawn on humanistic perspectives to delineate the various aspects or dimensions of eudaimonic well-being that all of us can seek to attain, whether religious or not.

Dimensions of Eudaimonic Well-being or "Flourishing"?

Positive psychologists have assessed a number of different aspects or dimensions of eudaimonic well-being, which can serve as a guide to how they define it. They most consistently mention having positive relationships, meaning or purpose in life, and a feeling of mastery or competence. Some also refer to the importance of self-acceptance or self-esteem; active engagement; autonomy or control; and optimism. Also mentioned, but less consistently, are aspects that refer to vitality, empathy, resilience, and social well-being.[48]

Some psychologists have used people's scores on these dimensions or aspects of eudaimonic well-being to classify individuals as flourishing, moderately mentally healthy, or languishing. People classified as flourishing are thought to exhibit especially positive or optimal mental health. People classified as languishing are assessed to have poor mental health. In the middle are people classified as moderately mentally healthy.[49] I think there are limits to what research along these lines can tell us for two reasons. First, the classification procedures are somewhat subjective. Second, the criteria or scores used appear to set a rather high bar for flourishing, while excluding significant numbers of people who are at least "moderately" healthy psychologically. Nonetheless, the studies provide some comparative information on levels of eudaimonic well-being or flourishing in various cultures. Here are some examples:

- In studies of American adults, about 17-20% have been classified as flourishing, 55-65% as moderately mentally healthy, and 12-16% as languishing.[50]

- In a national sample of American college students, 51.8% were classified as flourishing, 44.6% as moderately mentally healthy, and 3.6% as languishing.

- In a sample of Christian clergy in the United States, a much higher percentage (70%) were classified as flourishing, which the researchers attributed to the fact that most clergy view their career as a calling.[51]

- In a study involving 23 European countries, only 15.8% of the total sample was classified as flourishing. However, percentages ranged from 40.6% in Denmark, 30.2% in Switzerland, and 27.6% in Austria, to about 9% each in Slovakia, Russia, and Portugal.

- In New Zealand adults, the percentages of adults identified as flourishing depended on which researchers' dimensions and classification criteria were used, but ranged from 24% to 47%.[52]

Overall, then, the percentages of ordinary adults classified as flourishing in different countries has varied substantially, ranging from about 8% to 50%.

If we take these findings at face value, they suggest that only a minority of typical adults in various countries experience the optimal levels of eudaimonic well-being that researchers describe as flourishing. However, more educated adults such as college students and clergy are more likely to be so classified. Indeed, among the more consistent demographic findings in these studies is that "flourishing" individuals are more likely to be married, not living alone, and have higher levels of education. This suggests that the availability of social support and economic resources are important in one's ability to "flourish."[53]

Unfortunately, I could not identify any studies that examined whether religious people in general are more likely to "flourish" than fully secular people. The "flourishing" clergy investigated in one study is a rather select group and may not be typical of religious people in general.

Importantly, however, there is growing evidence that higher scores on these aspects of eudaimonic well-being are, in fact, associated with a variety of positive health, productivity, mortality, and relationship outcomes.[54] The people classified as moderately mentally healthy have shown somewhat reduced positive outcomes compared to flourishing individuals, but much better outcomes than people classified as languishing.

In addition to these studies, many psychologists have investigated specific goals, motives, emotions, sources of meaning, or character strengths thought to contribute to eudaimonic living and well-being. I describe these efforts in the following sections. Again, keep in mind that these sources of eudaimonic well-being are potentially available to both religious and non-religious individuals.

What Goals or Motives are Associated with Eudaimonic Living?

Goal attainment in itself can contribute to well-being. However, psychologists have found that well-being is best achieved when we pursue goals that are *intrinsic* or *self-concordant*—that is, goals that are ends in themselves, fulfill basic needs, and express our deeply held interests, values, or dispositions.[55] For example, such goals might include personal growth, self-acceptance, close interpersonal relationships, contributions to one's community, and physical health. In contrast, *extrinsic* goals, which are less likely to lead to eudaimonic well-being, are motivated by external factors or pressures such as achieving recognition and wealth, maintaining status or the approval of others, and avoiding punishment, guilt, or anxiety. Extrinsic goals may be motivated by defensiveness or needs for security.[56]

According to psychologists, intrinsic goals lead to better well-being and vitality because they satisfy three basic, universal needs: autonomy—the person's sense of choice and volition in regulating behavior; competence—a sense of efficacy or effectiveness in one's environment; and relatedness—feeling connected to and cared about by others.[57] That is, we are more likely to feel authentic and fulfilled when we are able to freely choose our goals, and when pursuit of these goals leads to feelings of competence and connectedness to others.

Of course, the selection of intrinsic goals requires that we have accurate awareness of our true feelings, interests, and values. Thus, *mindfulness* is also important. Mindfulness involves being attentive to the present moment, to our inner experiences and feelings, and to both internal and external events.

A great deal of research has supported these ideas. For example, studies show that:

- When we pursue intrinsic or self-concordant goals—or participate in activities that express "who we really are"—we are more likely to satisfy our needs for autonomy; attain and persist in our goals; experience feelings of vitality, creativity, and subjective well-being; feel better about ourselves; achieve better quality relationships; and attain various positive educational and work outcomes;[58]
- When we perceive that our needs for autonomy, competence, and relatedness are being satisfied, we are more likely to experience both hedonic and eudaimonic well-being;[59]
- When we are more mindful, we are more likely to experience greater hedonic and eudaimonic well-being, lower levels of depression and anxiety, more rapid recovery from emotional upsets, and greater openness and reduced defensiveness in relationships;[60]

- Mindfulness meditation and training increases positive affect, reduces anxiety and depression, and improves physical health.[61]

In addition, when we pursue intrinsically motivated activities, we can also experience what Mihaly Csikszentmihalyi has called *flow*. In the state of flow, we experience complete absorption or engagement in the activity. We lose track of time. We feel in control. And we feel that the activity is intrinsically rewarding or an end in itself. According to Csikszentmihalyi, we are more likely to experience flow when we take on challenging tasks, yet have the necessary skills to meet the challenge. When we experience flow, we are more likely to persist in the activity and further master the associated skills.

Not surprisingly, then, frequent experience of flow in relevant activities has been linked to greater academic commitment and achievement, satisfaction with work, perceived competence, self-esteem, and life satisfaction. Although anyone can experience flow, some of us are more prone to do so. For example, based on interview studies, Csikszentmihalyi reported that about 87% of Americans report having experienced flow.[62]

Generativity is another motive or goal that contributes to eudaimonic living or a life well lived. Psychologists Dan McAdams and Ed de St. Aubin described highly generative individuals as concerned for the well-being of the next generation. They desire to pass on knowledge and skills to others through parenting, teaching, and mentoring. They aim to make significant contributions to improve their community and society. And they seek to create or do things that have a lasting impact or legacy.[63] People with greater generativity tend to experience a variety of positive psychosocial outcomes including more extensive social support networks; higher levels of civic engagement and volunteerism; greater environmental concern and action; and greater hedonic and eudaimonic well-being.[64]

In short, psychologists have identified a number of goals or motives that can promote eudaimonic living and well-being for both religious and nonreligious individuals. For most people, including secular humanists, a more fulfilling life can be attained by pursuing intrinsic or self-concordant goals, practicing mindfulness, engaging in activities than elicit flow, and contributing in a generative manner to their community, society, and future generations.

Authenticity and Well-being

Another central component of eudaimonic living is authenticity. Indeed, authenticity, or acting in accordance with one's "true self," has long been viewed by philosophers and humanistic psychologists as central to a life well lived.[65] Although various psychologists approach the concept differently,

> ...at its heart, authenticity involves the degree to which people behave in ways that are congruent with "how they really are," that is, congruently with their personal characteristics, attitudes, beliefs, values, and motives.[66]

We are more likely to feel authentic when we pursue intrinsic goals and in environments that support our needs for autonomy. Authentic behaviors feel "self-authored" and genuine. In contrast, we experience inauthenticity when our behavior feels forced or imposed—for example, by social norms, societal demands, or pressure from others—or when we are deceptive, phony, or defensive.[67]

Some psychologists acknowledge that the concept of true self is "fuzzy" and "elusive," with limited consensus on how best to measure it. Indeed, we can ask whether there is such a thing as a true self, and, if so, whether people are actually capable of knowing it. If not, then it will be difficult for us to accurately judge the authenticity of our behavior. Our self-knowledge is likely partial and biased and we are rarely fully conscious of the motives behind our behavior.[68] Thus, we may not have an *objective* true self that can be accurately assessed or discovered. However, our *subjective* sense of authenticity may have significant implications for our well-being because it serves as a cue to whether we are living a good and culturally valued life.

To assess subjective authenticity, psychologists would typically ask you to rate how well you are described by statements such as the following: "I am true to myself in most situations;" or "I think it is better to be yourself than to be popular."[69] Studies have shown that people who report greater subjective authenticity also tend to report experiencing a variety of outcomes associated with positive hedonic and eudaimonic well-being.[70] Some studies indicate that these outcomes of authenticity hold across diverse cultures.[71] Thus, for both religious people and secular humanists, striving for authenticity provides another element in living a fulfilled life.

Self-Transcendent Emotions and Well-being

Another aspect of eudaimonic living or a life well lived is the experience of *self-transcendent emotions*. Psychologist Patty Van Cappellen defined self-transcendent emotions as uplifting positive emotions that transcend the self by reducing self-focus and increasing feelings of connectedness with others, the world, and—in a religious context—a Higher Power. Such emotions are thought to promote prosocial behavior.[72] Although there is no consensus list of such emotions, Van Cappellen includes admiration, elevation, gratitude, awe, love, compassion, and peacefulness. Not all of these emotions have been investigated extensively. While several of them can be found at the heart of religious traditions, they can also arise in secular contexts.

Admiration, elevation, and gratitude have been referred to as other-praising emotions. *Admiration* describes our emotional response to viewing extraordinary displays of skill or achievement—for example, the remarkable musical talent of cellist Yo-yo Ma. When we experience admiration of others, it can energize us to work harder on our own goals or talents.

Elevation describes our emotional response to witnessing virtuous or moral behavior—for example, acts of charity or extraordinary service. When we experience this emotion, it can motivate our own altruistic behavior, sense of purpose, and desire to be a better person.[73]

Among the most extensively researched self-transcendent emotions is *gratitude*. Gratitude refers to the emotion we experience in response to the helpful actions or gifts we receive from others.[74] Gratitude can also refer to a more general disposition or "life orientation towards noticing and appreciating the positive in life."[75] The tendency to experience gratitude has been associated with a host of positive outcomes, including greater hedonic and eudaimonic well-being, prosociality and social adjustment, authenticity, goal progress and satisfaction, and various favorable academic and work outcomes.[76]

The self-transcendent emotion of *awe* is of particular interest given the contention of secular humanists that experiences of awe or wonder are not limited to religious people. First-hand accounts of awe experiences often describe them as including several aspects. First, when we experience awe, we encounter feelings of wonder and amazement (and in some cases confusion or surprise) that are brought about by exposure to events or stimuli that are vast or powerful and outside our typical experience or frames of reference. Second, we experience a sense of smallness in the presence of something greater than ourselves. Third, we undergo an "accommodation" process in which our mental schemas or structures are adjusted in order to assimilate or make sense of the experience.[77]

Within a religious or spiritual framework, feelings of awe are associated with perceived encounters with the supernatural and other mystical experiences.[78] In a secular context, such experiences are reported in response to vast natural phenomena such as panoramic views of mountains and oceans; impressive objects in the built environment such as skyscrapers and cathedrals; inspiring music and art; grand scientific discoveries, theories, or epiphanies; and other extraordinary human accomplishments and events such as child-birth or exceptional athletic abilities. At least in ancient times, awe in the perceived presence of gods and powerful authorities would have involved reverence, submission, and fear. However, in modern secular settings, awe has generally been described as having a positive tone.[79]

Do all people—whether religious or fully secular—experience a sense of awe, at least on occasion? Apparently, yes. When people are asked to recall and write about a previous awe-eliciting experience, they have no difficulty doing so.[80] Even in a sample of confirmed American atheists, when asked, "Have you ever felt wonderment or felt as if you were part of something greater than yourself?" 71% said yes. Feelings of wonderment were most often elicited by nature (54%), with science the next most common source (29%), followed by music and art (12%).[81]

Psychological research has related the experience of awe to a range of generally positive psychosocial outcomes. For example, several studies have confirmed that experiences of awe cause people, at least momentarily, to feel smaller and less significant in the grand scheme of things. They also feel less self-entitled, part of something greater than themself, and less focused on personal day-to-day concerns. This reduced emphasis on self-oriented concerns turns our attention to other-oriented concerns and hence greater prosocial behavior.[82] Indeed, research has linked the induction of awe-eliciting experiences to greater feelings of connection to others, greater generosity and helping behavior, more ethical decision-making, and greater willingness to volunteer time for a worthy cause.[83]

Cognitive outcomes of awe experiences have also been observed, including increased tolerance for ambiguity, an expanded time perspective, and momentary judgments of greater life satisfaction.[84] Awe-eliciting experiences may also induce greater preference for experiential activities over material goods.[85] At least among religious people, awe-inducing interventions can strengthen their beliefs in God, supernatural control, and purposeful design.[86]

In sum, most if not all people—whether religious or fully secular—report experiences of awe, which, in turn, can promote a variety of positive cognitive and prosocial outcomes. Thus, exposure to awe-inducing experiences is another way for both religious people and secular humanists to achieve greater eudaimonic well-being and a host of positive psychosocial and cognitive outcomes.

Meaning in Life as an Essential Component of Eudaimonic Well-being

Perhaps most essential for eudaimonic well-being or a life well lived is having a sense of meaning or purpose. In the previous chapter I noted a multitude of secular sources of meaning or "ways to live" that have been advocated over time by artists, writers, philosophers, scientists, and proponents of secular humanism. Psychologists have investigated how people attain meaning or purpose in life more systematically and empirically. Here I ask three questions. What do we mean by "meaning in life?" Do most people experience meaning in their lives? What contributes to our sense of meaning in life? In addressing these questions, I am mindful of any implications for secular living or a life without religion.

What do we mean *by "meaning in life?"*

Following in the footsteps of Austrian psychiatrist and Holocaust survivor Victor Frankl, many psychologists have argued that we all have an inherent motive or need to seek meaning.[87] We experience meaning in our lives when we feel our lives have *purpose, coherence*, and *significance*. That is, we have goals and direction in our lives (i.e., purpose). We experience our lives and the world as having some predictability, regularity, and order (i.e., coherence). And we believe that our lives have importance or value (i.e., significance).[88]

There are two general perspectives or approaches in the psychological study of meaning. One approach has focused on how we make sense of, or find meaning in, highly stressful or traumatic events. For example, how might we make sense of, or finding meaning in, being diagnosed with cancer. Being able to find such meaning can serve as a "buffer" against these negative events, and help us cope with them. In some cases, it can even lead to greater personal resilience or what is referred to as post-traumatic growth.[89] Indeed, although the evidence is not entirely consistent, research suggests that the vast majority of us attempt to make sense of stressful life events and when we are able to do so—for example, through acceptance, reappraising the events, or modifying our general beliefs or goals—we can achieve increased levels of adjustment or well-being.[90]

Other scholars—particularly positive psychologists—have adopted an alternative perspective or approach in the study of meaning. They focus on how a sense of meaning and purpose in life can promote happiness, optimal functioning, or flourishing in general, while generally downplaying the negative or traumatic aspects of human existence. In this approach, your perceived sense of meaning in life would be assessed by asking you to rate your level of agreement with statements such as "I have a good sense of what makes my life meaningful," "I have a sense of direction and purpose in life," and "What I do matters to society."[91]

The two approaches can be seen as complementary rather than conflicting, and some psychologists have attempted to integrate them.[92]

Do most people experience meaning in their lives?

Yes, they do. This is probably not surprising since most of us experience the typical contributors to meaning in life—for example, supportive social relationships, intrinsic goals, and positive emotions. Indeed, psychologists Samantha Heintzelman and Laura King, in an article titled "Life is pretty meaningful," reviewed several large-scale surveys of Americans and found that most people agreed or strongly agreed that their lives are meaningful. Relatively few people described their lives as lacking meaning. For example, in a national survey of Americans over 50, 95% responded "yes" when asked whether they felt that their life had meaning over the past 12 months.[93]

Similarly, in an international survey of respondents in 132 countries, 91% answered "yes" to the question "Do you feel your life has an important purpose or meaning?"[94] Even in an interview study of 518 American atheists, sociologist Jerome Baggett reported that 80% of his interviewees agreed that their lives have "real purpose."[95]

Results such as these reveal that the vast majority of both religious and nonreligious people report experiencing a sense of meaning or purpose in life. This provides strong evidence against the claim that the secular life is impoverished or lacking in meaning or purpose.

What contributes to a sense of meaning in life?

Major religions address each of the components of meaning noted above. A sense of *purpose* is achieved by living a good or moral life in accordance with one's religion, and seeking salvation. Religions offer a sense of *coherence* by providing a ready-made worldview and belief system through which one can interpret one's life and the world. Finally, religions address *significance* by placing us within a larger cosmic context. God loves us and we are made in His image.[96] Indeed, in Chapter 4, I noted that in many studies, people who report greater religiosity tend to report a greater sense of meaning or purpose in their lives. In turn, this can contribute to greater overall psychological well-being.[97] In addition, the higher average meaning in life reported in poorer countries can be partially explained by the greater average religiosity of people in those countries.[98]

But what about people who are not religious? For both religious and nonreligious people, psychologists have found evidence for alternative sources of meaning in life. For example, the pursuit of intrinsic or autonomous goals and activities, generativity, authenticity, and certain character strengths have all been linked to a greater sense of meaning in life. In addition, when people are asked to describe what gives their lives meaning, among the most frequently mentioned is interpersonal relationships, particularly with family and friends.[99] Indeed, research has linked greater meaning in life to greater satisfaction of needs for relatedness, sense of belonging, and quality of social relationships. Conversely, feelings of loneliness and social exclusion are associated with lower perceived meaning in life.[100]

Another strong predictor of perceived meaning in life is positive emotions. Research has linked the experience of positive emotions to global feelings of meaning in life. In addition, daily reports of meaning in life are strongly related to how much positive affect is experienced that day.[101] In short, "When we are in a good mood, then life feels more meaningful."[102] Indeed, there is some evidence that high levels of positive affect can compensate for lack of religiosity, feelings of loneliness, and lower income in facilitating a sense of meaning in life.[103]

Finally, psychologists have investigated whether viewing one's work as a *calling* promotes a sense of meaning in life. The concept of a calling was originally presented in the context of religious vocations, with God calling one to serve. Protestant theologians John Calvin and Martin Luther subsequently extended the idea of calling to include any productive or "honest" work that serves society and God. In psychological science today, the concept of calling is typically interpreted in a more secular manner to include work that is personally meaningful, intrinsically motivating and engaging, and that contributes in some way to society or the greater good. Having a calling can be contrasted with having a "job," which may merely provide a paycheck, or having a "career," with its emphasis on ongoing personal advancement.[104] Researchers typically assess whether we have a calling by asking us to rate our agreement with statements such as "I have a calling to a particular kind of work," "My work is one of the most important things in my life," and "My work makes the world a better place."[105]

Depending on how people are asked, at least one-third and perhaps as high as one-half of Americans report that they have a calling.[106] And the outcomes of having a calling are generally positive. For example, university students who perceive themselves as having a calling report greater academic satisfaction, clarity and comfort with their vocational choice, optimism about career outcomes, and sense of meaning in life. Adults who describe their work as a calling report greater career and organizational commitment, work engagement and meaningfulness, perceived fit of their work with their preferences, and job and life satisfaction. Not surprisingly, there is some evidence that these positive outcomes are even more likely for peo-

307

ple who have the resources and opportunity to actually live out or implement their calling.[107]

More generally, regardless of the source of one's sense of meaning and purpose, those of us who report experiencing greater meaning in our lives also tend to report greater life satisfaction; less depression and suicide ideation; greater eudaimonic well-being; a more positive self-concept; and better health outcomes, among other positive outcomes. In the work domain, greater meaning in life is associated with better occupational adjustment. In the social domain, it is associated with reduced loneliness and higher ratings by others of social appeal.[108]

In summary, most of us—whether religious or fully secular—report experiencing a sense of meaning in our lives. While religion provides a ready-made sense of purpose, coherence, and significance, alternative sources of meaning and purpose are available for both religious and nonreligious individuals.

Are Certain Virtues and Character Strengths Associated with Well-being?

Recall that some conceptions of eudaimonic living include the pursuit of virtue, excellence, and the realization of one's talents and capabilities. Accordingly, psychologists have investigated numerous proposed *character strengths* and their implications for well-being. Most prominent among these efforts is Chris Peterson and Martin Seligman's Values in Action classification of 24 character strengths. They identified the 24 strengths by drawing on diverse religious and philosophical traditions, the scientific literature, lists of virtues offered by historical figures, and popular literature and media.

The strengths are organized conceptually under the following six *virtues*, with the associated character strengths in parentheses: Wisdom/knowledge (creativity, curiosity, open-mindedness, love of learning, perspective); Courage (authenticity, bravery, persistence, zest); Humanity (kindness, love, social intelligence); Justice (fairness, leadership, teamwork); Temperance (forgiveness, modesty, prudence, self-regulation); and Transcendence (appreciation of beauty and excellence, gratitude, hope, humor, spirituality).[109] When interviewed, people have typically been able to identify three to seven *signature strengths* that they possess and frequently exercise.[110] Readers may want to identify their own perceived strengths using this list.

Are these strengths applicable across different cultures? Indeed, cross-cultural research indicates that the meaningfulness and desirability of these strengths are acknowledged in such vastly different cultural groups as American university students; Kenyan Maasai, a traditional pastoralist group; and Inuit in Northern Greenland, who retain elements of a hunting lifestyle.[111] In addition, in 74 different countries, people's ratings of their perceived strengths were quite similar, although some cultural differences were also observed. On average in each country, the top five perceived strengths were honesty, fairness, kindness, judgment, and curiosity, in some order. The least endorsed strengths were also similar across countries and generally included self-regulation, modesty, prudence, spirituality, and zest. Spirituality, however, showed considerable variability within and across countries. For example, in Indonesia, Kenya, and Pakistan, spirituality was among the top five self-perceived strengths.[112]

Importantly, people who report various character strengths—for example, the tendency to be optimistic, grateful, and so forth—tend to report a variety of similar positive outcomes, typically including greater hedonic well-being, aspects of eudaimonic well-being, and various positive social, health, educational, and work outcomes. Among the most extensively researched strengths are gratitude, forgiveness, optimism, hope, and, more recently, patience and humility.[113] The character strengths as a group are more strongly associated with aspects of eudaimonic well-being than hedonic well-being. This supports the view that these strengths refer to important aspects in eudaimonic living.

Importantly, these findings demonstrate that—*for both religious and nonreligious individuals*—identifying and building on one's strengths provides another "ingredient" in achieving a sense of well-being.[114]

In this regard, it is noteworthy that many of the virtues and character strengths investigated by psychologists have long been promoted within religious contexts. Indeed, some psychologists have begun to trace how virtues such as patience, gratitude, love, hope, admiration, awe, kindness, forgiveness, humility, and wisdom are interpreted within Christian and other religious traditions, including by tracing their expression in sacred texts.[115] The following question is thus relevant: *Might certain virtues or strengths take on additional meaning or have greater impact in religious, as compared to secular, contexts—at least for religious individuals?*

For example, in the Christian tradition, the virtue of patience takes on additional references to suffering, redemption, and Christ's own submission to God.[116] The virtue of hope points toward a final fulfillment of the good, grounded in the life, death, and resurrection of Jesus.[117] Gratitude towards God is at the heart of religious faith, whereas secular conceptions of gratitude emphasize interpersonal aspects.[118] The concept of grace is foundational to Christianity, but it has been largely ignored by psychologists.[119] In addition, whereas positive psychologists have tended to investigate various virtues and character strengths in isolation, the virtue theory of Catholic theologian Thomas Aquinas sees practical wisdom and Christian love-friendship as integrating other virtues.[120]

More generally, positive psychologists tend to believe that virtues are developed through personal agency and willpower, with the goal of increasing individual and interpersonal success and well-being. In contrast, Christians may believe their virtues are gifts from God that are nurtured in religious communities and that facilitate love of God and others.[121] Differences such as these raise the possibility that the link between various virtues and well-being may differ for religious and nonreligious individuals, although there is presently little research on this possibility.

Several studies do show, however, that religion can contribute to, or amplify, selected virtues and emotions. For example, several studies have linked greater religiosity or frequency of prayer to self-reports of more frequent positive emotions and greater patience and gratitude.[122] In one study, *secular* forms of gratitude predicted hedonic well-being for *both* religious and nonreligious individuals, whereas *religious* gratitude contributed additional prediction of well-being only for religious individuals.[123]

Interestingly, the relationship between religiosity and the virtue of humility is inconsistent. One possible explanation is as follows: In more fundamentalist or conservative forms of religion, humility may take a different form, reflecting submission to authority structures and conformity to one's religious community, norms, and scriptures.[124] Indeed, increasing evidence indicates that people who have less humility regarding their religious beliefs and values tend to be less tolerant of, and more aggressive towards, members of other religious groups.[125]

Conversely, people with greater intellectual humility about their religion show greater tolerance of other religious groups and react less negatively to having their religious beliefs challenged. These people are more willing to acknowledge the limitations or fallibility of their religious perspective. They are more open to the possibility that others' religious views have some merit. And, they might even be open to changing their views if warranted.[126] In addition, while exposure to religious diversity can increase religious tolerance, this appears to be more the case for people who are already high in intellectual humility about their religion.[127]

In short, intellectual humility regarding one's religious or secular beliefs would appear to be important in promoting common ground and tolerance among people with different religious and secular perspectives. I will revisit this possibility in the Conclusion of this book.

To sum up: Some limitations or criticisms of the research on virtues and character strengths have been noted.[128] Nonetheless, the overall evidence points to the value of identifying and applying one's character strengths as yet another tool in the pursuit of well-being or a life well lived.

For religious individuals, some virtues and strengths may play out in a religious context, but they are also relevant in a variety of secular contexts.

WHAT PSYCHOSOCIAL INTERVENTIONS CAN INCREASE WELL-BEING?

For many religious and fully secular people, interventions to increase well-being may not be needed. They may already be attaining well-being by pursuing intrinsic or self-concordant goals, behaving authentically, experiencing close relationships and self-transcendent emotions, and applying their character strengths. For others, positive psychologists have devised and tested a variety of interventions or intentional activities that increase hedonic and eudaimonic well-being, at least in the short-term. Examples include (a) assisting individuals in identifying intrinsic goals and pathways to their achievement; (b) to increase gratitude, maintaining a daily diary of things one is grateful for; (c) to increase optimism, visualizing one's ideal future self; (d) to increase hope, writing about times that "one door closed" and "another door opened;" (e) to increase positive emotions, writing about one's positive experiences; (f) writing letters of forgiveness; (g) performing acts of kindness; (h) participating in mindfulness training or meditation; (i) savoring the present moment; and (j) helping people identify and cultivate their signature strengths. Activities such as these have also been incorporated into forms of individual therapy.[129]

A number of reviews indicate that, on average, such interventions and activities have small to moderate positive effects on hedonic and eudaimonic well-being in a variety of Western and non-Western countries and populations. Retention of beneficial effects for up to about 6 months has been demonstrated. Benefits tend to be larger, on average, when interventions or activities are longer in duration, of greater variety, when participants are highly motivated, and when the activities are a good fit to the participant's personality. For example, regarding personality-activity fit, extraverts may benefit more from gratitude visits, whereas introverts may prefer writing about things for which they are grateful.[130]

In sum, despite some limitations or concerns regarding these intervention studies,[131] growing evidence suggests that a variety of intentional activities are reasonably effective in increasing well-being, at least in the short term. People can thus select from these activities as appropriate in their everyday lives. And, of course, many of us—both religious and nonreligious—experience positive well-being through our normal routines without needing to purposefully draw on such activities or interventions.

TAKEAWAYS

The overarching question in this chapter was the following: What can the psychological science of well-being tell us about how to live a fulfilling and meaningful life—with or without religion. I do not present psychology as a kind of secular alternative to religion, as some critics have accused positive psychology of doing.[132] Rather, I draw on this research to make some inferences about the viability of the secular humanist life stance, while refuting claims that such a life stance is necessarily impoverished or unfulfilling.

Research on well-being shows us the following: Many, if not most, people—particularly in the absence of significant personal or societal adversity—report feeling mildly to moderately happy; are more satisfied than dissatisfied with their lives; experience a sense of meaning or purpose, and even a calling; and, at least on occasion, experience a sense of awe and wonder. Many of these people are secular humanists. Indeed, average well-being appears to be higher in relatively secular cultures. In addition, as noted in Chapter 9, there is growing evidence that nonbelievers who are confident and comfortable with their belief system experience levels of psychological and physical well-being comparable to religiously committed individuals.

In short, there is little evidence from psychological science for claims that the secular humanist life stance is necessarily, or even typically, an impoverished, flat, or empty one.

For those secular humanists (or anyone else) that experience lower levels of well-being, psychological research offers evidence on how to increase well-being. For individuals, this would include the following:

- Cultivating close and supportive relationships with others;
- Pursuing intrinsic goals;
- Engaging in activities that express one's authentic or true interests and values;
- Working for the betterment of one's community or the next generation;
- Seeking opportunities to experience positive emotions, including awe and gratitude, that reduce self-focus and increase connectedness to others and the world;
- Identifying and using one's talents or strengths;
- Seeking out vocational or avocational pursuits that one sees as a calling;
- Practicing certain intentional activities that increase feelings of well-being such as meditation, mindfulness practices, savoring the moment, and practicing gratitude or forgiveness in one's life.

Research indicates that such pursuits reliably promote hedonic and eudaimonic well-being, as well as a variety of physical health outcomes.

For religious people, certain emotions or strengths that enhance well-being such as gratitude, patience, hope, and love might be amplified and take on additional religious meaning or significance. For example, whereas secular humanists talk about experiencing self-transcendent emotions in a this-worldly context, Christians seek to experience "something unique and ineffable that is unpredictable and beyond our horizon."[133] In addition, religion provides a ready-made source of meaning, morality, and community. Nonetheless, the above secular paths to well-being are effective for people who find religion incompatible with their worldview or belief system. In addition, even if there is no ultimate or divine purpose for us in the universe—other than our evolution as a species—the scientific and

314

humanistic perspectives of secular humanists offer frameworks for understanding and interpreting the universe and our place in it.

Research also indicates that it may be better for secular humanists (and anyone else) to actively pursue eudaimonic outcomes such as self-actualization, intimate relationships, purpose in life, and personal growth—and experience happiness as a by-product of doing so—rather than focusing predominantly on the pursuit of happiness or hedonic well-being. By focusing on hedonic well-being and more extrinsic goals such as wealth, recognition, popularity, and power, people may be diverted from more meaningful eudaimonic outcomes. At the same time, secular humanists should not underestimate the benefit of positive emotions, an aspect of hedonic well-being. As outlined in broaden-and-build theory, frequent experience of positive emotions can broaden our awareness and action-tendencies. Over time, this helps us build psychosocial resources that are important for eudaimonic well-being and life satisfaction. Fortunately, we have learned that most of us do not need to choose between a happy life and a meaningful live, as hedonic and eudaimonic well-being tend to go together.

For secular humanists (and, again, anyone else) with fewer advantages and resources, interventions at the societal level can increase opportunities to fulfill basic and social needs and to pursue intrinsic and meaningful goals. Indeed, a number of societal interventions can promote these outcomes and higher average well-being. These include efforts to improve economic development; reduce income and health inequities; promote effective governments that support human rights, social justice, and political freedoms; and provide healthier natural environments. Although societal level change can be slow and challenging to achieve, secular humanists tend to favor such efforts. Indeed, dissatisfaction with specific aspects of society can motivate secular humanists to seek such changes.

Conclusion

In this Conclusion, I provide (a) a summary discussion of the plausible origins and persistence of religion, (b) a more complete pragmatic comparison of the relative merits and viability of religion and secular humanism from the perspective of the psychological and social sciences, and (c) some evidence–based proposals to improve individual and societal well-being, while reducing religious-secular conflict.

Perhaps faith is…an ability that comes easily and naturally to some people and comes only with great difficulty for other people.

— William Irwin[1]

Building a fully satisfying, fully secular world will take time, effort, and perhaps luck. But there is no strong evidence for supposing the task to be impossible.

— Philip Kitcher[2]

In the Introduction to this book, I noted the significant gap and cross-pressures between those who find their answers in religion and those who are indifferent or even hostile to it. On the one hand, several billion people around the world see religion as a divinely inspired source of comfort, meaning, belonging, and moral guidance. Some of these people reject scientific findings that call into question central religious tenets. On the other hand, increasing numbers of people see religion as human-made, infused with superstitious and irrational elements, and potentially divisive, intolerant, and violent. Many people in this latter group view science as the best way to understand the world and ourselves.

Given this gap between religious and secular belief systems, I sought in this book to address the following pragmatic question: *What can the psychological and social sciences tell us about the relative merits and viability of religion versus secular humanism?*

As I noted in the Introduction, such a pragmatic approach was advocated by American psychologist and philosopher William James—who argued that religion should be judged by its results—and by Dutch-American primatologist Frans de Waal, for whom the most relevant questions are "What good does religion do for us?" and "What might possibly take its place?"[3] Evolutionary scientists have also noted that in a contest between what is *true* or accurate about reality and what is biologically or culturally *adaptive* for survival and well-being, the latter is bound to win out in human evolution. That is, even if many religious beliefs provide false or illusory descriptions of the world, they may have contributed—and may continue to contribute—to the survival and well-being of individuals and societies.[4]

Previously, I noted some of the limitations of any scientific analysis. First, scientific findings are not always definitive or replicated. They frequently need to be qualified. And, they may evolve over time as better methods are developed and more refined questions are addressed. In my summary discussion here, I try to rely on the best supported or consensus findings.

Second, science cannot prove or disprove the existence of God or the truth or falsity of some religious claims. Nonetheless, for some readers, the findings of the psychological and social sciences may impact *perceptions* of the likely origins, functions, validity, utility, and persistence of religion, and the viability or even preferability of an alternative secular humanist life stance.

Third, the persuasiveness of my analysis is likely to depend to some extent on one's existing worldview or belief system—for example, one's religious commitments, openness to secular values, and attitudes towards science. That is, any comparison of the relative merits of religion and secular

317

humanism is likely to be seen through the lens of prior ideological commitments and values.

For people who are open to scientific perspectives and secular values, the overall findings reported here should be encouraging. They reveal that the secular humanist life stance, in comparison to religion, can be associated with comparable levels of well-being, meaning and purpose, and belonging and community, and—in comparison to some religious orientations—reduced levels of prejudice, intolerance, and violence. Even for people with various levels of religious faith and commitment, the findings may be of interest and stimulate reflection regarding the merits and viability of the religious and secular humanist life stances.

THE ORIGIN AND FUNCTIONS OF RELIGION: HUMAN-MADE OR DIVINELY INSPIRED?

One central question alluded to in the book is whether religion has a divine source or emerged naturalistically to meet the needs of individuals or groups via biological and cultural evolution. Naturalistic accounts of religion attempt to explain its origins and functions without recourse to supernatural phenomena. Neither science nor theology can answer the question of origins with certainty. However, many of the scientific findings reviewed in this book suggest—or, at a minimum, may persuade some readers—that religion is a naturalistic and human-made phenomenon that evolved to meet certain human needs. If so, this may impact personal perceptions of the cogency of religious versus secular belief systems.

Here are some of the findings I have in mind:

- The great diversity of religious forms across human history, including animism, shamanism, *mana*, ancestor worship, naturism, totemism, polytheism, monotheism;
- The apparent association of these religious forms with evolving cultural and ecological conditions;

318

- The diverse and somewhat contradictory beliefs and doctrines associated with current religions;
- Psychological findings that are consistent with the long-held views of philosophers and social scientists regarding the psychosocial origins and functions of religion and the human needs it satisfies;
- The plausible role of evolved cognitive and cultural learning mechanisms in the adoption of religion generally, as well as specific religious beliefs, affiliations, and practices;
- Scientific accounts of the origins of the universe (i.e., the Big Bang) and living things (i.e., evolutionary theory) that can be viewed as incompatible with religious Creation accounts.

For many people, the changing theological interpretation and status of various religious doctrines over time may also suggest that they are human-made, rather than divine, in origin or inspiration.[5]

Of course, theological or religious explanations of these findings can be offered. For example, God may have intentionally developed and tailored the diverse and evolving forms of religion to fit the developing capacities of humans in a process of divine accommodation. Alternatively, more "primitive" forms of religion could reflect "degeneration" from an original Supreme Being as a result of human error, sin, or a human preference for more permissive gods.[6] Also, the finding that religions function to meet certain psychological needs does not preclude a divine origin or basis for religion.

In addition, the diversity of major world religions, and their incompatible tenets, may be less problematic for the truth claims and viability of religion if we adopt the "pluralistic" position endorsed by some theologians. These theologians argue that all religions—while reflecting differences in the historical and cultural contexts in which they evolved—are human responses to the same divine or ultimate reality and equally valid paths to salvation.[7] Indeed, most Americans are pluralists in this sense, as only about one-fourth think that their religion is the one true faith leading to eternal life.[8] The pluralistic perspective may alleviate somewhat concerns about the differences between religions. However, it does not resolve the fact that different religions make conflicting claims and thus cannot all be correct in their specifics.[9]

Similarly, one can offer religious interpretations that attempt to reduce apparent conflicts between religious and scientific accounts of creation and evolution. For example, such conflicts can be resolved to some extent by interpreting religious creation stories as myths or metaphors rather than literal truths. (Still, as of 2014, 28% of Americans believed that the Bible is the actual word of God and should be interpreted literally.)[10] Alternatively, the origins of the universe and the evolution of all living things can be described as under God's direct or indirect guidance, as proposed by various *theistic evolution* accounts.[11]

In this book I have focused on psychological and social science perspectives, not theology, which is beyond the book's scope and my areas of expertise. However, the few examples just cited make clear that religious interpretations of the origin, evolution, and diversity of religions—as well as the creation of the universe and all living things—are available as alternatives to purely naturalistic and scientific accounts. People who view these questions through a religious lens may find the theological accounts more compelling. Nonetheless, I suspect that many readers, including some with varying levels of religious commitment, will find the naturalistic accounts of the origin and functions of religion presented in this book to be plausible and persuasive. And, of course, *these naturalistic accounts are quite compatible with an alternative secular humanist worldview.*

WILL RELIGION PERSIST?

Two important questions are relevant in any discussion of the viability of religion going forward. First, *will* religion persist forever, or at least well into the future? Second, *should* religion persist? That is, should we encourage either its persistence or demise? I address the first question in this section and postpone the second question until later in this Conclusion.

As noted previously, psychologists and social scientists that study religion are generally reticent to offer predictions regarding the fate of religion. However, the majority appears to view religion's eventual demise as unlikely. They offer a variety of reasons for thinking so, including the following: Most people like their religion. Religion meets important needs. Huge numbers of people in the world currently see life through a religious lens. Human brains may be hard-wired for the kinds of cognitive mechanisms and emotions that promote religion. Religion is a central component of socialization and identity in many cultures. Religious beliefs are important in galvanizing cooperation and group cohesion. And, it is difficult to see what could fill the void if religion disappeared.

Indeed, history has convincingly demonstrated that attempts to eliminate religion by force have eventually failed. This is illustrated most recently by the resurgence of religion in some former communist countries, which officially promoted atheism. Other scholars counter, however, that millions of Westerners have already abandoned religion without much difficulty.[12]

In Chapter 8, I offered my own predictions, given available evidence. I noted that secularization trends are likely to continue, at least in the near term and in more existentially secure societies. At the same time, given the higher fertility rates among more religious people, the overall percentage of religious people around the world is likely to increase, at least over the next several decades. Thus, at least in the near future, we are likely to see a continuing—and perhaps growing—gap between predominantly secular and religious societies and between religious and secular communities within some societies. I also noted, however, that long-term predictions are more precarious given the possibility of major disruptions or crises in the future that significantly decrease societal and personal security and thus increase the drawing power of religion.

In any case, it seems unlikely that religion will ever disappear entirely. The needs it fulfills and the functions it serves are likely to persist for many people. At the same time, it is unlikely that the world will ever be "re-enchanted" by ever-present spirits in those parts of the world that have experienced a "disenchantment of the world" over the past several centuries. Advances in science are likely to further reduce the credibility of some religious tenets, as the physiological basis of consciousness (aka the soul) and the origin and nature of the universe are further elaborated.[13] Secular humanism as an alternative belief system will likely be found persuasive by increasing numbers of people around the world, even in countries that are currently devoutly religious. Some critics view atheism as an impoverished "wasteland" that many will eventually reject. However, secular humanists—and psychological studies of well-being—make a persuasive case for the viability of secular humanism as a fulfilling way to live.

In sum, given the probable persistence of both religion and secular humanism, efforts to increase tolerance and dialogue between the two perspectives will be important.

RELIGION VERSUS SECULAR HUMANISM: A PRAGMATIC COMPARISON

In previous chapters, I reviewed findings that are relevant to a pragmatic assessment of the relative merits and viability of religion versus secular humanism from the perspective of the psychological and social sciences. Therefore, I offer only brief summaries. To foreshadow my bottom line: *In my opinion—based on available research—it is not possible to make a definitive case for the superiority of religion over secular humanism.*

Well-being. On the one hand, when religion is applied in a positive manner—for example, through positive methods of religious coping—it can have a generally beneficial albeit modest impact on physical health and psychological well-being, particularly for individuals with more intrinsic and committed religious orientations. In addition, people with firm religious convictions have additional sources of coping that are not available to the nonbeliever.

On the other hand, some people experience religious struggles or conflicts, or apply negative methods of religious coping that can adversely impact psychological well-being. In addition, research suggests that people with relatively weak or uncertain religious commitments may average no higher in well-being, and perhaps even lower, than committed secularists. Apparently, having an affirmative belief system, whether based on religion or secular humanism, is what is important. Psychological science offers a variety of intentional or therapeutic activities than can increase well-being for both secular humanists and religious individuals who might benefit from such activities. Finally—and importantly—any advantages of religion for psychological well-being appear to accrue primarily in relatively religious countries or regions, and in contexts in which life circumstances are difficult. This is consistent with research showing that the highest average levels of life satisfaction and well-being are reported in well-off, secular countries, not in the most religious countries.

Death anxiety. On the one hand, several studies have found that people high in intrinsic religiosity (but not extrinsic religiosity) report lower levels of death anxiety and reduced need to defend their cultural or religious worldviews when reminded of their mortality. Certainly, only religion offers the prospect of literal immortality in an afterlife.

On the other hand, religion's protective function against death anxiety or mortality awareness can result in aggression or intolerance towards out-groups. In addition, some studies reveal that buttressing secular worldviews can also protect against death anxiety and reminders of one's mortality. A variety of positive secular responses to mortality awareness are available to the secular humanist, such as pursuing meaningful goals, relationships, and achievements, which can provide a degree of symbolic immortality. Finally, lack of belief in an afterlife can provide a powerful incentive for secular humanists to make the most of the one finite life they have.

Uncertainty and needs for control. On the one hand, research indicates that religion can provide a buffer or shield against the inevitable uncertainties in life. It can also help to satisfy our need for perceived control over our lives. Identifying with a religious group can provide structure and reduce feelings of uncertainty.

On the other hand, strongly identifying with a particular religious group can promote an "us" versus "them" mentality in which members of other groups are depersonalized or perceived in stereotypical terms rather than as unique individuals. This can lead to intolerance, extremism, and violence. In addition, research suggests that three potential sources of perceived control—personal, religious, and governmental—can be largely substituted for each other in meeting needs for order, structure, and certainty. Thus, individuals can draw on either religious or secular means to achieve a sense of control. Nonetheless, religious communities may be particularly advantageous for this purpose, given their explicit focus on existential and sacred concerns, well-defined authority structures and rituals, and supportive communities.

Prosociality. On the one hand, research indicates that, on average, more religious people report making greater donations to charity, volunteering more, and possibly being more civically engaged—likely in part because their religious communities organize and promote such activities. They also report modestly higher levels of prosocial personality dispositions such as agreeableness and conscientiousness.

On the other hand, research indicates that the impact of religiosity on actual prosocial behavior is (a) generally modest; (b) often limited to members of relevant ingroups such as family, friends, and co-religionists; (c) motivated, at least in part, by the desire to view oneself as altruistic and to maintain a positive image; and (d) more induced by the presence of religious cues or reminders than by one's own religious disposition. In addition, to the extent that charity, volunteer activity, and civic engagement are associated with organized group membership, members of secular groups with a humanistic and social outreach focus could also serve these functions. Indeed, there is some evidence that they do.

In countries with strong social safety nets, secular governments and civic institutions have taken on many of the prosocial functions originally performed by religious institutions. Of course, history abounds with examples of prosocial contributions to society and humanity that were inspired by religion. However, many nonbelievers have also made significant contributions to social reform and justice efforts, presumably motivated by their perception that it is up to us humans to improve our condition. Indeed, research indicates that secular people are as motivated as religious people by compassion and concerns for fairness and justice. Along with moral intuitions and rational consideration of mutual human interests, these values can provide sufficient secular bases for moral or prosocial behavior.

Meaning in life. On the one hand, religion provides a ready-made, comprehensive, and God-given meaning system that addresses ultimate questions of existence, purpose, and morality. This meaning system can help believers interpret and cope with stressful circumstances, traumas, and death. Even in the worst moments, people of faith can find consolation in the belief that God has a plan for them and for the world. This may account for the finding that average levels of self-reported meaning in life are actually higher in poorer countries, where religion tends to be more central to people's lives.

On the other hand, secular humanism also provides a relatively comprehensive belief or meaning system. In addition, psychological research has identified a variety of paths to a life of meaning and fulfillment that do not require belief in gods or spirits—such as pursuing intrinsic and generative goals, meaningful relationships, authenticity, a calling, and signature character strengths.

Self-transcendent emotions. On the one hand, religion provides spiritual, interpersonal, and physical contexts that promote the experience of self-transcendent emotions such as joy, love, gratitude, awe, and wonder. This includes, for example, rituals, inspiring music, magnificent structures, a community of believers, and a personal relationship with God.

On the other hand, secular humanists are able to experience self-transcendent emotions through their encounters with inspiring natural phenomena (e.g., the cosmos, oceans, mountains) and human pursuits (e.g., art, music, literature, science, leisure, relationships). It is possible that the transcendent emotions experienced through religion are deeper or more expansive than those made possible through more naturalistic and humanistic means. However, most secular individuals do not report feeling that their lives are impoverished or lacking in meaning or inspiration.

Sense of community and belonging. On the one hand, religious denominations offer established, deep-rooted communities in which committed members share important beliefs and values, intimate emotional connections, feelings of belonging and identity, and assurances of mutual help. In most cases, secular groups and organizations are unlikely to adequately replace religious communities as a source of spiritual, social, and emotional support.

On the other hand, exceptions may be found among some secular "congregations" such as Sunday Assemblies and Ethical Culture societies. And some denominations, such as the Unitarian-Universalist Association, are open to both believers and nonbelievers. In any case, increasing numbers of people have turned away from organized religious communities in favor of more personal or individualized religious, spiritual, or secular perspectives. This indicates that for many people religious communities are not felt to be essential for well-being, a sense of purpose, or personal fulfillment.

Prejudice. Most religious communities discourage some forms of prejudice and promote acceptance and outreach towards marginalized or disadvantaged groups such as refugees, immigrants, and the poor. Nonetheless, research has linked conservative or fundamentalist religious orientations to prejudice against members of the LGBTQ+ community; various racial groups; immigrants and refugees; religious outgroups, including atheists and the nonreligious; and feminists.

In contrast, individuals with a more open and questioning (e.g., quest) religious orientation are more likely to be tolerant and accepting of these groups. Nonreligious people also tend to exhibit bias or prejudice towards groups that violate their social or political values. However, there is some evidence that people high in religious fundamentalism and with the greatest certainty about their religious beliefs show the most prejudice.

Violence. On the one hand, some violent conflicts can be linked to secular political agendas. In addition, religion has been used to promote peace, reconciliation, and transitional justice efforts. On the other hand, religion is often used to motivate and justify violence and terrorism and can exacerbate conflicts, making them more intense, uncompromising, and resistant to resolution. In addition, research indicates that secular or nonreligious individuals are, on average, less supportive of terrorism or political violence than are religious individuals.

So, what does this all mean for my pragmatic comparison of religion versus secular humanism?

It is only natural that people with religious commitments currently view religion, as compared to secular humanism, as a superior belief system. Indeed, some religious people view secular humanism as a source of great evil in the world. At the same time, most secular humanists view their secular life stance as fully capable of leading to moral and ethical, and rich and meaningful, lives. They hold a variety of views about religion, ranging from relatively tolerant and accommodating to strident and confrontational. Importantly, from a purely pragmatic perspective, *neither religion nor secular humanism appears to be definitively superior overall* when judged in terms of the psychological and social science evidence reviewed in this book and summarized in the previous section. Thus, claims of the superiority of religion over secular humanism can be made based on theological arguments, but such claims would not definitively follow from scientific research.

But Are There Other Important Considerations?

Indeed, an evaluation of the relative merits and viability of religion versus secular humanism should also take into account (a) the societal context; (b) for believers, the nature of their religious orientation; and (c) for people

327

generally, differences in their proneness to religious or spiritual experiences and their readiness or capacity to accept religious tenets.

Regarding the societal context: Some research suggests that the benefits of religion for well-being are more prominent in societies in which religion is more valued or normative. Thus, not surprisingly, religion is more likely to be perceived as superior to secular humanism in relatively religious societies—which also tend to be less existentially secure. In contrast, in relatively secular societies—which tend to be more existentially secure—the perceived benefits of religion over secular humanism will be less evident.

Regarding religious orientations: The most consistent finding is that people with more conservative or fundamentalist religious orientations are the most inclined towards intolerance or prejudice towards individuals or groups they view as violating their beliefs and values. They are also most inclined to support or participate in religion-inspired violence or terrorism. This suggests that the best religion has to offer can be attained by promoting more moderate, liberal, or "refined" forms of religion.

Finally, regarding individual differences in proneness to religious or spiritual experiences: A comparison of the relative merits of religion and secular humanism may be moot for people who find themselves unable to believe in the supernatural or in the various promises of religion. They will have little choice but to seek secular means to reduce existential anxieties and uncertainties, motivate prosocial behavior, and attain a sense of meaning, belonging, and control.

As alluded to in previous chapters, there are numerous reasons why some people find religious belief or faith difficult or impossible. They may have had limited exposure to credible learning experiences associated with religion, for example, because they were brought up in nonreligious environments. They may have weaker needs for religion because they feel existentially secure. They may be less susceptible to the cognitive biases or mechanisms associated with religious belief such as mind-body dualism or purpose-based (teleological) thinking. They may be more open to doubt and tolerant of ambiguity, and have weaker needs for order and certainty.

Their dispositions for analytic and independent thinking may lead them to question or reject central religious doctrines as superstitious or irrational. They may have concluded that moral and ethical behavior is possible based solely on humanistic principles. Or, they may not have had—or are not susceptible to—the mystical or spiritual experiences that some people interpret in religious terms.

Regarding the last point, prominent theologians, philosophers, and psychologists have all noted the greater importance of religious or spiritual experiences over rational or philosophical arguments as the basis for religious belief.[14] For example, William James observed that mystical experiences "carry an enormous sense of inner authority and illumination" for individuals who experience them, although such experiences are rare and not encountered by everyone.[15] Similarly, humanistic psychologist Abraham Maslow offered the following summary of his ideas on religion and peak experiences:

> To sum it up, from this point of view, the two religions of mankind tend to be the peakers and the non-peakers, that is to say, those who have private, personal, transcendent, core-religious experiences easily and often and who accept them and make use of them, and, on the other hand, those who have never had them or who repress or suppress them, and who, therefore, cannot make use of them for their personal therapy, personal growth, or personal fulfillment.[16]

More recently, psychological anthropologist Tanya Marie Luhrmann, Kara Weisman, and colleagues have observed that spiritual experiences involve an intuition that the boundary between mind and the world is at least somewhat porous or permeable. This intuition facilitates the kinds of extraordinary sensory experiences that are important to many religious people, such as sensing the presence of the Holy Spirit. Importantly, these researchers have shown, in several cultures, that there are reliable differences between people in their capacity to immerse themselves in such experiences and perceive them as real.[17]

Similarly, theologians contend that at least part of what is meant by "faith" involves a relaxing of one's need for control and allowing oneself "to be grasped by a deeper dimension of reality than ordinary experience."[18] For many of the reasons noted above, however, people differ in their willingness or ability to take this "leap of faith."

In short, people who have not had transcendent spiritual experiences, or are disinclined to interpret them in religious terms, may find it more difficult to embrace religious faith. Some people are disposed to enrich or "enchant" reality with supernatural beliefs in God and an afterlife. But others value the pursuit of what they see as a more true and accurate naturalistic view of reality.

Questioning the Rationality of Religious Claims

Indeed, for many people, any evaluation of the relative merits and viability of religion must consider the rationality or believability of its claims. For many secular humanists this is a paramount consideration.

Rational or philosophical "proofs" of God's existence have existed for centuries, but have generally proven unconvincing other than to some believers.[19] Prominent theologians and philosophers have argued with some persuasiveness that religious belief can be rational, justified, and warranted, at least under certain conditions.[20] Nonetheless, when analytic or critical thinking is applied to religious doctrines or concepts, apparent violations of reason abound, at least for some people. For example, many people find it difficult to accept the credibility of supernatural ideas such as the Incarnation, the Trinity, the virgin birth of Jesus, the resurrection of the body, or the plethora of reported miracles in the Bible.

Other questions—although perhaps simplistic from the perspective of a theologian—pressure the credibility of religion for some people. For example, "Why does God no longer reveal himself in grand fashion as he once did?"[21] Why did God not spare his creatures the suffering and extinction of species that results from the process of natural selection? Are the millions of nonbelievers in the world destined for external suffering in Hell? How are we to conceive of God? On the one hand, the popular anthropomorphic view of God seems to reinforce the idea of God as a human projection. On the other hand, impersonal conceptions of God (e.g., the Ground of Being, Ultimate Concern) seem incomprehensible and distant to many. And, of course, there is the difficult problem of evil and suffering in a world created and overseen by an all-powerful, all-knowing, and benevolent God. Philosopher Roberto Mangbeira Unger refers to such questions as "scandals of reason" associated with religion.[22]

Again, religious answers can be offered. For example, theologians have debated the problem of evil and suffering for centuries, offering explanations such as the following: God gave humans free will that is often misused. Evil is the result of human sin and Adam's fall from innocence. Evil or suffering are prerequisites for spiritual growth and development. God's creation is unfinished. Evil results from the work of Satan, the limits of God's powers, or God's curse on creation after the "fall."[23] Or—as depicted in the book of Job—the purpose of evil and suffering is described as beyond the limits of human reason or comprehension.

Importantly, however, many reflective people find such accounts unpersuasive.

Should Religion Persist?

Given all of the considerations above, I can now return to the question raised earlier—whether religion *should* persist or be discouraged. Some atheists, particularly of the more confrontational sort, are certain that the world would be a better place without religion. Other nonreligious scholars are not so sure. They note that religion can be useful in promoting well-being or prosocial behavior in some people. In addition, having a religious belief system might be better than having none at all or adopting a less desirable one such as QAnon or White supremacist ideologies. Furthermore, for some scholars, it is unclear what would take religion's place, or whether its replacement would be superior. Rather than trying to banish religion entirely, it might be better to encourage its better forms.[24] Alternatively, as I have argued in this book, secular humanism may provide a viable replacement for religion, at least for many people.

Also relevant here is the question of where the values of secular humanism come from. Secular humanists tend to attribute these values to the Enlightenment, reason, and our evolved history as social animals. In contrast, some theologians and historians have argued that secular values such as moral universalism and the dignity and worth of all humans have their roots in Christianity.[25] To the extent that these latter scholars are correct—and they make a plausible case—it raises the question of whether these "secular" values can be sustained, or will dissipate, over time if religion recedes significantly.

In my view, rather than attempting a definitive answer now, the question of whether religion *should* be encouraged or discouraged *should be answered empirically over time* in response to various interventions. That is, we can promote various actions designed to improve individual and societal well-being generally, while monitoring the evolving impact on well-being and the perceived merits of religion and secular humanism as alternative life stances. This recommendation is not a copout, but a sensible proposal given the current state of the religion-secular debate and existing empirical knowledge.

To some extent, a cultural experiment is already underway as secular institutions replace some of the traditional roles of religion and some modern societies become increasingly secular. For example, the high average levels of individual and societal well-being experienced in the highly secular Scandinavian countries suggest that a gradual erosion or diminishment of religion may not have significant detrimental effects on the well-being and morality of individuals and societies. However, might it be possible—as feared by some prominent religious figures and conservative commentators—that society without religion, or with a significantly diminished role for religion, will eventually lead to "tyranny," "anarchy," "nihilism," and the "full weight of God's wrath," as the foundations of morality and cooperation are presumably eroded?[26]

332

I think such catastrophic outcomes are unlikely. Indeed, as already noted, the happiest and most functional countries in the world are currently among the most secular. Nonetheless, it is not entirely unreasonable to ask whether this will continue to be the case as these secular cultures move further away in time from their religious roots. Might some form of value "replenishment" be needed?[27] Similarly, we can ask whether secular humanism—which I view as a viable alternative to religion—is now sufficiently mature or advanced to replace religion entirely, and, if not, when it might be.

One possibility is that religion—preferably in "better" or more refined forms—will come to co-exist in mutual toleration and dialogue with secular humanism, thus better meeting the varied needs of different individuals and societies. Again, my approach is a pragmatic one, offering proposals that improve human well-being and reduce religious-secular conflict—both worthwhile goals in any case—while monitoring the evolving impact on the well-being and religiosity of individuals and societies. In the following section, I offer a set of such evidence-based proposals.

PROPOSALS GOING FORWARD

Promoting Existential Security

The promotion of greater existential security for individuals and societies is inherently desirable and humane. Therefore, it is a worthwhile goal regardless of its potential impact on religion. As I noted in Chapter 10, higher average levels of individual well-being are found in countries with greater existential security as assessed by such indicators as economic development, income security, and health care, among others. At the same time, there is a fairly strong relationship between these indicators of existential security and reduced religiosity. Presumably, people who have their economic, social, and psychological needs met through effective governments and institutions have less need to rely on religion to do so.

333

Countries in northern Europe, and Scandinavia in particular, are frequently cited as examples of countries that rank high in prosperity, health, education, childcare, social security, gender equality, environmental protection, democracy, social solidarity, and trust. These are also among the least religious countries. Withholding these positive outcomes from individuals and societies—even if they might reduce religiosity in the long-term—makes little sense, unless one is focused exclusively on salvation in an afterlife at the expense of people's well-being in their present lives.

It is possible that alternative political and economic models can achieve some of these healthy individual and societal outcomes. Presently, however, we have the example of the "Nordic model" as one strategy that has been effective in achieving many of these outcomes. The Nordic model combines a capitalist system with a strong social safety net. A reasonable expectation is that individual and societal well-being will be increased—and the importance of religion gradually and naturally reduced—in other countries that pursue similar political and economic social policies, even if perhaps to a lesser extent.[28]

Promoting the "Best" Forms of Religion

Many scholars have suggested that we should seek not to eliminate religion but to encourage its best forms. In doing so, we might be able to benefit from religion's positive features while avoiding its potential harmful effects. The harmful effects of religion—for example, prejudice towards selected groups, "us" versus "them" thinking, and support for violence and terrorism—have been linked most consistently to more conservative or fundamentalist versions of religion. Therefore, a seemingly logical step would be to promote more liberal, moderate, or refined forms of religion.

At first glance, the fruitfulness of such a recommendation can be questioned on several counts. First, as noted previously, relatively conservative religious denominations with the most demanding requirements or signals of commitment have tended in the past to thrive better than more liberal denominations, such as mainline Protestants, which appear to be more fragile in terms of membership retention and renewal.[29] Indeed, for some critics, liberal or moderate religion represents "a largely vapid and irrelevant force"[30] that is less able to inspire commitment and less emotionally satisfying than rapidly growing movements such as Pentecostalism.[31]

Second, some critics argue that "moderate religion" requires people to ignore or loosely interpret those aspects of doctrine and scripture they find difficult to accept given reason and modern secular knowledge.[32] In this view, the result is a watered-down version of religion that falls short of true or orthodox faith, while also falling short of a fuller secular humanism. For philosopher Roberto Mangabeira Unger, this "halfway house" between true faith and secular humanism is self-deceptive and reveals "a loss of faith disguised as faith within the bounds of reason."[33]

Third, as noted in Chapter 7, some scholars, particularly the New Atheists, have argued that religious moderation is itself problematic, if not dangerous. In this view, the tolerance or political correctness of religious moderates enables a climate that inhibits justified criticism of more extreme or violent forms of religion.

Several counterarguments to these criticisms of moderate or liberal religion can be offered, however. First, although conservative denominations have, in the past, shown greater resiliency than more liberal denominations, they have not escaped the most recent secularization trends.[34] For example, David Gushee, past president of the American Academy of Religion and a former self-identified evangelical, observed that evangelicals used to think they were immune from the overall trend of religious decline. However, Gushee now sees White evangelicalism as being in trouble. For example, he cites data showing that from 2006 to 2016 the percentage of White Evangelicals in the United States population declined from 23% to 17%.[35] Similarly, a 2021 Public Religion Research Institute survey reported that White Evangelicals declined from 23% to 14.6% of the United States population between 2006 and 2021.[36]

Furthermore, the Unitarian-Universalist Association (UUA)—arguably the most liberal religious denomination—has defied the decline in membership experienced by mainline Protestant churches in the past several decades. Indeed, between 1980 and 2010, during which mainline Protestant congregations were declining by 30%, the UUA grew by 35%, adding ninety congregations, doubling its number of clergy, and expanding by 55,320 members. The significant growth of the UUA disputes the idea that only strict or conservative churches can grow. Interestingly, at least part of this success might be attributable to the UUA's welcoming attitude towards both believers and nonbelievers.[37]

Second, the claim that mainline Christianity is a vapid force with little influence is overstated. Although declining in membership—concomitant with the overall decline of religion in modern secular countries—many people still find emotional satisfaction, intellectual stimulation, a sense of purpose, supportive communities, and a home for social justice activism in these congregations.

Third, although religion may sometimes be treated as a "sacred cow" that is not to be criticized, there are many examples of religious moderates calling out more extreme forms of religion. For example, numerous Christian leaders and lay people have pushed back against Christian nationalism as a distortion of both Christianity and America's constitutional democracy—as well as its presence at the January 6, 2021 attack on the U.S. capital.[38] (At the same time, some have acknowledged the many ways in which mainline Protestants have inadvertently aided the Christian nationalist cause.)[39] Similarly, after reports that 81% of evangelicals voted for Donald Trump in 2016, some evangelicals, referring to themselves as "the 19 percent," expressed opposition to what they viewed as the reactionary politics of many evangelicals.[40] Indeed, a number of faith groups have been organizing and cooperating with secular groups both nationally and at the local level to counter the impact of Christian nationalism on Christianity and U.S. democracy.[41]

Although scholars in this debate often distinguish conservative or fundamentalist forms of religion from moderate or "liberalized" forms, it is not always clear how they are defining these different forms. As an exception, Philip Kitcher defines what he refers to as "refined religion," which many would consider moderate or liberal religion. In Kitcher's conception of refined religion, the emphasis is on practices and commitments, not a collection of doctrines. Doctrinal statements are interpreted symbolically as allegories or metaphors rather than literally. In addition, the basic commitment is to values and an ethical order that is identified independently rather than through a search of the scriptures.[42]

Similarly, Christian ethicist David Gushee has described a post-evangelical Christian humanist theology that might qualify as a more "refined religion." The approach is centered in Jesus and traditional theological sources. However, it appears to downplay doctrinal purity and ideology in favor of a number of principles that would be accepted by most secular humanists. These include a sense of common humanity; freedom of conscience; the holistic well-being of all humans; seeking common ground and peaceful solutions to human problems; and a humble, open posture in the quest for knowledge.[43]

In any case, it does not seem possible to definitively define the distinction between fundamentalist, conservative, moderate, or liberal forms of religion by referring to particular religions or religious denominations.[44] There *are* denominational differences in average scores on measures of religious fundamentalism.[45] However, fundamentalism is not exclusively linked to a specific religion or denomination. Similarly, although the predominant strand of American evangelicalism can at times be difficult to distinguish from fundamentalism, there is also a significant history of more progressive evangelical dissent and reform.[46]

It is also true that some religious traditions such as Evangelical Protestants and Mormons tend to be more politically conservative, on average, than other groups, for example, Jews and the religiously unaffiliated. For example, about 80% of White Evangelical Protestants have voted for the Republican candidate in the last three U.S. presidential elections.[47] Indeed, some critics, including some theologians, have lamented the apparent fusion between American evangelical and Republican identities.[48]

However, political conservatism and religious conservatism—although somewhat correlated—are not the same thing. For example, mainline Protestants are frequently viewed as representing moderate or liberal religion. However, in a survey of mainline Protestants, 37% reported being politically conservative, 38% reported being politically moderate, and 20% reported being liberal in their political ideology.[49]

Because of these complexities, it is challenging to define or specify the "best" forms of religion. Nonetheless, I offer one possible approach here.

Recall that the potential harmful effects of religion have been most definitively linked to religious fundamentalism. Therefore, it seems reasonable to define the "best" forms of religion in contrast to fundamentalism. Also, given the overlap between fundamentalism and Christian nationalism (see Chapter 6)—and the latter's tendency to fuse church and state—the "best" forms of religion would exclude Christian nationalism as well.

As described in Chapter 6, fundamentalists have an unquestioning belief "that there is one set of religious teachings that clearly contains the fundamental, basic, intrinsic, essential, inerrant truth about humanity and the deity."[50] In addition, psychological research has identified a "fundamentalist mindset" characterized by dogmatism, authoritarianism, intolerance of ambiguity, needs for closure, preference for consistency, and reduced integrative complexity and flexibility of thought regarding moral and existential issues. Thus, by defining the "best" forms of religion in contrast to these fundamentalist tendencies, we would include religions or religious communities that encourage an open, reflective, nonjudgmental, non-dogmatic, and even questioning approach to religion. Ideally, believers can find a "sweet spot" that incorporates a set of reflectively considered religious beliefs and practices that provide moral guidance, meaning, community, and inspiration without becoming dogmatic or intolerant of others' religious or nonreligious beliefs.

Adherents of these "best" forms of religion would likely exhibit several other positive characteristics. For example, they would be more open to diverse religious (and nonreligious) perspectives and thus less likely to engage in prejudice, intolerance, and violence. They would be more likely to seek dialogue and common cause with others, including secular humanists, who share important humanistic and social justice values. And, they would likely be more open to science, given their rejection or questioning of the inerrancy or literal truth of religious scriptures. An important element of this conception of the best forms of religion is intellectual humility regarding one's beliefs.

Promoting Intellectual Humility

Is it possible that our beliefs are wrong? Intellectual humility regarding our religious beliefs, or lack thereof, involves an acknowledgement of this possibility. Although we may feel strongly about our religious or secular views, we cannot be absolutely certain that our beliefs are more correct than, or superior to, those of other people.

Under these circumstances, a degree of intellectual humility—rather than dogmatic certainty—regarding our beliefs is an appropriate and pragmatic virtue. If we accept the premise that most people are sincere in their efforts to make sense of their existence, find meaning in their lives, and cope with life's difficulties—all of which can be challenging tasks—a degree of tolerance and understanding, and perhaps even respect, for those who hold different beliefs is warranted and might be attainable.

Of course, it may be more difficult to offer this respect and tolerance when we suspect that a person's belief system is not based on a degree of autonomous and genuine reflection or the person is dogmatic and unquestioning about their own belief system. For this reason, we need to also promote genuine self-reflection among both religious and nonreligious people. As philosopher William Irwin has noted, intellectual humility is closely tied to intellectual honesty. We need to be self-reflective and intellectually honest about our own beliefs and our basis for holding them.[51]

Are you a religious believer? Then, intellectual humility would include recognition that humility is a religious virtue; genuine faith can involve questions and doubt; and having faith does not prove the truth of your religious beliefs.

Are you a secular humanist? Then, intellectual humility would include an understanding of the following: Some people find great comfort, meaning, and community in their religious faith. Some people have spiritual experiences that they might reasonably interpret in religious terms. Science cannot prove there is no God or spiritual realm beyond observable nature. And, a secular humanist might conceivably experience a religious conversion in the future, even if this might seem unlikely.

For secularists, intellectual humility is probably more consistent with agnosticism than definitive atheism, and an accommodationist rather than confrontational approach to religion. The intellectually humble nonbeliever is open to the possibility, even if remote, that God exists or that evidence of religious claims could emerge in the future.[52]

Conversely, what intellectual humility does *not* require is treating religion (or secular humanism) as sacred cows that cannot be evaluated and criticized, particularly in their more dogmatic and unquestioning forms. In fact, this "permission" to evaluate and criticize is essential to the pragmatic approach I am promoting in evaluating the merits and viability of religion and secular humanism in the long term.

In this sense, intellectual humility subsumes the metabelief that "*beliefs should change in response to evidence*" and that we should be open to such evidence. Indeed, as described by biological anthropologist David Samson, this metabelief is our "primary defense against mind parasites like fake news, misinformation, science denial, propaganda, fundamentalism, and extreme divisive ideologies" and an important "vaccine" against our evolved "us" versus "them" tribal drives.[53]

Finally, intellectual humility does not mean we have to accept others' views as valid. Nonetheless, as reviewed in the previous chapter, research indicates that people with greater intellectual humility about their religion show greater tolerance of other religious groups and react less negatively to having their religious beliefs challenged. This will be important in promoting tolerance among people with different religious and secular perspectives.

Presenting Secular Humanism as an Alternative Belief System

People need a positive worldview or belief system that provides an account of the world and our place in it. Such a belief system, even if not explicitly articulated, provides structure and a sense of meaning or purpose for our lives. If religion diminishes in importance, we will need a replacement belief system. Mere rejection of God or religion is unlikely to be sufficient.

I do not wish to proselytize on behalf of secular humanism. However, I believe that it provides a positive worldview that is consistent with reason, science, and well-being for those who seek an alternative to religion.[54] I have described how secular humanism provides a basis for well-being or personal fulfillment; moral and ethical behavior; and a sense of meaning, purpose, and even awe. The material in this book should provide readers with sufficient information to form some impressions regarding the viability of secular humanism as a belief system or "way to live."

As I noted previously, acceptance of a secular humanist stance does not require that we abandon enjoyment of the inspirational art, literature, music, architecture, or history that is part of our religious cultural heritage. If nothing else, they remain part of our historical and cultural heritage. However, they can be studied and appreciated without endorsing the associated religious beliefs or doctrines. For many people, it will be sad to think how the magnificent churches, temples, and mosques around the world might be repurposed if religion continues to lose its influence in the future. However, these repurposed structures could still serve the public good, for example, as affordable housing or community centers.

Religious conservatives sometimes portray secular humanism as an evil that will lead to a chaotic, impoverished, or immoral world. Hopefully, however, you will be able to get beyond such polemics and make a reasonably objective assessment of secular humanism and its potential advantages and disadvantages. To do so, you can draw in part on the evidence and discussion presented in this book.

Secular humanism need not be promoted in a confrontational manner, nor as necessarily opposed to religion. As I discussed previously, a confrontational approach can be counterproductive. Rather, secular humanism can be "promoted" in a positive manner by providing information about it. It can also be promoted indirectly as more people "come out" as secular humanists, making it evident that secular humanism is compatible with moral and prosocial behavior, and with meaningful and fulfilling lives.

Promoting Dialogue Among Diverse Groups

Many religious figures and umbrella organizations, as well as philosophers and social scientists, have promoted the idea of dialogue or ecumenical efforts among religious and nonreligious groups. They also acknowledge that dialogue can be difficult.[55] For example, both Pope Francis and Pope Benedict XVI promoted the idea of dialogue between believers and nonbelievers.[56] Humanists UK, with a designated Dialogue Officer, offers training for dialogue between humanists and diverse religious communities with the aim to "build mutual understanding, identify common ground and, where it makes sense, engage in shared action."[57] There is also some recognition among those promoting dialogue that it is more likely to be fruitful between reflective and open-minded representatives of their respective perspectives. In particular, it might be difficult to dialogue with dogmatic individuals from either perspective, or those who are less interested in mutual understanding than in "scoring points" for their side.

In short, dialogue is most likely to be productive among people capable of intellectual humility, mutual respect, and civility on both "sides" of the discussion.

What can religious people learn from dialogue with secular humanists? That most secular people have nuanced views of religion and are not interested in destroying it or banishing it from society.[58] That most secular humanists feel that their lives have meaning and purpose and are not deficient in some way. That moral and ethical behavior does not need to be based on religion. And, why separation of church and state is important to secular humanists.

Conversely, what can secular humanists gain from dialogue with religious people? They can determine what, if anything, they might wish to retain or refine from religious traditions. They may come to appreciate that some of the values associated with secular humanism—for example, moral universalism and the dignity and worth of all humans—may have emerged, at least in part, from within Christian traditions.[59] They may attain a better understanding of the spiritual experiences that some religious individuals report. And, they may better understand what religious people mean by religious liberty and why it is important to them.

From each other, religious and secular individuals can clarify what values and causes they may share; how they might build mutual trust and act together in some instances; and how they both occasionally experience questions or doubts about their beliefs or strategies. In addition, by listening to others' perspectives (even if we think they are wrong), we can better understand and refine our *own* perspectives. Importantly, dialogue may also facilitate some convergence on a shared set of facts or truths, which can be important in combating polarization and tribalism.

From such dialogue, we would hope for a reduction in tensions and the perceived gap between religion and secular humanism. Indeed, serious religious people and secular humanists might share more than they think. For example, this could include certain humanistic values, concern for the human condition, and a reflective or probing approach to life's big questions. Indeed, historian Jennifer Michael Hecht observed that: "Great doubters are often more invested in religious questions than is the average believer."[60]

Finally, when it comes to improving society, we can ask the following question: Is it more important to debate and resolve differences in doctrines or beliefs or to determine how religious and secular individuals can work together on common causes? As atheist philosopher Louise Antony asks:

> Why do theists care so much about belief in God? Disagreement over that question is really no more than a difference in philosophical opinion....Why should a disagreement like that bear any moral significance? Why shouldn't theists just look for allies among us atheists in the battles that matter—the ones concerned with justice, civil rights, peace, etc.—and forget about our differences with respect to such arcane matters as the origins of the universe?[61]

Many religious believers will disagree with Antony's minimizing of the importance of their belief in, or relationship with, God. However, her pragmatic point about working together on shared causes is well taken. Dialogue between religious and secular communities might even lead to compromises on issues involving religious liberty, church-state separation, and other intractable issues at the intersection of religion and politics such as abortion.[62]

Interfaith activist Chris Stedman, in his book *Faitheist: How an Atheist Found Common Ground with the Religious*, provides a personal and inspirational account of the potential of interfaith dialogue that includes atheists and humanists. Based on his experiences, he concludes that "atheists and the religious need to find better ways to talk to one another, and they need to identify the areas of shared humanity that will enable mutually enriching collaboration."[63]

Promoting Education and Critical Thinking

Many if not most people probably agree: Efforts to increase levels of education, scientific literacy, and critical or analytical thinking are inherently worthwhile. Indeed, for decades, educators have been talking about educating for critical thinking skills. Today, such skills remain badly needed to counteract the avalanche of misinformation and conspiracy theories circulating on social media and elsewhere.[64] Fortunately, research indicates that critical thinking skills can be successfully taught at any level of the education system using a variety of strategies.[65] This introduces a potential dilemma for religion, however. Increases in education, scientific literacy, and critical thinking all tend to be associated with reduced religiosity.

We can also promote religious literacy. Religious education often refers to learning about one's *own* religion in school or a religious context. However, religious literacy can also refer to learning about different religions, and could be extended to include alternative belief systems such as secular humanism and ethical culture. Indeed, with some success (as well as pushback), humanists in the United Kingdom have in recent years sought to have humanism included as an alternative life stance in religious education curricula.[66]

A case can be made for offering a course in comparative belief systems during the high school years, because the majority of people do not pursue college degrees. Less ideally—but more pragmatically, given curriculum constraints in high school—briefer discussions, for example, based on relevant supplemental readings, could take place in social studies or history classes. Critical thinking could also be applied in these courses as participants discuss—hopefully with a degree of tolerance and intellectual humility—the pragmatic advantages and disadvantages of different belief systems. Research could be conducted to determine whether such courses impact individuals' existing religious or nonreligious commitments.

On the one hand, we would expect some individuals to question their religious or nonreligious commitments as a result of their increasing literacy. On the other hand, for some individuals, such experiences might reinforce and provide a more solid grounding for their existing belief system, so that it is not simply based on where they were born or socialized. Arguably, a faith that cannot survive exposure to, and critical thinking about, alternative belief systems is not well grounded. In any case, increasing knowledge and understanding of others' religious or nonreligious belief systems could help to bridge differences and reduce the polarizing impact that religion can have in society.[67]

At a minimum, we already know that participation in such educational instruction can lead to greater tolerance of other religions. For example, in one study, 10th grade Omani students participated in a 10-week educational intervention titled "Our brothers and sisters in humanity" that included information and learning activities about the world's major religions (Christianity, Islam, Judaism, Hinduism, Sikhism, and Buddhism). The focus was on identifying similarities between the religions. The educational intervention had a large positive impact on tolerance towards the other religions, including perceptions of the acceptability of the other religions having freedom of worship in the country.[68]

More generally, research suggests that more positive attitudes and reduced prejudice towards members of other religious (or nonreligious) groups can be achieved with children beginning as early as elementary school. Curricula or training programs have involved direct contact among members of diverse groups or promotion of empathy and perspective taking.[69]

Weakening Religion's Links to Politics and Political Affiliation

U.S. politics is already polarized. The increasing alignment of the Republican Party with religious conservatives—particularly White Evangelical Protestants—and the Democratic Party with minorities, the nonreligious, and liberal Whites, aggravates this situation and has the potential to further divide the parties ideologically and increase political gridlock.[70] Similarly, around the world, the increasing ideological and economic gaps between religious and secular countries will continue to impact world politics. Finally, research reviewed in Chapter 6 reveals that religious violence is greater when religious infusion—that is, religion's public role in politics and daily life—is greater.

These considerations warrant efforts to weaken the link between religion and political affiliation and to maintain or enhance the separation of church and state. Both of these efforts may reduce political polarization, as well as religious-secular conflict. Indeed, most secularists in the United States do not think that people are better off without religion (only 37% say that people would be), but a clear majority (67%) think that religion has too much influence in society.[71] One encouraging sign is that younger adults are less comfortable with the link between religion and politics, which may help to break down religion-related polarization in the future.[72]

Several of the proposals described in this chapter, if implemented, might weaken religion's links with politics and political affiliation. By promoting more open and tolerant forms of religion, greater intellectual humility by religious and nonreligious individuals, and greater pursuit of shared social causes, it should be possible to reduce polarization, conflict, and the growing link between religion and political affiliation. This does not mean that our beliefs cannot be expressed in political contexts or inform our voting patterns. However, we should resist a "fusion" of our religious and political identities if it makes our votes largely automatic and unreflective.

Writing from the perspective of a Christian ethicist, David Gushee has also pointed to the dangers of Christianity becoming fused with a political identity. Importantly, he offers several recommendations for a "healthy Christian politics." For example, Christians need to protect the primacy and independence of their Christian identity and not fuse this identity with a political party. They should avoid over investment in the political arena and maintain distance from "all earthly powers." They should adopt a global rather than parochial or nationalist perspective. And, they should prioritize the common good over the church's self-interest. If followed, suggestions such as these could help to weaken the link between religion and political affiliation.[73]

ANTICIPATED PUSHBACK

I anticipate some pushback on the above proposals. For example, government interventions that seek to strengthen the existential security of its citizens may be lambasted as "socialism" by some political or economic conservatives, despite the fact that many capitalist countries have achieved strong social safety nets promoting existential security while maintaining strong market economies. In addition, religious conservatives can rightly note that their religious communities have proven as least as viable as more liberal or moderate forms of religion and that religious conservatism is undergirded by a vast network of religious communities, book publishers, and media networks.[74]

For some believers, intellectual humility about their religious belief system may be perceived as weak faith or commitment, or even apostasy.[75] For some committed atheists, intellectual humility may be viewed as cowardly agnosticism or as overly accommodating towards religion. For everyone, tolerance and respect for others' views can be difficult amid strong disagreements. For some religious conservatives, dialogue with secular humanists—whom they have long vilified—may be viewed as off limits.

The proposed educational interventions have the potential to improve critical thinking, scientific and religious literacy, and religious tolerance. However, advocates of private religion-affiliated education or home schooling—particularly those who wish to promote Creationism or Intelligent Design as science—may resist such interventions.

Politicians will continue to cater to policies or agendas that appeal to particular religious or secular groups. This will make it more difficult to loosen the ties between politics and religion and reduce political polarization.

In short, it will be challenging to implement the proposals offered here. Nonetheless, they seem important in improving the human condition and deriving a more harmonious relationship between religion and secular humanism.

FINAL COMMENTS

As noted, the proposals presented above are likely to face challenges and pushback. However, I believe they will contribute to the increased well-being of individuals and societies, while also reducing religious-secular conflict and political polarization.

As a secondary or indirect effect, research suggests that most if not all of these proposals, if successfully implemented, might also reduce the religiosity of individuals and societies over time. Presently, different individuals and societies will have vastly different views on whether or not this secondary effect on religion would be a good thing.

My own (pragmatic) perspective is as follows:

First, since successful implementation of these proposals is likely to have a largely positive impact on the well-being of individuals and societies over time, it makes sense to pursue them.

Second, the question of whether any secondary or indirect effects on religiosity are largely good or bad for individuals or societies can be investigated and evaluated over time. As already noted, from the perspective of the psychological and social sciences, there is presently no definitive basis for concluding that a religious or secular humanist belief system is superior overall. Each may have its advantages and disadvantages, depending on the individual and society. There is evidence that individual and societal well-being are actually better in some of the most secular countries, which also have greater existential security. This finding offers at least the possibility that a less religious world would be a positive thing, assuming that a viable and positive alternative belief system can take hold. As discussed in this book, secular humanism appears to be such a positive belief system or life stance.

Third, assuming that religion will likely persist in the long term, we can at least pursue proposals that seek to increase tolerance and reduce religious-secular conflict by pursuing the "best" forms of religion and by in-

349

creasing intellectual humility and dialogue among both religious and secular individuals.

In any case, the ultimate goal is to achieve the highest levels of individual and societal well-being possible, with or without religion.

Acknowledgments

I am grateful to the many people whose support over the years made this book possible. First and foremost, I thank my wife Marcia Katigbak Church, for her support, patience, and collaboration in both family and career matters for over 40 years. She has supported my efforts and tolerated the extensive time I have spent on this book and on career activities generally. She is an excellent researcher in her own right and was my primary collaborator on many international studies of culture and personality. She was also the first to read and comment on each of the chapters of this book.

A special thanks also to Sara Church and Brad Church for reading later versions of the book and offering feedback from the perspective of inquisitive and reflective lay people. I am also grateful to my extended family, which has provided exemplars of the full range of religious and irreligious belief systems, including individuals identifying as devout born-again evangelicals, practicing Catholics and Protestants, liberal religious and secular humanists, spiritual-but-not-religious individuals, and confirmed atheists.

I would not have had the expertise necessary to review the large number of scientific articles and books I read during my research for this book if not for my doctoral training in psychology at the University of Minnesota. Among the professors who influenced me most were Auke Tellegen, Eric Klinger, Mark Davison, René Dawis, David Weiss, James Butcher, and Thomas Bouchard. Of course, one's ongoing mastery of state-of-the-art research methods is a matter of life-long learning and continued active scholarship. In this regard, I want to acknowledge the support of Washington State University, the National Science Foundation, and the National

Institute of Mental Health in the United States, which supported much of my collaborative research on personality across cultures.

Much of the research for this book took place during the COVID-19 pandemic and after I had retired away from the Washington State University (WSU) campus. Thus, I am especially appreciative of the WSU library staff that so promptly located and forwarded many books and articles needed for my research.

Finally, I would like to thank David G. McAfee of Hypatia Press for showing interest in the book, and both David G. McAfee and Sarah Hembrow, Publishing Director of Ockham Publishing, for their assistance in preparing the book for publication.

Notes

Introduction

[1] Dewey (1934, pp. 1-2).

[2] For example, a 2019 Pew Research Center (2020a) survey found that, across 34 countries spanning 6 continents, medians of 62%, 61%, and 53% of respondents, respectively, said that religion, God, and prayer play an important role in their lives.

[3] For reviews of relevant surveys, see D. E. Campbell, Layman, & Green (2021); Kasselstrand, Zuckerman, & Cragun (2023, pp. 88-94); Putnam & Campbell (2010).

[4] According to a 2024 Pew Research Center report, 28% of U.S. adults are currently unaffiliated with a religion, about 5% are self-identified atheists, and about 6% are self-identified agnostics.

[5] D. E. Campbell et al. (2021, see footnote 3, p. 23).

[6] P. Zuckerman, Galen, & Pasquale (2016, p. 5).

[7] Karim & Saroglou (2023).

[8] Keysar (2017, p. 41).

[9] For example, in a recent Pew Research Center survey, 48% of U.S. adults said there's "a great deal" of or "some" conflict between their religious beliefs and mainstream American culture. Forty-nine percent believe that religion is losing its influence in American society and that this is a bad thing (Pew Research Center, 2024a).

[10] Wellman (2008, p. xii).

[11] Elie (2003, p. 472).

[12] James (1902/1985, pp. 18-21, italics in original).

[13] de Waal (2013, pp. 94-95, 216).

[14] Küng (1988, pp. 237-245).

[15] For a discussion of the relationship between science and religion, see Ferngren (2017).

[16] Coyne (2015). American paleontologist Stephen Jay Gould (1941-2002) was the best-known proponent of the separate-spheres position, arguing that science and religion represent "non-overlapping magisteria"—that is, distinct domains of authority—that should not conflict because they do not overlap.

[17] For example, see Craig (2008); A. McGrath (2017, pp. 109-114); Plantinga (2015); Polkinghorne (2009).

[18] Jeeves & Ludwig (2018); A. McGrath (2017, pp. 159-163, 178-180); Worthington (2010).

[19] Jeeves & Brown (2009); Jeeves & Ludwig (2018); A. McGrath (2017); Polkinghorne (2009); Worthington (2010). Biologos, founded by Francis Collins, former director of the National Institutes of Health, and the Templeton Foundation both encourage dialogue and engagement between science and religion.

[20] Given the already broad scope of this book and my limited expertise in the natural sciences, I do not address unresolved issues in the natural sciences that often appear in religious-secular debates, such as "Why is there something rather than nothing?" "What, if anything, caused the Big Bang?" "Is the universe fine-tuned for life on earth?" "Why do science and mathematics do such a good job of describing and predicting phenomena in the natural world?" (see Brierly, 2023; Collins, 2006; Holt, 2012; Krauss, 2012, for diverse perspectives on these questions).

[21] Tylor (1871/1958, p. 8).

[22] Durkheim (1912/2001, p. 46, italics in original).

[23] Kasselstrand et al. (2023, p. 9, italics in original).

[24] Saroglou (2021).

[25] Humanists International Minimum Statement on Humanism. Retrieved from https://humanists.international/what-is-humanism on March 31, 2022.

[26] The overview of Humanism offered in these paragraphs draws primarily on the following sources: *A Secular Humanist Declaration*, issued in 1980 by

The Council for Democratic and Secular Humanism (now the Council for Secular Humanism); *Secular Humanism Defined*, retrieved from the Council of Secular Humanism website https://secularhumanism.org/what-is-secular-humanism/secular-humanism-defined/; *Humanism and its Aspirations* (Humanistic Manifesto III), published in 2003 by the American Humanist Association; The Amsterdam Declaration 2002, published by the International Humanist and Ethical Union; *Declaration of Modern Humanism*, agreed at the General Assembly of Humanists International, Glasgow, United Kingdom, 2022; and Herrick (2005).

[27] Herrick (2005, p. 27).

[28] See https://americanhumanistcenterforeducation.org/ten-commitments/. Similarly, P. Zuckerman (2019, pp. 157-180) has described seven "cardinal virtues" of a humanistic worldview: free-thinking; living in reality; here-and-nowness; acceptance of existential mystery; scientific empiricism; cosmopolitanism; and empathy/compassion.

[29] Other labels include freethinker, rationalist, materialist, philosophical naturalist, nontheist, nonbeliever, and irreligionist. See Blankholm (2022, pp. 6-12, 34-56, 178) for a discussion. Although the existence of different labels for nonbelievers can be advantageous in offering options with some distinct connotations, it can also make it more difficult to unify nonbelievers under a shared identity.

[30] Pinker (2018, p. 430).

[31] See Flynn (2013) for a discussion.

[32] Doerr (2013, p. 17).

[33] Hedges (2008, p. 9).

[34] Hobson (2018, p. 118).

[35] Ozment (2016, p. 131). Cimino & Smith (2014) describe ongoing debates in the secularist movement about which label might promote a more positive self-image in the larger population than labels such as secular humanist or atheist.

[36] However, see Wixwat & Saucier (2021) for a recent review.

[37] Eberstadt (2013, p. 56).

[38] Beck (2010, p. 85); C. G. Brown (2017, p. 105); Bruce (2017, p. 68); Dennett (2006, pp. 302-303); Mercadante (2014, p. 72); Mercadante (2018, p. 122).

CHAPTER 1: ORIGIN AND FUNCTIONS OF RELIGION: EARLY NATURALISTIC ACCOUNTS

[1] Firth (1951, p. 247).

[2] Haught (2008, pp. 53-54).

[3] Pals (2015, p. 2).

[4] Pals (2015, p. 3).

[5] Preus (1987, pp. 84-99).

[6] Evans-Pritchard (1965, p. 20).

[7] Spencer (1898, pp. 285-305); Stark (2007, pp. 29-32). The term "primitive" was commonly used—particularly in previous centuries—to refer to the religious practices of traditional peoples (generally hunter-gatherers). I use the term when describing the perspectives of early philosophers and social scientists, but wish to avoid any evaluative or ethnocentric sense of the term.

[8] Preus (1987, pp. 59-60, 113, 124-125). Comte's Religion of Humanity had some success in other countries such as Brazil and England, but was criticized for adopting secular analogs of Catholic rituals (e.g., an idealized feminine figure in place of Mary; secular artists, writers, scientists, and so forth as secular substitutes for saints) (Bakewell, 2023, pp. 273-274).

[9] Eliade (1949/1974, pp. 95, 98); Malinowski (1925/1954, pp. 40, 51-53); T. Parsons (1958); Radcliffe-Brown (1952, pp. 164, 177).

[10] Pals (2015, Chapter 4).

[11] Firth (1951, p. 250).

[12] Firth (1951, p. 250).

[13] Preus (1987, pp. 45-46, 51, 74).

[14] Preus (1987, p. 18).

[15] Tylor (1871/1958, p. 12).

[16] Tylor (1871/1958, Ch. XVI and XVII).

[17] Lessa and Vogt (1958, p. 12); Lowie (1924/1952, pp. 108-109, 122-123; Malinowski (1925/1954, pp. 2, 18); Marett (1916, p. 2). Sir James Frazer, an English protégé of Tylor, also proposed an evolutionary model in which modes of human thought were posited to progress from magic to religion to science (Lowie, 1924/1952, pp. 138-139).

[18] A. Lang (1898/1968, p. 334).

[19] Stark (2007, pp. 61-62).

[20] A. Lang (1898/1968, pp. 184, 206, 224-225, 280-291); Schmidt (1931/1958, pp. 24-25). Among modern scholars, sociologist of religion Rodney Stark (2007, p. 63) appears to be the most supportive of the idea that active High Gods were common among primitive groups.

[21] Firth (1951, p. 244); Lowie (1924/1952, p. 132); Pettazzoni (1954/1958, p. 43).

[22] Pettazzoni (1954/1958, p. 43).

[23] Marett (1916, p. 2) referred to this pre-animistic concept as *animatism*.

[24] Marett (1916, p. 22).

[25] Marett (1916, p. 105).

[26] Codrington (1891/1957, pp. 118-119).

[27] Tomlinson & Makihara (2009). For a review, see Rumsey (2016).

[28] Firth (1940).

[29] Keesing (1984). Keesing argued that Codrington's (and hence Marett's) flawed conception of *mana* was based on limited ethnographic evidence and pervasive translation errors.

[30] Tomlinson & Kāwika-Tengan (2016, p. 1).

[31] Durkheim (1912/2001, p. 9).

[32] Durkheim (1912/2001, pp. 47-75).

[33] Durkheim (1912/2001, p. 154).

[34] For example, Lowie (1924/1952, pp. 113-114) argued that the aboriginal Australian tribes were not more primitive than tribes such as the Andaman Islanders, the Semang of the Malay Peninsula, or the Paviotso of Nevada,

groups in which totemism did not occur. Thus, it was unwarranted to infer primeval conceptions from Australian conditions.

[35] Lévi-Strauss (1962, pp. 3-5).

[36] Lévi-Strauss (1962, p. 45). Palmer, Begley, & Coe (2015) proposed an alternative function of totemism as a long-term strategy for identifying and supporting descendants and thus the survival of one's clan.

[37] Freud (1928/1961, p. 43). In *Totem and Taboo*, Freud (1918/1998) also offered a speculative hypothesis regarding the origins of religion based on the psychoanalytic principle of the Oedipus complex, involving murder, cannibalism, and totem animals as father substitutes. Not surprisingly, the hypothesis was rejected as an implausible "fantasy" or "fairy-tale" (Evans-Pritchard, 1965, p. 42), so I do not present it here.

[38] Lightner, Bendixen, & Purzycki (2023).

[39] Peoples, Duda, & Marlowe (2016); Peoples & Marlowe (2012); Sanderson & Roberts (2008); Steadman, Palmer, & Tilley (1996); Swanson (1960); Winkelman (1990).

[40] McClenon (2002); Winkelman (1990, 2015, p. 267).

[41] McClenon (2002, p. 6). Others argue that shamanism is not a distinct form of religion in an organized or institutional sense, but rather coexists as a technique with other forms of magic and religion (Peoples et al., 2016, p. 274; Townsend, 1997, p. 431).

[42] Steadman et al. (1996).

[43] Rossano (2007, 2009).

[44] Dunbar (2022, p. 163).

[45] Pargament (2002).

[46] Evans-Pritchard (1965, p. 15).

[47] Bellah (2011); Hayden (2003). More evidence for this claim will be presented in Chapter 3 of this book.

[48] Haught (2008, p. 98).

[49] C. Geertz (1973, p. 88).

[50] Guthrie (1993, p. 10).

CHAPTER 2: ARE WE BIOLOGICALLY PREPARED FOR RELIGION?

[1] J. Barrett (2004, p. 21).

[2] L. Turner (2014, p. 5).

[3] Kandler (2021).

[4] Atran (2002); J. Barrett (2004); Bloom (2009, p. 120); Boyer (2001, pp. 116-120); Gervais (2013); Greenway & Barrett (2021); Guthrie (1993, 2021). Alternative labels for these mechanisms or modules include mental tools or structures, intuitive inference systems, habits of mind, or thought processes.

[5] Boyer (2001, pp. 279-281); McCauley (2011). The intuitive-reflective distinction is frequently referred to as the *dual-processing model*. Some CSR proponents have pointed to the apparent readiness of young children to conceptualize supernatural agents and to perceive purpose and design in their environments and concluded that children may be "born believers" or "intuitive theists" (J. Barrett, 2012, p. 3; Kelemen, 2004).

[6] Boyer (2001, p. 311).

[7] J. H. Turner, Maryanski, Petersen, & Geertz (2018, pp. 134-135).

[8] Deacon & Cashman (2010, p. 3). A third possibility is that religion was initially a by-product of evolved cognitive mechanisms, which subsequently became adaptive in its own right. A fourth possibility is that religion is a "vestigial trait" or "behavioral fossil," that is, a trait that was once adaptive but is no longer (Schloss, 2009, p. 20).

[9] Richerson & Newson (2009); Wilson (2002). Dawkins (1976, Chapter 11) coined the term *memes* to refer to units of cultural inheritance that might replicate in a manner analogous to genes, although some critics have questioned the analogy.

[10] D. Johnson (2016); Norenzayan (2013); Norenzayan, Shariff, Gervais, Willard, McNamara, Slingerland, & Henrich (2016); Shariff (2011).

[11] Dawkins (2006, p. 188).

[12] Even so, some philosophers of religion continue to debate whether the adaptive nature of religious beliefs (or the evolved cognitive mechanisms underlying such beliefs) implies the truth of those beliefs. For a recent example, see Van Eyghen & Bennett (2022).

[13] For a succinct review of the most frequently mentioned cognitive mechanisms or processes, see also Greenway & Barrett (2021).

[14] Atran (2002); Atran & Norenzayan (2004); J. Barrett (2004); Guthrie (1993, 2021).

[15] Atran (2002, p. 71).

[16] Maij, van Harreveld, Gervais, Schragg, Mohr, & van Elk (2017, Study 4); Maij & van Elk (2019); Riekki, Lindeman, Aleneff, Halme, & Nuortimo (2013); Scholl & Tremoulet (2000).

[17] Rochat, Morgan, & Carpenter (1997).

[18] Petrican & Burris (2012); Riekki et al. (2013); Riekki, Lindeman, & Riaj (2014).

[19] Van Elk, Rutjens, van der Pligt, & van Harreveld (2016).

[20] A. R. Atkinson (2023).

[21] Banerjee & Bloom (2014, 2015); J. Barrett (2012); Bering (2011, pp. 55-59); E. M. Evans (2001); Gervais (2013); Kelemen (2004); Norenzayan (2016).

[22] Legare & Gelman (2008).

[23] Banerjee & Bloom (2014); Heywood & Bering (2014); Schachner, Zhu, Li, & Kelemen (2017); White, Willard, Baimel, & Norenzayan (2021); Willard, Cingl, & Norenzayan (2020).

[24] Banerjee & Bloom (2015); Kelemen (1999a, b; 2004); Kelemen & DiYanni (2005).

[25] Casler & Kelemen (2008); Kelemen & Rosset (2009); Kelemen, Rottman, & Seston (2013).

[26] E. M. Evans (2001). For the fundamentalist group, this preference for creationist accounts was consistent across all age groups, whereas some age differences were observed in the non-fundamentalist group.

[27] E. M. Evans (2001).

[28] Kelemen & Rossett (2009, p. 142).

[29] J. Barrett (2012, p. 73); Bloom (2009, p. 123).

[30] Atran (2002); J. Barrett (2009); Bering (2011); Boyer (2001); Gervais (2013); Greenway & Barrett (2021, pp. 72-74); Norenzayan (2016). Mind perception is a prerequisite for religion in other ways. For example, without mind perception we would not be able to communicate our ideas to others and potentially agree on the tenets that constitute formal religions (Dunbar, 2022, pp. 116-117).

[31] Gervais (2013, p. 380).

[32] Greenway & Barrett (2021, pp. 72-74); Shtulman & Lindeman (2016).

[33] Schjoedt, Stodkilde-Jorgensen, Geertz, & Roepstorff (2009).

[34] White, Bamiel, & Norenzayan (2021). Ishii & Watanabe (2023) report weaker or less definitive findings in Japanese samples.

[35] Riekki et al. (2014).

[36] Maij et al. (2017); Norenzayan, Gervais, & Trzesniewski (2012); Reddish, Tok, & Kundt (2016); Schaap-Jonker, Sizoo, van Schothorst-van Roekel, & Corveleyn (2013).

[37] For example, see Burdett, Wigger, & Barrett (2021); Willard & McNamara (2019).

[38] Boyer (2001, p. 142); Guthrie (1993, 2021).

[39] Tillich (1957).

[40] Shaman, Saide, & Richert (2018); Shtulman & Lindeman (2016); Willard et al. (2020); Willard & Norenzayan (2013).

[41] J. Barrett & Keil (1996); Heiphetz, Lane, Waytz, & Young (2016). Still other studies suggest that adults conceive of God's mind not only anthropomorphically, but also egocentrically—that is, by projecting or attributing their *own* beliefs onto God (e.g., Epley, Converse, Delbosc, Monteleone, & Cacioppo, 2009).

[42] Bloom (2004, 2009); Gervais (2013); Greenway & Barrett (2021, pp. 75-77); Norenzayan (2016).

[43] Bering (2011); Bloom (2004, 2009, pp. 123-124).

[44] Astuti & Harris (2008); Bering & Borklund (2004); Bering, Hernández Blasi, & Bjorklund (2005); Greenway & Barrett (2021, pp. 75-77); P. L. Harris & Giménez (2005); Watson-Jones, Busch, Harris, & Legare (2017).

[45] Bering (2011, p. 119).

[46] Jensen (2023).

[47] White, Willard, Baimel, & Norenzayan (2021); Willard et al. (2020).

[48] Astuti & Harris (2008); P. L. Harris & Giménez (2005); Watson-Jones et al. (2017).

[49] Astuti & Harris (2008); Jensen (2023); Watson-Jones et al. (2017).

[50] Jensen (2023).

[51] Haught (2008, p. 98); Jeeves & Ludwig (2018, pp. 133-135, 169).

[52] Atran (2002); Boyer (2001).

[53] J. Barrett (2009, p. 85); Swan & Halberstadt (2019).

[54] Atran & Norenzayan (2004); J. Barrett & Nyhof (2001); Boyer & Ramble (2001).

[55] Atran (2002, pp. 86, 97); Beebe & Duffy (2020); Sommer, Musolino, & Hemmer (2023). See Purzycki & Willard (2016) for a review.

[56] Bendixen & Purzycki (2021, p. 308).

[57] Gervais (2021); Gervais & Henrich (2010).

[58] Purzycki & Willard (2016, p. 29).

[59] J. Barrett (2009, pp. 88-89); Boyer (2001, pp. 189-191); Haidt (2001, 2007, 2009); Pyysiäinen & Hauser (2010).

[60] Haidt (2007, p. 998).

[61] Haidt (2009, p. 283). Haidt (2012, pp. 197-216) subsequently added a sixth moral dimension, Liberty/oppression.

[62] de Waal (2013); B. King (2017). See also Boehm (2012).

[63] de Waal (2013, p. 228).

[64] de Waal (2013, p. 238).

[65] Saroglou (2021, p. 55).

[66] See Teehan (2021) for a recent review.

[67] Bloom (2012); Haidt (2007).

[68] Polkinghorne (2009, pp. 95, 128).

[69] Bowlby (1969).

[70] Granqvist & Kirkpatrick (2013); Kirkpatrick (2005, 2012).

[71] Granqvist (2020).

[72] Greenway & Barrett (2021, pp. 70, 78).

[73] Banerjee & Bloom (2014); White, Willard, et al. (2021); Willard et al. (2020); Willard & Norenzayan (2013).

[74] Granqvist (2020, p. 342); Visala (2011, Chapter 1); F. Watts (2014, p. 118). The former view is sometimes referred to as the *massive modularity hypothesis* (Tooby & Cosmides, 1992).

[75] Jeeves & Brown (2009); P. McNamara (2006, Vols. II and III). For a recent review, see Grafman, Cristofori, Zhong, & Bulbulia (2020), who acknowledge that the neural basis of religious cognition and beliefs remains only "partially understood" (p. 131).

[76] See Norenzayan et al. (2016) for a theoretical approach that integrates cognitive and cultural learning mechanisms in cultural evolution.

[77] Beit-Hallahmi (2021, p. 358).

[78] Gervais (2021, pp. 23-24); Gervais & Najle (2015); Gervais, Shariff, & Norenzayan (2011); Gervais, Willard, Norenzayan, & Henrich (2011); Henrich (2009); Henrich & Gil-White (2001); Norenzayan (2016); White, Baimel, & Norenzayan (2021); Willard, Henrich, & Norenzayan (2016); Willard & Norenzayan (2013). According to CSR proponents, these various learning mechanisms have themselves evolved through a process of natural selection, enabling humans to more effectively acquire cultural information such as ideas, beliefs, and values.

[79] Gervais & Najle (2015).

[80] Gervais Shariff, & Norenzayan (2011, p. 404).

[81] Hitzeman & Wastell (2017); Lanman (2012); Lanman & Buhrmester (2017); Lowicki & Zajenkowski (2020); Maij et al. (2017).

[82] Lowicki & Zajenkowski (2020); Maij et al. (2017); White, Baimel, & Norenzayan (2021).

[83] Gervais, Shariff, & Norenzayan (2011, p. 403); Hitzeman & Wastell (2017); Shariff & Norenzayan (2007, Study 2); Uzarevic & Coleman (2021).

[84] Gervais et al. (2011, p. 404). Indeed, a number of findings call into question the contention that religion is natural, while atheism is not. These include the long history of religious skepticism and doubt (see Chapter 7); the prevalence of nonbelievers in the world today (see Chapter 8); the fact that more than half of people in some countries today are nonreligious; and evidence that most children who are raised as secular or nonreligious remain so as adults. See Kasselstrand et al. (2023, Chapter 4) for a discussion and evidence.

[85] M. J. Murray & Goldberg (2009, p. 194).

[86] Dennett (2006, p. 25, italics in original).

[87] Atran (2002, p. 4).

[88] Bulbulia (2009, p. 74).

[89] Bering (2011, p. 202).

[90] Visala (2014).

[91] J. Barrett (2009, p. 97).

[92] M. J. Murray (2009, p. 178).

[93] J. Barrett (2009, p. 98); A. McGrath (2017, p. 157); Plantinga (2015, pp. 33-35); Visala (2014, pp. 67-68).

[94] A. McGrath (2017, p. 105).

[95] Ruse (2014, p. 52).

[96] Bering (2011, p. 200).

CHAPTER 3: EVOLUTION AND CHANGE IN RELIGIOUS BEHAVIOR

[1] Dunbar (2022, p. 129).

[2] D. Johnson (2016, p. 206).

[3] N. F. Barrett (2014, p. 106).

[4] Rappaport (1999, pp. 22-26). More recently, D. H. Stein, Hobson, & Schroeder (2021, p. 114) offered a similar definition of rituals as "predefined sequences of action characterized by rigidity, formality, and repetition that are embedded in a larger system of symbolism and meaning."

[5] Henrich (2020, pp. 76-78).

[6] S. D. Piven et al. (2022). For recent reviews, see Abrams, Jackson, & Gray (2021); McKay & Whitehouse (2015, pp. 457-458); and Mogan, Fischer, & Bulbulia (2017).

[7] See Dunbar (2022, pp. 137-148) for a review of relevant studies.

[8] See M. Lang & Chvaja (2023) for a discussion and review of evidence.

[9] Sosis & Handwerker (2011). See also M. Lang, Krátký, & Xygalatas (2020).

[10] The basic approach has appeared under additional names or guises, including hard-to-fake sign of commitment model (Iron, 2001), honest signaling theory (Bulbulia & Sosis (2011), and commitment theory (Atran & Norenzayan, 2004).

[11] Alcorta & Sosis (2005); Bulbulia (2009); Bulbulia & Sosis (2011); Irons (2001); M. Lang & Kundt (2023); Purzycki, Haque, & Sosis (2014); Sosis (2006, 2023).

[12] Bulbulia (2009, p. 75). Sterelny (2020) observes that types of costly signals change as societies scale-up from egalitarian forager to more complex, hierarchical societies.

[13] Irons (2001, pp. 298-299). Some scholars have suggested that costly signaling displays might also involve sexual selection, in that particular displays could indicate that the individual possesses good genes or the kinds of traits that signal mate quality (e.g., see Liddle & Shackelford, 2021, p. 12).

[14] Rossano (2012).

[15] Henrich (2020, pp. 144-145).

[16] Iannaccone (1994).

[17] Wellman (2008). Wellman conclusions were based on an extensive study of evangelical and liberal Protestant churches in the American Pacific Northwest. The evangelical churches also adopted more aggressive growth strategies.

[18] Sosis (2006, p. 79).

[19] As will be noted later in this book, these past findings may need to be qualified somewhat by more recent trends. For example, more conservative religious denominations have not been immune from the most recent secu-

larization trends in the United States. Also, the Unitarian-Universalist community—in contrast to the declines seen in most mainline Protestant churches—has shown considerable growth in the past several decades (Baker & Smith, 2015, pp. 214-215).

[20] Sosis & Bressler (2003). Dunbar (2022, p. 92) cites additional studies that compared religious and secular communes and concluded that the generally larger size and longevity of religious communes, as compared to secular communes, suggests "that a religious ethos somehow enables the members to keep a lid on the fractiousness and squabbles that inevitably arise in small communities, thereby preventing the community from tearing itself apart."

[21] Soler (2012).

[22] Power (2017).

[23] P. Singh, Tewari, Kesberg, Karl, Bulbulia, & Fischer (2020).

[24] Hall, Cohen, Meyer, Varley, & Brewer (2015).

[25] Sosis, Kress, & Boster (2007, p. 244). Not surprisingly, costly signals may take on different forms depending on the resources of participants (Xygalatas et al., 2021; Xygalatas et al., 2013). The value of costly signaling also applies to religious or spiritual leaders (M. Singh & Henrich, 2020).

[26] Ginges, Hansen, & Norenzayan (2009). Frequency of prayer did not predict suicide attacks. The results supported the researchers' *coalitional-commitment hypothesis*, which proposes that religion's relationship to suicide attacks is independent of religious belief per se, but rather derives from the ability of collective ritual to strengthen commitment to coalitional identities.

[27] Sosis et al. (2007, p. 235). Whereas costly signaling theories have largely focused on rituals as an *external* signal of commitment to one's group, rituals may also enhance participants' *internal* commitment to the group—and thus the group's long-term survival (D. H. Stein et al., 2021).

[28] Gervais (2021); Richerson et al. (2016); Wilson (2002).

[29] Harari (2015, xiii); B. King (2017, pp. 6, 63); McBrearty & Brooks (2000); Smithsonian National Museum of Natural History web site: https://humanorigins.si.edu/evidence/human-fossils/species/homo-sapiens.

[30] In current usage, the term *hominin* refers to current humans (*Homo sapiens*) and our ancestors in the human lineage after separation from the Great Apes about six million years ago. In contrast, the term *hominid* refers to all Great Apes, including humans.

[31] McClenon (2002).

[32] Winkelman (2015).

[33] Alcorta & Sosis (2005, p. 269); Bellah (2011, Chapter 2).

[34] Asma (2018); Boehm (2012); de Waal (2013); B. King (2017, pp. 33-44).

[35] de Waal (2013, p. 20).

[36] Boehm (2012, pp. 94-130).

[37] de Waal (2013, pp. 17, 42).

[38] Rossano & Vandewalle (2021, pp. 83-85).

[39] J. H. Turner et al. (2018, see especially Tables 6.1 and 6.2) offer a comprehensive model of pre-adaptations and behavioral propensities and capacities our human ancestors inherited from the Great Apes. With increasing brain size, emotional and cognitive development, and language facility, these inherited propensities would have enabled religion and morality to eventually emerge in *Homo sapiens*. These pre-adaptations and propensities include, among others, basic primary emotions and the experience of collective emotional arousal, empathy, role-taking abilities, ritual and play behaviors, perceptions of fairness and justice, reciprocity, understanding of status relationships, and a sense of self in relation to others.

[40] Bellah (2011); Deacon & Cashman (2010); Dunbar (2022, pp. 153-175); McClenon (2002); Mithen (1996); Rappaport (1999); Torrey (2017); J. H. Turner et al. (2018, p. 134); Winkelman (2015); Wunn (2000).

[41] Rappaport (1999, p. 26).

[42] Bellah (2011, Chapter 3).

[43] Bellah (2011, Chapters 6-9). Recently, Australian philosopher Kim Sterelny (2020) has described similar phases in the evolution of religion, which he has labeled *embodied religion* (analogous to mimetic culture); *articulated religion* (analogous to mythic culture); and *ideological religion* (similar to theoretic culture), characterized by the more elaborate, centralized, and moralized narratives associated with the emergence of more complex hierarchical societies.

[44] Mithen (1996). German religious scholar Ina Wunn (2000) agrees with Mithen that there is no paleoanthropological evidence of religious practice prior to *Homo sapiens*. Wunn argues that neither *Homo habilis* nor *Homo erectus* were capable of the complex symbolic thinking required for religious expression. Although Neanderthals developed advanced intellectual abilities, Wunn views as mere speculation claims by some scholars that Neanderthals believed in a soul or afterlife. See also McBrearty & Brooks (2000, p. 519).

[45] Torrey (2017). By tracing the archeological evidence of ceremonial sites and temples, Torrey estimates the emergence of ancestor worship at about 11,000 years ago and the emergence of the first higher gods at sometime before 7000 years ago, as some ancestors were gradually elevated to deities.

[46] Rossano & Vandewalle (2021, p. 93).

[47] Rossano & Vandewalle (2021).

[48] Whitehouse & Hodder (2010, p. 127).

[49] Boyer (2005, p. 26); Hinde (2005, pp. 36-37).

[50] For a recent comprehensive review, see Whitehouse (2021).

[51] Whitehouse (2005, pp. 226-227).

[52] Q. D. Atkinson & Whitehouse (2011); Whitehouse & Hodder (2010); Whitehouse (2021, pp. 74-80).

[53] McClenon (2002); Winkelman (2015).

[54] Indeed, Dunbar (2022, pp. 32-33) cites a survey of 488 ethnographic societies around the world, in which "no less than 90 per cent incorporated altered states of consciousness into their belief systems."

[55] McClenon (2002). Unlike some other scholars cited in this chapter, McClenon contends that basic forms of religious behavior were present among Neanderthals, who would have experienced pre-linguistic and early-linguistic forms of hominid anomalous experience.

[56] Asma (2018); B. King (2017); J. H. Turner et al. (2018).

[57] B. King (2017, p. 156).

[58] Hayden (2003, Chapter 4).

[59] Hayden (2003, pp. 120-121).

[60] Hayden (2003, Chapter 5).

[61] See also Bellah (2011, Chapter 5) for a description of religious expression in chiefdoms and kingdoms.

[62] Hayden (2003, Chapter 11).

[63] Hayden (2003, Chapters 11, 12).

[64] Norenzayan (2013).

[65] Norenzayan (2013, p. 7).

[66] Henrich (2020, pp. 131-132).

[67] Norenzayan (2013, p. 28).

[68] Norenzayan (2013, p. 24).

[69] Norenzayan (2013, pp. 8-9). D. Johnson (2011) and Henrich (2020) offer similar views regarding the cultural evolution of Big Moralizing Gods. See also Fitouchi & Singh (2022).

[70] For a succinct recent discussion, see Lior (2023).

[71] Norenzayan (2013, pp. 120-121). Indeed, Norenzayan hypothesized that the Big Gods were one important factor contributing to the rise of agriculture and the large-scale societies that agriculture enabled.

[72] Boyer & Baumard (2021).

[73] Dunbar (2022, pp. 191-201); Henrich (2020, pp. 146-148). Dunbar views the emergence of Big Moralizing Gods as a way for societies to cope with the stresses associated with dramatically increased population sizes and socio-political complexity. In addition, he presents evidence linking rapid population growth, and the subsequent emergence of moralizing high gods, to the positive conditions (i.e., longer growing seasons, reduced pathogen prevalence) associated with the northern subtropical zone immediately

above the tropics during the Axial Age. This is where nearly all of the monotheistic religions first emerged.

[74] Turchin et al. (2023); Whitehouse et al. (2023).

[75] Lior (2023, p. 304).

[76] Rattfield, Price, & Collard (2019); Turchin et al. (2023); Whitehouse et al. (2023).

[77] Turchin et al. (2023).

[78] Peoples & Marlowe (2012); Turchin et al. (2023).

[79] Fitouchi & Singh (2022, pp. 252-253); Lightner, Bendixen, & Purzycki (2023); Purzycki, Willard, et al. (2022).

[80] Fitouchi & Singh (2022, pp. 252-253); Purzycki, Willard, et al. (2022).

[81] J. Watts, Greenhill, Atkinson, Currie, Bulbulia, & Gray (2015). There is also some evidence, at least in traditional Austronesian cultures, that ritual human sacrifice, performed by elites as a means of divinely sanctioned social control, played a role in sustaining social stratification (J. Watts, Sheehan, Atkinson, Bulbulia, & Gray, 2016).

[82] Dunbar (2022, pp. 163-175).

[83] Stark (2007, p. 6, italics in original).

[84] J. Barrett (2009, p. 97).

[85] A. McGrath (2001); Ryrie (2017).

[86] See M. Lang & Chvaja (2023) for a discussion and review of evidence.

[87] Richerson et al. (2016).

[88] Saroglou (2021, pp. 98-99).

CHAPTER 4: THE PSYCHOSOCIAL FUNCTIONS OF RELIGION

[1] Evolutionary adaptationist accounts of religion, as discussed in Chapter 3, offer "ultimate" explanations of religion, because they link religion to the survival and reproduction of individuals or groups. Yet, to the extent that people are consciously aware of—and can articulate—their reasons for religious belief and practice, they are more likely to draw on either religious explanations, such as their belief that God exists, or more "proximal" expla-

nations addressing the psychological functions or role of religion in their everyday lives.

[2] Quoted in Vail, Rothschild, Weise, Solomon, Pyszczynski, & Greenberg (2010, p. 84). Statius was a Roman poet of the 1st century AD.

[3] Roth (2001, p. 15).

[4] Tolstoy (1957/1983, p. 35).

[5] For a review, see Jong, Ross, Philip, Chang, Simons, & Halberstadt (2018).

[6] Mitchell (2004).

[7] Sample questions adapted from Batson & Stocks (2014, p. 142, Table 9.1).

[8] Bentzen, J. S. (2019); Höllinger & Muckenhuber (2019); Myers (2020); Norris & Inglehart (2011, pp. 61-65); Ruiter & van Tubergen (2009). Results from a recent study in 14 diverse societies, ranging from hunter-gatherer groups to market-integrated urban samples, suggested a possible qualification to these findings: Greater insecurity—in this case, food insecurity—was associated with greater religious commitment towards powerful, moralistic gods such as the Christian God or Hindu Shiva, but *not* towards less powerful local deities such as ancestors and spirits, presumably because only the former gods were seen as powerful enough to address individuals' insecurities (Baimel et al., 2022).

[9] Norris & Inglehart (2011, pp. 61-65).

[10] Stolz (2020).

[11] Fincher & Thornhill (2008); D. R. Murray & Schaller (2017).

[12] See D. R. Murray & Schaller (2017) and Terrizzi & Shook (2021) for reviews.

[13] Becker (1973, p. xvii).

[14] According to TMT, cultural worldviews imbue the world with a sense of order, meaning, and permanence. They also provide a set of standards and values (e.g., a moral code) through which we can attain a sense of personal value or self-esteem by meeting or exceeding these standards. For general

discussions of Terror Management Theory, see Greenberg, Vail, & Pyszczynski (2014); Soenke, Landau, & Greenberg (2013).

[15] See Soenke et al. (2013) for citations to relevant studies.

[16] Sibley & Bulbulia (2012).

[17] Christian Science Monitor (2024).

[18] Burke, Martens, & Faucher (2010).

[19] Norenzayan & Hansen (2006).

[20] Pyszczynski, Abdollahi, Solomon, Greenberg, Cohen, & Weise (2006, Study 1). Presently, however, it is not definitive that worldview defenses against mortality salience are universal around the world and, if they are, they may take different forms in different cultures (Burke et al., 2010; Ma-Kellams & Blascovich, 2012).

[21] Allport & Ross (1967).

[22] Jonas & Fischer (2006); Jong (2021); Jong et al. (2018); Soenke et al. (2013); Van Tongeren, Raad, McIntosh, & Pae (2013).

[23] Jong et al. (2018).

[24] Jong et al. (2018).

[25] Vail, Juhl, Arndt, Vess, Routledge, & Rutjens (2012).

[26] Rutjens, van Harreveld, van der Pligt, van Elk, & Pyszczynski (2016).

[27] Frankl (1963, p. 164).

[28] Quoted in E. F. Church (1987, p. 1).

[29] Frankl (1963).

[30] Frankl (1963, p. 157).

[31] Frankl (1963, p. 172, italics in original).

[32] Baumeister (1991); Emmons (1999); C. L. Park (2010, 2013); C. L. Park, Edmondson, & Hale-Smith (2013); Wong (2012).

[33] Emmons (1999, p. 138); C. L. Park et al. (2013).

[34] Heine, Proulx, & Vohs (2006); C. L. Park (2010); C. L. Park et al. (2013).

[35] L. A. King & Hicks (2012); Klinger (2012).

[36] Baumeister (1991, pp. 40-41, 195-196, 203).

[37] C. L. Park et al. (2013, p. 164).

[38] Stephens, Fryberg, Markus, & Hamedani (2012).

[39] McIntosh, Poulin, Silver, & Homan (2011).

[40] McIntosh, Silver, & Wortman (1993).

[41] Chamberlain & Zika (1988); Cranney (2013); French & Joseph (1999); Galek, Flannelly, Ellison, Silton, & Jankowski (2015); Peterson & Park (2012); Martos, Barna, & Steger (2010); Steger & Frazier (2005).

[42] Chamberlain & Zika (1988); French & Joseph (1999); Steger & Frazier (2005). However, see Galek et al. (2015).

[43] Emmons (1999, 2005); Mahoney, Wong, Pomerleau, & Pargament (2022); Schnitker & Emmons (2013); Tix & Frazier (2005).

[44] Steger, Frazier, Oishi, & Kaler (2006); Martos et al. (2010).

[45] Oishi & Diener (2014).

[46] Kay, Gaucher, McGregor, & Nash (2010, p. 40).

[47] Juergensmeyer (2020, Chapter 3); Kay, Gaucher, et al. (2010).

[48] Kay, Whitson, Gaucher, & Galinsky (2009); Kay, Gaucher, et al. (2010).

[49] Hogg (2014); Hogg, Adelman, & Blagg (2010)

[50] Van den Bos, Van Ameijde, & Van Gorp (2006).

[51] Hogg (2014); Hogg et al. (2010); McGregor, Haji, Nash, & Teper (2008).

[52] Kay, Gaucher, Napier, Callan, & Laurin (2008); Kay, Shepherd, Blatz, Chua, & Galinsky (2010); Laurin, Kay, & Moscovitch (2008). For reviews, see Kay, Whitson, Gaucher, & Galinsky (2009); Kay, Gaucher, et al. (2010). Hoogeveen, Wagenmakers, Kay, & Van Elk (2018) failed to find that a threat to personal control increased belief in a God who can control events. However, they did find that people in the United States (but not the Netherlands) with general feelings of low personal control reported greater belief in a controlling God.

[53] Sorrentino & Roney (2000, p. 37, Figure 2.3).

[54] McGregor et al. (2008); McGregor, Nash, & Prentice (2010).

[55] Summarized in Hogg & Adelman (2013).

[56] Carlucci, Albaghli, Saggino, & Balsamo (2021); Saroglou (2002a).

[57] Wellman, Corcoran, & Stockly (2020, pp. 143-147). These authors contrast the more certain and unambiguous messaging of these megachurches to the more abstract, questioning, and ambiguous messaging typical of more liberal Protestant churches.

[58] Kay et al. (2008, Studies 3 and 4).

[59] Kay et al. (2008, Study 3); See also Kay, Shepherd, et al. (2010, Studies 1 and 4).

[60] M. Zuckerman, Li, & Diener (2018).

[61] McGregor et al. (2010); Rutjens, van Harreveld, & van der Pligt (2013).

[62] Baumeister & Leary (1995, p. 497).

[63] Granqvist & Kirkpatrick (2013, p. 141).

[64] Maslow (1954).

[65] Baumeister & Leary (1995).

[66] Granqvist et al. (2010); Granqvist (2020); Granqvist & Kirkpatrick (2013); Kirkpatrick (2005).

[67] Cherniak, Mikulincer, Shaver, & Granqvist (2021).

[68] Kirkpatrick, Shillito, & Kellas (1999).

[69] Granqvist (2020). See also Cherniak et al. (2021) for a review.

[70] Granqvist & Hagekull (2000).

[71] Kirkpatrick et al. (1999).

[72] Krause & Wulff (2005).

[73] Aydin, Fischer, & Frey (2010, Study 1).

[74] Aydin et al. (2010, Study 2); Epley, Akalis, Waytz, & Cacioppo (2008).

[75] D. Johnson (2016, p. 94).

[76] White & Norenzayan (2022).

[77] D. Johnson (2016, pp. 74-75); D. Johnson (2018).

[78] Hartberg, Cox, & Villamayor-Tomas (2016).

[79] Xygalatas et al. (2018).

[80] Purzycki, Apicella, et al. (2016). However, in a comparison of small villages and large cities in China, Ge, Chen, Wu, & Mace (2019) concluded that reputational concerns, not belief in supernatural rewards and punishments, impacted generosity and honesty in charitable donations. In addi-

tion, in studies of 15 diverse populations that included pastoralists, foragers, horticulturalists, and wage laborers practicing Buddhism, Christianity, or Hinduism, it was less clear that generous or cooperative behavior extends to members of other religions (i.e., religious outgroups) (M. Lang et al., 2019) or is linked to the perceived moral concerns of the deities (Bendixen et al., 2023).

[81] Bolyanatz (2022); Hadnes & Schumacher (2012); Shariff & Norenzayan (2007); White, Kelly, Shariff, & Norenzayan (2019); Yilmaz & Bahçekapili (2016). Less supportive results have been reported in some cultural contexts (Soler, Purzycki, & Lang, 2022). Other researchers have investigated whether the mere presence of artificial cues of surveillance in one's environment (e.g., images of eyes) can lead to more prosocial behavior, but the results have been mixed (Dear, Dutton, & Fox, 2019; Northover, Pedersen, Cohen, & Andrews, 2017).

[82] DeBono, Shariff, Poole, & Muraven (2017); Shariff, & Norenzayan (2011). Quote is from Shariff & Rhemtulla (2012, p. 4). R. A. McNamara, Norenzayan, & Henrich (2016) showed in a study of Fiji villagers that the influence of supernatural punishment on prosocial behavior towards ingroup and outgroup members can depend on the nature of the God believed to be doing the punishing (i.e., the Bible God vs. a local ancestral god), as well as the extent of material insecurity in the community.

[83] Shariff & Norenzayan (2007); Yilmaz & Bahçekapili (2016).

[84] Fehr & Gächter (2002); Henrich, McElreath et al. (2006); Herrmann, Thöni, & Gächter (2008).

[85] Laurin, Shariff, Henrich, & Kay (2012, pp. 3272-3281).

[86] Norris & Inglehart (2011); P. Zuckerman (2014, pp. 42-52); P. Zuckerman et al. (2016, Chapter 4).

[87] Indeed, there is extensive research indicating that people tend to attribute their religiosity to the actual existence of God, their spiritual experiences to the presence of the Holy Spirit, their morality to their religious beliefs, and their conversion to divine influences, while being unaware of the unconscious cognitive, personality, socialization, and situational factors that are involved (see Galen, 2023, for a review).

[88] Galen (2023, pp. 44-45).

[89] DeBono, Poepsel, & Corley (2020); Public Religion Research Institute (2015).

[90] Baumeister (1991, p. 183).

[91] Asma (2018).

[92] A. McGrath (2001); Polkinghorne (2009).

[93] Baumeister (1991, p. 283).

[94] McGregor et al. (2010).

[95] Edmondson, Park, Blank, Fenster, & Mills (2008); Steger & Frazier (2005).

[96] For discussions of this point, see Allport (1950, p. 79); Baumeister (1991, p. 195); Emmons (1999).

CHAPTER 5: THE PSYCHOSOCIAL BENEFITS OF RELIGION

[1] Abu-Raiya, Pargament, & Krause (2016, p. 1272).

[2] Abrams, Jackson, & Gray (2021).

[3] Koenig, King, & Carson (2012); Masters, Boehm, Boylan, Vagnini, & Rush (2023); Powell, Shahabi, & Thoresen (2003); VanderWeele (2017).

[4] Koenig et al. (2012). For meta-analytic reviews of religion's impact on mortality, see also Chida & Steptoe (2008) and Powell et al. (2003).

[5] Koenig et al. (2012, p. 467).

[6] Koenig et al. (2012); Pargament (2013).

[7] Long & VanderWeele (2023); Powell et al. (2003); VanderWeele (2017).

[8] VanderWeele (2017).

[9] Ebert, Gebauer, Talman, & Rentfrow (2020).

[10] Garssen, Visser, & Pool (2021); Koenig et al. (2012, pp. 602-603); Saroglou (2021, p. 82).

[11] Clobert (2021); A. B. Cohen & Johnson (2017); Garssen et al. (2021); Koenig et al. (2012); T. B. Smith, McCullough, & Poll (2003); VanderWeele (2017); Yonker, Schnabelrauch, & DeHaan (2012). My focus in this chapter is on the relationship between religiosity and psychological well-being in relatively normal (i.e., nonclinical) samples. For a succinct

discussion of how religiosity relates to psychopathology, obsessive-compulsive disorders, and sexual repression, see Saroglou (2021, pp. 76-81). In general, Saroglou concludes that religion can interact with, or amplify, preexisting psychopathology, but is not its underlying cause.

[12] T. B. Smith et al. (2003).

[13] Russell, Yu, Thompson, Sussman, & Barry (2020); Yonker et al. (2012).

[14] Salsman et al. (2015).

[15] Garssen et al. (2021); Joshanloo (2023). In longitudinal studies, the relationship between religion and well-being is investigated over extended periods of time (rather than a single point in time), enabling stronger conclusions regarding the causal and predictive relationships between religion and well-being.

[16] Cragun & Speed (2022, p. 186).

[17] Garssen et al. (2021); VanderWeele (2017).

[18] VanderWeele (2017).

[19] Batson, Schoenrade, & Ventis (1993); A. B. Cohen & Johnson (2017); T. B. Smith et al. (2003).

[20] Batson et al. (1993, pp. 290-291).

[21] Mochon, Norton, & Ariely (2011).

[22] Berthold & Ruch (2014). See Vilchinsky & Kravetz (2005) for similar results with Israelis.

[23] Diener, Tay, & Myers (2011); Gebauer, Sedikides, Schonbrodt, Bleidorn, Renfrow, Potter, & Gosling (2017); Lun & Bond (2013); Stavrova, Fetchenhauer, & Schlösser (2012); Stoop & Baker (2018). In addition, Pearson, Lo, & Sasaki (2023) showed that cultural norms favoring religion (or not) may be more important for individual well-being in "tight" cultures, where cultural norms are more strongly enforced.

[24] Gebauer, Sedikides, Schonbrodt, et al. (2017, Study 1).

[25] Stavrova et al. (2012, p. 99).

[26] Diener, Tay, & Myers (2011).

[27] Ellison (2020).

[28] Mochon et al. (2011); Uzarevic & Coleman (2021).

[29] Pargament (1997).

[30] Pargament, Koenig, & Perez (2000). See also Vishkin (2021), who reviewed research showing that more religious people differ from less religious people in several aspects of emotion regulation, which can also be viewed as an aspect of coping.

[31] Abu-Raiya et al. (2016); Exline (2013); Exline, Przeworski, Peterson, Turnamian, Stauner, & Uzdavines (2021); Exline, Wilt, Stauner, & Pargament (2021).

[32] For example, see Exline, Wilt, et al. (2021).

[33] Abu-Raiya et al. (2016); Ano & Vasconcelles (2005); Gall & Guirguis-Younger (2013); Koenig et al. (2012); Pargament et al. (2000); C. L. Park, Holt, Le, Christie, & Williams (2018); Tix & Frazier (1998).

[34] Bockrath et al. (2022); Exline (2013); C. L. Park (2007); Voytenko et al. (2023).

[35] Askwith (2024); Winell (2017). Askwith defines "high-control" religious communities as those with rigid beliefs and authoritarian demands, and that use threats of divine punishment or social shunning to instill fear and to control thoughts and emotions.

[36] Exline (2013); Krause (2006); Tix & Frazier (1998); Krumrei, Mahoney, & Pargament (2009).

[37] For recent reviews, see Shariff & Mercier (2021); Tsang, Al-Kire, & Ratchford (2021).

[38] R. D. Carlisle & Tsang (2013); Chaves (2010); Galen (2012); Norenzayan (2014); Norenzayan & Shariff (2008); Preston, Ritter, & Hernandez (2010); Shariff (2015).

[39] R. D. Carlisle & Tsang (2013); McCullough & Worthington (1999, p. 1151); Tsang, McCullough, & Hoyt (2005). This apparent contradiction has been referred to as the *religion-forgiveness discrepancy*.

[40] Chaves (2010, p. 2).

[41] J. B. Johnson (2013); D. E. Campbell et al. (2021, Chapter 4); Myers (2012, 2020); Putnam & Campbell (2010); Petrovic, Chapman, & Schofield (2021). For qualifications and complexities, see Galen (2012,

2023, pp. 151-155); Reddish & Tong (2023); P. Zuckerman et al. (2016, pp. 163-165).

[42] See Galen (2023, pp. 151-155); Speed & Edgell (2023); P. Zuckerman et al. (2016, p. 165).

[43] Pew Research Center (2024c).

[44] D. E. Campbell et al. (2021, p. 71); Galen (2012, 2023, p. 150); J. B. Johnson (2013); Speed & Edgell (2023).

[45] Speed & Edgell (2023, p. 265).

[46] Uzarevic & Coleman (2021).

[47] Putnam & Campbell (2010).

[48] Malka, Soto, Cohen, & Miller (2011). For example, sociologist of religion James K. Wellman (2008, pp. 62-63) has noted the ambivalence of American evangelicals towards secular social programs, which are viewed as superficial and destined to fail. Instead, evangelicals prioritize personal conversion, repentance of sins, and one's relationship with Jesus Christ as "the necessary engine of personal transformation" and social change. There is also evidence that religious conservatives are more likely to place blame on the poor for their plight (Galen, 2023, pp. 52-53).

[49] P. Zuckerman et al. (2016, pp. 167-168).

[50] D. E. Campbell et al. (2021, see especially Chapter 4).

[51] D. E. Campbell et al. (2021, p. 81).

[52] Saroglou, Delpierre, & Dernelle (2004); Schwartz (2017); Saroglou & Craninx (2021).

[53] Saroglou et al. (2004); Saroglou & Craninx (2021).

[54] Clobert (2021).

[55] Graham & Haidt (2010); Graham, Nosek, Haidt, Iyer, Koleva, & Ditto (2011); Saroglou & Craninx (2021).

[56] See Saroglou & Craninx (2021) for citations to relevant studies. There is also some evidence of cultural differences in the strength of the link between religiosity and morality (Clobert, 2021). For example, the link may be stronger in relatively secular countries in which religion is more of a per-

sonal choice, as compared to those countries in which religious norms are more strongly enforced for everyone (Stavrova & Siegers, 2014).

[57] McCrae (2017).

[58] Ashton & Lee (2021); Saroglou (2002b). However, several researchers have questioned this finding. When the relevant studies compared people of high versus low religiosity they did not—at the low end of religiosity—distinguish atheists from people with merely weak or marginal religiosity, groups that might differ in these personality traits (Streib & Klein, 2013; P. Zuckerman et al., 2016, pp. 117-118). P. Zuckerman et al. have suggested that the relationship between religiosity and Conscientiousness might actually be curvilinear, "such that those who are strongly religious *or* strongly nonreligious score higher on Conscientiousness than those who are only somewhat religious or indifferent" (p. 118). For example, see Galen & Kloet (2011).

[59] When personality is measured using the alternative HEXACO personality model, comprised of Honesty, Emotional Stability, Extraversion, Agreeableness, Conscientiousness, and Openness dimensions, greater religiosity is also associated with greater self-reported Honesty, a trait that is subsumed under Agreeableness in the Big Five model (Ashton & Lee, 2021).

[60] Ashton & Lee (2021); Entringer et al. (2021).

[61] Saroglou (2017); Saucier & Skrzypińska (2006).

[62] Ashton & Lee (2021).

[63] Ashton & Lee (2021); Clobert (2021); Entringer et al. (2021); Gebauer, Bleidorn, et al. (2014); Gebauer, Paulhus, & Neberich (2013).

[64] Ashton & Lee (2021); Gebauer et al. (2013); McCullough, Tsang, & Brion (2003); Saroglou (2017, 2021).

[65] Gebauer, Sedikides, & Schrade (2017); Sedikides & Gebauer (2010, 2021).

[66] Galen (2012, 2023, pp. 159-162); Norenzayan (2014); Shariff, Willard, Anderson, & Norenzayan (2016).

[67] Sosis & Alcorta (2003).

[68] Sosis & Ruffle (2003).

[69] Baier & Wright (2001); Koenig et al. (2012, Chapter 12).

[70] P. Zuckerman et al. (2016, pp. 155-159).

[71] Malhotra (2008, p. 140).

[72] Hofmann, Wisneski, Brandt, & Skitka (2014).

[73] Norenzayan & Shariff (2008, p. 62). For comparable conclusions, see Galen (2012); Galen, Kurby, & Fles (2022); Norenzayan (2014); Saroglou (2012); Tsang et al. (2021).

[74] These priming methods vary in the likelihood that participants will become consciously aware of the priming content or the religious focus of the study. Such awareness could bias their behavior in the subsequent tasks assessing prosociality.

[75] Shariff et al. (2016). See also Billingsley, Gomes, & McCullough (2018) and Willard, Shariff, & Norenzayan (2016). More recent studies have generally replicated these findings (e.g., Nichols, Lang, Kavanagh, Kundt, Yamada, Ariely, & Mitkidis, 2020). However, Purzycki, Lang, Henrich, & Norenzayan (2022) concluded there is no clear support for a causal connection between priming moralizing gods and more prosocial action, and raised questions about the ecological validity and cross-cultural equivalence of the primes.

[76] Ahmed & Salas (2013).

[77] Xygalatas (2013).

[78] Duhaime (2015).

[79] Xygalatas et al. (2016).

[80] Norenzayan & Shariff (2008, p. 62, italics added).

[81] For a recent review, see Mancuso & Lorona (2023).

[82] Steger & Frazier (2005); Vilchinsky & Kravetz (2005).

[83] Ellison (2020); Krause (2022); C. L. Park (2007); VanderWeele (2017).

[84] Mollidor, Hancock, & Pepper (2015); Salsman, Brown, Brechting, & Carlson (2005); Speed, Barry, & Cragun (2020).

[85] D. E. Campbell et al. (2021, pp. 72-76); Graham & Haidt (2010); Putnam & Campbell (2010); Van Cappellen, Fredrickson, Saroglou, & Corneille (2017); Van Cappellen, Saroglou, & Toth-Gauthier (2016).

[86] McCullough & Willoughby (2009); C. Wood (2017); Zell & Baumeister (2013). Religion can promote self-regulation by providing clear standards for moral behavior; encouraging self-monitoring, aided by the specter of supernatural monitoring; building self-regulatory strength through rituals, prayer, and meditation; and reducing the emotional distress or suffering that can lead to impulsive behavior.

[87] Marcus & McCullough (2021).

[88] McCullough & Carter (2013); Ramsay, Tong, Chowdhury, & Ho (2017); Van Cappellen, Edwards, & Fredrickson (2021); Van Cappellen, Toth-Gauthier, Saroglou, & Fredrickson (2016); Van Cappellen, Zhang, & Fredrickson (2023); C. Wood (2017).

[89] Cauble et al. (2023); Koenig et al. (2012, Chapter 28); Washington-Nortey, Worthington, & Ahmed (2023). In most studies, participants self-reported these virtues, raising the possibility of social desirability bias.

[90] Krause (2022).

[91] Ellison (2020); Pargament et al. (2000).

[92] Ahmed & Salas (2013); Norenzayan (2014); Norenzayan & Shariff (2008); Preston, Ritter, & Hernandez (2010); Saleam & Moustafa (2016); Shariff (2015); Xygalatas (2013).

[93] Galen (2012, 2023, pp. 151-155); Saroglou (2012).

[94] Saroglou (2012, p. 907).

[95] Samson (2023, pp. 293-314).

[96] Shariff (2020).

[97] Pasek et al. (2023); J. M. Smith, Pasek, Vishkin, Johnson, Shackleford, & Ginges (2022).

[98] Inglehart (2021, pp. 134-143).

[99] Lim & Putnam (2010); C. L. Park (2007); VanderWeele (2017).

[100] Lim & Putnam (2010). In a recent study by J. E. Brown and colleagues (2023), participants in traditional religious services reported somewhat higher satisfaction with the quality of their social relationships than did participants in secular Sunday Assemblies, but did not differ in their overall quality of life or psychological health ratings. The researchers noted that the

differences in social relationship quality might have been due, in part, to the fact that Sunday Assemblies only meet once a month, whereas many churchgoers attend more frequently.

[101] Lim & Putnam (2010, p. 929). VanderWeele (2017) draws similar conclusions.

[102] Indeed, in a series of studies of American adults, researchers found that having a compassionate disposition, or compassionate feelings induced in a situation, were more important in predicting generosity for less religious Americans than for more religious Americans. The researchers inferred that for secular Americans one's level of compassion is important in motivating prosocial behavior, whereas for more religious Americans other factors such as religious doctrine, communal identity, or reputational concerns may be more important motivators (Saslow, Willer, Feinberg, Piff, Clark, Keltner, & Saturn, 2013).

[103] Putnam (2000, pp. 116-122); P. Zuckerman (2019, pp. 4-5) notes that when it comes to charitable giving, "community is more important than faith."

[104] Norenzayan (2014, p. 380).

[105] Shariff (2020, p. 191).

[106] Moon, Cohen, Laurin, & MacKinnon (2023).

CHAPTER 6: IS RELIGION HARMFUL?

[1] S. Evans (2024). The countries in which more than 60% shared this view were India, Sweden, Great Britain, Belgium, Netherlands, and France.

[2] Shariff (2020). In addition, P. Zuckerman (2019, p. 19) cites evidence that Christian fundamentalists in the United States, as compared to nonreligious Americans, are more supportive of corporal punishment of children.

[3] Wellman et al. (2020, Chapter 14, Appendix C).

[4] For example, P. Jenkins (2020, p. 89) refers to such scandals in Thailand and other Buddhist nations. See also, Wellman et al. (2020, Appendix C).

[5] Shariff (2020). Some evangelicals have supported climate action. For example, in September 2021, Young Evangelicals for Climate Action, a minis-

try of the Evangelical Environmental Network, hosted a rally in Washington, DC, to promote climate action (Pally, 2022, p. 107).

[6] Koenig et al. (2012, p. 73).

[7] Shimron (2023, February 23).

[8] Allport (1954/1979, p. 444).

[9] Brandt & Van Tongeren (2017, p. 77).

[10] The percentage of evangelicals who believe the Bible contains the literal word of God ranges from about 55 to 65% (Burge, 2021, p. 15).

[11] Batson et al. (1993).

[12] Tajfel & Turner (1986). Such research supported what has been referred to as *social identity theory*. For a recent discussion, see Galen (2023, pp. 95-99).

[13] Altemeyer & Hunsberger (1992, p. 118).

[14] Sample items are from the Revised 12-Item Religious Fundamentalism scale (Altemeyer & Hunsberger, 2004) and the RF Scale (Altemeyer & Hunsberger, 1992). Although individual variability exists within all religious denominations, some research indicates that scores on religious fundamentalism scales are highest, on average, in congregations of Evangelicals, Pentecostals, Baptists, and Jehovah's Witnesses, and lowest among Jews and the nonreligiously affiliated, with Catholics and mainline Protestants in between (Altemeyer & Hunsberger, 1992).

[15] For reviews, see Batson et al. (1993); Hall, Marz, & Wood (2010); Hunsberger & Jackson (2005); Rowatt, Shen, LaBouff, & Gonzalez (2013); Rowatt, Carpenter, & Haggard (2014); Whitley (2009).

[16] German Professor of Religious Education Heinz Streib and colleagues have described an alternative but similar set of religious orientations or "schemas" that can make or unmake prejudice. The *truth of texts and teachings* (*ttt*) schema is highly similar to fundamentalism. Individuals with this schema tend to exhibit Islamophobia, anti-Semitism, general racism, anti-black prejudice, sexism, homophobia, and a less welcoming attitude towards refugees. In contrast, individuals who exhibit the *fairness, tolerance, rational choice* (*ftr*) schema endorse fair, just, and rational consideration of

diverse perspectives, and individuals who exhibit the *xenosophia/inter-religious dialogue* (*xenos*) schema are open to inter-religious encounters and dialogue, are willing to reexamine their own truths or worldviews, and find inspiration and creativity in their interactions with those with different perspectives. The descriptions of the latter two schemas suggest some similarity with the quest orientation to religion, which, as noted here, has been linked to tolerance rather than prejudice towards various outgroups (Streib, Hood, & Klein, 2010; Streib & Klein, 2014, 2018).

[17] M. Campbell et al. (2019); Clobert (2021); Hoffarth, Hodson, & Molnar (2018); Jäckle & Wenzelburger (2015); Rowatt, LaBouff, Johnson, Froese, & Tsang (2009); Van Droogenbroeck, Spruyt, Siongers, & Keppens (2016); van der Toorn, Jost, Packer, Noorbaloochi, & Van Bavel (2017); Whitehead & Perry (2020). For reviews, see Etengoff & Lefevor (2021); Hunsberger & Jackson (2005); Whitley (2009).

[18] Jäckle & Wenzelburger (2015).

[19] Human Rights Watch (n.d.).

[20] Etengoff & Lefevor (2021).

[21] M. Campbell et al. (2019); Exline, Przeworski et al. (2021).

[22] Miller (2023, February 2).

[23] RNS Staff (2022, December 29). For example, as of January, 2024, more than 7,650 U.S. churches have departed the United Methodist Church, most of which are likely to join the new, more conservative Global Methodist Church (Crary, 2024, January 9).

[24] Shimron & Dell'orto (2022, December 5).

[25] Pew Research Center (2013).

[26] Lefevor, Milburn, Sheffield, & Tamez Guerrero (2023); Lefevor, Sorrell, Virk, Huynh, Paiz, Stone, & Franklin (2021).

[27] R. P. Jones (2017, pp. 116-120); Whitley (2009). Lefevor et al. (2023) found that the strongest predictor of homonegativity in a sample of U.S. congregations was the extent to which they endorsed literal interpretation of the scriptures, one indicator of religious fundamentalism.

[28] Etengoff & Lefevor (2021); Labouff, Rowatt, Johnson, & Finkle (2012).

[29] Hoffarth et al. (2018).

[30] Thomas & Whitehead (2015).

[31] Pally (2022, p. 112).

[32] For reviews, see Batson et al. (1993); Hall et al. (2010); Whitley (2009).

[33] Pally (2022); Tisby (2019). Pally (2022, Chapter 7) traces efforts within the Southern Baptist Convention (SBC) to address racism and White supremacy attitudes, but also the continuing racial animus within the church.

[34] Even the relationship between fundamentalism and racial prejudice may need to be qualified, however. Brandt & Reyna (2014) found that fundamentalists expressed prejudice towards African Americans when they were seen as violating important values (e.g., needing to work harder, having gotten more than they deserve), but otherwise did not express negative feelings towards African Americans.

[35] Batson et al. (1993); Ekici & Yucel (2015); Hall et al. (2010).

[36] Smietana (2022, February 7).

[37] Smietana (2023, August 28).

[38] Cowling, Anderson, & Ferguson (2019); Deslandes & Anderson (2019); Scheepers, Gijsberts, & Hello (2002). In a 2018 Pew Research Center survey of Western Europeans, the percentages who stated that immigration should be reduced were 40% for Church-attending Christians, 37% for non-practicing Christians, and 28% for religiously unaffiliated (Pew Research Center, 2018a). However, a study by Ekici & Yucel (2015) involving 37 European countries did not find a relationship between religious affiliation and prejudice towards immigrants.

[39] Rowatt (2019); Scheepers et al. (2002).

[40] Pew Research Center (2018b).

[41] Pally (2022, p. 99).

[42] Cowling et al. (2019). See also Rowatt (2019).

[43] Gushee (2020, pp. 152-154, 168).

[44] Pally (2022, p. 106).

[45] R. P. Jones (2017, pp. 163-166); Wright, Wallace, Wisnesky, Donnelly, Missari, Wisnesky, & Zozula (2015).

386

[46] M. K. Johnson, Rowatt, & LaBouff (2012b); Kossowska & Sekerdej (2015); Uzarevic & Saroglou (2020). There may be East-West cultural differences in the relationship between religiosity and prejudice towards religious outgroups (Clobert, 2021; Clobert, Saroglou, & Hwang, 2017; Saroglou et al., 2022).

[47] M. K. Johnson, Rowatt, & LaBouff (2012a); LaBouff et al. (2012).

[48] LaBouff et al. (2012).

[49] Rowatt & Al-Kire (2021).

[50] Saroglou et al. (2022); Van Tongeren, Hakim, Hook, Johnson, Green, Hulsey, & Davis, (2016).

[51] Neuberg et al. (2014); Stewart, Edgell, & Delehanty (2018).

[52] Neuberg et al. (2014).

[53] Brandt & Van Tongeren (2017); Clobert et al. (2017); Edgell, Hartmann, Stewart, & Gerteis (2016); Doane & Elliott (2015); Gervais, Shariff, & Norenzayan (2011); M. K. Johnson et al. (2012b); Saroglou et al. (2022).

[54] Humanists UK (2022).

[55] Gervais et al. (2011); Mallinis & Conway (2022).

[56] Edgell et al. (2016).

[57] D. E. Campbell et al. (2021, Chapter 10); Gervais et al. (2011).

[58] Edgell et al. (2016); Gervais et al. (2017).

[59] Pew Research Center (2020a).

[60] Gervais et al. (2011); Gervais et al. (2017). Belief in God may be a more important factor in trust than religious affiliation. For example, in one laboratory study, Christians more readily trusted a believing Muslim over a Christian who reported disbelief in God (Shariff & Mercier, 2021, p. 253).

[61] Brown-Iannuzzi, McKee, & Gervais (2018); Dubendorff & Luchner (2017). Baggett (2019, pp. 7-34) describes a number of misperceptions that Americans have of atheists, among them the view that atheists constitute a monolithic group, that atheism is a relatively new phenomenon, and that atheists represent an insignificant minority.

[62] Baggett (2019); D. E. Campbell et al. (2021, p. 186).

[63] Doane & Elliott (2015); Frost, Scheitle, & Ecklund (2022).

[64] Baggett (2019, p. 24) cites survey results suggesting that about two-thirds of atheists never or seldom discuss their religious views with religious people they encounter.

[65] Frost et al. (2022).

[66] Cragun, Kosmin, Keysar, Hammer, & Nielson (2012).

[67] Hunsberger & Jackson (2005); Rowatt et al. (2014).

[68] Altemeyer & Hunsberger (1992, 2005); Blogowska & Saroglou (2013); Brandt & Reyna (2010, 2014); Hall et al. (2010); Saroglou et al. (2022).

[69] Brandt & Reyna (2010, 2014); Clobert et al. (2017); Rowatt (2019).

[70] Brandt & Reyna (2014); Clobert et al. (2017); M. K. Johnson, Rowatt, Barnard-Brak, Patok-Peckham, LaBouff, & Carlisle (2011); Mavor, Macleod, Boal, & Louis (2009); Rowatt et al. (2013).

[71] Whitehead & Perry (2020). Ironically, Perry, Braunstein, Gorski, & Grubbs (2022) have found that endorsement of Christian nationalism predicts greater tendencies to affirm factually *incorrect* statements about religion's place in America's founding documents, policies, and court decisions, probably due to Christian nationalists' greater exposure to misinformation on these topics and their embrace of the Christian nationalist narrative.

[72] Whitehead & Perry (2020, pp. 10, 86, 105).

[73] Shimron (2023, February 8). Similar estimates of Christian nationalist adherents (11%) and sympathizers (19%) were derived in a survey conducted by Neighborly Faith (2023, December).

[74] Indeed, Whitehead & Perry (2020, p. 124) have noted that descriptions of fundamentalism "align perfectly" with what they observe for Christian nationalism.

[75] Whitehead & Perry (2020, pp. 16, 99).

[76] Kossowska, Czernatowicz-Kukuczka, & Sekerdej (2017).

[77] Uzarevic & Saroglou (2020); Uzarevic et al. (2021).

[78] D. E. Campbell et al. (2021, p. 220). See also Brandt & Van Tongeren (2017).

[79] Meral (2018, p. 20).

[80] Armstrong (2014, p. 15).

[81] Pew Research Center (2014).

[82] Pape (2005, pp. 16-17).

[83] Atran (2006, p. 127) cites 2005 data indicating that "80 percent of suicide attacks since 1968 occurred after the September 11 attacks, with jihadis representing 31 of the 35 responsible groups."

[84] Miller, E. M. (2023, January 17).

[85] S. Harris (2005, p. 27).

[86] Hitchens (2007a, p. 25).

[87] Dawkins (2006, pp. 260-261).

[88] For examples in the Bible, see Deuteronomy 13:6-11, 32:39-42; Jude 1:5; 2 Chronicles 15:12-13; Hebrews 3:12; 2 Peter 2:1; Leviticus 20:10, 20:13; 24:16, 25:44-46; Colossians 3:22, 4:1; 2 Samuel 13; Exodus 1:3-8, 21:17, 31:15. For examples in the Quran, see 2:96, 2:193, 3:86-91; 3:139-142, 3:169-170; 4:95-101, 9:23, 9:29, 9:73, 9:123, and 98.6. In *The End of Faith*, Sam Harris (2005) compiled a list of Quranic verses vilifying nonbelievers in the Islamic faith that filled more than five pages.

[89] Cavanaugh (2009, Chapter 3).

[90] Cavanaugh (2009, Chapter 1).

[91] Huntington (1996).

[92] For example, an analysis of all militarized interstate conflicts between 1950 and 1992 found that geographical contiguity was a much better predictor of conflict than was civilizational membership, and that conflicts were not significantly more frequent between states from different civilizational boundaries than between other pairs of states (Russett, Oneal, & Cox, 2000).

[93] Armstrong (2014, p. 395).

[94] Armstrong (2014, pp. 315-316, 379).

[95] Meral (2018).

[96] Meral (2018, Chapter 4, pp. 133-146).

[97] For example, see Dawson (2019); De Graaf & van den Bos (2021).

[98] J. W. Jones (2013); Stern (2003).

[99] Gregg (2016); Juergensmeyer (2000, 2020).

[100] Gregg (2016, p. 350).

[101] S. Stein (2011).

[102] Stern (2003, pp. 70-72).

[103] Basedau, Pfeiffer, & Vüllers (2016); J. W. Jones (2013); Meral (2018); Sells (2003).

[104] Ryrie (2017).

[105] Atran (2016); Atran & Ginges (2012); Atran, Sheikh, & Gomez (2014).

[106] Stern (2003, p. xix). Stern also notes the use of selective interpretation of religious texts to justify violence (p. 31).

[107] J. S. Piven (2017, p. 97, italics in original).

[108] For further discussion of this issue, see Dawson (2019); De Graaf & van den Bos (2021).

[109] Huntington (1996, p. 271); J. W. Jones (2013, p. 360); Meral (2018, p. 166).

[110] Sells (2003).

[111] Atran (2016); Swann, Buhrmester, Gómez, Jetten, Bastian, Vázquez, & Zhang (2014); Whitehouse (2018).

[112] Bonnin & Lane (2023); Whitehouse (2018); Whitehouse (2021, Chapter 3).

[113] J. W. Jones (2013, p. 365); Stern (2003, pp. 26-31).

[114] Stern (2003, p. 26).

[115] Waller (2013).

[116] Canetti, Hobfoll, Pedahzur, & Zaidise (2010); Mayer & Koizumi (2017); Sirgy, Joshanloo, & Estes (2019).

[117] Mayer & Koizumi (2017).

[118] Beller & Kröger (2018); Canetti et al. (2010); Sirgy et al. (2019).

[119] Armaly, Buckley, & Enders (2022).

[120] Adamczyk & LaFree (2015).

[121] Henrich, Bauer, Cassar, Chytilová, & Purzycki (2019).

[122] Echeverría Vicente, Hemmerechts, & Kavadias (2022).

[123] Basedau et al. (2016). Examples of countries meeting these conditions were Côte d'Ivoire, Nigeria, the Philippines, and Sudan prior to partition.

[124] Neuberg et al. (2014).

[125] Saiya (2017).

[126] For example, Ryrie (2017, p. 460) refers to the "divine summons to battle on all sides of World War I." Several scholars have noted that Nazi leaders during World War II made frequent references to the Christian God and hatred of Jews in their speeches and writings (Beit-Hallahmi, 2010; Epstein, 2009, p. 5; Neiblum, 2023, pp. 297-302). Beit-Hallahmi (2010) observed that religious polemicists have ignored the record of official Roman Catholic collaboration with dictators such as Francisco Franco in Spain, Antonio Salazar in Portugal, Josip Tito in Yugoslavia, and Benito Mussolini in Italy. P. Jenkins (2020, p. 85) argues that Japan also invoked religious justifications for their involvement in World War II.

[127] Labov (January 12, 2023).

[128] Pew Research Center (2024b).

[129] Doosje, Moghaddam, Kruglanski, de Wolf, Mann, & Feddes (2016); Post (2007).

[130] Fox (2004).

[131] Kiper & Sosis (2021).

[132] Meral (2018, pp. 142-143).

[133] Waller (2013).

[134] Philpott (2009).

[135] Silberman, Higgins, & Dweck (2005).

[136] https://www.rfp.org/

[137] Jain (2023, July 17).

[138] https://mfnn.org.

[139] Indeed, there is evidence that when American and Israeli Jews and Palestinian Muslims acknowledge their shared Abrahamic roots, they show more positive attitudes towards the other religious group, greater support for peacemaking, and greater willingness to make compromises on territorial issues such as a two-state solution to the Israeli/Palestinian conflict (Kunst, Kimel, Shani, Alayan, & Thomsen, 2019).

140 Banks (2023, June 9).

141 Smietana (2023, August 14).

142 Hertzler-McCain (2024, March 27).

143 Banks (2023, February 20).

144 Psychologists and social scientists have discussed a number of ways in which religion and its institutions can effectively promote conflict resolution, peace, and reduced polarization (Cavendish, 2023; Silberman et al., 2005).

145 VanderWeele (2020a).

146 Pally (2022, p. 105).

147 Dein, Loewenthal, Lewis, & Pargament (2020); Kanol & Michalowski (2023); Ruan, Vaughan, & Han (2023); Schnabel & Schieman (2022); VanderWeele (2020a); Wildman, Bulbulia, Sosis, & Schjoedt (2020).

148 See Dein et al. (2020) for examples. See also Pew Research Center (2021).

149 Pew Research Center (2020b).

150 Dias & Graham (2021). As of this writing, it was not clear how much this percentage was reduced by the implementation of vaccine mandates in subsequent months.

151 Dein et al. (2020); Olagoke, Olagoke, & Hughes (2021).

152 Dein et al. (2020).

153 CNN (2021).

154 Plohl & Musil (2021).

155 DiGregorio, Corcoran, & Scheitle (2022); Kranz, Niepel, Botes, & Greiff (2023); Olagoke et al. (2021).

156 Freeman et al. (2022).

157 DiGregorio, Corcoran, & Scheitle (2022); Levin & Bradshaw (2022); Perry, Whitehead, & Grubbs (2020); Schnabel & Schieman (2022).

158 Abrams et al. (2021). The authors acknowledge that these three types of moral character are not mutually exclusive and that people can shift between them depending on the situation.

159 J. C. Jackson & Gray (2019).

[160] Chaves (2010).

[161] Van Droogenbroeck et al. (2016, p. 797).

[162] Shariff (2020, p. 193).

[163] Burch-Brown & Baker (2016). See also Rowatt et al. (2014).

[164] Edgell et al. (2016).

[165] Gervais (2011); LaBouff & Ledoux (2016); Simpson, McCurrie, & Rios (2019).

CHAPTER 7: A BRIEF HISTORY OF HUMANISM AND RELIGIOUS SKEPTICISM

[1] Grayling (2013, p. 149).

[2] Hecht (2003, p. xii).

[3] C. G. Brown, Nash, & Lynch (2023, p. 30); Blankholm (2017); Epstein (2009, pp. 59-60). In Britain, Frederick James Gould, Ethical Culture vice-president, referred to "us Humanists" as early as 1909. Unitarian minister John H. Dietrich began using the term *humanism* around 1915. The English journal *The Humanist* was first published in 1917. The term *secularism* was first popularized by British freethinker George Jacob Holyoake in 1851. During the 19th century, the term *freethinker* was a common label for a variety of religious and political dissenters.

[4] For additional overviews of this topic, see Epstein (2009, pp. 38-60); Herrick (2005, pp. 4-11); G. H. Smith (2000, pp. 173-216).

[5] Baggett (2019, pp. 12-14).

[6] Hecht (2003, Chapter 1, pp. 1-44).

[7] Hecht (2003, pp. 95-98).

[8] Hecht (2003, pp. 102-111, quotation is on p. 108).

[9] Hecht (2003, Chapter 2, pp. 45-85).

[10] Hecht (2003, p. 145).

[11] Quoted in Hecht (2003, p. 151).

[12] Hecht (2003, pp. 155-162).

[13] Hecht (2003, p. 263).

14 Epstein (2009, pp. 45-47).

15 Hecht (2003, pp. 223-229).

16 Hecht (2003, pp. 227-230).

17 Hecht (2003, pp. 239-240).

18 Hecht (2003, p. 242).

19 Hecht (2003, p. 241).

20 In Anselm's argument, we can purportedly conclude that God exists from the concept of God as the greatest or most perfect being. Subsequent thinkers have pointed out the logical flaws in this argument.

21 Hecht (2003, pp. 250-263).

22 Hecht (2003, p. 261).

23 Grayling (2013, p. 141).

24 Grayling (2013, p. 142); Hecht (2003, pp. 274-275); Ryrie (2017, pp. 20-21). Theologian Hans Küng (1988, p. 20) described Erasmus as "a reformer before the [Protestant] reformers."

25 Hecht (2003, pp. 269-296).

26 In the 20th century, Albert Einstein famously reported that he believed in the God of Spinoza.

27 Quoted in Nadler (2011, p. 157).

28 Nadler (2011, p. 240).

29 Lilla (2007, pp. 78-80, 218); Nadler (2011, p. 55).

30 Lilla (2007, p. 78).

31 Lilla (2007, p. 75). Hobbes referred to the medieval theological-political system as a "Kingdom of Darkness."

32 Lilla (2007, p. 125). See also Hecht (2003, pp. 319-333).

33 Hecht (2003, pp. 341-355).

34 Walters (2011, p. 7). Walters notes the prominent influence on Deism of three 17th-century Enlightenment figures, Francis Bacon, Isaac Newton, and John Locke.

35 Joshi (2011, p. 8).

36 Walters (2011, pp. 269-272).

37 Walters (2011, p. 78).

[38] Walters (2011, pp. 40-43); Wills (2007, pp. 100-103). According to Walters (2011), the most influential British Deist was Matthew Tindal, whose book *Christianity as Old as the Creation,* published in 1730, became known as the Deist Bible.

[39] Wills (2007, p. 125).

[40] Wills (2007, p. 125).

[41] Walters (2011, pp. 51-85).

[42] Walters (2011, pp. 87-94). Quoted material is on p. 94.

[43] Walters (2011, pp. 113-144).

[44] Walters (2011, pp. 145-177).

[45] Epstein (2009, p. 51).

[46] Walters (2011, pp. 179-211). See also Wills (2007, pp. 152-171).

[47] Jacoby (2004, p. 51).

[48] Jacoby (2004, p. 52).

[49] Wills (2007, p. 171).

[50] Walters (2011, pp. 247-248, 264); Wills (2007).

[51] Hecht (2003, p. 371).

[52] Coles (1999, pp. 49-50).

[53] Hecht (2003, p. 441).

[54] Hecht (2003, pp. 391-392).

[55] Jacoby (2004, pp. 68-77).

[56] Jacoby (2004, p. 205).

[57] Jacoby (2004, p. 158).

[58] Hecht (2003, p. 417).

[59] Hecht (2003, pp. 414-416).

[60] Quoted in Blankholm (2017, p. 690). See also, C. G. Brown et al. (2023, p. 49).

[61] Hecht (2003, pp. 393-401).

[62] A. McGrath (2006, pp. 51-60).

[63] A. McGrath (2006, p. 57).

[64] C. Carlisle (2019, see especially Chapter 15).

[65] Hecht (2003, pp. 393-401).

[66] Joshi (2011, p. 89).

[67] Joshi (2011, pp. 55-75).

[68] Hecht (2003, pp. 419-427); Wills (2007, pp. 271-282).

[69] Wills (2007, pp. 263-266).

[70] Quoted in Jacoby (2004, pp. 214-215).

[71] Joshi (2011, pp. 92-93).

[72] Joshi (2011, pp. 41-53).

[73] Joshi (2011, p. 23).

[74] Quoted in Joshi (2011, p. 31).

[75] Joshi (2011, pp. 39-40).

[76] Coit was involved in the establishment of forty Ethical Culture societies in Britain, and in 1896 the umbrella Union of Ethical Societies (later the Ethical Union) (C. G. Brown et al., 2023, p. 56).

[77] Blankholm (2017) cites Adler's experiences with the Free Religious Association as part of the inspiration for his Ethical Culture movement. The Free Religious Association had been formed in the United States in 1867 by more radical Unitarians in response to the adoption of a more explicitly Christian platform by the American Unitarian Association.

[78] Quoted in Blankholm (2017, p. 695).

[79] Quoted in C. G. Brown et al. (2023, p. 50).

[80] C. G. Brown et al. (2023).

[81] Blankholm (2017, pp. 696-697).

[82] Epstein (2009, p. 171).

[83] Blankholm (2017, p. 701).

[84] Hecht (2003, p. 440).

[85] Joshi (2011, pp. 167-177).

[86] Jacoby (2004, pp. 338-347).

[87] Joshi (2011, pp. 103-117, 119-139).

[88] C. G. Brown et al. (2023).

[89] Joshi (2011, pp. 155-166).

[90] Camus (1955); Sartre (1946/2007).

[91] Quoted in Joshi (2011, p. 150).

[92] Joshi (2011, pp. 181-193).

[93] Sagan (2006/2007). Sagan did not self-identify as an atheist, viewing that label as too definite or absolute to describe his position, which was open to compelling evidence one way or another.

[94] Weinberg (1992/2007).

[95] See, for example, the collection of reflections by prominent philosophers edited by Antony (2007). In the opening sentence of his book *Nothing to be Frightened Of*, English novelist Julian Barnes expresses a similar sentiment when he writes that "I don't believe in God, but I miss Him" (Barnes, 2009, p. 3).

[96] Weinberg (1992/2007, p. 379).

[97] The works of the New Atheists have come under considerable criticism. For a representative critique, see Eller (2010).

[98] Stenger (2008, p. 199).

[99] Dennett (2006, p. 279). Sam Harris supplements this analysis by refuting the idea of moral relativism, arguing that it is possible to discern that some behaviors are objectively more ethical or moral than others, independently of religious faith (S. Harris, 2005, pp. 178-182).

[100] Stenger (2008, pp. 126-127). See also Holt (2012) and Krauss (2012).

[101] Stenger (2008, pp. 77-93).

[102] Hitchens (2007a, Chapters 4 and 16). See also Pinker (2018, p. 432).

[103] Dennett (2006, pp. 291-300); S. Harris (2005, pp. 16-23).

[104] Dennett (2006, p. 300).

[105] Warraq (1995/2020).

[106] Warraq (1995/2020, pp. 355-356).

[107] Ali (2015).

[108] See Pinker (2018, pp. 442-443) for an extensive list of such Muslim intellectuals.

[109] See Fidalgo (2023) for a discussion.

[110] Grayling (2013, p. 42).

[111] Grayling (2013, p. 13).

[112] Grayling (2013, pp. 238-239).

[113] Grayling (2013, pp. 18-21).
[114] Grayling (2013, pp. 238, 151-174). See Neiblum (2023) for another wide-ranging critique of the Abrahamic religions. Neiblum points to our increasingly naturalistic and scientific perspective, while emphasizing the need to move beyond religion in order to continue our progress in morality, social justice, and other human values.
[115] Blankholm (2022, p. 172) noted that during his fieldwork with secular people, most of them reported "that the New Atheists were a catalyst in their lives—whether for leaving religion, 'coming out' as a nonbeliever, joining a nonbeliever community, or becoming involved in secular activism."
[116] For example, see Brierly (2023, pp. 106-110); Haught (2008); McGrath & McGrath (2007).
[117] Hedges (2008); McGrath & McGrath (2007). For a discussion, see Cimino & Smith (2014, pp. 58-65).
[118] Brierly (2023, Chapter 1).
[119] Bruenig (2015); McDade (2023).
[120] Kitcher (2014).
[121] Epstein (2009).
[122] Pinker (2018, p. 431).
[123] Pinker (2018, p. 429). See also Grayling (2013, p. 14) for a similar view.
[124] For additional names of influential humanists, atheists, and agnostics, both historic and recent, see Bakewell (2023), Grayling (2013, p. 145), Hitchens (2007b), Joshi (2007), Hecht (2003, p. 483), Pinker (2018, pp. 442-443), and Ali (2015, Appendix). The latter two references list religious reformers, skeptics, and humanists in the Islamic world. The emphasis in Bakewell is on literary or "humanities humanists."
[125] Haught (2008); McGrath (2001).
[126] Polkinghorne (2009, pp. 145-147).

CHAPTER 8: IS THE WORLD BECOMING MORE SECULAR?

[1] P. Zuckerman (2008, p. 110).

[2] Norris & Inglehart (2011, p. 217, quotation is italicized in original).

[3] A. McGrath (2006, p. 242).

[4] Bruce (2002, 2017); Norris & Inglehart (2011, p. 3); Stark (1999); Eberstadt (2013).

[5] Copson (2017).

[6] In this sense, sociologists Kasselstrand et al. (2023) define secularization as *"[t]he process of shifting from beliefs, values, and behaviors rooted in the supernatural to beliefs, values, and behaviors rooted in the natural."* (p. 22, italics in original).

[7] Taylor (2007, p. 25).

[8] Taylor (2007, p. 3).

[9] Henrich (2020).

[10] Henrich (2020, p. 416). Other scholars have also linked secularization to pre-Protestant influences (Berger, 1967/1990; Hobson, 2018; Taylor, 2007). For example, Taylor (2007, pp. 154-155) described how spiritualities associated with the Axial Age brought about "a certain form of religious individualism," in which ideas of a good life were revised to include human flourishing that "can be carried through by individuals on their own." However, Taylor also viewed the Protestant Reformation as key in the winding path towards exclusive humanism. Hobson (2018, pp. 44-50) traces a number of pre-Reformation influences leading eventually to secular humanism, including the concept of rights, individual conscience, moral universalism, and the idea that all souls are of equal worth.

[11] Baggett (2019, pp. 19-20); Berger (1967/1990); Bruce (2002, 2017); Gregory (2012); Lilla (2007); Taylor (2007); Weber (1904/2003).

[12] Berger (1967/1990); Gorski (2000); Gregory (2012, p. 231); Taylor (2007). Max Weber apparently initiated the concept using the German term *Entzauberung* (Burge, 2021, p. 38).

[13] Berger (1967/1990, p. 111).

[14] Taylor (2007, pp. 80, 134, 266). Taylor (2007, p. 247) argues that this turn towards humanism would nonetheless need to have come through Christianity, with the Christian idea of universal love translated into a more

secular striving for altruism and mutual benefit. See also Hobson (2018) for a detailed argument regarding the roots of secular humanistic values in Christianity.

[15] A. McGrath (2006, pp. 206-207).

[16] Berger (1967/1990, pp. 158-159); Lilla (2007, pp. 226-228).

[17] Lilla (2007, p. 248).

[18] Baggett (2019, pp. 21-22).

[19] Gorski (2000, p. 148).

[20] Berger (1967/1990); Norris & Inglehart (2011, p. 7); Weber (1904/2003).

[21] Henrich (2020, p. 454).

[22] Taylor (2007, pp. 226-227, 234).

[23] Taylor (2007, p. 75).

[24] Joshi (2011, pp. 8-11).

[25] Fuller (2017, p. 572).

[26] Gifford (2019, especially Chapter 2).

[27] Bruce (2017, p. 65).

[28] Ryrie (2019).

[29] Weber (1904/2003). See also Bruce (2017); Taylor (2007, p. 179).

[30] Bruce (2017); Inglehart (2021); Norris & Inglehart (2011).

[31] Bruce (2002, p. 8); Bruce (2017); Norris & Inglehart (2011, p. 9).

[32] Jacoby (2016); Kaufmann (2010); Stolz (2020). Although the question of whether religious pluralism or diversity increases or decreases religiosity in the population was a question of significant debate among sociologists, particularly in the 1990s, recent research is consistent with the traditional view that pluralism has a negative impact on religiosity (Olson, Marshall, Jung, & Voas, 2020).

[33] Bruce (2017, pp. 59-60); Davie (1999, p. 76); Gorski (2000).

[34] Gregory (2012).

[35] Beck (2010, p. 106); Lilla (2007, p. 198); A. McGrath (2006, p. 119).

[36] Weber (1904/2003, p. 104).

[37] Friedman (2021/2022, see especially chapters 6 and 7).

[38] Taylor (2007, p. 68). See also Bruce (2017, pp. 58-60).

[39] Taylor (2007, Chapter 3).

[40] Bruce (2017, p. 60); Henrich (2020, pp. 10-16, 464).

[41] Beck (2010, pp. 39-40).

[42] Beck (2010, pp. 16, 86).

[43] Norris & Inglehart (2011, p. 53).

[44] Norris & Inglehart (2011, p. 220).

[45] Bentzen, J. S. (2019); Delamontagne (2010); Höllinger & Muckenhuber (2019); Paul (2009); Ruiter & van Tubergen (2009). Although existential security is confounded with a number of other factors, Inglehart (2021, pp. 63-66) reviews additional studies supporting the view that existential insecurity is a better predictor of religiosity than other relevant factors such as education and urbanization.

[46] Höllinger & Muckenhuber (2019).

[47] Delamontagne (2010).

[48] Gill & Lundsgaarde (2004). Also see Granqvist (2020, Chapter 11) for a review of relevant studies.

[49] Inglehart (2021).

[50] Inglehart (2021, pp. 1-8).

[51] Inglehart (2021, pp. 12-16).

[52] Inglehart (2021, pp. 66-71). Sociologists Kasselstrand, Zuckerman, & Cragun (2023) have recently proposed a rather comprehensive theory of secularization that integrates many of the components discussed here, including economic development, differentiation, rationalization, religious pluralism, existential security, and childhood autonomy. The new component, childhood autonomy, proposes that "children who are granted higher levels of autonomy regarding their religiosity will generally be less religious than are the parents" (p. 36).

[53] P. Zuckerman (2008). For example, in a global ranking of the peace and security of nations, Denmark ranked third, Sweden seventh, and Norway first.

[54] Research generally shows that women are more religious, on average, than men; that women play a greater role in support of religion in the family; and that working women are less religious than non-working women (e.g., P. Zuckerman, 2008, pp. 115-116). C. G. Brown (2017) describes how female narratives of their journey toward atheism often mention the impact on family relations, changing mores regarding marriage and heterosexual activity, and feminism generally.

[55] Burge (2021, Chapter 2); Baggett (2019, pp. 4-5); Inglehart (2021, pp. 2-3, 84); Pinker (2018, pp. 438-439); P. Zuckerman (2014, pp. 66-72); P. Zuckerman (2019, pp. xiv-xxi).

[56] Kasselstrand et al. (2023, pp. 53-70); Norris & Inglehart (2011); Roberts (2023); Voas (2009); P. Zuckerman et al. (2016, pp. 4-6).

[57] P. Zuckerman et al. (2016, p. 5). At the high end of disbelief are France (40%) and the Czech Republic (37%).

[58] Burge (2021, p. 39, Figure 2.1).

[59] Norris & Inglehart (2011, p. 86); Voas (2009).

[60] Eberstadt (2013, p. 9).

[61] Davie (1999, p. 83).

[62] For example, survey evidence suggests that historically Protestant countries such as Britain and the Scandinavian countries secularized first. However, more recently, the most religious countries, including predominantly Catholic nations, have been showing the greatest declines in religiosity (Eberstadt, 2013, p. 53; Norris & Inglehart, 2011; Voas, 2009). For example, the more recent collapse of religiosity in predominantly Catholic Ireland—where, for example, rates of mass attendance plunged from 91% in 1973 to 34% in 2005—has been particularly noteworthy (Eberstadt, 2013, pp. 111-114; Voas, 2009). In recent years, Catholic Poland appears to be following a similar trend, with young people, in particular, leaving the church is large numbers (Piela, 2023, October 18).

[63] Voas (2009). See also Stolz (2020).

[64] Stolz (2020).

[65] Inglehart (2021); Kasselstrand et al. (2023, pp. 53-70); Roberts (2023).

[66] Inglehart (2021, pp. 85-86).

[67] Roberts (2023).

[68] Kasselstrand et al. (2023, pp. 53-70). The authors note the following non-European countries that show meaningful declines in belief in God: South Korea, Hong Kong, Japan, New Zealand, Australia, India, Uruguay, Singapore, Chile, Malaysia, Columbia, and Indonesia. We also see declines in religious affiliation in most European countries, Canada and the United States, South American countries, and modern countries in Asia (i.e., Australia, New Zealand, Japan, and South Korea). Religious affiliation can be a less definitive indicator of secularization because in many countries identification with a religion may reflect a cultural identity, rather than religious belief or practice.

[69] Roberts (2023, p. 667).

[70] Keysar (2017, p. 41); Pinker (2018, pp. 436-437).

[71] Keysar & Navarro-Rivera (2013); P. Zuckerman (2008, p. 96). Drawing on numerous international surveys, P. Zuckerman (2014, p. 46) concluded that the most secular nations on earth—that is, those with the highest rates of atheism, agnosticism, or theological indifference—include Sweden, Denmark, the Czech Republic, Japan, Canada, Norway, Finland, China, New Zealand, South Korea, Estonia, France, Vietnam, Russia, Bulgaria, Netherlands, Slovenia, Germany, Hungary, Great Britain, Australia, and Belgium. The most religious nations on earth—those highest in theism—include Nigeria, Uganda, the Philippines, Pakistan, Morocco, Egypt, Zimbabwe, Bangladesh, El Salvador, Columbia, Senegal, Malawi, Indonesia, Brazil, Peru, Jordan, Algeria, Ghana, Venezuela, Mexico, and Sierra Leone.

[72] Stark (1999).

[73] Norris & Inglehart (2011, pp. 108, 226); Delamontagne (2010); Paul (2009).

[74] P. Jenkins (2020, pp. 112-114); Norris & Inglehart (2011, p. 226).

[75] Eberstadt (2013) attributed the relatively greater religiosity of the United States, as compared to Europe, to the greater relative strength of the natural family in the United States. P. Jenkins (2020, p. 111) points to the decen-

tralized nature of American society and media, enabling religious broadcasters to flourish in many parts of the country.

[76] Burge (2021, p. 40, Figure 2.2).

[77] Kasselstrand et al. (2023, pp. 88-94); Norris & Inglehart (2011, p. 268); Voas & Chaves (2016). In addition, whether Americans *perceive* the U.S. as predominantly religious or secular may depend on where they live, with evangelicals more heavily concentrated in small towns and rural areas, particularly in the South and Midwest, and secularists more concentrated in urban cities in the North East and on the Pacific Coast (Norris & Inglehart, 2011, p. 94).

[78] Putnam & Campbell (2010).

[79] Smietana (2024, March 25).

[80] Burge (2021, pp. 29-33); D. E. Campbell et al. (2021, p. 3); Pew Research Center (2024c).

[81] Kasselstrand et al. (2023, p. 21).

[82] See Burge (2021, pp. 15-29) for detailed graphs and analyses of which religious groups have shown the most (e.g., mainline Protestants) and least (e.g., Evangelical Protestants, Black Protestants, Jews) decline in recent decades. Catholics show a moderate decline, particularly in the last decade. Some other faith traditions, including Mormons, have shown increases in membership in recent years.

[83] Inglehart (2021, p. 42). See Kasselstrand et al. (2023, pp. 88-94) and Pew Research Center (2019) for similar evidence of decline of religiosity in the United States. In addition, a decline in specific beliefs was reported in a 2023 Pew Research Center survey of 1,011 American adults, which showed drops from 2001 to 2023 in the percentages of Americans believing in God (from 90% to 74%), Heaven (83% to 67%), angels (79% to 69%), Hell (71% to 59%) and the Devil (68% to 58%) (Pew Research Center, 2023a).

[84] Pew Research Center (2022). In making these projections, the Pew Research Center took into account realistic projections regarding religious switching.

[85] R. P. Jones (2017, p. 49).

[86] R. P. Jones (2017, p. 51).

[87] Inglehart (2021, pp. 27-28).

[88] Inglehart (2021, p. 97).

[89] A. McGrath (2006, pp. 192-197); Ryrie (2017, Chapter 16).

[90] Eberstadt (2013, p. 30); A. McGrath (2006, pp. 192-197).

[91] Ryrie (2017, Chapter 16). Quoted material is on pp. 426, 462.

[92] Beck (2010, p. 30).

[93] Molina (2023, January 30).

[94] Bird & Thumma (2020); Wellman et al. (2020).

[95] Somewhat distinct from the question of whether religiosity is growing or declining around the world is the extent of religion's influence in the public sphere. For example, ongoing debates over abortion, LGBTQ+ rights, religious freedom, and other social issues reveal the continuing influence of religion in politics and society. Andrew Copson, Chief Executive of Humanists UK, noted a resurgence of transnational religious NGOs in the 21st century and their efforts to "roll back secularism in national laws and constitutions" (Copson, 2017, p. 134).

[96] Fox (2004); Kaufmann (2010). Inglehart (2021, pp. 30-33) disagrees that fundamentalism is growing throughout the world, instead viewing it, demographically, as in retreat. However, fundamentalist movements will continue to arise in less secure sectors of advanced societies.

[97] Similarly, Charles Taylor (2007, p. 95) depicted the path towards secularity as a "zig-zag" process.

[98] Berger (1967/1990, pp. 161-166). See also Lilla (2007, pp. 261-275).

[99] Wills (2007, pp. 100-117, 287-302).

[100] Baker & Smith (2015, pp. 67-80); Bruinius (2024); R. P. Jones (2017); Wills (2007, pp. 480-494).

[101] Pew Research Center (2021). At the same time, however, church attendance in the United States has not fully recovered from the pandemic and it is likely that some people—particularly among the young and those with more marginal ties to religious communities—have severed ties completely (Smietana, 2023, January 5).

[102] Jacoby (2016).

[103] Sandage & Moe (2013, p. 408) cite national survey data showing that such "switching" is common in the United States.

[104] Jacoby (2016). Prominent examples include the English writers G. K. Chesterton and C. S. Lewis, author of the *Narnia* novels, and American physician and geneticist Francis Collins, former head of the Human Genome Project. Brierly (2023) and McDade (2023) note a number of recent examples of individuals who have converted from atheism to religion. Some recent commentators have pointed to religious conversions among people who have listened to Jordan Peterson's lectures on the Book of Genesis and young men's character, referring to a "Jordan Peterson Effect" (Saliashvili, 2024, February 15).

[105] T. W. Smith (2006).

[106] For a review, see Sandage & Moe (2013). For common antecedent personal problems associated with religious/spiritual conversions, see T. W. Smith (2006). The classical perspective is illustrated by the work of American philosopher and psychologist William James (1902/1985).

[107] Beck (2010). Fuller (2017, p. 578) expresses a similar idea with the phrase "spiritual niche picking."

[108] Davie (1999); Stark (1999). This phenomenon is sometimes referred to as "believing without belonging."

[109] Fuller (2017, p. 575); W. B. Parsons (2018).

[110] A. McGrath (2006, pp. 189-191).

[111] Eberstadt (2013, p. 56).

[112] Tillich (1957).

[113] Fuller (2017, p. 579). See also chapters in Van Ness (1996).

[114] Kasselstrand et al. (2023, pp. 40-45).

[115] Hackett, Stonawski, Potancoková, Grim, & Skirbekk (2015).

[116] P. Jenkins (2020, pp. 127-129); World Fact Book, Central Intelligence Agency, https://www.cia.gov/the-world-factbook/field/total-fertility-rate/country-comparisons.

[117] Kaufmann (2010); Shariff & Mercier (2021, p. 256). The causal relations between religiosity and fertility may be bi-directional or religiosity and fertility may share a common underlying cause such as modernization and existential security (P. Jenkins, 2020; Voas, 2022).

[118] Kaufmann (2010).

[119] P. Jenkins (2020).

[120] Hackett et al. (2015); Kaufmann (2010); Peri-Rotem (2022).

[121] Hackett et al. (2015); Pew Research Center (2015).

[122] P. Zuckerman (2008, p. 196, endnote 5).

[123] Bruce (2017, p. 69).

[124] Ryrie (2019, p. 206).

[125] Paul (2009, p. 424).

[126] Berger (1999, pp. 12-13).

[127] A. McGrath (2006, p. 271).

[128] Fuller (2017, p. 573).

[129] Taylor (2007, p. 677).

[130] Taylor (2007, p. 770).

[131] For example, see Berger (1999, p. 13); A. McGrath (2006, p. 187); Taylor (2007, p. 770).

[132] Gregory (2012, p. 383).

[133] Norris & Inglehart (2011).

[134] Berger (1999, pp. 4-6); Davie (1999, p. 76); Kaufmann (2010); A. McGrath (2006, pp. 213-215).

[135] Bruce (2017, p. 67); Kaufmann (2010); Norris & Inglehart (2011, p. 221).

[136] J. Barrett (2004).

[137] For example, see Coleman, Messick, & van Mulukom (2023); A. W. Geertz & Markússon (2010); D. Johnson (2012). For a review, see Caldwell-Harris (2012).

CHAPTER 9: SECULAR LIVING

[1] P. Zuckerman (2014, p. 3).

[2] Epstein (2009, p. 66).

[3] Grayling (2013, p. 4).

[4] Pew Research Center (2024c).

[5] Baker & Smith (2015); Burge (2021, Chapter 3); Caldwell-Harris (2012); Galen (2009); J. M. Smith (2017); Streib & Klein (2013); P. Zuckerman et al. (2016, pp. 106-112).

[6] Blankholm (2022, pp. 86-94); C. G. Brown (2017, pp. 139-143).

[7] Blankholm (2022, pp. 80-86). There are other complexities involving ethnicity. For example, among Latinos, rates of nonreligion are higher among the more assimilated. Among Asian Americans, second-generation and more assimilated individuals are more likely to be nonreligious (Baker & Smith, 2015).

[8] For explanations of gender differences in secularity or atheism, see Beit-Hallahmi (2021, pp. 358-360); Ozment (2016, p. 212); Willard & Norenzayan (2013); P. Zuckerman et al. (2016, pp. 105-106). Blankholm (2022, p. 21) has also noted that, traditionally, women have felt less at home in secular organizations, which have been dominated by White men.

[9] Vardy et al. (2022).

[10] Stolz (2020).

[11] See Stolz (2020, pp. 5-6) for citations to relevant studies.

[12] van Mulukom et al. (2023).

[13] Kasselstrand et al. (2023, pp. 59-60, Figure 2.3).

[14] M. Zuckerman, Li, Lin, & Hall (2020); M. Zuckerman, Silberman, & Hall (2013).

[15] Baggett (2019, p. 122); Caldwell-Harris (2012); Sherkat (2011); Stagnaro & Rand (2021, pp. 162-163); Uzarevic & Coleman (2021); M. Zuckerman et al. (2020); P. Zuckerman et al. (2016, pp. 112-116). The relationship between intelligence and nonreligiosity does not appear to be fully

accounted for by differences between religious and nonreligious people in levels of education (e.g., M. Zuckerman et al., 2020).

[16] Sherkat (2022).

[17] Yilmaz (2021); M. Zuckerman et al. (2013); P. Zuckerman et al. (2016, pp. 112-116).

[18] Pennycook, Ross, Koehler, & Fugelsang (2016). See also Gervais & Norenzayan (2012); Karim & Saroglou (2023); Pennycook, Cheyne, Koehler, & Fugelsang (2020); Ritter, Preston, & Hernandez (2014); Shenhav, Rand, & Greene (2012).

[19] Pennycook, Cheyne, Seli, Koehler, & Fugelsang (2012); Saribay & Yilmaz (2017). See Yilmaz (2021) for a review of relevant studies.

[20] M. Zuckerman et al. (2020).

[21] See Yilmax (2021, p. 151) for a review of relevant studies.

[22] See Clobert (2021) for citations to relevant studies. There is also some evidence, although not entirely consistent, that priming participants to elicit analytic thinking can decrease religious belief, whereas priming participants to elicit intuitive thinking can increase religious belief (Gervais & Norenzayan, 2012; Shenhav et al. 2012; Yilmaz, Karadöller, & Sofuoglu, 2016; Yonker, Edman, Cresswell, & Barrett, 2016).

[23] Gervais et al. (2018).

[24] Bahçekapili & Yilmaz (2017); Stagnaro, Ross, Pennycook, & Rand (2019).

[25] Bahçekapili & Yilmaz (2017).

[26] Caldwell-Harris (2012); Galen (2009); Galen & Kloet (2011); Streib & Klein (2013); P. Zuckerman et al. (2016, pp. 116-120).

[27] See Kasselstrand et al. (2023, pp. 128-132) for a review of the child-rearing values of secular parents in various countries.

[28] Pew Research Center (2023b).

[29] Norris, & Inglehart (2011); P. Zuckerman (2014, pp. 42-52); P. Zuckerman et al. (2016, Chapter 4).

[30] Epstein (2009, p. xiii).

³¹ Baggett (2019, pp. 212-215); Epstein (2009, pp. 34-37, 118-121); Grayling (2013, Chapter 17); P. Zuckerman (2014, pp. 12-13); P. Zuckerman (2019, Chapter 7).

³² Grayling (2013, p. 246).

³³ Shariff & Mercier (2021, pp. 258-259). P. Zuckerman et al. (2016, p. 172) contrasts this consequentialist perspective with religious perspectives, which tend to be more rule-based (e.g., "What does my religion say about this behavior?) and deontological (i.e., based on a behavior's inherent goodness or badness).

³⁴ Aronson (2008, pp. 86-87).

³⁵ Baggett (2019, p. 210).

³⁶ Grayling (2013, p. 185); Kitcher (2014, pp. 46-51). For a critique of this position, see MacIntyre (2007).

³⁷ Curry, Mullins, & Whitehouse (2019).

³⁸ https://www.un.org/en/about-us/universal-declaration-of-human-rights. Examples include the right to life, liberty, and security; freedom of opinion and expression; and prohibitions against slavery, torture, discrimination, arbitrary arrest or detention.

³⁹ Critics of religion as an independent source of universal moral values also point to the so-called *Euthyphro problem* introduced by Plato in the fourth century BCE, which raises the question: "Is something moral because God approves of it and commands it, or does God approve of it and command it because it is moral?" If the former is the case, then religious people would be obligated to follow any (perhaps arbitrary) moral commands made by God, including some rather distasteful commands presented in the Bible. If the latter, then we do not need God as an independent source of moral guidelines.

⁴⁰ Uzarevic & Coleman (2021); van Mulukom et al. (2023); P. Zuckerman et al. (2016, pp. 175-192).

⁴¹ For example, see Harris (2010).

[42] Arli, van Esch, & Cui (2023); Caldwell-Harris (2012); D. E. Campbell et al. (2021, Chapter 3); Epstein (2009, pp. 148-150); Keysar (2017, p. 52); P. Zuckerman et al. (2016, pp. 175-192).

[43] P. Zuckerman (2019, pp. 171-175).

[44] D. E. Campbell et al. (2021, pp. 87-89).

[45] Baker & Smith (2015, p. 186). In another national survey, Americans also *perceived* religion and secularity as linked to the major political parties, with religious people, and especially evangelical Christians, perceived as more likely to be Republicans, and nonreligious people and atheists perceived as more likely to be Democrats (D. E. Campbell et al., 2021, pp. 83-84).

[46] Hazleton (2016, p. 128),

[47] Epstein (2009, p. 8).

[48] Ruse (2019, Chapter 4).

[49] P. Watson (2014/2016).

[50] P. Watson (2014/2016, p. 149).

[50] Dreyfus & Kelly (2011, p. 102).

[51] P. Watson (2014/2016, p. 476). Philip Kitcher (2014, pp. 94, 158) also proposes that the secular life is diminished if we don't engage with great writers who have explored the human condition.

[52] Dreyfus & Kelly (2011, p. 102).

[53] For brevity, I have attempted to reduce and organize the proposed "ways to live" of the many artists, philosophers, and scientists that P. Watson reviews in his extensive book. My purpose is to provide some idea of the range of ideas proposed in the past few centuries as possible substitute sources of meaning offered by those who no longer found religion persuasive.

[54] P. Watson (2014/2016, p. 549).

[55] Epstein (2009, pp. 98-103); Grayling (2013, pp. 161-162); Kitcher (2014, Chapter 4); Ozment (2016, p. 240); Yaden, Iwry, Smith, & Pawelski (2017, pp. 558-565); P. Zuckerman (2014, p. 102).

[56] Grayling (2013, p. 148).

[57] See Uzarevic & Coleman (2021) for a review.

[58] Schnell & Keenan (2011).

[59] Uzarevic & Coleman (2021, p. 134). Atheist psychiatrist Ralph Lewis (2021) also argues that the increasing secular trend in modern societies is not leading to an alienated or nihilistic feeling of purposelessness or meaninglessness.

[60] Aronson (2008, pp. 56-63); Maslow (1964/1970); Vernon (2008, p. 70); Yaden et al. (2017, pp. 564-565); P. Zuckerman (2014, p. 209).

[61] Baker & Smith (2015, p. 92).

[62] Baggett (2019, Chapter 2); Baker & Smith (2015, p. 102); Epstein (2009, p. 28). See Streib (2021) for a review of the traits and values of people who deconvert or leave their religion.

[63] Baggett (2019, p. 73, Table 2.1); P. Zuckerman et al. (2016, pp. 97-100).

[64] Aronson (2008, p. 183); Grayling (2013, p. 217); Hazleton (2016, p. 154); Ozment (2016, p. 244); P. Zuckerman (2014, p. 197).

[65] Epstein (2009, p. xiii, italics in original).

[66] Hazleton (2016, p. 154).

[67] Baggett (2019, pp. 183-193).

[68] P. Zuckerman (2014, p. 192).

[69] For reviews, see Streib & Klein (2013), Uzarevic & Coleman (2021), and P. Zuckerman et al. (2016, pp. 131-132).

[70] Baker & Smith (2015, p. 95).

[71] Baker, Stroope, & Walker (2018).

[72] Speed (2022).

[73] P. Zuckerman et al. (2016, p. 144).

[74] Major international organizations include Humanists International (formerly the International Humanist and Ethical Union) and Atheists Alliance International. Major organizations in the United States include the Center for Inquiry/Council for Secular Humanism, American Humanist Association, American Atheists, American Ethical Union, Skeptics Society, Freedom from Religion Foundation, United Coalition of Reason, Unitarian

Universalist Humanist Association, and Society for Humanistic Judaism. The Secular Student Alliance is a college campus organization for nonbelievers, with locations throughout North America. Smaller organizations include Hispanic American Freethinkers, Black Nonbelievers, Black Secular Collective, Ex-Muslims of North America, Secular Woman, and Foundation Beyond Belief (Blankholm, 2022, p. 14). Many of the U.S. groups associate with the Secular Coalition of America, a political and cultural advocacy group on behalf of the nontheist community in the United States. In the United Kingdom, major organizations include Humanists UK and the National Secular Society. Based on first-hand interviews, Blankholm (2022) reports on the views of many of the leaders and activist members of these organizations.

[75] Humanist or secular holidays include World Humanist Day, celebrated on June 21; the National Day of Reason, held annually on the same day as the National Day of Prayer; Darwin Day, which celebrates Charles Darwin's February 12 birthday and reason and science generally; International Atheist Day, which on March 23 raises awareness about atheism and encourages nonbelievers to "come out" as atheist; Atheist Pride Day, celebrated on June 6; and International Blasphemy Rights Day, which on September 30 celebrates free expression, including the right to criticize or satirize religion.

[76] The Sunday Assembly organization was founded in London in 2013 and describes itself as "a network of secular (non-religious) communities who gather to celebrate this one life we know we have," and as "a global movement for wonder and good." (https://www.sundayassembly.org/). A similar group, the Oasis Network, was founded in Houston in 2012 and has a modest number of member groups in the United States and Canada.

[77] By one estimate, there are about 3,100 groups of various types catering to secular individuals in the United States (Baggett, 2019, p. 77).

[78] Stanton & Spratt (2023, June 28).

[79] For descriptions of many of these groups and their missions, see Cimino & Smith (2014) and the appendix in Epstein (2009). Ozment (2016)

draws on first-hand interview accounts to describe how various individuals are seeking secular replacements for religious meaning and community.

[80] D. E. Campbell et al. (2021, pp. 213-215).

[81] Blankholm (2022, p. 66).

[82] Epstein (2009, p. 217).

[83] P. Zuckerman et al. (2016, p. 207).

[84] Epstein (2009, p. 175); P. Zuckerman et al. (2016, p. 215).

[85] Cimino & Smith (2014, pp. 34, 81, 108, 158).

[86] J. E. Brown, van Mulukom, Charles, & Farias (2023); Charles, van Mulukom, Brown, Watts, Dunbar, & Farias (2021); Frost (2023); Price & Launay (2018).

[87] Galen & Kloet (2011).

[88] Karim & Saroglou (2023).

[89] I have drawn primarily on the following researchers in selecting and organizing the labels and varieties of secularity described here: Ammerman (2013); Baker & Smith (2015); Eller (2010, p. 5); Galen (2009); Hecht (2003, p. 485); Manning (2010); Najle & Gervais (2017); Sheridan (2021); Silver, Coleman, Hood, & Holcombe (2014); J. M. Smith (2017, pp. 520-521); P. Zuckerman (2008, pp. 98-106); P. Zuckerman (2014, pp. 63-64).

[90] Baker & Smith (2015); Galen (2009); Karim & Saroglou (2023); Lindeman, van Elk, Lipsanen, Marin, & Schjodt (2019); Schnell, de Boer, & Alma (2023); Silver et al. (2014); van Elk & Naaman (2021).

[91] Galen (2009); Schnell et al. (2023).

[92] Blankholm (2022, p. 52).

[93] Hazleton (2016, pp. 5-6, 21, 58-59, 65).

[94] Vernon (2008, pp. 53-56, 88).

[95] Kitcher (2014, pp. 23-25, 63, 124).

[96] Hazleton (2016, p. 79).

[97] Vernon (2008, p. 178).

[98] Karim & Saroglou (2023); Schnell et al. (2023).

[99] Van Ness (1996, p. 7).

[100] Fuller & Parsons (2018); Mercadante (2018); Pew Research Center (2017). Ammerman (2013), based on a qualitative study of religious and

nonreligious Americans, described the prevalence of SBNR people as quite small—at most 5 of 95 in her sample.

[101] Pew Research Center (2018a).

[102] Fitzpatrick & Parsons (2018); Fuller (2018); Mercadante (2014, 2018); Saucier & Skrzypińska (2006); Willard & Norenzayan (2017); Wixwat & Saucier (2021).

[103] Willard & Norenzayan (2017).

[104] Fuller (2018, p. 97).

[105] Jacoby (2016, p. 274); Ozment (2016, p. 210); Hazleton (2016, p. 115). Mercadante (2018) cites the following stereotypes she has heard about spiritual-but-not-religious people: "salad-bar spiritualists," "narcissistic commitment-phobes," and "anti-dogma experience seekers."

[106] Cragun & Kosmin (2011).

[107] Beck (2010, p. 85); Bruce (2017, p. 68).

[108] Mercadante (2014, p. 72).

[109] Mercadante (2018, p. 122). Based on interviews with American adults, Mercadante (2014, pp. 53-66, 68-91) identified at least five different categories of self-identified SBNR individuals, as well as some shared themes among them.

[110] Dennett (2006, pp. 302-303).

[111] Fuller (2017, p. 584).

[112] For example, see S. Harris (2014).

[113] Masters, Emerson, & Hooker (2022).

[114] See Galen (2023, pp. 127-139) for a review of relevant studies.

[115] Cimino & Smith (2014, pp. 124-125).

[116] Fuller (2017, p. 583).

[117] For a good example of an accommodationist approach, see Stedman (2012). For essays on this topic see the special issue of *Free Inquiry*, 2011, *31*(4).

[118] C. G. Brown et al. (2023).

[119] Kasselstrand et al. (2023, p. 116).

[120] Epstein (2009); Irwin (2019); Kitcher (2014); Stedman (2012).

[121] Moore (2023, p. 191).

[122] van Mulukom et al. (2023).

[123] Hobson (2018); A. McGrath (2006); Taylor (2007); Vernon (2008, p. 4). Throughout his book, Hobson (2018) describes secular humanism using terms such as *shallow, thin, insubstantial, hollow, superficial, and theoretically weak.*

[124] A. McGrath (2015, p. 223).

[125] A. McGrath (2006, pp. 187-188, 271-272).

[126] A. McGrath (2015, pp. 11-13).

[127] Taylor (2007, pp. 37-42, 302-309, 596-607).

[128] Taylor (2007, p. 307).

[129] Taylor (2007, pp. 299-313).

[130] de Botton (2013).

[131] Kitcher (2014, p. 122).

[132] Kitcher (2014, p. 122).

[133] Ozment (2016, p. 229).

[134] Blankholm (2022).

[135] In his interviews with American atheists, Baggett (2019, pp. 107-108) reports that some report experiencing such feelings of regret.

[136] For example, see MacIntrye (2007).

[137] P. Zuckerman (2014, p. 61).

[138] Some critics depict a rather narrow conception of secularity, for example, focusing on the limitations of atheism, while largely ignoring the many secular humanist writers who describe a broader humanistic life stance. This broader stance includes experiences of awe and wonder at the natural world, the arts, science, and so forth. For example, humanist Philip Kitcher (2014, pp. 124-133) argues that Charles Taylor's (2007) supposition that the lives of the nonreligious are somehow "flattened" is simply conjecture.

[139] P. Zuckerman (2008).

CHAPTER 10: THE PSYCHOLOGY OF WELL-BEING (WITH OR WITHOUT RELIGION)

[1] James (1902/1985, p. 78).

[2] R. M. Ryan, Curren, & Deci (2013, p. 64).

[3] For general reviews of the origins, progress, and future directions of positive psychology, see Csikszentmihalyi & Nakamura (2011); Diener (2009); Seligman (2019); Seligman & Csikszentmihalyi (2000).

[4] Recently, Shigehiro Oishi and colleagues have introduced the concept of the "psychologically rich life" and shown that it is related to but distinct from hedonic and eudaimonic well-being (Oishi & Westgate, 2022). Because research on this new conception of "the good life" is just emerging, I focus in this chapter on hedonic and eudaimonic well-being, both of which have been extensively studied.

[5] Diener, Oishi, & Lucas (2009); Peterson, Park, & Seligman (2005); R. M. Ryan & Deci (2001); Waterman (2013a).

[6] Accordingly, researchers sometimes combine these three components into a single index of hedonic or subjective well-being. However, because the components relate differently to some phenomena, it is often appropriate to treat them separately (Diener, Heintzelman, Kushlev, Tay, Wirtz, Lutes, & Oishi, 2017; Heintzelman & Tay, 2018).

[7] Deci & Ryan (2008); Huta (2013); R. M. Ryan & Deci (2001); Ryff (2013); Ryff & Singer (2008); Schlegel, Hirsch, & Smith (2013); Waterman & Schwartz (2013).

[8] Baumeister, Vohs, Aaker, & Garbinsky (2013); R. M. Ryan, Huta, & Deci (2008); For example, see Gruber, Mauss, and Tamir (2011, pp. 226-227) on "the wrong ways to pursue happiness."

[9] Butler & Kern (2016); Marsh, Huppert, Donald, Horwood, & Sahdra (2020).

[10] VanderWeele (2020b); Volf, Croasmun, & McAnnally-Linz (2020).

[11] VanderWeele (2020b, p. 46).

12 Diener, Oishi, & Lucas (2015); Myers (2000).

13 Diener, Diener, Choi, & Oishi (2018).

14 Paradoxically, some evidence suggests that people who are *moderately* happy may actually be better off in some ways—for example, in terms of income, education, and political participation—than people who are *very* happy. This could be because moderately happy people are more motivated to improve skills and performance, whereas very happy people may be more complacent in this regard. For reviews, see Diener, Kushlev, Tay, Wirtz, Lutes, & Oishi (2017); Diener & Chan (2011); Oishi, Diener, & Lucas (2007); Oishi & Kurtz (2011).

15 Brickman, Coates, & Janoff-Bulman (1978); Diener, Lucas, & Scollon (2006); Myers (2000). This proposition has been variously referred to as *adaption-level, set-point,* or *hedonic treadmill theory.*

16 McCrae & Costa (1991); D. Watson & Clark (1992). Indeed, an estimated 40-50% of the personality variability among people can be attributed to genetic factors (Vukasović & Bratko, 2015). The estimated heritability of SWB is in a similar range and, indeed, personality traits and SWB share some genetic influences (Diener et al., 2017; Ng, 2017; Tay & Kuykendall, 2013).

17 Diener et al. (2018).

18 For reviews see Diener et al. (2017); Heintzelman & Tay (2018); Luhmann, Hofmann, Eid, & Lucas (2012); Tay & Kuykendall (2013).

19 Bolier, Haverman, Westerhof, Smit, & Bohlmeijer (2013); Diener et al. (2017); Heintzelman & Tay (2018); Lyubomirsky & Layous (2013); Sin & Lyubomirsky (2009).

20 Cuijpers et al. (2021); Spielmans & Flückiger (2018).

21 For reviews, see Lomas & Vanderweele (2023); Myers (2000); Oishi & Westgate (2022); R. M. Ryan & Deci (2001); Tay & Diener (2011).

22 Lyubomirsky (2001); Tay & Diener (2011).

23 Kuykendall, Tay, & Ng (2015).

24 Diener & Biswas-Diener (2002); Lomas & Vanderweele (2023); Myers (2000); R. M. Ryan & Deci (2001). Seligman (2019, p. 5) cited a salary of

about $100,000 per year in the United States as "the inflection point at which markedly diminishing increases in happiness occur with increasing income."

[25] Lucas & Schimmack (2009).

[26] Lomas & Vanderweele (2023); R. M. Ryan & Deci (2001); Van Boven (2005).

[27] Kuykendall et al. (2015).

[28] Lomas & Vanderweele (2023).

[29] Lyubomirsky (2001); Oishi & Westgate (2022); R. M. Ryan & Deci (2001).

[30] Diener, Oishi, & Lucas (2015); Heintzelman & Tay (2018); Lomas & VanderWeele (2023); Tay, Herian, & Diener (2014); Tay & Kuykendall (2013).

[31] Lomas & VanderWeele (2023). For example, in the 2024 World Happiness Report, the ten most happy countries, based on average life evaluations for 2021 through 2023, were Finland, Denmark, Iceland, Sweden, Israel, Netherlands, Norway, Luxembourg, Switzerland, and Australia, while the 10 least happy countries were Afghanistan, Lebanon, Lesotho, Sierra Leone, Congo (Kinshasa), Zimbabwe, Botswana, Malawi, Eswatini (formerly Swaziland), and Zambia.

[32] For explorations of cultural universals and differences in the factors associated with happiness or subjective well-being, see Diener et al. (2017); Lyubomirsky et al. (2005); Oishi & Gilbert (2016); Ng (2017).

[33] Masters et al. (2023).

[34] Chida & Steptoe (2008); S. Cohen & Pressman (2006); Diener & Chan (2011); Diener, Kanazawa, Suh, & Oishi (2015); Lyubomirsky, King, & Diener (2005).

[35] Diener & Chan (2011).

[36] Lawrence, Rogers, & Wadsworth (2015).

[37] Chida & Steptoe (2008); S. Cohen & Pressman (2006); Diener et al. (2017); Nguyen & Fredrickson (2018).

[38] Diener, Kanazawa, et al. (2015); Fredrickson (2013); Fredrickson, Cohn, Coffey, Pek, & Finkel (2008); Lyubomirsky et al. (2005); Nguyen & Fredrickson (2018).

[39] Fredrickson (2013); Fredrickson et al. (2008); Nguyen & Fredrickson (2018). A variety of positive emotions are viewed as relevant to the model, including, but not limited to amusement, awe, contentment, compassion, curiosity, elevation, gratitude, hope, interest, joy, love, and pride.

[40] Van Cappellen, Edwards, & Fredrickson (2021).

[41] Fredrickson (2013); Fredrickson et al. (2008); Van Cappellen et al. (2021).

[42] Fredrickson et al. (2008, p. 1057).

[43] House, Kalisch, & Maidman (2018); Waterman (2013b); Yalom (1980).

[44] Rogers (1961, pp. 183-196).

[45] Maslow (1968, pp. 26-27, 137-138).

[46] Maslow (1964/1970, p. 20).

[47] Seligman (2019); Seligman & Csikszentmihalyi (2000); Wong (2017); Yalom (1980, p. 20).

[48] Diener, Wirtz, Tov, Kim-Prieto, Choie, Oishi, & Biswas-Diener (2010); Huppert & So (2013); Keyes (1998, 2002); Marsh et al. (2020); Ryff (2013); Ryff & Singer (2008); Seligman (2011, 2018); Su, Tay, & Diener (2014). Different aspects of social well-being include social acceptance, social growth, social contribution, social coherence, and social integration. For those models that also include hedonic well-being, positive emotions or life satisfaction are usually incorporated.

[49] Keyes (2002); Keyes, Dhingra, & Simoes (2010); Keyes & Simoes (2012); Keyes, Yao, Hybels, Milstein, & Proeschold-Bell (2020); Hone, Jarden, Schofield, & Duncan (2014).

[50] Keyes (2002); Keyes & Simoes (2012).

[51] Keyes et al. (2010).

[52] Hone et al. (2014).

[53] Keyes (2002); Keyes & Simoes (2012); Marsh et al. (2020); Schotanus-Dijkstra et al. (2016).

[54] Keyes (2002); Keyes et al. (2010); Keyes et al. (2020); Keyes & Simoes (2012); Fuller-Thomson, Lung, West, Keyes, & Baiden (2020); Ryff (2013); Ryff & Singer (2008); Wissing, Schutte, Liversage, Entwisle, Gericke, & Keyes (2019).

[55] R. M. Ryan et al. (2013); R. M. Ryan et al. (2008); Sheldon (2014).

[56] Kasser & Ryan (1996); Sheldon & Kasser (2001).

[57] Deci & Ryan (2008); R. M. Ryan et al. (2013); R. M. Ryan et al. (2008); Sheldon (2013, 2014).

[58] K. W. Brown & Ryan (2003); Deci & Ryan (2000); Niemiec, Ryan, & Deci (2009); R. M. Ryan et al. (2008); R. M. Ryan et al. (2013); Waterman (2013b).

[59] This has been demonstrated in a number of cultures, although the strength of the effects sometimes differs across cultures (A. T. Church et al., 2013).

[60] K. W. Brown & Ryan (2003); Grossman, Niemann, Schmidt, & Walach (2004).

[61] K. W. Brown & Ryan (2003, Study 5); Fredrickson et al. (2016); Grossman et al. (2004); Khoury et al. (2013).

[62] Csikszentmihalyi (1975, 1993); Nakamura & Csikszentmihalyi (2009); Tse, Nakamura, & Csikszentmihalyi (2021).

[63] McAdams & de St. Aubin (1992). See also Cox, Wilt, Olson, & McAdams (2010).

[64] Cox et al. (2010); Matsuba, Pratt, Norris, Mohle, Alisat, & McAdams (2012).

[65] Hicks, Schlegel, & Newman (2019); Schlegel et al. (2013); A. M. Wood, Linley, Maltby, Baliousis, & Joseph (2008).

[66] Jongman-Sereno & Leary (2019, p. 235).

[67] W. S. Ryan & Ryan (2019); Schlegel & Hicks (2011); Schlegel et al. (2013).

[68] Hicks et al. (2019); Jongman-Sereno & Leary (2019); Rivera, Christy, Kim, Vess, Hicks, & Schlegel (2019); W. S. Ryan & Ryan (2019).

[69] For example, see the Authenticity Scale of A. M. Wood et al. (2008). Inversely, a lack of subjective authenticity (e.g., self-alienation, accepting external influences) can be assessed with items such as "I feel out of touch with the real me" or "I am strongly influenced by the opinions of others."

[70] Jongman-Sereno & Leary (2019); Rivera et al. (2019); W. S. Ryan & Ryan (2019); Schlegel & Hicks (2011); Schlegel et al. (2013).

[71] Rivera et al. (2019).

[72] Van Cappellen (2017, p. 254).

[73] Algoe & Haidt (2009); Van Cappellen (2017).

[74] Emmons & Mishra (2011); Van Cappellen (2017).

[75] A. M. Wood, Froh, & Geraghty (2010, p. 891).

[76] Emmons & Mishra (2011); Gulliford & Morgan (2018); Watkins, Van Gelder, & Frias (2009); A. M. Wood et al. (2010).

[77] Keltner & Haidt (2003); Piff, Dietze, Feinberg, Stancato, & Keltner (2015); Shiota, Keltner, & Mossman (2007).

[78] Van Cappellen, Edwards, & Fredrickson (2021).

[79] Perlin & Li (2020).

[80] Rudd, Vohs, & Aaker (2012).

[81] Caldwell-Harris (2012).

[82] Piff et al. (2015); Shiota et al. (2007).

[83] Piff et al. (2015); Rudd et al. (2012); Van Cappellen & Saroglou (2012).

[84] Rudd et al. (2012); Shiota et al. (2007); Valdesolo & Graham (2014).

[85] Rudd et al. (2012, Study 3).

[86] Vandesolo & Graham (2014).

[87] For example, see Baumeister (1991); Frankl (1963); Heine et al. (2006); C. L. Park (2010); Wong (2017); Yalom (1980).

[88] Baumeister (1991); Christy, Rivera, Chen, & Hicks (2018); L. A. King, Heintzelman, & Ward (2016); Heintzelman & King (2014); Steger, Shin, Shim, & Fitch-Martin (2013).

[89] See Halama (2014); C. L. Park (2010) for reviews.

[90] Batthyany & Russo-Netzer (2014); Halama (2014); C. L. Park (2010).

[91] The first sample item is from the Meaning in Life—Presence scale (MLQ-P; Steger, Frazier, Oishi, & Kaler, 2006); the second from Ward & King (2016); and the third from the Life of Meaning subscale of the Orientations to Happiness measure (Peterson et al., 2005).

[92] Wong (2014).

[93] Heintzelman & King (2014).

[94] Oishi & Diener (2014).

[95] Baggett (2019, p. 133).

[96] Baumeister (1991); Christy et al. (2018).

[97] Hicks & King (2008); Steger & Frazier (2005).

[98] Oishi & Diener (2014). As the researchers concluded: "As society becomes wealthier, religion becomes less central to people's life. As religion becomes less central to people's life, more people lose a sense of meaning in life" (p. 427).

[99] Mascaro (2014).

[100] Christy et al. (2018); A. T. Church et al. (2013); Heintzelman & King (2014); Hicks & King (2009); L. A. King, Heintzelman, & Ward (2016); Lambert, Stillman, Hicks, Kamble, Baumeister, & Fincham (2013); MacKenzie & Baumeister (2014).

[101] Christy et al. (2018); Heintzelman & King (2014); L. A. King et al. (2016); Ward & King (2016).

[102] Heintzelman & King (2014, p. 563).

[103] Christy et al. (2018); Hicks & King (2009); L. A. King et al. (2016); Ward & King (2016).

[104] Duffy & Dik (2013); Steger, Pickering, Shin, & Dik (2010); Wrzesniewski (2015); Yaden & Newberg (2015).

[105] The first sample item is from the Brief Calling Scale (Dik, Eldridge, Steger, & Duffy, 2012). The other sample items are cited in Yaden (2015).

[106] For a review of studies, see Duffy & Dik (2013).

[107] Duffy, Allan, Autin, & Bott (2013); Duffy & Dik (2013); Steger et al. (2010); Wrzesniewski (2015).

[108] Christy et al. (2018); Czekierda, Banik, Park, & Luszczynska (2017); Heintzelman & King (2014); Hill & Turiano (2014); MacKenzie & Baumeister (2014); Masters et al. (2023); Peterson et al. (2005); Ryff (1989); Steger et al. (2013).

[109] Peterson & Seligman (2004).

[110] Peterson & Park (2009, p. 29).

[111] Biswas-Diener (2006).

[112] R. E. McGrath (2015).

[113] Buschor, Proyer, & Ruch (2013); Peterson, Ruch, Beermann, Park, & Seligman (2007); Wagner, Gander, Proyer, & Ruch (2020). For gratitude outcomes specifically, see Emmons, Froh, & Rose (2019); Emmons & Mishra (2011); A. M. Wood et al. (2010). For optimism outcomes, see Baranski, Sweeney, Gardiner, Members of the International Situations Project, & Funder (2021); Bouchard, Carver, Mens, & Scheier (2018); Scheier, Swanson, Barlow, Greenhouse, Wrosch, & Tindle (2021). For hope outcomes, see Gallagher (2023). For forgiveness outcomes, see McCullough, Tabak, & Witvliet (2009); Wade, Hoyt, Kidwell, & Worthington (2014); Witvliet & Root Luna (2018). For patience outcomes, see Schnitker (2012); Schnitker, Houltberg, Dyrness, & Redmond (2017). For humility outcomes, see Paine, Moon, Hauge, & Sandage (2018); Tangney (2009); Worthington & Allison (2018).

[114] Some researchers have made a potentially important distinction between *having* positive character traits and actually *using* them. Studies have shown that perceived *use* of one's strengths is associated with greater goal progress, self-esteem, SWB, vitality, organismic valuing, and psychological well-being (see Linley, 2013, for a review).

[115] Berthold & Ruch (2014); D. E. Davis, Hook, McAnnaly-Linz, Choe, & Placeres (2017); Emmons & Kneezel (2005); Root Luna, van Tongeren, & Witvliet (2017); Schnitker et al. (2017); Van Cappellen (2017). Also see Part III in E. B. Davis, Worthington, & Schnitker (2023). Paralleling the development of positive psychology, Schnitker & Emmons (2017, p. 239) note the development within theology of a field of *positive theology*, which is

reorienting theology away from original sin and human failings towards human well-being and flourishing.

[116] Schnitker et al. (2017).

[117] Long & VanderWeele (2023).

[118] Emmons & Kneezel (2005).

[119] Emmons, Hill, Barrett, & Kapic (2017).

[120] Titus (2017).

[121] Hodge, Hook, Kim, Mosher, McLaughlin, Davis, & Van Tongeren (2023).

[122] Emmons & Kneezel (2005); Rosmarin, Pirutinsky, Cohen, Galler, & Krumrei (2011); Schnitker et al. (2017); Schnitker & Emmons (2017); Van Cappellen (2017).

[123] Rosmarin et al. (2011).

[124] D. E. Davis et al. (2017).

[125] Van Tongeren, Stafford, Hook, Green, David, & Johnson (2016).

[126] Hook, Farrell, Johnson, Van Tongeren, Davis, & Aten (2017); Hopkin, Hoyle, & Toner (2014).

[127] Hook et al. (2017).

[128] For analyses and criticisms, see Krause & Hayward (2014); Nelson & Slife (2017); Robbins & Friedman (2018); Snow (2019); Stichter & Saunders (2019); Titus (2017).

[129] For example, see Cheavens & Guter (2018); Fava & Ruini (2003); Magyar-Moe, Owens, & Conoley (2015).

[130] Bolier et al. (2013); Chakhssi, Kraiss, Sommers-Spijkerman, & Bohlmeijer (2018); Dickens (2017); Grossman et al. (2004); Hendriks, Schotanus-Dijkstra, Hassankhan, Graafsma, & Bohlmeijer (2018); Hendriks, Schotanus-Dijkstra, Hassankhan, Jong, & Bohlmeijer (2020); Lyubomirsky & Layous (2013); Seligman, Steen, Park, & Peterson (2005); Sin & Lyubomirsky (2009); Wade et al. (2014). Higher quality studies tend to show smaller effects (Bolier et al., 2013; Hendriks et al., 2018).

[131] For analyses and criticisms, see Dickens (2017); Emmons & Mishra (2011); Oishi & Kurtz (2011); Wong & Roy (2018); A. M. Wood et al. (2010).

[132] Lazarus (2003); Moreno-Jiménez & Aguirre-Camacho (2018).

[133] Nelson & Slife (2017, p. 461). Nelson and Slife refer to this distinction as weak and strong transcendence, respectively.

CONCLUSION

[1] Irwin (2019, p. 56).

[2] Kitcher (2014, p. 154).

[3] de Waal (2013, pp. 94-95, 216); James (1902/1985, pp. 18-21).

[4] D. Johnson (2016, p. 171); Wilson (2002, pp. 227-229).

[5] Indeed, some skeptics of religion have asked why an omnipotent God did not dispense with the need for humans to evolve (and in some cases suffer) through all these diverse forms of religion on the way to monotheism. Why did God not simply hard-wire our brains to believe in only Him rather than the plethora of other supernatural entities that have emerged across human history and cultures? And would vast numbers of people in the world—historically and presently—miss out on salvation through no fault of their own because they were not born or socialized into the "one true religion"?

[6] Stark (2007, pp. 5-8, 54-63).

[7] See D'Costa (1986, especially Chapter 2) for a review of prominent pluralist theologians and religious scholars. See also McGrath (2013, pp. 549-551).

[8] Baggett (2019, p. 30) cites relevant survey evidence.

[9] The *pluralistic* perspective can be contrasted with *exclusivist* and *inclusivist* perspectives. An exclusivist perspective views one's own religion as the only true one, offering the only path to salvation. An *inclusivist* perspective proposes that people of all religions can be saved through God's grace, but that (in the case of Christianity) Christ is the most definitive and authoritative revelation of God (D'Costa, 1986). See Hans Küng (1988, pp. 227-256)

for an example of a largely ecumenical, pluralistic perspective. Wellman (2008, p. 109), in his study of evangelical and liberal Protestant churches in the American Pacific Northwest, concluded that liberal churches generally adopt a pluralistic perspective, whereas evangelical churches generally adopt an exclusivist perspective.

[10] https://news.gallup.com/poll/170834/three-four-bible-word-god.aspx. In the same survey, about half of Americans viewed the Bible as inspired by God, but not to be taken literally, while about 20% viewed the Bible as reporting "ancient fables, legends, history, and precepts written by man."

[11] For a discussion and critique of alternative theistic evolution perspectives, see Moreland, Meyer, Shaw, Gauger, & Grudem (2017). In contrast, advocates of Intelligent Design propose that God created the universe and designed living things in their final form directly. Proponents of Intelligent Design argue that the *irreducible complexity* of biological organisms requires an intelligent designer, typically implied to be God (Behe, 2006).

[12] For example, see de Waal (2013, p. 21); Henrich (2009, p. 255); D. Johnson (2016, pp. 136, 238); A. McGrath (2006, p. 231); Pargament (2013, p. 269). See C. G. Brown (2017) for personal narratives of many who became atheist.

[13] For example, see Lewis (2021) for an accessible discussion of extant and emerging theories of the origins of the universe, life on earth, and human consciousness.

[14] James (1902/1985, p. 16); Maslow (1964/1970, p. 29); Plantinga (2015, pp. 11-18);

[15] James (1902/1985, p. 16).

[16] Maslow (1964/1970, p. 29).

[17] Luhrmann & Weisman (2022). The authors refer to this immersive orientation towards experience as the capacity for *absorption*.

[18] Haught (2008, p. 60).

[19] For a review and discussion of prominent arguments, see Grayling (2013). For a detailed critique of 36 arguments for the existence of God, see Goldstein (2010).

[20] For example, see Craig (2008), A. McGrath (2017), and Plantinga (2015).

[21] Irwin (2019, p. 38). Rather, God is hidden (or as Thomas Aquinas stated, God is *deus absconditus*). A common religious response is that God wants us to believe in Him based on faith.

[22] Unger (2016, pp. 264-275). Pearce (2011), in his book titled *The Little Book of Unholy Questions*, presents 501 detailed questions about God, Jesus, the Bible, the problem of evil, creationism versus evolution, ritual, morality, and so forth. Although some of the questions can be viewed as irreverent or tongue-in-cheek, many raise cogent questions about the rationality or credibility of the Christian faith. Similarly, McAfee (2019), in his book titled *Disproving Christianity and Other Secular Writings*, describes many of the contradictions, improbabilities, and logical weaknesses that call into question the authenticity and divine basis of the Christian scriptures and traditions.

[23] Haught (2008, pp. 106-107); A. McGrath (2001, pp. 292-295).

[24] For discussions on this issue, see de Waal (2013, pp. 216-218, 249-250); D. Johnson (2016, pp. 187-191, 233).

[25] Brierly (2023); Hobson (2018); Taylor (2007).

[26] P. Zuckerman (2008, pp. 19-20) offers quotes from Jerry Falwell, Pat Robertson, Ann Coulter, Bill O'Reilly, William Bennett, and Paul Weyrich that express such views.

[27] See Brierly (2023, pp. 56-64) for a discussion.

[28] For an overview of some of the successes of the Nordic Model, see P. Zuckerman (2019, pp. 248-256). Henrich (2020, p. 464) cites studies showing that stronger social safety nets actually spur innovation and that this was the case in premodern Europe and remains so today. They do so by enhancing average cognitive and social skills in the population and by promoting independence.

[29] Burge (2021, pp. 15-27); Iannacone (1994); Wellman (2008).

[30] Hedges (2008, p. 4).

[31] Lilla (2007, p. 301); A. McGrath (2006, pp. 213-216). Similarly, Wellman et al. (2020, p. 71) have argued that the success of megachurches in the United States is tied, in part, to the emotional energy their services generate among participants, whereas "the diminishing of emotion's importance in church life and practice has been one of the primary failings of mainline Protestants."

[32] For example, see S. Harris (2005, pp. 17-21).

[33] Unger (2016, p. 263).

[34] For example, see Burge (2021, pp. 17-18, Figure 1.2).

[35] Gushee (2020, p. 1).

[36] Public Religion Research Institute (2021).

[37] Baker & Smith (2015, pp. 214-215). Indeed, the UUA website contains a page titled "Atheist and Agnostic Unitarian-Universalists."

[38] See Christians against Christian nationalism (https://www.christiansagainstchristiannationalism.org); Molina (2023, January 5); Moore (2023); Pally (2022, Chapter 8);

[39] Moderate Protestant pastors Brian Kaylor and Beau Underwood (2023) noted many ways in which mainline Christians have inadvertently enabled Christian nationalism, for example, through its participation in congressional prayers, displaying of the U.S. flag in churches, singing of patriotic hymns, and, during the period after World War II, supporting the addition of "under God" to the Pledge of Allegiance and "In God We Trust" as the nation's motto.

[40] Whitehead & Perry (2020, p. 42).

[41] J. Jenkins (2023, August 11).

[42] Kitcher (2014, Chapter 3).

[43] Gushee (2020, p. 60).

[44] For example, see Burge (2021, pp. 15-29).

[45] Altemeyer & Hunsberger (1992).

[46] Gushee (2020, pp. 28, 68); Pally (2022, Chapter 8). Although the meaning of the term *evangelical* has been debated, a common scheme used with the General Social Survey in the United States classifies Southern Baptists, the Assemblies of God and other Pentecostal traditions, the Free Methodist

Church, the Lutheran Church-Missouri Synod, and some nondenominational churches as Evangelical Protestants. However, Black Southern Baptists are not classified as evangelicals. Among self-identified evangelicals in the United States, 70% are White, 14% are African-American, 12% are Hispanic, and 4% are other ethnicities (Pally, 2022, p. 68). The percentage of evangelicals who believe the Bible contains the literal word of God ranges from about 55% to 65% (Burge, 2021, p. 15).

[47] Burge (2021, p. 16).

[48] Gushee (2020, pp. 24, 142).

[49] Pew Research Center (n.d.). Similarly, Burge (2021, p. 18) reports that majorities of members of the Disciples of Christ, Episcopal Church, American Baptist Church, and the United Church of Christ identify as Democrats. However, among United Methodists, the largest mainline Protestant denomination, only 35.1% identify as Democrats and 53.7% identify as Republicans.

[50] Altermeyer & Hunsberger (1992, p. 118).

[51] Irwin (2019, p. 75).

[52] Similarly, Irwin (2019, p. 78) has referred to "honest atheism" as an openness to some uncertainty and doubt about God's existence. Philip Kitcher (2014, pp. 23-25) has referred to the "soft atheism" of secularists who are open to learning from and finding common cause with religion. Gary Gutting (2017, pp. 210-211) has referred to "religious agnosticism," which involves withholding judgment about God's existence, while finding it worthwhile to pursue the question.

[53] Samson (2023, pp. 343-355). Quoted material is on page 346, italics in original. Research indicates that people who believe more strongly that beliefs should change based on evidence are less religious and more supportive of scientific claims (Pennycook et al., 2020).

[54] As Blankholm (2022, pp. 166-175) has observed, the question of whether secular people should proselytize or explicitly promote secularity among religious people is a source of conflict among secular activists and organizations. While some atheists seek to do so, others view such efforts as too

analogous to religious evangelizing and as incompatible with secular values of individual autonomy and choice. According to Blankholm, national secular organizations "draw a sharp distinction between advocacy and evangelizing" (p. 175).

[55] For example, see Cimino & Smith (2014, pp. 162-164); Epstein (2009, Chapter 5, pp. 151-168); Irwin (2019, Chapter 6); Stedman (2012); Streib & Klein (2014, 2018). A number of umbrella organizations, including Interfaith America (formerly Interfaith Youth Corp), Christian Churches Together, the National Council of Churches, United Religions Initiative, and the World Council of Churches promote, as part of their mission, ecumenical efforts and dialogue, and working together towards unity, peace, and justice. Some of these groups include nonbelievers in these efforts. Interfaith America, the Deep Canvass Institute, and Humanists UK offer curricula and/or training to facilitate such discussions.

[56] Cimino & Smith (2014, p. 162).

[57] Rodell (2024).

[58] S. Evans (2024). Based on interviews with 518 American atheists, Baggett (2019, pp. 155-165) concluded that many atheists are understanding and empathetic towards religious individuals, particularly those closest to them, but are more disparaging of religious institutions.

[59] Hobson (2018); Taylor (2007).

[60] Hecht (2003, p. 364).

[61] Interview with Louise Antony in Gutting (2017, pp. 33-34).

[62] For example, see articles on the abortion debate by Kissling (2018), Beaty (2018), and C. Jackson (2018).

[63] Stedman (2012, p. 163).

[64] Critical thinking involves open-minded and well-informed analyses and judgments that are based on relevant and accurate information, reasoning, and awareness of one's personal biases (Abrami, Bernard, Borokhovski, Waddington, Wade, & Persson, 2015, p. 275).

[65] See Abrami et al. (2015) for a recent meta-analysis of available studies.

[66] C. G. Brown et al. (2023, pp. 228-229).

[67] In a 2019 contribution for the "How to Fix Polarization" segment in *Politico Magazine*, Zeenat Rahman, director of the Inclusive America Project at the Aspen Institute, promoted the teaching of religious literacy in the schools, as well as other forms of multifaith engagement, as a means to reduce polarization in America (https://www.politico.com/interactives/2019/how-to-fix-politics-in-america/polarization/religious-literacy-education).

[68] Al Sadi & Basit (2013).

[69] R. Berger, Benatov, Abu-Raiya, & Tadmore (2016). See Beelmann & Heinemann (2014) for a comprehensive meta-analytic review. As one way to foster a greater appreciation among Muslims of the value of secularism, Sirgy et al. (2019) have proposed that Muslim children and adolescents be given instruction in how modern society and democracy work, and how social and behavioral sciences can be used to solve national problems such as crime, unemployment, and corruption.

[70] Many scholars have raised this concern, including Baker & Smith (2015, pp. 182-183); D. E. Campbell et al. (2021, p. 106); Gushee (2020, pp. 142-143); R. P. Jones (2017, pp. 234-235).

[71] D. E. Campbell et al. (2021, pp. 43-44)

[72] Even among Latter-Day Saints (Mormons) in the United States, the decades-long tradition of voting Republican is breaking down, with only about half of younger generations of Mormons identifying as Republican. This suggests that it might be possible to weaken the link between religion and political affiliation over time.

[73] Gushee (2020, pp. 144-149).

[74] For example, see Burge (2021, p. 67, 131); Du Mez (2020); R. P. Jones (2017).

[75] For example, as Wellman (2008, p. 102) observes, whereas acceptance of doubt is an aspect of faith for many liberal Protestants, it is less consistent with the absolute truth claims and certainty of many evangelicals. For many evangelicals, questioning the authority of scripture can be seen as falling into error or even apostasy.

Bibliography

Abrami, P. C., Bernard, R. M., Borokhovski, E., Waddington, D. I., Wade, C. A., & Persson, T. (2015). Strategies for teaching students to think critically: A meta-analysis. *Review of Educational Research, 85,* 275-314.

Abrams, S., Jackson, J. C., & Gray, K. (2021). The new trinity of religious moral character: The Cooperator, the Crusader, and the Complicit. *Current Opinion in Psychology, 40,* 99-105.

Abu-Raiya, H., Pargament, K. I., & Krause, N. (2016). Religion as problem, religion as solution: Religious buffers of the links between religious/spiritual struggles and well-being/mental health. *Quality of Life Research, 25,* 1265-1274.

Adamczyk, A., & LaFree, G. (2015). Religiosity and reactions to terrorism. *Social Science Research, 51,* 17-29.

Ahmed, A., & Salas, O. (2013). Religious context and prosociality: An experimental study from Valparaíso, Chile. *Journal for the Scientific Study of Religion, 52,* 627-637.

Alcorta, C. S., & Sosis, R. (2005). Ritual, emotion, and sacred symbols: The evolution of religion as an adaptive complex. *Human Nature, 16,* 323-359.

Ali, A. H. (2015). *Heretic: Why Islam needs a reformation now.* New York, NY: Harper.

Algoe, S. B., & Haidt, J. (2009). Witnessing excellence in action: The "other-praising" emotions of elevation, gratitude, and admiration. *The Journal of Positive Psychology, 4,* 105–127.

Allport, G. W. (1979). *The nature of prejudice*. Reading, MA: Addison-Wesley Publishing Co. (Originally published in 1954)

Allport, G. W. (1962). *The individual and his religion: A psychological interpretation*. New York, NY: Macmillan.

Allport, G. W., & Ross, J. M. (1967). Personal religious orientation and prejudice. *Journal of Personality and Social Psychology, 5*, 432-443.

Al Sadi, F. H., & Basit, T. N. (2013). Religious tolerance in Oman: Addressing religious prejudice through educational intervention. *British Educational Research Journal, 39*, 447-472.

Altemeyer, B., & Hunsberger, B. (1992). Authoritarianism, religious fundamentalism, quest, and prejudice. *The International Journal for the Psychology of Religion, 2*, 113-133.

Altemeyer, B., & Hunsberger, B. (2004). A Revised Religious Fundamentalism Scale: The short and sweet of it. *The International Journal for the Psychology of Religion, 14*, 47-54.

Altemeyer, B., & Hunsberger, B. (2005). Fundamentalism and authoritarianism. In R. F. Paloutzian & C. L. Park (Eds.), *Handbook of the psychology of religion and spirituality* (pp. 378-393). New York, NY: Guilford.

Ammerman, N. T. (2013). Spiritual but not religious? Beyond binary choices in the study of religion. *Journal for the Scientific Study of Religion, 52*, 258-278.

Ano, G. G., & Vasconcelles, E. B. (2005). Religious coping and psychological adjustment to stress: A meta-analysis. *Journal of Clinical Psychology, 61*, 461-480.

Antony, L. M. (Ed.). (2007). *Philosophers without gods: Meditations on atheism and the secular life*. New York, NY: Oxford University Press.

Arli, D., van Esch, P., & Cui, Y. (2023). Who cares more about the environment, those with an intrinsic, an extrinsic, a quest, or an atheistic religious orientation?: Investigating the effect of religious ad appeals on attitudes toward the environment. *Journal of Business Ethics, 85*, 427-448.

Armaly, M. T., Buckley, D. T., & Enders, A. M. (2022). Christian nationalism and political violence: Victimhood, racial identity, conspiracy, and support for the capitol attacks. *Political Behavior, 44,* 937– 960.

Armstrong, K. (2014). *Fields of blood: Religion and the history of violence.* New York, NY: Alfred A. Knopf.

Aronson, R. (2008). *Living without God: New directions for atheists, agnostics, secularists, and the undecided.* Berkeley, CA: Counterpoint.

Ashton, M. C., & Lee, K. (2021). A review of personality/religiousness associations. *Current Opinion in Psychology, 40,* 51-55.

Askwith, G. (2024). Faith to faithless: The difficult process of leaving a high-control religion. *Humanistically Speaking,* January 31. https://www.humanisticallyspeaking.org/post/faith-to-faithless-the-difficult-process-of-leaving-a-high-control-religion

Asma, S. T. (2018). *Why we need religion.* New York, NY: Oxford University Press.

Astuti, R., & Harris, P. L. (2008). Understanding mortality and the life of the ancestors in rural Madagascar. *Cognitive Science, 32,* 713-740.

Atkinson, A. R. (2023). The places of agency detection and predictive processing in the ontogenesis of religious belief; and "Who put the 'H' in the HADD. *Religion, Brain & Behavior.* https://doi.org/10.1080/2153599X.2023.2168731

Atkinson, Q. D., & Bourrat, P. (2011). Beliefs about God, the afterlife and morality support the role of supernatural policing in human cooperation. *Evolution and Human Behavior, 32,* 41-49.

Atkinson, Q. D., & Whitehouse, H. (2011). The cultural morphospace of ritual form: Examining modes of religiosity cross-culturally. *Evolution and Human Behavior, 32,* 50-62.

Atran, S. (2002). *In gods we trust: The evolutionary landscape of religion.* New York, NY: Oxford University Press.

Atran, S. (2006). The moral logic and growth of suicide terrorism. *Washington Quarterly, 29,* 127-147.

435

Atran, S. (2016). The devoted actor: Unconditional commitment and intractable conflict across cultures. *Current Anthropology, 57*, 192-203.

Atran, S., & Ginges, J. (2012). Religious and sacred imperatives in human conflict. *Science, 336*(6083), 855-857.

Atran, S., & Norenzayan, A. (2004). Religion's evolutionary landscape: Counterintuition, commitment, compassion, communion. *Behavioural and Brain Sciences, 27*, 713-730.

Atran, S., Sheikh, H., & Gomez, A. (2014). Devoted actors sacrifice for close comrades and sacred cause. *Proceedings of the National. Academy of Sciences, 111*, 17702-17703.

Aydin, N., Fischer, P., & Frey, D. (2010). Turning to God in the face of ostracism: Effects of social exclusion on religiousness. *Personality and Social Psychology Bulletin, 36*, 742-753.

Baggett, J. R. (2019). *The varieties of nonreligious experience: Atheism in American* culture. New York, NY: New York University Press.

Bahçekapili, H., & Yilmaz, O. (2017). The relation between different types of religiosity and analytic thinking style. *Personality and Individual Differences, 117*, 267-272.

Baier, C. J., & Wright. B. R. E. (2001). "If you love me, keep my commandments": A meta-analysis of the effect of religion on crime. *Journal of Research in Crime and Delinquency, 38*, 3-21.

Baimel, A., Apicela, C., Atkinson, Q., Bolyanatz, A., Cohen, E., Handley, C., Henrich, J., Kundtová Klocová, E., Lang, M., Lesogorol, C., Mathew, S., McNamara, R., Moya, C., Norenzayan, A., Placek, C. D., Soler, M., Vardy, T., Weigel, J., Willard, A., Xygalatas, D., & Purzycki, B. (2022). Material insecurity predicts greater commitment to moralistic and less commitment to local deities: A cross-cultural investigation. *Religion, Brain & Behavior, 12*, 4-17.

Baker, J. O., & Smith, B. G. (2015). *American secularism: Cultural contours of nonreligious belief systems.* New York, NY: New York University Press.

Baker, J. O., Stroope, S., & Walker, M. H. (2018). Secularity, religiosity, and health: Physical and mental health differences between atheists, agnostics, and nonaffiliated theists compared to religiously affiliated individuals. *Social Science Research, 75*, 44-57.

Bakewell, S. (2023). *Humanly possible: Seven hundred years of humanist freethinking, inquiry, and hope.* New York, NY: Penguin Press.

Banerjee, K., & Bloom, P. (2014). Why did this happen to me? Religious believers' and non-believers' teleological reasoning about life events. *Cognition, 133*, 277-303.

Banerjee, K., & Bloom, P. (2015). "Everything happens for a reason:" Children's beliefs about purpose in life events. *Child Development, 86*, 503-518.

Banks, A. M. (2023, February 20). Harvard, National Council of Churches, and Reform Jews seeking reparations blueprint. *Religion News Service.* https://religionnews.com/2023/02/20/harvard-national-council-of-churches-reform-jews-seeking-reparations-blueprint

Banks, A. M. (2023, June 9). Three years after George Floyd's death, faith groups quietly advance racial healing. *Religion News Service.* https://religionnews.com/2023/06/09/questions-of-race-are-on-the-agenda-of-three-church-groups-in-early-june/

Baranski, E., Sweeny, K., Gardiner, G., Members of the International Situations Project, & Funder, D. C. (2021). International optimism: Correlates and consequences of dispositional optimism across 61 countries. *Journal of Personality, 89*, 288-304.

Barnes, J. (2009). *Nothing to be frightened of.* New York, NY: Vintage Books.

Barrett, J. (2004). *Why would anyone believe in God?* Walnut Creek, CA: AltaMira Press.

Barrett, J. (2009). Cognitive science, religion, and theology. In J. Schloss & M. J. Murray (Eds.), *The believing primate: Scientific, philosophical, and theological reflections on the origin of religion* (pp. 76-99). Oxford, UK: Oxford University Press.

Barrett, J. (2012). *Born believers: The science of children's religious belief.* New York, NY: Free Press.

Barrett, J., & Keil, F. C. (1996). Conceptualizing a non-natural entity: Anthropomorphism in God concepts. *Cognitive Psychology, 31*, 219-247.

Barrett, J., & Nyhof, M. (2001). Spreading non-natural concepts: The role of intuitive conceptual structures in memory and transmission of cultural materials. *Journal of Cognition and Culture, 1*, 69-100.

Barrett, N. F. (2014). Skilful engagement and the "effort after value:" An axiological theory of the origins of religion. In F. Watts & L. Turner (Eds.), *Evolution, religion, and cognitive science: Critical and constructive essays* (pp. 92-108). Oxford, UK: Oxford University Press.

Basedau, M., Pfeiffer, B., & Vüllers, J. (2016). Bad religion? Religion, collective action, and the onset of armed conflict in developing countries. *Journal of Conflict Resolution, 60*, 226-255.

Batson, C. D., Schoenrade, P. A., & Ventis, W. L. (1993). *Religion and the individual: A social-psychological perspective.* New York, NY: Oxford University Press.

Batson, C. D., & Stocks, E. L. (2014). Religion: Its core psychological functions. In J. Greenberg, S. L. Koole, & T. Pyszczynski (Eds.), *Handbook of experimental existential psychology* (pp. 141-155). New York, NY: Guilford.

Batthyany, A., & Russo-Netzer, P. (2014). *Meaning in positive and existential psychology.* New York, NY: Springer.

Baumeister, R. F. (1991). *Meanings in life.* New York, NY: Guilford Press.

Baumeister, R. F., & Leary, M. R. (1995). The need to belong: Desire for interpersonal attachments as a fundamental human motivation. *Psychological Bulletin, 117*, 497-529.

Baumeister, R. F., Vohs, K. D., Aaker, J. L., & Garbinsky, E. N. (2013). Some key differences between a happy life and a meaningful life. *Journal of Positive Psychology, 8*, 505-516.

Beaty, K. (2018, December 18). The abortion conversation needs new language. *Religion & Politics*. https://religionandpolitics.org/2018/12/18/the-abortion-conversation-needs-new-language

Beck, U. (2010). *A God of one's own: Religion's capacity for peace and potential for violence*. Cambridge, UK: Polity Press.

Becker, E. (1973). *The denial of death*. New York, NY: Free Press.

Beebe, J., & Duffy, L. (2020). The memorability of supernatural concepts: Effects of minimal counterintuitiveness, moral valence, and existential anxiety on recall. *The International Journal for the Psychology of Religion, 30*, 322-341.

Beelmann, A., & Heinemann, K. S. (2014) Preventing prejudice and improving intergroup attitudes: A meta-analysis of child and adolescent training programs. *Journal of Applied Developmental Psychology, 35*, 10-24.

Behe, M. J. (2006). *Darwin's black box: The biochemical challenge to evolution*. New York, NY: Free Press.

Beit-Hallahmi, B. (2010). Morality and immorality among the irreligious. In P. Zuckerman (Ed.), *Atheism and secularity. Vol. 1: Issues, concepts, and definitions* (pp. 113-148). Santa Barbara, CA: Praeger.

Beit-Hallahmi, B. (2021). Challenges to an evolutionary perspective on religion. In J. R. Liddle & T. K. Shackelford (Eds.), *The Oxford handbook of evolutionary psychology and religion* (pp. 356-373). New York, NY: Oxford University Press.

Bellah, R. N. (2011). *Religion in human evolution: From the Paleolithic to the axial age*. Cambridge, MA: Belknap Press of Harvard University Press.

Beller, J., & Kröger, C. (2018). Religiosity, religious fundamentalism, and perceived threat as predictors of Muslim support for extremist violence. *Psychology of Religion and Spirituality, 10*, 345-355.

Bendixen, T., Lightner, A. D., Apicella, C., Atkinson, Q., Bolyanatz, A., Cohen, E., Handley, C., Henrich, J., Kundtová Klocová, E., Lesorogol, C., Mathew, S., McNamara, R. A., Moya, C., Norenzayan, A., Placek, C., Soler, M., Vardy, T., Weigel, J., Willard, A. K., Xygalatas, D., Lang, M., & Purzycki, B. G. (2023). Gods are watching and so what? Moralistic supernatural punishment across 15 cultures. *Evolutionary Human Sciences, 5,* e18.

Bendixen, T., & Purzycki, B. G. (2021). Competing forces account for the stability and evolution of religious beliefs. *The International Journal for the Psychology of Religion, 31,* 307-312.

Bentzen, J. S. (2019). Acts of God? Religiosity and natural disasters across subnational world districts. *The Economic Journal, 129,* 2295-2321.

Berger, P. L. (1990). *The sacred canopy: Elements of a sociological theory of religion.* New York, NY: Anchor Books. (Original work published 1967)

Berger, P. L. (1999). The desecularization of the world: A global overview. In P. L. Berger (Ed.), *The desecularization of the world: Resurgent religion and world affairs* (pp. 1-18). Grand Rapids, MI: William B. Eerdmans.

Berger, R., Benatov, J., Abu-Raiya, H., & Tadmore, C. T. (2016). Reducing prejudice and promoting positive intergroup attitudes among elementary-school children in the context of the Israeli-Palestinian conflict. *Journal of School Psychology, 57,* 53-72.

Bering, J. (2006). The folk psychology of souls. *Behavioral and Brain Sciences, 29,* 453-498.

Bering, J. (2011). *The belief instinct: The psychology of souls, destiny, and the meaning of life.* New York, NY: W. W. Norton.

Bering, J., & Bjorklund, D. F. (2004). The natural emergence of reasoning about the afterlife as a developmental regularity. *Developmental Psychology, 40,* 217-233.

Bering, J., Hernández Blasi, C., & Bjorklund, D. F. (2005). The development of "afterlife" beliefs in secularly and religiously schooled children. *British Journal of Development Psychology, 23,* 587-607.

Bering, J., & Johnson, D. D. P. (2005). "O Lord. You perceive my thoughts from afar": Recursiveness and the evolution of supernatural agency. *Journal of Cognition and Culture, 5*, 118-142.

Berthold, A., & Ruch, W. (2014). Satisfaction with life and character strengths of non-religious and religious people: It's practicing one's religion that makes the difference. *Frontiers in Psychology, 5*, Article 876, 1-9.

Billingsley, J., Gomes, C. M., & McCullough, M. E. (2018). Implicit and explicit influences of religious cognition on dictator game transfers. *Royal Society Open Science, 5*, 170238.

Bird, W., & Thumma, S. (2020). *Megachurch 2020: The changing reality in America's largest churches.* Hartford Institute for Religion Research. http://hirr.hartsem.edu/megachurch/2020_Megachurch_Report.pdf

Biswas-Diener, R. (2006). From the equator to the north pole: A study of character strengths. *Journal of Happiness Studies, 7*, 293-310.

Biswas-Diener R., Vitterso, J., & Diener, E. (2005). Most people are pretty happy, but there is cultural variation: The Inughuit, the Amish, and the Maasai. *Journal of Happiness Studies, 6*, 205-226.

Blankholm, J. (2017). Secularism, humanism, and secular humanism. P. Zuckerman & J. R. Shook (Eds.), *The Oxford handbook of secularism* (pp. 687-705). New York, NY: Oxford University Press.

Blankholm, J. (2022). *The secular paradox: On the religiosity of the not religious.* New York, NY: New York University Press.

Blogowska, J., & Saroglou, V. (2013). For better or worse: Fundamentalists' attitudes towards outgroups as a function of exposure to authoritative religious texts. *The International Journal for the Psychology of Religion, 23*, 103-125.

Bloom, P. (2004). *Descartes' baby: How the science of child development explains what makes us human.* London, UK: William Heinemann.

Bloom, P. (2009). Religious belief as an evolutionary accident. In J. Schloss & M. J. Murray (Eds.), *The believing primate: Scientific, philosophi-*

cal, and theological reflections on the origin of religion (pp. 118-127). Oxford, UK: Oxford University Press.

Bloom, P. (2012). Religion, morality, evolution. *Annual Review of Psychology, 63,* 179-199.

Bockrath, M. F., Pargament, K. I., Wong, S., Harriott, V. A., Pomerleau, J. M., Homolka, S. J., Chaudhary, Z. B., & Exline, J. J. (2022). Religious and spiritual struggles and their links to psychological adjustment: A meta-analysis of longitudinal studies. *Psychology of Religion and Spirituality, 14,* 283-299.

Boehm, C. (2012). *Moral origins: The evolution of virtue, altruism, and shame.* New York, NY: Basic Books.

Bolier, L., Haverman, M., Westerhof, G., Smit, F., & Bohlmeijer, M. (2013). Positive psychology interventions: A meta-analysis of randomized controlled studies. *BMC Public Health, 13,* 119.

Bolyanatz, A. H. (2022). When god is watching: Dictator game results from the Sursurunga of New Ireland, Papua New Guinea. *Religion, Brain & Behavior, 12,* 61-78.

Bonnin, K., & Lane, J. (2023). Sacred values: Identity fusion, devotee actor theory, and extremism. In Y. Lior & J. Lane (Eds.), *The Routledge handbook of evolutionary approaches to religion* (pp. 46-64). London & New York: Routledge.

Bouchard, L. C., Carver, C. S., Mens, M. G., & Scheier, M. F. (2018). Optimism, health, and well-being. In D. S. Dunn (Ed.), *Positive psychology: Established and emerging issues* (pp. 112-130). New York, NY: Routledge.

Bowlby, J. (1969). *Attachment.* New York, NY: Basic Books.

Boyer, P. (2001). *Religion explained: The evolutionary origins of religious thought.* New York, NY: Basic Books.

Boyer, P. (2005). A reductionistic model of distinct modes of religious transmission. In H. Whitehouse & R. N. McCauley, *Mind and religion: Psychological and cognitive foundations of religiosity* (pp. 3-29). Walnut Creek, CA: AltaMira Press.

Boyer, P., & Baumard, N. (2021). The diversity of religion systems across history: An evolutionary cognitive approach. In J. R. Liddle & T. K. Shackelford (Eds.), *The Oxford handbook of evolutionary psychology and religion* (pp. 34-47). New York, NY: Oxford University Press.

Boyer, P., & Ramble, C. (2001). Cognitive templates for religious concepts: Cross-cultural evidence for recall of counter-intuitive representations. *Cognitive Science, 25*, 535-564.

Brandt, M. J., & Reyna, C. (2010). The role of prejudice and the need for closure in religious fundamentalists. *Personality and Social Psychology Bulletin, 36*, 715-725.

Brandt, M. J., & Reyna, C. (2014). To love or hate thy neighbor: The role of authoritarianism and traditionalism in explaining the link between fundamentalism and racial prejudice. *Political Psychology, 35*, 207-223.

Brandt, M. J., & Van Tongeren, D. R. (2017). People high and low on religious fundamentalism are prejudiced toward dissimilar groups. *Journal of Personality and Social Psychology, 112*, 76-97.

Brickman, P., Coates, D., & Janoff-Bulman, R. (1978). Lottery winners and accident victims: Is happiness relative? *Journal of Personality and Social Psychology, 36*, 917-927.

Brierly, J. (2023). *The surprising rebirth of God: Why new atheism grew old and secular thinkers are considering Christianity again.* Carol Stream, IL: Tyndale Elevate.

Brown, C. G. (2017). *Becoming atheist: Humanism and the secular West.* London, UK: Bloomsbury Academic.

Brown, C. G., Nash, D., & Lynch, C. (2023). *The humanist movement in modern Britain: A history of ethicists, rationalists and humanists.* London, UK: Bloomsbury.

Brown, J. E., van Mulukom, V., Charles, S. J., & Farias, M. (2023). Do you need religion to enjoy the benefits of church services? Social bonding, morality and quality of life among religious and secular congregations. *Psychology of Religion and Spirituality, 15*, 308-318.

Brown, K. W., & Ryan, R. M. (2003). The benefits of being present: Mindfulness and its role in psychological well-being. *Journal of Personality and Social Psychology, 84,* 822-848.

Brown-Iannuzzi, J. L., McKee, S., & Gervais, W. M. (2018). Atheist horns and religious halos: Mental representations of atheists and theists. *Journal of Experimental Psychology: General, 147,* 292-297.

Bruce, S. (2002). *God is dead: Secularization in the West.* Oxford, UK: Blackwell Publishing.

Bruce, S. (2017). Secularization and its consequences. In P. Zuckerman & J. R. Shook (Eds.), *The Oxford handbook of secularism* (pp. 53-70). New York, NY: Oxford University Press.

Bruenig, E. (2015, Nov. 4). Is the new atheism dead? How atheists and the religious are learning to get along. *New Republic.* https://newrepublic.com/article/123349/new-atheism-dead

Bruinius, H. (2024, January 29). Meet the post-Evangelical Christians. They're just getting started. *Christian Science Monitor,* 20-26.

Bulbulia, J. (2009). Religiosity as mental time-travel: Cognitive adaptations for religious behavior. In J. Schloss & M. J. Murray (Eds.), *The believing primate: Scientific, philosophical, and theological reflections on the origin of religion* (pp. 44-75). Oxford, UK: Oxford University Press.

Bulbulia, J., & Sosis, R. (2011). Signalling theory and the evolution of religious cooperation. *Religion, 41,* 363–88.

Burch-Brown, J., & Baker, W. (2016). Religion and reducing prejudice. *Group Processes & Intergroup Relations, 19,* 784-807.

Burdett, E. R. R., Wigger, J. B., & Barrett, J. L. (2021). The minds of God, mortals, and in-betweens: Children's developing understanding of extraordinary and ordinary minds across four countries. *Psychology of Religion and Spirituality, 13,* 212-221.

Burge, R. P. (2021). *The nones: Where they came from, who they are, and where they are going.* Minneapolis, MN: Fortress Press.

Burke, B. L., Martens, A., & Faucher, E. H. (2010). Two decades of terror management theory: A meta-analysis of mortality salience research. *Personality and Social Psychology Review*, *14*, 155-195.

Buschor, C., Proyer, R. T., & Ruch, W. (2013). Self- and peer-rated character strengths: How do they relate to satisfaction with life and orientations to happiness? *The Journal of Positive Psychology*, *8*, 116-127.

Butler, J., & Kern, M. L. (2016). The PERMA-Profiler: A brief multidimensional measure of flourishing. *International Journal of Wellbeing*, *6*, 1-48.

Caldwell-Harris, C. L. (2012). Understanding atheism/non-belief as an expected individual-differences variable. *Religion, Brain & Behavior*, *2*, 4-23.

Campbell, D. E., Layman, G. C., & Green, J. C. (2021). *Secular surge: A new fault line in American politics*. Cambridge, UK: Cambridge University Press.

Campbell, M., Hinton, J. D. X., & Anderson, J. R. (2019). A systematic review of the relationship between religion and attitudes toward transgender and gender-variant people. *International Journal of Transgenderism*, *20*, 21-38.

Camus, A. (1955). *The myth of Sisyphus and other essays*. (Justin O'Brien, Trans.). New York, NY: Alfred A. Knopf.

Canetti, D., Hobfoll, S. E., Pedahzur, A., & Zaidise, E. (2010). Much ado about religion: Religiosity, resource loss, and support for political violence. *Journal of Peace Research*, *47*, 575-587.

Carlisle, C. (2019). *Philosopher of the heart. The restless life of Søren Kierkegaard.* New York, NY: Farrar, Straus and Giroux.

Carlisle, R. D., & Tsang, J-A. (2013). The virtues: Gratitude and forgiveness. In K. I. Pargament (Editor-in-Chief), J. J. Exline, & J. W. Jones (Associate Editors), *APA handbook of psychology, religion, and spirituality: Vol. 1. Context, theory, and research* (pp. 423-438). Washington, DC: American Psychological Association.

Carlucci, L., Albaghli, B., Saggino, A., & Balsamo, M. (2021). Does a fundamentalist mindset predict a state or trait anxiety? The covariate role of dogmatism. *Journal of Religion and Health, 60,* 1029-1045.

Casler, K., & Kelemen, D. (2008). Developmental continuity in teleofunctional explanation: Reasoning about nature among Romanian Romani adults. *Journal of Cognition and Development, 9,* 340-362.

Cauble, M. R., Said, I. A., McLaughlin, A. T., Gazaway, S., Van Tongeren, D. R., Hook, J. N., Lacey, E. K., Davis, E. B., & Davis, D. E. (2023). Religion/spirituality and the twin virtues of humility and gratitude. In E. B. Davis, E. L. Worthington, Jr., & S. A. Schnitker (Eds.), *Handbook of positive psychology, religion, and spirituality* (pp. 379-393). Cham, Switzerland: Springer.

Cavanaugh, W. T. (2009). *The myth of religious violence: Secular ideology and the roots of modern conflict.* Oxford, UK: Oxford University Press.

Cavendish, J. (2023). Religion as a resource in an increasingly polarized society. *Sociology of Religion, 84,* 1-15.

Chakhssi, F., Kraiss, J. T., Sommers-Spijkerman, M., & Bohlmeijer, E. T. (2018). The effect of positive psychology interventions on well-being and distress in clinical samples with psychiatric or somatic disorders: A systematic review and meta-analysis. *BMC Psychiatry, 18,* 211.

Chamberlain, K., & Zika, S. (1988). Religiosity, life meaning, and well-being: Some relationships in a sample of women. *Journal for the Scientific Study of Religion, 27,* 411-420.

Charles, S. J., van Mulukom, V., Brown, J. E., Watts, F., Dunbar, R. I., & Farias, M. (2021). United on Sunday: The effects of secular rituals on social bonding and affect. *PLOS One, 16*(1), e0242546.

Chaves, M. (2010). SSSR presidential address: Rain dances in the dry season: Overcoming the religious congruence fallacy. *Journal for the Scientific Study of Religion, 49,* 1-14.

Cheavens, J. S., & Guter, M. M. (2018). Hope therapy. In M. W. Gallagher & S. J. Lopez (Eds.), *The Oxford handbook of hope* (pp. 133-142). Oxford, UK: Oxford University Press.

Cherniak, A. D., Mikulincer, M., Shaver, P. R., & Granqvist, P. (2021). Attachment theory and religion. *Current Opinion in Psychology, 40*, 126-130.

Chida, Y., & Steptoe, A. (2008). Positive psychological well-being and mortality: A quantitative review of prospective observational studies. *Psychosomatic Medicine, 70*, 741-756.

Christian Science Monitor (2024, January 29). Ukraine's other resistance: The monitor's view, 27.

Christy, A. G., Rivera, G., Chen, K., & Hicks, J. A. (2018). Existential meaning in life and positive psychological functioning. In D. S. Dunn (Ed.), *Positive psychology: Established and emerging issues* (pp. 220-235). New York, NY: Routledge.

Church, A. T., Katigbak, M. S., Locke, K. D., Zhang, H., Shen, J., Vargas-Flores, J., Ibañez-Reyes, J., Tanaka-Matsumi, J., Curtis, G. J., Cabrera, H. F., Mastor, K. A., Alvarez, J. M., Ortiz, F. A., Simon, J.-Y., & Ching, C. M. (2013). Need satisfaction and well-being: Testing self-determination theory in eight cultures. *Journal of Cross-Cultural Psychology, 44*, 507 - 535.

Church, E. F. (Ed.). (1987). *The essential Tillich: An anthology of the writings of Paul Tillich*. Chicago, IL: The University of Chicago Press.

Cimino, R., & Smith, C. (2014). *Atheist awakening: Secular activism and community in America*. New York, NY: Oxford University Press.

Clobert, M. (2021). East versus West: Psychology of religion in East Asian cultures. *Current Opinion in Psychology, 40*, 61-66.

Clobert, M., & Saroglou, V. (2015). Religion, paranormal beliefs, and distrust in science: Comparing East versus West. *Archive for the Psychology of Religion, 37*, 185-199.

Clobert, M., Saroglou, V., & Hwang, K.-K. (2017). East Asian religious tolerance versus Western monotheist prejudice: The role of (in)tolerance of contradiction. *Group Processes & Intergroup Relations, 20,* 216-236.

CNN (2021, April 12). Millions of Hindu pilgrims head to Ganges River as India's daily coronavirus cases continue to surge. https://www.cnn.com/2021/04/12/india/india-covid-kumbh-mela-crowd-intl-hnk-scli/index.html

Codrington, R. H. (1957). *The Melanesians: Studies in their anthropology and folk-lore.* New Haven, CT: HRAF Press. (Originally published in 1891 by The Clarendon Press, Oxford).

Cohen, A. B., & Johnson, K. A. (2017). The relation between religion and well-being. *Applied Research in Quality of Life, 12,* 533-547.

Cohen, S., & Pressman, S. D. (2006). Positive affect and health. *Current Directions in Psychological Science, 15,* 122-125.

Coleman, T. J., Messick, K. J., & van Mulukom, V. (2023). Atheism: A new evolutionary perspective on non-belief. In Y. Lior & J. Lane (Eds.), *The Routledge handbook of evolutionary approaches to religion* (pp. 130-150). London & New York: Routledge.

Coles, R. (1991). *The secular mind.* Princeton, NJ: Princeton University Press.

Collins, F. S. (2006). *The language of God: A scientist presents evidence for belief.* New York, NY: Free Press.

Copson, A. (2017). *Secularism: Politics, freedom, and religion.* Oxford, UK: Oxford University Press.

Cowling, M. M., Anderson, J. R., & Ferguson, R. (2019). Prejudice-relevant correlates of attitudes towards refugees: A meta-analysis. *Journal of Refugee Studies, 32,* 502-524.

Cox, K. S., Wilt, J., Olson, B., & McAdams, D. P. (2010). Generativity, the Big Five, and psychosocial adaptation in midlife adults. *Journal of Personality, 78,* 1185-1208.

Coyne, J. A. (2015). *Faith vs. fact: Why science and religion are incompatible*. New York, NY: Penguin Books.

Cragun, R., & Kosmin, B. (2011). Repackaging humanism as "spirituality." *Free Inquiry, 31*(4), 30-33.

Cragun, R., Kosmin, B. A., Keysar, A., Hammer, J., & Nielson, M. (2012). On the receiving end: Discrimination toward the non-religious in the United States. *Journal of Contemporary Religion, 27*, 105-127.

Cragun, R. T., & Speed, D. (2022). Religious and non-religious perspectives on happiness and well-being. In S. Sugirtharajah (Ed.), *Religious and secular perspectives on happiness and well-being* (pp. 167-191). London, UK: Routledge.

Craig, W. L. (2008). *Reasonable faith: Christian truth and apologetics* (3rd ed.). Wheaton, IL: Crossway.

Cranney, S. (2013). Do people who believe in God report more meaning in their lives? The existential effects of belief. *Journal for the Scientific Study of Religion, 52*, 638-646.

Crary, D. (2024, January 9). How to deal with same-sex unions? It's a question fracturing major Christian denominations. *Religion News Service.* https://religionnews.com/2024/01/09/how-to-deal-with-same-sex-unions-its-a-question-fracturing-major-christian-denominations/

Csikszentmihalyi, M. (1975). *Beyond boredom and anxiety*. San Francisco, CA: Jossey-Bass Publishers.

Csikszentmihalyi, M. (1993). *The evolving self: A psychology for the third millennium*. New York, NY: HarperCollins Publishers.

Csikszentmihalyi, M., & Nakamura, J. (2011). Positive psychology: Where did it come from, where is it going? In K. M. Sheldon, T. B. Kashdan, & M. F. Steger (Eds.), *Designing positive psychology: Taking stock and moving forward*. Oxford, UK: Oxford University Press.

Cuijpers, P., Quero, S., Noma, H., Ciharova, M., Miguel, C., Karyotaki, E., Cipriani, A., Cristea, I. A., & Furukawa, T. A. (2021). Psychotherapies for depression: A network meta-analysis covering efficacy, acceptability and long-term outcomes of all main treatment types. *World Psychiatry, 20,* 283-293.

Curry, O. S., Mullins, D. A., & Whitehouse, H. (2019). Is it good to co-operate? Testing the theory of morality-as-cooperation in 60 societies. *Current Anthropology, 60,* 47-69.

Czekierda, K., Banik, A., Park, C. L., & Luszczynska, A. (2017). Meaning in life and physical health: Systematic review and meta-analysis. *Health Psychology Review, 11,* 387-418.

Davie, G. (1999). Europe: The exception that proves the rule? In P. L. Berger (Ed.), *The desecularization of the world: Resurgent religion and world affairs* (pp. 65-83). Grand Rapids, MI: William B. Eerdmans.

Davis, D. E., Hook, J. N., McAnnaly-Linz, R., Choe, E., & Placeres, V. (2017). Humility, religion, and spirituality: A review of the literature. *Psychology of Religion and Spirituality, 9,* 242-253.

Davis, E. B., Worthington, E. L., Jr., & Schnitker, S. A. (Eds.) (2023). *Handbook of positive psychology, religion, and spirituality.* Cham, Switzerland: Springer.

Dawkins, R. (1976). *The selfish gene.* Oxford, UK: Oxford University Press.

Dawkins, R. (2006). *The God delusion.* Boston, MA: Houghton Mifflin Co.

Dawson, L. L. (2019). Taking terrorist accounts of their motivations seriously: An exploration of the hermeneutics of suspicion. *Perspectives on Terrorism, 13,* 74- 89.

D'Costa, G. (1986). *Theology and religious pluralism: The challenge of other religions.* Oxford, UK: Basil Blackwell.

Deacon, T., & Cashman, T. (2010). The role of symbolic capacity in the origins of religion. *Journal for the Study of Religion, Nature and Culture, 3,* 490-517.

Dear, K., Dutton, K., & Fox, E. (2019). Do "watching eyes" influence antisocial behavior? A systematic review and meta-analysis. *Evolution and Human Behavior, 40*, 269-280.

DeBono, A., Poepsel, D., & Corley, N. (2020). Thank God for my successes (not my failures): Feeling God's presence explains a God attribution bias. *Psychological Reports, 123*, 1663– 87.

DeBono, A., Shariff, A. F., Poole, S., & Muraven, M. (2017). Forgive us our trespasses: Priming a forgiving (but not a punishing) God increases unethical behavior. *Psychology of Religion and Spirituality, 9*, Supplement 1, S1-S10.

de Botton, A. (2013). *Religion for atheists. A non-believer's guide to the uses of religion.* New York, NY: Vintage International.

De Graaf, B. A., & van den Bos, K. (2021). Religious radicalization: Social appraisals and finding radical redemption in extreme beliefs. *Current Opinion in Psychology, 40*, 56-60.

Dechesne, M., Pyszczynski, T., Arndt, J., Ransom, S., Sheldon, K. M., van Knippenberg, A., & Janssen, J. (2003). Literal and symbolic immortality: The effect of evidence of literal immortality on self-esteem strivings in response to mortality salience. *Journal of Personality and Social Psychology, 84*, 722-737.

Deci, E. L., & Ryan, R. M. (2000). The "what" and "why" of goal pursuits: Human needs and the self-determination of behavior. *Psychological Inquiry, 11*, 227-268.

Deci, E. L., & Ryan, R. M. (2008). Hedonia, eudaimonia, and well-being: An introduction. *Journal of Happiness Studies, 9*, 1-11.

Dein, S., Loewenthal, K., Lewis, C. A., & Pargament, K. I. (2020). COVID-19, mental health and religion: An agenda for future research. *Mental Health, Religion & Culture, 23*, 1-9.

Delamontagne, R. G. (2010). High religiosity and societal dysfunction in the United States during the first decade of the twenty-first century. *Evolutionary Psychology, 8*, 617-657.

Dennett, D. C. (2006). *Breaking the spell: Religion as a natural phenomenon.* New York, NY: Viking.

Deslandes, C., & Anderson, J. (2019) Religion and prejudice towards immigrants and refugees: A meta-analytic review. *The International Journal of the Psychology of Religion, 29,* 128-145.

de Waal, F. (2013). *The bonobo and the atheist: In search of humanism among the primates.* New York, NY: W. W. Norton.

Dewey, J. (2013). *A common faith* (2nd ed.). New Haven, CT: Yale University Press. (Originally published in 1934)

Dias, E., & Graham, R. (2021, April 5). White evangelical resistance is obstacle in vaccination efforts. *New York Times.* https://www.nytimes.com/2021/04/05/us/covid-vaccine-evangelicals.html

Dickens, L. R. (2017). Using gratitude to promote positive change: A series of meta-analyses investigating the effectiveness of gratitude interventions. *Basic and Applied Social Psychology, 39,* 193–208.

Diener, E. (2009). Positive psychology: Past, present, and future. In C. R. Snyder & S. J. Lopez (Eds.), *Oxford handbook of positive psychology* (pp. 7-11). Oxford, UK: Oxford University Press.

Diener, E., & Biswas-Diener, R. (2002). Will money increase subjective well-being? A literature review and guide to needed research. *Social Indicators Research, 57,* 119-169.

Diener, E., & Chan, M. (2011). Happy people live longer: Subjective well-being contributes to health and longevity. *Applied Psychology: Health and Well-Being, 3,* 1–43.

Diener, E., Diener, C., Choi, H., & Oishi, S. (2018). Revisiting "Most people are happy"—and discovering when they are not. *Perspectives on Psychological Science, 13,* 166-170.

Diener, E., Heintzelman, S., Kushlev, K., Tay, L., Wirtz, L., Lutes, L. D., & Oishi, S. (2017). Findings all psychologists should know from the new science on subjective well-being. *Canadian Psychologist, 58,* 87-104.

Diener, E., Kanazawa, S., Suh, E. M., & Oishi, S. (2015). Why people are in a generally good mood. *Personality and Social Psychology Review, 19*, 235-256.

Diener, E., Lucas, R. E., & Scollon, C. N. (2006). Beyond the hedonic treadmill: Revising the adaptation theory of well-being. *American Psychologist, 61*, 305-314.

Diener, E., Oishi, S., & Lucas, R. E. (2009). Subjective well-being: The science of happiness and life satisfaction. In C. R. Snyder & S. J. Lopez (Eds.), *Oxford handbook of positive psychology* (pp. 187-194). Oxford, UK: Oxford University Press.

Diener, E., Oishi, S., & Lucas, R. E. (2015). National accounts of subjective well-being. *American Psychologist, 70*, 234-242.

Diener, E., Tay, L., & Myers, D. G. (2011). The religion paradox: If religion makes people happy, why are so many dropping out? *Journal of Personality and Social Psychology, 101*, 1278-1290.

Diener, E., Wirtz, D., Tov, W., Kim-Prieto, C., Choie, D. W., Oishi, S., & Biswas-Diener, R. (2010). New well-being measures: Short scales to assess flourishing and positive and negative feelings. *Social Indicators Research, 97*, 143-156.

DiGregorio, B. D., Corcoran, K. E., & Scheitle, C. B. (2022). 'God will protest us': Belief in God/higher power's ability to intervene and COVID-19 vaccine uptake. *Review of Religious Research, 64*, 475-495.

Dik, B. J., Eldridge, B. M., Steger, M. F., & Duffy, R. D. (2012). Development and validation of the Calling and Vocation Questionnaire (CVQ) and Brief Calling Sale (BCS). *Journal of Career Assessment, 20*, 242-263.

Doane, M. J., & Elliott, M. (2015). Perceptions of discrimination among atheists: Consequences for atheist identification, psychological and physical well-being. *Psychology of Religion and Spirituality, 7*, 130-141.

Doerr, E. (2013). Tracing 'secular humanism.' *Free Inquiry, 33*(3), 17.

Doosje, B., Moghaddam, F. M., Kruglanski, A. W., de Wolf, A., Mann, L., & Feddes, A. R. (2016). Terrorism, radicalization and de-radicalization. *Current Opinion in Psychology, 11,* 79-84.

Dreyfus, H., & Kelly, S. D. (2011). *All things shining: Reading the Western classics to find meaning in a secular age.* New York, NY: Free Press.

Du Mez, K. K. (2020). *Jesus and John Wayne: How White evangelicals corrupted a faith and fractured a nation.* New York, NY: Liveright Publishing Company.

Dubendorff, S. J., & Luchner, A. F. (2017). The perception of atheists as narcissistic. *Psychology of Religion and Spirituality, 9,* 368-376.

Duffy, R. D., Allan, B. A., Autin, K. L., & Bott, E. M. (2013). Calling and life satisfaction: It's not about having it, it's about living it. *Journal of Counseling Psychology, 60,* 42–52.

Duffy, R. D., & Dik, B. J. (2013). Research on calling: What have we learned and where are we going? *Journal of Vocational Behavior, 83,* 428-436.

Duhaime, E. P. (2015). Is the call to prayer a call to cooperate? A field experiment on the impact of religious salience on prosocial behavior. *Judgment and Decision-Making, 10,* 593-596.

Dunbar, R. (2022). *How religion evolved and why it endures.* New York, NY: Oxford University Press.

Durkheim, E. (2001). *The elementary forms of religious life* (C. Cosman, Trans.). Oxford, UK: Oxford University Press. (Original work published 1912)

Eberstadt, M. (2013). *How the West really lost God: A new theory of secularization.* West Conshohocken, PA: Templeton Press.

Ebert, T., Gebauer, J. E., Talman, J. R., & Rentfrow, P. J. (2020). Religious people only live longer in religious cultural contexts: A gravestone analysis. *Journal of Personality and Social Psychology, 119,* 1-6.

Echeverría Vicente, N. J., Hemmerechts, K., & Kavadias, D. (2022). Armed conflict and religious adherence across countries: A time series analysis. *Sociology of Religion, 83,* 371–401.

Edgell, P., Hartmann, D., Stewart, E., & Gerteis, J. (2016). Atheists and other cultural outsiders: Moral boundaries and the non-religious in the United States. *Social Forces, 95,* 607–638.

Edmondson, D., Park, C. L., Blank, T. O., Fenster, J. R., & Mills, M. A. (2008). Deconstructing spiritual well-being: Existential well-being and HRQOL in cancer survivors. *Psycho-Oncology, 17, 161-169.*

Ekici, T., & Yucel, D. (2015). What determines religious and racial prejudice in Europe? The effects of religiosity and trust. *Social Indicators Research, 122,* 105-133.

Eliade, M. (1974). *The myth of the eternal return or, cosmos and history* (W. R. Trask, Trans., Bollingen Series XLVI). New York, NY: Princeton University Press. (Original work published 1949)

Elie, P. (2003). *The life you save may be your own: An American pilgrimage.* New York, NY: Farrar, Straus and Giroux.

Eller, J. D. (2010). What is atheism? In P. Zuckerman (Ed.), *Atheism and secularity. Vol. 1: Issues, concepts, and definitions* (pp. 1-18). Santa Barbara, CA: Praeger.

Ellison, C. G. (2020). Religion's contribution to population health: Key theoretical and methodological considerations. In A. B. Cohen (Ed.), *Religion and human flourishing* (pp. 105-125). Waco, TX: Baylor University Press.

Emmons, R. A. (1999). *The psychology of ultimate concerns.* New York, NY: Guilford Press.

Emmons, R. A. (2005). Striving for the sacred: Personal goals, life meaning, and religion. *Journal of Social Issues, 61,* 731-745.

Emmons, R. A., Froh, J., & Rose, R. (2019). Gratitude. In M. W. Gallagher & S. J. Lopez (Eds.), *Positive psychological assessment: A handbook of models and measures* (2nd ed., pp. 317-332). Washington, DC: American Psychological Association.

Emmons, R. A., Hill, P. C., Barrett, J. L., & Kapic, K. M. (2017). Psychological and theological reflections on grace and its relevance for science and practice. *Psychology of Religion and Spirituality, 9*, 276-284.

Emmons, R. A., & Kneezel, T. T. (2005). Giving thanks: Spiritual and religious correlates of gratitude. *Journal of Psychology and Christianity, 24*, 140-148.

Emmons, R. A., & Mishra, A. (2011). Why gratitude enhances well-being: What we know, what we need to know. In K. M. Sheldon, T. B. Kashdan, & M. F. Steger (Eds.), *Designing positive psychology: Taking stock and moving forward* (pp. 248-262). New York, NY: Oxford University Press.

Entringer, T. M., Gebauer, J. E., Eck, J., Bleidorn, W., Rentfrow, P. J., Potter, J., & Gosling, S. D. (2021). Big five facets and religiosity: Three large-scale, cross-cultural, theory-driven, and process-attentive tests. *Journal of Personality and Social Psychology, 120*, 1662-1695.

Epley, N., Akalis, S., Waytz, A., & Cacioppo, J. T. (2008). Creating social connection through inferential production: Loneliness and perceived agency in gadgets, gods, and greyhounds. *Psychological Science, 19*, 114-120.

Epley, N., Converse, B. A., Delbosc, A., Monteleone, G. A., & Cacioppo, J. T. (2009). Believer's estimates of God's beliefs are more egocentric than estimates of others people's beliefs. *Proceedings of the National Academy of Sciences, 106*, 21533-21538.

Epstein, G. M. (2009). *Good without God: What a billion nonreligious people do believe.* New York, NY: William Morrow.

Etengoff, C., & Lefevor, T. G. (2021). Sexual prejudice, sexism, and religion. *Current Opinion in Psychology, 40*, 45-50.

Evans, E. M. (2001). Cognitive and contextual factors in the emergence of diverse belief systems: Creation versus evolution. *Cognitive Psychology, 42*, 217-266.

Evans, S. (2024, January 31). Secularists do not wish to banish religion from the public square but do insist on the separation of church and state. *Humanistically Speaking*. https://www.humanisticallyspeaking.org/post/why-secularists-want-a-state-free-from-religion

Evans-Pritchard, E. E. (1965). *Theories of primitive religion*. London, UK: Oxford University Press.

Exline, J. J. (2013). Religious and spiritual struggles. In K. I. Pargament (Editor-in-Chief), J. J. Exline, & J. W. Jones (Associate Editors), *APA handbook of psychology, religion, and spirituality: Vol. 1. Context, theory, and research* (pp. 459-476). Washington, DC: American Psychological Association.

Exline, J. J., Przeworski, A., Peterson, E. K., Turnamian, M. R., Stauner, N., & Uzdavines, A. (2021). Religious and spiritual struggles among transgender and gender-nonconforming adults. *Psychology of Religion and Spirituality, 13*, 276-286.

Exline, J. J., Wilt, J. A., Stauner, N., & Pargament, K. I. (2021). Approach, disengagement, protest, and suppression: Four behaviors toward God in the context of religious/spiritual struggle. *Psychology of Religion and Spirituality, 15*, 491-503.

Fava, G. A., & Ruini, C. (2003). Development and characteristics of a well-being enhancing psychotherapeutic strategy: Well-being therapy. *Journal of Behavior Therapy and Experimental Psychiatry, 34*, 45-63.

Fehr, E., & Gächter, S. (2002). Altruistic punishment in humans. *Nature, 415*, 137-140.

Ferngren, G. B. (Ed.). (2017). *Science and religion: A historical introduction* (2nd ed.). Baltimore, MD: Johns Hopkins University Press.

Fidalgo, P. (2023, Nov. 27). The enemy of her enemy. https://secularhumanism.org/exclusive/the-enemy-of-her-enemy/

Fincher, C. L., & Thornhill, R. (2008). Assortative sociality, limited dispersal, infectious disease and the genesis of the global pattern of religion diversity. *Proceedings of the Royal Society B, 275*, 2587-2594.

Firth, R. (1940). The analysis of *mana*: An empirical approach. *The Journal of the Polynesian Society, 49,* 482-510.

Firth, R. (1951). *Elements of social organization.* New York, NY: The Philosophical Library.

Fitouchi, L., & Singh, M. (2022). Supernatural punishment beliefs as cognitively compelling tools of social control. *Current Opinion in Psychology, 44,* 252-257.

Fitzpatrick, S., & Parsons, W. B. (2018). The triumph of the therapeutic and being spiritual but not religious. In W. B. Parsons (Ed.), *Being spiritual but not religious: Past, present, future(s)* (pp. 30-44). New York, NY: Routledge.

Flynn, T. (2013). Religious humanism: Dead, alive, or bifurcating: Introduction. *Free Inquiry, 33*(6), 18-22.

Fox, J. (2004). Religion and state failure: An examination of the extent and magnitude of religious conflict from 1950 to 1996. *International Political Science Review, 25,* 55-76.

Frankl, V. E. (1963). *Man's search for meaning: An introduction to logotherapy.* Boston, MA: Beacon Press.

Fredrickson, B. L. (2013). Positive emotions broaden and build. *Advances in experimental social psychology, 47,* 1-53.

Fredrickson, B. L., Boulton, A. J., Firestine, A. M., Van Cappellen, P., Algoe, S. B., Brantley, M. M., Kim, S. L., Brantley, J., & Salzberg, S. (2016). Positive emotion correlates of meditation practice: A comparison of mindfulness meditation and loving-kindness meditation. *Mindfulness, 8,* 1623–1633.

Fredrickson, B. L., Cohn, M. A., Coffey, K. A., Pek, J., & Finkel, S. M. (2008). Open hearts build lives: Positive emotions, induced through loving-kindness meditation, build consequential personal resources. *Journal of Personality and Social Psychology, 95,* 1045-1062.

Freeman, D., Waite, F., Rosebrock, L., Petit, A., Causier, C., East, A., Jenner, L., Teale, A.-L., Carr, L., Mulhall, S., Bold, E., & Lambe, S.

(2022). Coronavirus conspiracy beliefs, mistrust, and compliance with government guidelines in England. *Psychological Medicine*, *52*, 251-263.

French, S., & Joseph, S. (1999). Religiosity and its association with happiness, purpose in life, and self-actualisation. *Mental Health, Religion & Culture*, *2*, 117-120.

Freud, S. (1961). *The future of an illusion* (J. Strachey, Trans. & Ed.). New York, NY: W. W. Norton. (Original work published in 1928)

Freud, S. (1998). *Totem and taboo: Resemblances between the psychic lives of savages and neurotics* (A. A. Brill, Trans.). Mineola, NY: Dover Publications. (Original work published in 1918)

Friedman, B. M. (2022). Religion and the rise of capitalism. New York, NY: Vintage Books. (Originally published in 2021 by Alfred A. Knopf)

Frost, J. (2023). Ritualizing nonreligion: Cultivating rational rituals in secular spaces. *Social Forces, 101*, 2013-2033.

Frost, J., Scheitle, C. P., & Ecklund, E. H. (2022). Patterns of perceived hostility and identity concealment among self-identified atheists. *Social Forces, 101*, 1580-1605.

Fuller, R. C. (2017). Secular spirituality. In P. Zuckerman & J. R. Shook (Eds.). *The Oxford handbook of secularism* (pp. 571-586). New York, NY: Oxford University Press.

Fuller, R. C. (2018). Minds of their own: Psychological substrates of the spiritual but not religious sensibility. In W. B. Parsons (Ed.), *Being spiritual but not religious: Past, present, future(s)* (pp. 89-109). New York, NY: Routledge.

Fuller, R. C., & Parsons, W. B. (2018). Spiritual but not religious: A brief introduction. In W. B. Parsons (Ed.), *Being spiritual but not religious: Past, present, future(s)* (pp. 15-29). New York, NY: Routledge.

Fuller-Thomson, E., Lung, Y., West, K. J., Keyes, C. L. M., & Baiden, P. (2020). Suboptimal baseline mental health associated with 4-month premature all-cause mortality: Findings from 18 years of follow-up of the Canadian National Population Health Survey. *Journal of Psychosomatic Research, 136,* 110176.

Galek, K., Flannelly, K. J., Ellison, C. G., Silton, N. R., & Jankowski, K. R. B. (2015). Religion, meaning and purpose, and mental health. *Psychology of Religion and Spirituality, 7,* 1-12.

Galen, L. W. (2009). Profiles of the Godless: Results from a survey of the nonreligious. *Free Inquiry, 29*(5), 41-45.

Galen, L. W. (2012). Does religious belief promote prosociality? A critical examination. *Psychological Bulletin, 138,* 876-906.

Galen, L. W. (2023). *A social cognition perspective of the psychology of religion: "Why God thinks like you."* London, UK: Bloomsbury Academic.

Galen, L. W., & Kloet, J. (2011). Personality and social integration factors distinguishing nonreligious from religious groups: The important of controlling for attendance and demographics. *Archive for the Psychology of Religion/Archiv für Religionspsychologie, 33,* 205-228.

Galen, L. W., Kurby, C. A., & Fles, E. H. (2022). Religiosity, shared identity, trust, and punishment of norm violations: No evidence of generalized prosociality. *Psychology of Religion and Spirituality, 14,* 260-272.

Gall, T. L., & Guirguis-Younger, M. (2013). Religious and spiritual coping: Current theory and research. In K. I. Pargament (Editor-in-Chief), J. J. Exline, & J. W. Jones (Associate Editors), *APA handbook of psychology, religion, and spirituality: Vol. 1. Context, theory, and research* (pp. 349-364). Washington, DC: American Psychological Association.

Gallagher, M. W. (2023). The scientific status of the psychology of hope. *Current Opinion in Psychology, 53,* Article 101684.

Garssen, B., Visser, A., & Pool, G. (2021). Does spirituality or religion positively affect mental health? Meta-analysis of longitudinal studies. *The International Journal for the Psychology of Religion, 31,* 4-20.

Ge, E., Chen, Y., Wu, J., & Mace, R. (2019). Large-scale cooperation driven by reputation, not fear of divine punishment. *Royal Society Open Science, 6:* 190991.

Gebauer, J. E., Bleidorn, W., Gosling, S. D., Rentfrow, P. J., Lamb, M. E., & Potter, J. (2014). Cross-cultural variations in big five relationships with religiosity: A sociocultural motives perspective. *Journal of Personality and Social Psychology, 107,* 1064-1091.

Gebauer, J. E., Paulhus, D. L., & Neberich, W. (2013). Big Two personality and religiosity across cultures: Communals as religious conformists and agentics as religious contrarians. *Social and Personality Science, 4,* 21-30.

Gebauer, J. E., Sedikides, C., Schönbrodt, F. D., Bleidorn, W., Renfrow, P. J, Potter, J., & Gosling, S. D. (2017). The religiosity as social value hypothesis: A multi-method replication and extension across 65 countries and three levels of spatial aggregation. *Journal of Personality and Social Psychology, 113,* e18-e39.

Gebauer, J. E., Sedikides, C., & Schrade, A. (2017). Christian self-enhancement. *Journal of Personality and Social Psychology, 113,* 786-809.

Geertz, A. W., & Markússon, G. I. (2010). Religion is natural, atheism is not: On why everybody is both right and wrong. *Religion, 40,* 152-165.

Geertz, C. (1973). *The interpretation of cultures: Selected essays.* New York, NY: Basic Books.

Gervais, W. M. (2011). Finding the faithless: Perceived atheist prevalence reduces anti-atheist prejudice. *Personality and Social Psychology Bulletin, 37,* 543–556.

Gervais, W. M. (2013). Perceiving minds and gods: How mind perception enables, constrains, and is triggered by belief in gods. *Perspectives on Psychological Science, 8,* 380-394.

Gervais, W. M. (2021). Mickey, Yahweh, and Zeus: Why cultural learning is essential for the evolutionary study of religion. In J. R. Liddle & T. K. Shackelford (Eds.), *The Oxford handbook of evolutionary psychology and religion* (pp. 18-33). New York, NY: Oxford University Press.

Gervais, W. M., & Henrich, J. (2010). The Zeus problem: Why representational content biases cannot explain faith in gods. *Journal of Cognition and Culture, 10,* 383-389.

Gervais, W. M., & Najle, M. B. (2015). Learned faith: The influences of evolved cultural learning mechanisms on belief in gods. *Psychology of Religion and Spirituality, 7,* 327-335.

Gervais, W. M., & Norenzayan, A. (2012). Analytic thinking promotes religious disbelief. *Science, 336* (6080), 493-496.

Gervais, W. M., Shariff, A. F., & Norenzayan, A. (2011). Do you believe in atheists? Distrust is central to anti-atheist prejudice. *Journal of Personality and Social Psychology, 101,* 1189-1206.

Gervais, W. M., van Elk, M., Xygalatas, D., McKay, R. T., Aveyard, M., Buchtel, E. E., Dar-Nimrod, I., Kundtová Klocová, E., Ramsay, J. E., Riekki, T., Svedholm-Häkkinen, A. M., & Bulbulia, J. (2018). Analytic atheism: A cross-culturally weak and fickle phenomenon? *Judgment and Decision Making, 13,* 268-274.

Gervais, W. M., Willard, A. K., Norenzayan, A., & Henrich, J. (2011). The cultural transmission of faith: Why innate intuitions are necessary, but insufficient, to explain religious belief. *Religion, 41,* 389-410.

Gervais, W. M., Xygalatas, D., McKay, R. T., van Elk, M., Buchtel, E. E., Aveyard, M., Schiavone, S. R., Dar-Nimrod, I., Svedholm-Häkkinen, A. M., Riekki, T., Kundtová Klocová, E., Ramsay, J. E., & Bulbulia, J. (2017). Global evidence of extreme intuitive moral prejudice against atheists. *Nature Human Behaviour, 1,* Article 0151.

Gifford, P. (2019). *The plight of Western religion: The eclipse of the otherworldly.* Oxford, UK: Oxford University Press.

Gill, A., & Lundsgaarde, E. (2004). State welfare spending and religiosity: A cross-national analysis. *Rationality and Society, 16,* 399-436.

Ginges, J., Hansen, I., & Norenzayan, A. (2009). Religion and support for suicide attacks. *Psychological Science, 20,* 224-230.

Goldstein, R. N. (2010). *36 arguments for the existence of God: A work of fiction.* New York, NY: Pantheon Books.

Gorski, P. S. (2000). Historicizing the secularization debate. *American Sociological Review, 65,* 142.

Grafman, J., Cristofori, I., Zhong, W., & Bulbulia, J. (2020). The neural basis of religious cognition. *Current Directions in Psychological Science, 29,* 126-133.

Graham, J., & Haidt, J. (2010). Beyond beliefs: Religions bind individuals into moral communities. *Personality and Social Psychology Review, 14,* 140-150.

Graham, J., Nosek, B. A., Haidt, J., Iyer, R., Koleva, S., & Ditto, P. H. (2011). Mapping the moral domain. *Journal of Personality and Social Psychology, 101,* 366-385.

Granqvist, P. (2020). *Attachment in religion and spirituality: A wider view.* New York, NY: Guilford Press.

Granqvist, P., & Hagekull, B. (2000). Religiosity, adult attachment, and why "singles" are more religious. *The International Journal for the Psychology of Religion, 10,* 111-123.

Granqvist, P., & Kirkpatrick, L. A. (2013). Religion, spirituality, and attachment. In K. I. Pargament (Editor-in-Chief), J. J. Exline, & J. W. Jones (Associate Editors), *APA handbook of psychology, religion, and spirituality. Vol. 1. Context, theory, and research* (pp. 139-155). Washington, DC: American Psychological Association.

Grayling, A. C. (2013). *The God argument: The case against religion and for humanism.* New York, NY: Bloomsbury.

Greenberg, J., Vail, K., & Pyszczynski, T. (2014). Terror management theory and research: How the desire for death transcendence drives our strivings for meaning and significance. In A. J. Elliot (Ed.), *Advances in motivation science* (Vol. 1, pp. 85-134). San Diego, CA: Elsevier Academic Press.

Greenway, T. S., & Barrett, J. L. (2021). Evolutionary developmental psychology of children's religious beliefs. In J. R. Liddle & T. K. Shackelford (Eds.), *The Oxford handbook of evolutionary psychology and religion* (pp. 69-82). New York, NY: Oxford University Press.

Gregg, H. S. (2016). Three theories of religious activism and violence: Social movements, fundamentalists, and apocalyptic warriors. *Terrorism and Political Violence, 28*, 338-360.

Gregory, B. S. (2012). *The unintended Reformation: How a religious revolution secularized society.* Cambridge, MA: Harvard University Press.

Grossman, P., Niemann, L., Schmidt, S., & Walach, H. (2004). Mindfulness-based stress reduction and health benefits: A meta-analysis. *Journal of Psychosomatic Research, 57*, 35-43.

Gruber, J., Mauss, I. B., & Tamir, M. (2011). A dark side of happiness? How, when, and why happiness is not always good. *Perspectives on Psychological Science, 6*, 222-233.

Gulliford, L., & Morgan, B. (2018). The meaning and valence of gratitude in positive psychology. In N. Brown, R. Lomas, & F. J. Eiroa-Orosa (Eds.), *The Routledge international handbook of critical positive psychology* (pp. 53-69). New York, NY: Routledge/Taylor & Francis Group.

Gushee, D. P. (2020). *After evangelicalism: The path to a new Christianity.* Louisville, KY: Westminster John Knox Press.

Guthrie, S. E. (1993). *Faces in the clouds: A new theory of religion.* New York, NY: Oxford University Press.

Guthrie, S. E. (2021). Religion as anthropomorphism: A cognitive theory. In J. R. Liddle & T. K. Shackelford (Eds.), *The Oxford handbook of evolutionary psychology and religion* (pp. 48-68). New York, NY: Oxford University Press.

Gutting, G. (Ed., interviewer). (2017). *Talking God: Philosophers on belief.* New York, NY: W.W. Norton & Company.

Hackett, C., Stonawski, M., Potancoková, M., Grim, B. J., & Skirbekk, V. (2015). The future size of religiously affiliated and unaffiliated populations. *Demographic Research, 32*, 829-842.

Hadnes, M., & Schumacher, H. (2012). The gods are watching: An experimental study of religion and traditional belief in Burkina Faso. *Journal for the Scientific Study of Religion, 41*, 689-704.

Haidt, J. (2001). The emotional dog and its irrational tail: A social intuitionist approach to moral judgment. *Psychological Review, 108*, 814-834.

Haidt, J. (2007). The new synthesis in moral psychology. *Science, 316*, no. 5827, 998-1002.

Haidt, J. (2009). Moral psychology and the misunderstanding of religion. In J. Schloss & M. J. Murray (Eds.), *The believing primate: Scientific, philosophical, and theological reflections on the origin of religion* (pp. 278-291). Oxford, UK: Oxford University Press.

Haidt, J. (2012). *The righteous mind: Why good people are divided by politics and religion.* New York, NY: Vintage.

Halama, P. (2014). Meaning in life and coping. Sense of meaning as a buffer against stress. In A. Batthyany & P. Russo-Netzer, P. (Eds.), *Meaning in positive and existential psychology* (pp. 239-250). New York, NY: Springer.

Hall, D. L., Cohen, A. B., Meyer, K. K., Varley, A. H., & Brewer, G. A. (2015). Costly signaling increases trust, even across religious affiliations. *Psychological Science, 26*, 1368-1376.

Hall, D. L., Marz, D. C., & Wood, W. (2010). Why don't we practice what we preach? A meta-analytic review of religious racism. *Personality and Social Psychology Review, 14*, 126-139.

Harari, Y. N. (2015). *Sapiens: A brief history of humankind.* New York, NY: HarperCollins.

Harris, P. L., & Giménez, M. (2005). Children's acceptance of conflicting testimony: The case of death. *Journal of Cognition and Culture, 5*, 143-164.

Harris, S. (2005). *The end of faith: Religion, terror, and the future of reason.* New York, NY: W. W. Norton & Company.

Harris, S. (2010). *The moral landscape: How science could determine human values.* New York, NY: Free Press.

Harris, S. (2014). *Waking up: A guide to spirituality without religion.* New York, NY: Simon & Schuster Paperbacks.

Hartberg, Y., Cox, M., & Villamayor-Tomas, S. (2016). Supernatural monitoring and sanctioning in community-shared resource management. *Religion, Brain & Behavior, 6,* 95-111.

Haught, J. F. (2008). *God and the New Atheism: A critical response to Dawkins, Harris, and Hitchens.* Louisville, KY: Westminster John Knox Press.

Hayden, B. (2003). *Shamans, sorcerers, and saints: A prehistory of religion.* Washington, D.C.: Smithsonian Books.

Hazleton, L. (2016). *Agnostic: A spirited manifesto.* New York, NY: Riverhead Books.

Hecht, J. M. (2003). *Doubt: A history.* New York, NY: HarperSanFrancisco.

Hedges, C. (2008). *When atheism becomes religion: America's new fundamentalists.* New York, NY: Free Press.

Heine, S. J., Proulx, T., & Vohs, K. D. (2006). The meaning maintenance model: On the coherence of social motivations. *Personality and Social Psychology Review, 10,* 88-110.

Heintzelman, S. J., & King, L. A. (2014). Life is pretty meaningful. *American Psychologist, 69,* 561-574.

Heintzelman, S. J., & Tay, L. (2018). Subjective well-being: Payoffs of being happy and ways to promote happiness. In D. S. Dunn (Ed.), *Positive psychology: Established and emerging issues* (pp. 9-28). New York, NY: Routledge.

Heiphetz, L., Lane, J. D., Waytz, A., & Young, L. L. (2016). How children and adults represent God's mind. *Cognitive Science, 40,* 121-144.

Hendriks, T., Schotanus-Dijkstra, M., Hassankhan, A., Graafsma, T., Bohlmeijer, E. T., & de Jong, J. (2018). The efficacy of positive psychology interventions from non-Western countries: A systematic review and meta-analysis. *International Journal of Wellbeing, 8,* 71–98.

Hendriks, T., Schotanus-Dijkstra, M., Hassankhan, A., Jong, J., & Bohlmeijer, E. (2020). The efficacy of multi-component positive psychology interventions: A systematic review and meta-analysis of randomized controlled trials. *Journal of Happiness Studies, 21,* 357-390.

Henrich, J. (2009). The evolution of costly displays, cooperation and religion: Credibility enhancing displays and their implications for cultural evolution. *Evolution and Human Behavior, 30,* 244-260.

Henrich, J. (2020). *The weirdest people in the world: How the West became psychologically peculiar and particularly prosperous.* New York, NY: Picador/Farrar, Straus and Giroux.

Henrich, J., Bauer, M., Cassar, A., Chytilová, J., & Purzycki, B. G. (2019). War increases religion. *Nature Human Behaviour, 32,* 129-135.

Henrich, J., Ensimger, J., McElreath, R., Barr, A., Barrett, C., Bolyanatz, A., Cardenas, J. C., Gurven, M., Gwako, E., Henrich, N., Lesorogol, C., Marlowe, F., & Ziker, J. (2010). Markets, religion, community size, and the evolution of fairness and punishment. *Science, 327,* 1480-1484.

Henrich, J., & Gil-White, F. J. (2001). The evolution of prestige: Freely conferred deference as a mechanism for enhancing the benefits of cultural transmission. *Evolution and Human Behavior, 22,* 165–196.

Henrich, J., McElreath, R., Barr, A., Ensminger, J. Barrett, C., Bolyanatz, A., Cardenas, J. C., Gurven, M., Gwako, E., Henrich, N., Lesorogol, C., Marlowe, F., Tracer, D., & Ziker, J. (2006). Costly punishment across human societies. *Science, 312,* 1767-1770.

Herrick, J. (2005). *Humanism: An introduction.* Amherst, NY: Prometheus Books.

Herrmann, B., Thöni, C., & Gächter, S. (2008). Antisocial punishment across societies. *Science, 319,* 1362-1367.

Hertzler-McCain, A. (2024, March 26). More than 140 global Christian leaders call for Gaza cease-fire in Holy Week letter. *Religion News Service.* https://religionnews.com/2024/03/26/more-than-140-global-christian-leaders-call-for-gaza-cease-fire-in-holy-week-letter/

Heywood, B. T., & Bering, J. M. (2014). "Meant to be": How religious beliefs and cultural religiosity affect the implicit bias to think teleologically. *Religion, Brain & Behavior, 4*, 183-201.

Hicks, J. A., & King, L. A. (2008). Religious commitment and positive mood as information about meaning in life. *Journal of Research in Personality, 42*, 43-57.

Hicks, J. A., & King, L. A. (2009). Positive mood and social relatedness as information about meaning in life. *Journal of Positive Psychology, 4*, 471-482.

Hicks, J. A., Schlegel, R. J., & Newman, G. E. (2019). Introduction to the special issue: Authenticity: Novel insights into a valued, yet elusive, concept. *Review of General Psychology, 23*, 3-7.

Hill, P. L., & Turiano, N. A. (2014). Purpose in life as a predictor of mortality across adulthood. *Psychological Science, 25*, 1482-1486.

Hinde, R. A. (2005). Modes theory: Some theoretical considerations. In H. Whitehouse & R. N. McCauley, *Mind and religion: Psychological and cognitive foundations of religiosity* (pp. 31-55). Walnut Creek, CA: AltaMira Press.

Hitchens, C. (2007a). *God is not great: How religion poisons everything.* New York, NY: Grand Central Publishing.

Hitchens, C. (Ed.). (2007b). *The portable atheist: Essential readings for the nonbeliever.* Philadelphia, PA: Da Capo Press.

Hitzeman, C., & Wastell, C. (2017). Are atheists implicit theists? *Journal of Cognition and Culture, 17*, 27-50.

Hobson, T. (2018). *God created humanism: The Christian basis of secular values.* London, UK: SPCK.

Hodge, A. S., Hook, J. N., Kim, J. J., Mosher, D. K., McLaughlin, A. T., Davis, D. E., & Van Tongeren, D. R. (2023). Positive psychology and Christianity. In E. B. Davis, E. L. Worthington, Jr., & S. A. Schnitker (Eds.), *Handbook of positive psychology, religion, and spirituality* (pp. 147-161). Cham, Switzerland: Springer.

Hoffarth, M. R., Hodson, G., & Molnar, D. S. (2018). When and why is religious attendance associated with antigay bias and gay rights opposition? A justification-suppression model approach. *Journal of Personality and Social Psychology, 115,* 526-563.

Hofman, W., Wisneski, D. C., Brandt, M. J., & Skitka, L. J. (2014). Morality in everyday life. *Science, 345,* 6202.

Hogg, M. A. (2014). From uncertainty to extremism: Social categorization and identity processes. *Current Directions in Psychological Science, 23,* 338-342.

Hogg, M. A., & Adelman, J. (2013). Uncertainty-identity theory: Extreme groups, radical behavior, and authoritarian leadership. *Journal of Social Issues, 69,* 436-454.

Hogg, M. A., Adelman, J., & Blagg, R. (2010). Religion in the face of uncertainty: An uncertainty-identity theory account of religiousness. *Personality and Social Psychology Review, 14,* 72-83.

Höllinger, F., & Muckenhuber, J. (2019). Religiousness and existential insecurity: A cross-national comparative analysis on the macro- and micro-level. *International Sociology, 34,* 19-37.

Holt, J. (2012). *Why does the world exist? An existential detective story.* New York, NY: Liveright Publishing Corporation.

Hone, L. C., Jarden, A., Schofield, G. M., & Duncan, S. (2014). Measuring flourishing: The impact of operational definitions on the prevalence of high levels of wellbeing. *International Journal of Wellbeing, 4,* 62-90.

Hoogeveen, S., Wagenmakers, E. J., Kay, A. C., & Van Elk, M. (2018). Compensatory control and religious beliefs: A registered replication report across two countries. *Comprehensive Results in Social Psychology, 3,* 240–65.

Hook, J. N., Farrell, J. E., Johnson, K. A., Van Tongeren, D. R., Davis, D. E., & Aten, J. D. (2017). Intellectual humility and religious tolerance. *The Journal of Positive Psychology, 12,* 29-35.

Hopkin, C. R., Hoyle, R. H., & Toner, K. (2014). Intellectual humility and reactions to opinions about religious beliefs. *Journal of Psychology and Theology, 42*, 50-61.

House, R., Kalisch, D., & Maidman, J. (2018). *Humanistic psychology: Current trends and future prospects.* New York, NY: Routledge.

Human Rights Watch (n.d.). LGBT Rights: #Outlawed: "The love that dare not speak its name." https://internap.hrw.org/features/features/lgbt_laws/

Humanists UK (2022, December 8). Over 70% of people live in countries that "severely discriminate" against the non-religious—report. https://humanists.uk/2022/12/08/over-70-of-people-live-in-countries-that-severely-discriminate-against-the-non-religious-report

Hunsberger, B., & Jackson, L. M. (2005). Religion, meaning, and prejudice. *Journal of Social Issues, 61*, 807-826.

Huntington, S. P. (1996). *The clash of civilizations and the remaking of world order.* New York, NY: Simon & Schuster.

Huppert, F. A., & So, T. C. (2013). Flourishing across Europe: Application of a new conceptual framework for defining well-being. *Social Indicators Research, 110*, 837-861.

Huta, V. (2013). Pursuing eudaimonia versus hedonia: Distinctions, similarities, and relationships. In A. S. Waterman (Ed.), *The best within us: Positive psychology perspectives on eudaimonia* (pp. 139-158). Washington, DC: American Psychological Association.

Iannacone, L. R. (1994). Why strict churches are strong. *American Journal of Sociology, 99*, 1180-1211.

Inglehart, R. F. (2021). *Religion's sudden decline: What's causing it, and what comes next?* New York, NY: Oxford University Press.

Irons, W. (2001). Religion as a hard-to-fake sign of commitment. In R. Nesse (Ed.), *Evolution and the capacity for commitment* (pp. 292-309). New York: Russell Sage Foundation.

Irwin, W. (2019). *God is a question, not an answer: Finding common ground in our uncertainty.* London, UK: Rowman & Littlefield.

Ishii, T., & Watanabe, K. (2023). Do empathetic people have strong religious beliefs? Survey studies with large Japanese samples. *The International Journal for the Psychology of Religion, 33,* 1-18.

Jäckle, S., & Wenzelburger, G. (2015). Religion, religiosity, and the attitudes toward homosexuality: A multilevel analysis of 79 countries. *Journal of Homosexuality, 62,* 207-241.

Jackson, C. (2018, December 18). We must engage with shared values in the abortion debate. *Religion & Politics.* https://religionandpolitics.org/2018/12/18/we-must-engage-with-shared-values-in-the-abortion-debate

Jackson, J. C., & Gray, K. (2019). When a good god makes bad people: Testing a theory of religion and immorality. *Journal of Personality and Social Psychology, 117,* 1203-1230.

Jacoby, S. (2004). *Freethinkers: A history of American secularism.* New York, NY: Metropolitan Books.

Jacoby, S. (2016). *Strange gods: A secular history of conversion.* New York, NY: Vintage books.

Jain, K. (2023, July 17). In Thailand, 'socially engaged Buddhism' goes beyond meditation to seek justice. *Religion News Service.* https://religionnews.com/2023/07/17/in-thailand-socially-engaged-buddhism-goes-beyond-meditation-to-seek-justice/

James, W. (1985). *The varieties of religious experience.* New York, NY: Penguin Books. (Original published in 1902)

Jeeves, M., & Brown, W. S. (2009). *Neuroscience, psychology, and religion: Illusions, delusions, and realities about human nature.* West Conshohocken, PA: Templeton Press.

Jeeves, M. A., & Ludwig, T. E. (2018). *Psychological science and Christian faith: Insights and enrichments from constructive dialogue.* West Conshohocken, PA: Templeton Press.

Jenkins, J. (2023, August 11). Christian nationalist's opponents are getting organized. *Religion News Service.* https://religionnews.com/2023/08/11/christian-nationalisms-opponents-are-getting-organized/

Jenkins, P. (2020). *Fertility and faith: The demographic revolution and the transformation of world religions.* Waco, TX: Baylor University Press.

Jensen, L. A. (2023). Afterlife beliefs among evangelical and mainline Protestant children, adolescents, and adults: A cultural–developmental study in the U.S. *Psychology of Religion and Spirituality, 15,* 94-104.

Johnson, D. (2005). God's punishment and public goods: A test of the supernatural punishment hypothesis in 186 world cultures. *Human Nature, 16,* 410-446.

Johnson, D. (2011). Why God is the best punisher. *Religion, Brain & Behavior, 1,* 77-84.

Johnson, D. (2012). What are atheists for? Hypotheses on the functions of non-belief in the evolution of religion. *Religion, Brain & Behavior, 2,* 48-70.

Johnson, D. (2016). *God is watching you: How the fear of God makes us human.* New York, NY: Oxford University Press.

Johnson, D. (2018). The wrath of the academics: Criticisms, applications, and extensions of the supernatural punishment hypothesis. *Religion, Brain & Behavior, 8,* 320-350.

Johnson, J. B. (2013). Religion and volunteering over the adult life course. *Journal for the Scientific Study of Religion, 52,* 733-752.

Johnson, K. A. (2021). God…karma, jinn, spirits, and other metaphysical forces. *Current Opinion in Psychology, 40,* 10-14.

Johnson, M. K., Rowatt, W. C., Barnard-Brak, L. M., Patok-Peckham, J. A., LaBouff, J. P. & Carlisle, R. D. (2011). A mediational analysis of the role of right-wing authoritarianism and religious fundamentalism in the religiosity-prejudice link. *Personality and Individual Differences, 50,* 851-856.

Johnson, M. K., Rowatt, W. C., & LaBouff, J. P. (2012a). Priming Christian religious concepts increases racial prejudice. *Social Psychological and Personality Science, 1*, 119-126.

Johnson, M. K., Rowatt, W. C., & LaBouff, J. P. (2012b). Religiosity and prejudice revisited: In-group favoritism, out-group derogation, or both? *Psychology of Religion and Spirituality, 4*, 154-168.

Jonas, E., & Fischer, P. (2006). Terror management and religion: Evidence that intrinsic religiousness mitigates worldview defense following mortality salience. *Journal of Personality and Social Psychology, 91*, 553-567.

Jones, J. W. (2013). The psychology of contemporary religious violence: A multidimensional approach. In K. I. Pargament (Editor-in-Chief), A. Mahoney & E. P. Shafranske (Associate Editors), *APA handbook of psychology, religion, and spirituality: Vol. 2: An applied psychology of religion and spirituality* (pp. 355-370). Washington, D. C.: American Psychological Association.

Jones, R. P. (2017). *The end of White Christian America*. New York, NY: Simon & Schuster Paperbacks.

Jong, J. (2021). Death anxiety and religion. *Current Opinion in Psychology, 40*, 40-44.

Jong, J., Ross, R., Philip, T., Chang, S.-H., Simons, N., & Halberstadt, J. (2018). The religious correlates of death anxiety: A systematic review and meta-analysis. *Religion, Brain & Behavior, 8*, 4-20.

Jongman-Sereno, K. P., & Leary, M. R. (2019). The enigma of being yourself: A critical examination of the concept of authenticity. *Review of General Psychology, 23*, 113-142.

Joshanloo, M. (2023). Temporal associations between religiosity and subjective well-being in a nationally representative Australian sample. *The International Journal for the Psychology of Religion, 33*, 107-114.

Joshi, S. T. (Ed.) (2007). *The agnostic reader*. Amherst, NY: Prometheus Books.

Joshi, S. T. (2011). *The unbelievers: The evolution of modern atheism*. Amherst, NY: Prometheus Books.

Juergensmeyer, M. (2000). *Terror in the mind of God: The global rise of religious violence*. Berkeley, CA: University of California Press.

Juergensmeyer, M. (2020). *God at war: A meditation on religion and warfare*. New York, NY: Oxford University Press.

Kandler, C. (2021). A meta-analytic review of nature and nurture in religiousness across the lifespan. *Current Opinion in Psychology, 40*, 106-113.

Kanol, E., & Michalowski, I. (2023). Impact of COVID-19 pandemic on religiosity: Evidence from Germany. *Journal for the Scientific Study of Religion, 62*, 293-311.

Karim, M., & Saroglou, V. (2023). Being agnostic, not atheist: Personality, cognitive, and ideological differences. *Psychology of Religion and Spirituality, 15*, 118-127.

Kasselstrand, I., Zuckerman, P., & Cragun, R. T. (2023). *Beyond doubt: The secularization of society*. New York, NY: New York University Press.

Kasser, T., & Ryan, R. M. (1996). Further examining the American dream: Well-being correlates of intrinsic and extrinsic goals. *Personality and Social Psychology Bulletin 22*, 281-288.

Kaufmann, E. P. (2010). *Shall the religious inherit the earth? Demography and politics in the twenty-first century*. London, UK: Profile Books.

Kay, A. C., Gaucher, D., McGregor, I., & Nash, K. (2010). Religious belief as compensatory control. *Personality and Social Psychology Review, 14*, 37-48.

Kay, A. C., Gaucher, D., Napier, J. L., Callan, M. J., & Laurin, K. (2008). God and the government: Testing a compensatory control mechanism for the support of external systems. *Journal of Personality and Social Psychology, 95*, 18-35.

Kay, A. C., Shepherd, S., Blatz, C.W., Chua, S.N., & Galinsky, A.D. (2010). For God (or) country: The hydraulic relation between government instability and belief in religious sources of control. *Journal of Personality and Social Psychology, 99*, 725–739.

Kay, A. C., Whitson, J. A., Gaucher, D., & Galinsky, A. D. (2009). Compensatory control: Achieving order through the mind, our institutions, and the heavens. *Current Directions in Psychological Science, 18*, 264-268.

Kaylor, B., & Underwood, B. (2023, January 4). How mainline Protestants help build Christian nationalism. *Religion & Politics*. https://religionandpolitics.org/2023/01/04/how-mainline-protestants-help-build-christian-nationalism

Keesing, R. M. (1984). Rethinking *mana. Journal of Anthropological Research, 40*, 137-156.

Kelemen, D. (1999a). The scope of teleological thinking in preschool children. *Cognition, 70*, 241-272.

Kelemen, D. (1999b). Why are rocks pointy? Children's preference for teleological explanations of the natural world. *Developmental Psychology, 35*, 1440-1453.

Kelemen, D. (2004). Are children "intuitive theists"? *Psychological Science, 15*, 295-301.

Kelemen, D., & DiYanni, C. (2005). Intuitions about origins: Purpose and intelligent design in children's reasoning about nature. *Journal of Cognition and Development, 6*, 3-31.

Kelemen, D., & Rosset, E. (2009). The human function compunction: Teleological explanation in adults. *Cognition, 111*, 138-143.

Kelemen, D., Rottman, J., & Seston, R. (2013). Professional physical scientists display tenacious teleological tendencies: Purpose-based reasoning as a cognitive default. *Journal of Experimental Psychology: General, 142*, 1074-1083.

Keltner, D., & Haidt, J. (2003). Approaching awe, a moral, spiritual, and aesthetic emotion. *Cognition and Emotion, 17*, 2997-314.

Keyes, C. L. M. (1998). Social well-being. *Social Psychology Quarterly, 61*, 121-140.

Keyes, C. L. M. (2002). The Mental Health Continuum: From languishing to flourishing in life. *Journal of Health and Social Behavior, 43,* 207-222.

Keyes, C. L. M., Dhingra, S. S., & Simoes, E. J. (2010). Change in level of positive mental health as a predictor of future risk of mental illness. *American Journal of Public Health, 100,* 2366-2371.

Keyes, C. L. M., & Simoes, E. J. (2012). To flourish or not: Positive mental health and all-cause mortality. *American Journal of Public Health, 102,* 2164-2172.

Keyes, C. L. M., Yao, J., Hybels, C. F., Milstein, G., & Proeschold-Bell, R. J. (2020). Are changes in positive mental health associated with increased likelihood of depression over a two year period? A test of the mental health promotion and protection hypothesis. *Journal of Affective Disorders, 270,* 136-142.

Keysar, A. (2017). Religious/nonreligious demography and religion versus science. In P. Zuckerman & J. R. Shook (Eds.), *The Oxford handbook of secularism* (pp. 40-54). New York, NY: Oxford University Press.

Keysar, A., & Navarro-Rivera, J. (2013). A world of atheism: Global demographics. In S. Bullivant & M. Ruse (Eds.), *The Oxford handbook of atheism* (pp. 553-586), Oxford: Oxford University Press.

Khoury, B., Lecomte, T., Fortin, G., Masse, M., Therien, P., Bouchard, V., Chapleau, M.-A., Paquin, K., & Hofmann, S. G. (2013). Mindfulness-based therapy: A comprehensive meta-analysis. *Clinical Psychology Review, 33,* 763-771.

King, B. (2017). *Evolving God: A provocative view of the origins of religion* (Expanded edition). Chicago, IL: The University of Chicago Press.

King, L. A., Heintzelman, S. J., & Ward, S. J. (2016). Beyond the search for meaning: A contemporary science of the experience of meaning in life. *Current Directions in Psychological Science, 25,* 211-216.

King, L A., & Hicks, J. A. (2012). Positive affect and meaning in life: The intersection of hedonism and eudaimonia. In P. T. P. Wong (Ed.), *The human quest for meaning: Theories, research, and applications* (2nd ed., pp. 125-142). New York, NY: Routledge.

Kiper, J., & Sosis, R. (2021). The roots of intergroup conflict and the co-optation of the religious system: An evolutionary perspective on religious terrorism. In J. R. Liddle & T. K. Shackelford (Eds.), *The Oxford handbook of evolutionary psychology and religion* (pp. 265-281). New York, NY: Oxford University Press.

Kirkpatrick, L. A. (2005). *Attachment, evolution, and the psychology of religion.* New York, NY: Guilford Press.

Kirkpatrick, L. A. (2012). Attachment theory and the evolutionary psychology of religion. *The International Journal for the Psychology of Religion, 22,* 231-241.

Kirkpatrick, L. A., Shillito, D. J., & Kellas, S. L. (1999). Loneliness, social support, and perceived relationships with God. *Journal of Social and Personal Relationships, 16,* 13-22.

Kissling, F. (2018, December 18). We should be peacemakers in the abortion wars. *Religion & Politics.* https://religionandpolitics.org/2018/12/18/we-should-be-peacemakers-in-the-abortion-wars/

Kitcher, P. (2014). *Life after faith: The case for secular humanism.* New Haven, CT: Yale University Press.

Klinger, E. (2012). The search for meaning in evolutionary goal-theory perspective and its clinical implications. In P. T. P. Wong (Ed.), *The human quest for meaning: Theories, research, and applications* (2nd ed., pp. 23-56). New York, NY: Routledge.

Koenig, H. G., King, D. E., & Carson, V. B. (2012). *Handbook of religion and health* (2nd ed.), Oxford, UK: Oxford University Press.

Kossowska, M., Czernatowicz-Kukuczka, A., & Sekerdej, M. (2017). Many faces of dogmatism: Prejudice as a way of protecting certainty against value violators among dogmatic believers and atheists. *British Journal of Psychology, 108,* 127-147.

Kossowska, M., & Sekerdej, M. (2015). Searching for certainty: Religious beliefs and intolerance toward value-violating groups. *Personality and Individual Differences, 83*, 72-76.

Kranz, D., Niepel, C., Botes, E., & Greiff, S. (2023). Religiosity predicts unreasonable coping with COVID-19. *Psychology of Religion and Spirituality, 15*, 1-5.

Krause, N. (2006). Exploring the stress-buffering effects of church-based and secular social support on self-rated health in late life. *Journal of Gerontology, 61B*, S35-43.

Krause, N. (2022). *Religion, virtues, and health: New directions in theory construction and model development.* New York, NY: Oxford University Press.

Krause, N., & Hayward, R. (2014). Virtues, practical wisdom, and psychological well-being: A Christian perspective. *Social Indicators Research, 122*, 735-755.

Krause, N., & Wulff, K. M. (2005). Church-based social ties, a sense of belonging in a congregation, and physical health status. *The International Journal for the Psychology of Religion, 15*, 73-79.

Krauss, L. M. (2012). *A universe from nothing: Why there is something rather than nothing.* New York, NY: Free Press.

Krumrei, E. J., Mahoney, A., & Pargament, K. I. (2009). Divorce and the divine: The role of spirituality in adjustment to divorce. *Journal of Marriage and Family, 71*, 373-383.

Küng, H. (1988). *Theology for the third millennium: An ecumenical view.* New York, NY: Doubleday.

Kunst, J. R., Kimel, S. Y., Shani, M., Alayan, R., & Thomsen, L. (2019). Can Abraham bring peace? The relationship between acknowledging shared religious roots and intergroup conflict. *Psychology of Religion and Spirituality, 11*, 417-432.

Kuykendall, L., Tay, L, & Ng, V. (2015). Leisure engagement and subjective well-being: A meta-analysis. *Psychological Bulletin, 141*, 364-403.

LaBouff, J. P., & Ledoux, A. M. (2016). Imagining atheists: Reducing fundamental distrust in atheist intergroup attitudes. *Psychology of Religion and Spirituality, 8,* 330-340.

LaBouff, J. P., Rowatt, W. C., Johnson, M. K., & Finkle, C. (2012). Differences in attitudes toward outgroups in religious and nonreligious contexts in a multinational sample: A situational context priming study. *The International Journal for the Psychology of Religion, 22,* 109.

Labov, D. C. (2023, January 12). Advancing religious freedom despite persecutions on the rise. *Vatican News.* https://www.vaticannews.va/en/church/news/2023-01/advancing-religious-freedom-despite-persecutions-on-the-rise.html

Lambert, N. M., Stillman, T. F., Hicks, J. A., Kamble, S., Baumeister, R. F., & Fincham, F. D. (2013). To belong is to matter: Sense of belonging enhances meaning in life. *Personality and Social Psychology Bulletin, 39,* 1418-1427.

Lang, A. (1968). *The making of religion.* New York, NY: AMS Press. (Original work published 1898)

Lang, M., & Chvaja, R. (2023). Hazard precaution: Examining the possible adaptive value of ritualized behavior. In Y. Lior & J. Lane (Eds.), *The Routledge handbook of evolutionary approaches to religion* (pp. 164-184). London & New York: Routledge.

Lang, M., Krátký, J., & Xygalatas, D. (2020). The role of ritual behaviour in anxiety reduction: An investigation of Marathi religious practices in Mauritius. *Philosophical Transactions of the Royal Society B, 375,* Article 20190431.

Lang, M., & Kundt, R. (2023). The evolution of human ritual behavior as a cooperative signaling platform. *Religion, Brain & Behavior.* DOI: 10.1080/2153599X.2023.2197977

Lang, M., Purzycki, B. G., Apicella, C. L., Atkinson, Q. D., Bolyanatz, A., Cohen, E., Handley, C., Kundtová Klocová, E., Lesorogol, C., Mathew, S., McNamara, R. A., Moya, C., Placek, C. D., Soler, M., Vardy, T., Weigel, J. L., Willard, A. K., Xygalatas, D., Norenzayan, A., & Henrich, J.

(2019). Moralizing gods, impartiality and religious parochialism across 15 societies. *Proceedings of the Royal Society B, 286*, 20190202.

Lanman, J. A. (2012). The importance of religious displays for belief acquisition and secularization. *Journal of Contemporary Religion, 27*, 49-65.

Lanman, J. A., & Buhrmester, M. D. (2017). Religious actions speak louder than words: Exposure to credibility-enhancing displays predicts theism. *Religion, Brain & Behavior, 7*, 3-16.

Laurin, K., Kay, A. C., & Moscovitch, D. A. (2008). On the belief in God: Towards an understanding of the emotional substrates of compensatory control. *Journal of Experimental Social Psychology, 44*, 1559-1562.

Laurin, K., Shariff, A. F., Henrich, J., & Kay, A. C. (2012). Outsourcing punishment to God: Beliefs in divine control reduce earthly punishment. *Proceedings of the Royal Society B: Biological Sciences, 279*, 3272-3281.

Lawrence, E. M., Rogers, R. G., & Wadsworth, T. (2015). Happiness and longevity in the United States. *Social Science & Medicine, 145*, 115–119.

Lazarus, R. S. (2003). The Lazarus manifesto for positive psychology and psychology in general. *Psychological Inquiry, 14*, 173-189.

Lefevor, G. T., Milburn, H. E., Sheffield, P. E., & Tamez Guerrero, N. A. (2023). Religiousness and homonegativity in congregations: The role of individual, congregational, and clergy characteristics. *Psychology of Religion and Spirituality, 15*, 195-205.

Lefevor, G. T., Sorrell, S. A., Virk, H. E., Huynh, K. D., Paiz, J. Y., Stone, W.-M., & Franklin, A. (2021). How do religious congregations affect congregants' attitudes toward lesbian women and gay men? *Psychology of Religion and Spirituality, 13*, 184-193.

Legare, C. H., & Gelman, S. A. (2008). Bewitchment, biology, or both: The co-existence of natural and supernatural explanatory frameworks across development. *Cognitive Science, 32*, 607-642.

Lessa, W. A., & Vogt, E. Z. (1958). *Reader in comparative religion: An anthropological approach*. Evanston, IL: Row, Peterson and Company.

Lévi-Strauss, C. (1962). *Totemism* (R. Needham, Trans.). Boston, MA: Beacon Press.

Levin, J., & Bradshaw, M. (2022). Determinants of COVID-10 skepticism and SARS-CoV-2 vaccine hesitancy: Findings from a national population survey of U.S. adults. *BMC Public Health, 22,* 1047.

Lewis, R. (2021). *Finding purpose in a Godless world: Why we care even if the universe doesn't.* Amherst, NY: Prometheus Books.

Liddle, J. R., & Shackelford, T. K. (2021). An introduction to evolutionary perspectives on religion. In J. R. Liddle & T. K. Shackelford (Eds.), *The Oxford handbook of evolutionary psychology and religion* (pp. 1-17). New York, NY: Oxford University Press.

Lightner, A. D., Bendixen, T., & Purzycki, B. G. (2023). Moralistic supernatural punishment is probably not associated with social complexity. *Evolution and Human Behavior, 44,* 555-565.

Lilla, M. (2007). *The stillborn God: Religion, politics, and the modern West.* New York, NY: Vintage Books.

Lim, C., & Putnam, R. D. (2010). Religion, social networks, and life satisfaction. *American Sociological Review, 75,* 914-933.

Lindeman, M., van Elk, M., Lipsanen, J., Marin, P., & Schjodt, U. (2019). Religious unbelief in three Western European countries: Identifying and characterizing unbeliever types using latent class analysis. *The International Journal for the Psychology of Religion, 29,* 184-203.

Linley, P. A. (2013). Human strengths and well-being: Finding the best within us at the intersection of eudaimonic philosophy, humanistic psychology, and positive psychology. In A. S. Waterman (Ed.), *The best within us: Positive psychology perspectives on eudaimonia* (pp. 269-285). Washington, DC: American Psychological Association.

Lior, Y. (2023). Big Gods and the cultural evolution of social complexity. In Y. Lior & J. Lane (Eds.), *The Routledge handbook of evolutionary approaches to religion* (pp. 298-316). London & New York: Routledge.

Lomas, T., & Vanderweele, T. J. (2023). The complex creation of happiness: Multidimensional conditionality in the drivers of happy people and societies. *Journal of Positive Psychology, 18,* 15-33.

Long, K. N. G., & VanderWeele, T. J. (2023). Theological virtues, health, and well-being: Theory, research, and public health. In E. B. Davis, E. L. Worthington, Jr., & S. A. Schnitker (Eds.), *Handbook of positive psychology, religion, and spirituality* (pp. 395-409). Cham, Switzerland: Springer.

Lowicki, P., & Zajenkowski, M. (2020). Empathy and exposure to credible religious acts during childhood independently predict religiosity. *The International Journal for the Psychology of Religion, 30,* 128-141.

Lowie, R. H. (1952). *Primitive religion.* New York, NY: Liveright Publishing Corporation. [Originally published in 1924]

Lucas, R. E., & Schimmack, U. (2009). Income and wellbeing: How big is the gap between the rich and the poor? *Journal of Research in Personality, 43,* 75–78.

Luhmann, M., Hofmann, W., Eid, M., & Lucas, R. E. (2012). Subjective well-being and adaptation to life events: A meta-analysis. *Journal of Personality and Social Psychology, 102,* 592-615.

Luhrmann, T. M., & Weisman, K. (2022). Porosity is the heart of religion. *Current Directions in Psychological Science, 31,* 247-253.

Lun, V. M.-C., & Bond, M. H. (2013). Examining the relation of religion and spirituality to subjective well-being across national cultures. *Psychology of Religion and Spirituality, 5,* 304-315.

Lyubomirsky, S. (2001). Why are some people happier than others? *American Psychologist, 56,* 239-249.

Lyubomirsky, S., King, L. A., & Diener, E. (2005). The benefits of frequent positive affect: Does happiness lead to success? *Psychological Bulletin, 131,* 803-855.

Lyubomirsky, S., & Layous, K. (2013). How do simple positive activities increase well-being? *Current Directions in Psychological Science, 22,* 57-62.

Ma-Kellams, C., & Blascovich, J. (2012). Enjoying life in the face of death: East-west differences in the response to mortality salience. *Journal of Personality and Social Psychology, 103*, 773-786.

MacIntyre, A. C. (2007). *After virtue: A study in moral theory* (3rd ed.). Notre Dame, IN: University of Notre Dame Press.

MacKenzie, M. J., & Baumeister, R. F. (2014). Meaning in life: Nature, needs, and myths. In A. Batthyany & P. Russo-Netzer, P. (Eds.), *Meaning in positive and existential psychology* (pp. 25-37). New York, NY: Springer.

Magyar-Moe, J. L., Owens, R. L., & Conoley, C. W. (2015). Positive psychological interventions in counseling: What every counseling psychologist should know. *The Counseling Psychologist, 43*, 508-557.

Mahoney, A., Wong, S., Pomerleau, J. M., & Pargament, K. I. (2022). Sanctification of diverse aspects of life and psychosocial functioning: A meta-analysis of studies from 1999 to 2019. *Psychology of Religion and Spirituality, 14*, 585-598.

Maij, D. L. R., & van Elk, M. (2019). The boundary conditions of the hypersensitive agency detection device: An empirical investigation of agency detection in threatening situations. *Religion, Brain & Behavior, 9*, 23-51.

Maij, D. L. R., van Harreveld, F., Gervais, W., Schragg, Y., Mohr, C., & van Elk, M. (2017). Mentalizing skills do not differentiate believers from non-believers, but credibility enhancing displays do. *PLOS ONE, 12*, Article e0182764.

Malhotra, D. (2010). (When) are religious people nicer? Religious salience and the "Sunday effect" on pro-social behavior. *Judgment and Decision Making, 5*, 138-143.

Malinowski, B. (1954). *Magic, science and religion.* Garden City, NY: Doubleday Anchor Books. (Original work published 1925)

Malka, A., Soto, C. J., Cohen, A. B., & Miller, D. T. (2011). Religiosity and social welfare: Competing influences of cultural conservatism and pro-social value orientation. *Journal of Personality, 79*, 763-792.

Mallinas, S. R., & Conway, P. (2022). If you don't believe in God, do you at least believe in Aristotle? Evaluations of religious outgroup members hinge upon moral perceptions. *The International Journal for the Psychology of Religion, 32*, 127– 49.

Mancuso, E. K., & Lorona, R. T. (2023). The scientific study of life satisfaction and religion/spirituality. In E. B. Davis, E. L. Worthington, Jr., & S. A. Schnitker (Eds.), *Handbook of positive psychology, religion, and spirituality* (pp. 299-313). Cham, Switzerland: Springer.

Manning, C. (2010). Atheism, secularity, the family, and children. In P. Zuckerman (Ed.), *Atheism and secularity. Vol. 1: Issues, concepts, and definitions* (pp. 19-41). Santa Barbara, CA: Praeger.

Marcus, Z. J., & McCullough, M. E. (2021). Does religion make people more self-controlled? A review of research from the lab and life. *Current Opinion in Psychology, 40*, 167-170.

Marett, R. R. (1916). *The threshold of religion* (3rd edition). London, UK: Methuen & Co. Ltd.

Marsh, H. W., Huppert, F. A., Donald, J. N., Horwood, M. S., & Sahdra, B. K. (2020). The Well-Being Profile (WB-Pro): Creating a theoretically based multidimensional measure of well-being to advance theory, research, policy, and practice. *Psychological Assessment, 32*, 294-313.

Martos, T., Barna, K. T., & Steger, M. F. (2010). It's not only what you hold, it's how you hold it: Dimensions of religiosity and meaning in life. *Personality and Individual Differences, 49*, 863-868.

Mascaro, N. (2014). Meaning sensitive psychotherapy: Binding clinical, existential, and positive psychological perspectives. In A. Batthyany & P. Russo-Netzer (Eds.), *Meaning in positive and existential psychology* (pp. 269-289). New York, NY: Springer.

Maslow, A. H. (1954). *Motivation and personality.* New York, NY: Harper & Row.

Maslow, A. H. (1968). *Toward a psychology of being* (2nd ed.). New York, NY: D. Van Nostrand.

Maslow, A. H. (1970). *Religions, values, and peak-experiences*. New York, NY: The Viking Press. (Original work published 1964)

Masters, K. S., Boehm, J. K., Boylan, J. M., Vagnini, K. M., & Rush, C. L. (2023). The scientific study of positive psychology, religion/spirituality, and physical health. In E. B. Davis, E. L. Worthington, Jr., & S. A. Schnitker (Eds.), *Handbook of positive psychology, religion, and spirituality* (pp. 329-343). Cham, Switzerland: Springer.

Masters, K. S., Emerson, R. W., IV, & Hooker, S. A. (2022). Effects of devotional prayer and secular meditation on cardiovascular response to a faith challenge among Christians. *Psychology of Religion and Spirituality, 14*, 251-259.

Matsuba, M. K., Pratt, M. W., Norris, J. E., Mohle, E., Alisat, S., & McAdams, D. P. (2012). Environmentalism as a context for expressing identity and generativity: Patterns among activists and uninvolved youth and midlife adults. *Journal of Personality, 80*, 1091-1115.

Mavor, K. I., Macleod, C. J., Boal, M. J., & Louis, W. R. (2009). Right-wing authoritarianism, fundamentalism and prejudice revisited: Removing suppression and statistical artefact. *Personality and Individual Differences, 46*, 592-597.

Mayer, J. D., & Koizumi, N. (2017). Is there a culture or religion of torture? International support for brutal treatment of suspected terrorists. *Studies in Conflict Resolution, 40*, 758-771.

McAdams, D. P., & de St. Aubin, E. (1992). A theory of generativity and its assessment through self-report, behavioral acts, and narrative themes in autobiography. *Journal of Personality and Social Psychology, 62*, 1003-1015.

McAfee, D. G. (2019). *Disproving Christianity and other secular writings* (3rd ed.). Hypatia Press.

McBrearty, S., & Brooks, A. S. (2000). The revolution that wasn't: A new interpretation of the origin of modern human behavior. *Journal of Human Evolution, 39*, 453-563.

McCauley, R. N. (2011). *Why religion is natural and science is not*. Oxford, UK: Oxford University Press.

McClenon, J. (2002). *Wondrous healing: Shamanism, human evolution, and the origin of religion*. DeKalb, IL: Northern Illinois University Press.

McCrae, R. R. (2017). The five-factor model across cultures. In A. T. Church (Ed.), *The Praeger handbook of personality across cultures: Vol. 1. Trait psychology across cultures* (pp. 47-71). Santa Barbara, CA: Praeger.

McCrae, R. R., & Costa, P. T., Jr. (1991). Adding liebe und arbeit: The full five-factor model and well-being. *Personality and Social Psychology Bulletin, 17*, 227-232.

McCullough, M. E., & Carter, E. C. (2013). Religion, self-control, and self-regulation: How and why are they related? In K. I. Pargament (Editor-in-Chief), J. J. Exline, & J. W. Jones (Associate Editors), *APA handbook of psychology, religion, and spirituality: Vol. 1. Context, theory, and research* (pp. 123-138). Washington, DC: American Psychological Association.

McCullough, M. E., Tsang, J.-A., & Brion, S. (2003). Personality traits in adolescence as predictors of religiousness in early adulthood: Findings from the Terman longitudinal study. *Personality and Social Psychology Bulletin, 29*, 980-991.

McCullough, M. E., & Willoughby, B. L. B. (2009). Religion, self-regulation, and self-control: Associations, explanations, and implications. *Psychological Bulletin, 135*, 69-93.

McCullough, M. E., & Worthington, E. L., Jr. (1999). Religion and the forgiving personality. *Journal of Personality, 67*, 1141-1164.

McDade, S. (2023, August 14). New atheism is dead. What's the new atheism? *Christianity Today*. https://www.christianitytoday.com/ct/2023/september/new-atheism-is-dead

McGrath, A. (2001). *Christian theology: An introduction* (3rd ed.). Malden, MA: Blackwell.

McGrath, A. (2006). *The twilight of atheism: The rise and fall of disbelief in the modern world.* New York, NY: Galilee.

McGrath, A. (2015). *The big question: Why we can't stop talking about science, faith and God.* New York, NY: St. Martin's Press.

McGrath, A. (2017). *Enriching our vision of reality: Theology and the natural sciences in dialogue.* West Conshohocken, PA: Templeton Press.

McGrath, A., & McGrath, J. C. (2007). *The Dawkins delusion: Atheist fundamentalism and the denial of the divine.* Downers Grove, IL: IVP Books.

McGrath, R. E. (2015). Character strengths in 75 nations: An update. *The Journal of Positive Psychology, 10,* 1-12.

McGregor, I., Haji, R., Nash, K. A., & Teper, R. (2008). Religious zeal and the uncertain self. *Basic and Applied Social Psychology, 30,* 183-188.

McGregor, I., Nash, K., & Prentice, M. (2010). Reactive approach motivation (RAM) for religion. *Journal of Personality and Social Psychology, 99,* 148-161.

McIntosh, D. N., Poulin, M. J., Silver, R. C., & Homan, E. A. (2011). The distinct roles of spirituality and religiosity in physical and mental health after collective trauma: A national longitudinal study of responses to the 9/11 attacks. *Journal of Behavioral Medicine, 34,* 497-507.

McIntosh, D. N., Silver, R. C., & Wortman, C. B. (1993). Religion's role in adjustment to a negative life event: Coping with the loss of a child. *Journal of Personality and Social Psychology, 65,* 812-821.

McKay, R., & Whitehouse, H. (2015). Religion and morality. *Psychological Bulletin, 141,* 447-473.

McNamara, P. (Ed.). (2006). *Where God and science meet: How brain and evolutionary studies alter our understanding of religion* (Vol. II and III). Westport, CT: Praeger.

McNamara, R. A., Norenzayan, A., & Henrich, J. (2016). Supernatural punishment, in-group biases, and material insecurity: Experiments and ethnography from Yasawa, Fiji. *Religion, Brain & Behavior, 6,* 34-55.

Mercadante, L. A. (2014). *Belief without borders: Inside the minds of the spiritual but not religious.* New York, NY: Oxford University Press.

Mercadante, L. (2018). Belief without borders: Inside the minds of the spiritual but not religious. In W. B. Parsons (Ed.), *Being spiritual but not religious: Past, present, future(s)* (pp. 110-127). New York, NY: Routledge.

Meral, Z. (2018). *How violence shapes religion: Belief and conflict in the Middle East and Africa.* Cambridge, UK: Cambridge University Press.

Miller, E. M. (2023, January 17). Christian persecution higher than ever as Open Doors' World Watch List marks 30 years. *Religion News Service.* https://religionnews.com/2023/01/17/christian-persecution-higher-than-ever-as-open-doors-world-watch-list-marks-30-years

Miller, E. M. (2023, February 2). Clergy protest legislation targeting transgender children in Missouri. *Religion News Service.* https://religionnews.com/2023/02/02/clergy-protest-legislation-targeting-transgender-children-in-missouri

Mitchell, S. (2004). *Gilgamesh.* New York, NY: Atria Paperback.

Mithen, S. (1996). *The prehistory of the mind: The cognitive origins of art, religion and science.* London, UK: Thames and Hudson.

Mochon, D., Norton, M. I., & Ariely, D. (2011). Who benefits from religion? *Social Indicators Research, 101,* 1-15.

Mogan, R., Fischer, R., & Bulbulia, J. A. (2017). To be in synchrony or not? A meta-analysis of synchrony's effects on behavior, perception, cognition and affect. *Journal of Experimental Social Psychology, 72,* 13-20.

Molina, A. (2023, January 5). Faith leaders hold prayer vigils to mark second anniversary of Jan. 6 insurrection. *Religion News Service.* https://religionnews.com/2023/01/05/faith-leaders-hold-prayer-vigils-to-mark-second-anniversary-of-jan-6-insurrection

Molina, A. (2023, January 30). US Hispanic Protestant churches are young, growing and largely new to the country. *Religion News Service.* https://religionnews.com/2023/01/30/u-s-hispanic-protestant-churches-are-growing-and-largely-new-to-the-u-s.

Mollidor, C., Hancock, N., & Pepper, M. (2015). Volunteering, religiosity and well-being: Interrelationships among Australian churchgoers. *Mental Health, Religion & Culture, 18,* 20-32.

Moon, J. W., Cohen, A. B., Laurin, K., & MacKinnon, D. P. (2023). Is religion special? *Perspectives on Psychological Science, 18,* 340-357.

Moore, R. (2023). *Losing our religion: An altar call for evangelical America.* New York, NY: Sentinel.

Moreno-Jiménez, B., & Aguirre-Camacho, A. (2018). Positive psychology: Intellectual, scientific, or ideological movement? In N. Brown, R. Lomas, & F. J. Eiroa-Orosa (Eds.), *The Routledge international handbook of critical positive psychology* (pp. 117-183). New York, NY: Routledge/Taylor & Francis Group.

Moreland, J. P., Meyer, S. C., Shaw, C., Gauger, A. K., & Grudem, W. (Eds.). (2017). *Theistic evolution: A scientific, philosophical, and theological critique.* Wheaton, IL: Crossway.

Murray, M. J. (2009). Scientific explanations of religion and the justification of religious belief. In J. Schloss & M. J. Murray (Eds.), *The believing primate: Scientific, philosophical, and theological reflections on the origin of religion* (pp. 168-178). Oxford, UK: Oxford University Press.

Murray, M. J., & Goldberg, A. (2009). Evolutionary accounts of religion: Explaining and explaining away. In J. Schloss & M. J. Murray (Eds.), *The believing primate: Scientific, philosophical, and theological reflections on the origin of religion* (pp. 179-199). Oxford, UK: Oxford University Press.

Murray, D. R., & Schaller, M. (2017). Pathogens, personality, and culture. In A. T. Church (Ed.), *The Praeger handbook of personality across cultures* (Vol. 3, pp. 87-116). Santa Barbara, CA: Praeger.

Myers, D. G. (2000). The funds, friends, and faith of happy people. *American Psychologist, 55,* 56-67.

Myers, D. G. (2012). Reflections on religious belief and prosociality: Comment on Galen (2012). *Psychological Bulletin, 138,* 913-917.

Myers, D. G. (2020). Some big-data lessons about religion and human flourishing. In A. B. Cohen (Ed.), *Religion and human flourishing* (pp. 145-163). Waco, TX: Baylor University Press.

Nadler, S. (2011). *A book forged in Hell: Spinoza's scandalous treatise and the birth of the secular age.* Princeton, NJ: Princeton University Press.

Najle, M. B., & Gervais, W. M. (2017). Nonreligious people in religious societies. In P. Zuckerman & J. Shook (Eds.), *The Oxford handbook of secularism* (pp. 587-602). New York, NY: Oxford University Press.

Nakamura, J., & Csikszentmihalyi, M. (2009). Flow theory and research. In C. R. Snyder & S. Lopez (Eds.), *The Oxford handbook of positive psychology* (2nd ed., pp. 195-206). New York, NY: Oxford University Press.

Neiblum, A. (2023). *Rise of the nones: The importance of freedom from religion.* Hypatia Press.

Neighborly Faith (2023, December). *Christian nationalism: A new approach.* https://www.neighborlyfaith.org/cn-report-2023

Nelson, J. M., & Slife, B. D. (2017). A new positive psychology: A critique of the movement based on early Christian thought. *The Journal of Positive Psychology, 12,* 459-467.

Neuberg, S. L., Warner, C., Mistler, S., Berlin, A., Hill, E., Johnson, J., Filip-Crawford, G., Millsap, B., Thomas, G. M., Winkelman, M., Broome, B., Taylor, T., & Schober, J. (2014). Religion and intergroup conflict: Findings from the Global Group Relations Project. *Psychological Science, 25,* 198-206.

Nguyen, K. D. L., & Fredrickson, B. L. (2018). Positive emotions and well-being. In D. S. Dunn (Ed.), *Positive psychology: Established and emerging Issues* (pp. 29-45). New York, NY: Routledge.

Nichols, A. D., Lang, M., Kavanagh, C., Kundt, R., Yamada, J., Ariely, D., & Mitkidis, P. (2020). Replicating and extending the effects of auditory religious cues on dishonest behavior. *PLOS ONE, 15,* Article e0237007.

Niemiec, C. P., Ryan, R. M., & Deci, E. L. (2009). The path taken: Consequences of attaining intrinsic and extrinsic aspirations in post-college life. *Journal of Research in Personality, 43,* 291-306.

Norenzayan, A. (2013). *Big gods: How religion transformed cooperation and conflict.* Princeton, NJ: Princeton University Press.

Norenzayan, A. (2014). Does religion make people moral? *Behaviour, 151,* 365-384.

Norenzayan, A. (2016). Theodiversity. *Annual Review of Psychology, 67,* 465-488.

Norenzayan, A., Gervais, W. M., & Trzesniewski, K. H. (2012). Mentalizing deficits constrain belief in a personal god. *PLOS ONE, 7,* Article e36880.

Norenzayan, A., & Hansen, I. G. (2006). Belief in supernatural agents in the face of death. *Personality and Social Psychology Bulletin, 32,* 174-187.

Norenzayan, A., & Shariff, A. F. (2008). The origin and evolution of religious prosociality. *Science, 322,* 58-62.

Norenzayan, A., Shariff, A. F., Gervais, W. M., Willard, A. K., McNamara, R., Slingerland, E., & Henrich, J. (2016). The cultural evolution of prosocial religions. *Behavioral and Brain Sciences, 39,* Article e1.

Norris, P., & Inglehart, R. (2011). *Sacred and secular: Religion and politics worldwide* (2nd ed.). New York, NY: Cambridge University Press.

Northover, S. B., Pedersen, W. C., Cohen, A. B., & Andrews, P. W. (2017). Artificial surveillance cues do not increase generosity: Two meta-analyses. *Evolution and Human Behavior, 38,* 144-153.

Oishi, S., & Diener, E. (2014). Residents of poor nations have a greater sense of meaning in life than residents of wealthy nations. *Psychological Science, 25,* 422-430.

Oishi, S., Diener, E., & Lucas, R. E. (2007). The optimal level of well-being: Can people be too happy? *Perspectives on Psychological Science, 2,* 346-360.

Oishi, S., & Gilbert, E. A. (2016). Current and future directions of culture and happiness research. *Current Opinion in Psychology, 8*, 54-58.

Oishi, S., & Kurtz, J. L. (2011). The positive psychology of positive emotions: An avuncular view. In K. M. Sheldon, T. B. Kashdan, & M. F. Steger (Eds.), *Designing positive psychology: Taking stock and moving forward* (pp. 101-114). New York, NY: Oxford University Press.

Oishi, S., & Westgate, E. C. (2022). A psychologically rich life: Beyond happiness and meaning. *Psychological Review, 129*, 790-811.

Olagoke, A. A., Olagoke, O. O., & Hughes, A. M. (2021). Intention to vaccinate against the novel 2019 coronavirus disease: The role of health locus of control and religiosity. *Journal of Religion and Health, 60*, 65-80.

Olson, D. V. A., Marshall, J., Jung, J. H., & Voas, D. (2020). Sacred canopies or religious markets? The effect of county-level religious diversity on later changes in religious involvement. *Journal for the Scientific Study of Religion, 59*, 227-246.

Ozment, K. (2016). *Grace without God: The search for meaning, purpose, and belonging in a secular age.* New York, NY: HarperCollins.

Paine, D. R., Moon, S. H., Hauge, D. J., & Sandage, S. J. (2018). Cultural and racial perspectives on positive psychologies of humility. In N. Brown, R. Lomas, & F. J. Eiroa-Orosa (Eds.), *The Routledge international handbook of critical positive psychology* (pp. 281-298). New York, NY: Routledge/Taylor & Francis Group.

Pally, M. (2022). *White evangelicals and right-wing populism: How did we get here?* London and New York: Routledge.

Palmer, C. T., Begley, R. O., & Coe, K. (2015). Totemism and long-term evolutionary success. *Psychology of Religion and Spirituality 7*, 286-294.

Pals, D. L. (2015). *Nine theories of religion* (3rd ed.). New York, NY: Oxford University Press.

Pape, R. A. (2005). *Dying to win: The strategic logic of suicide terrorism.* New York, NY: Random House.

Pargament, K. I. (1997). *The psychology of religion and coping: Theory, research, and practice.* New York, NY: Guilford Press.

Pargament, K. I. (2002). Is religion nothing but...? Explaining religion versus explaining away. *Psychological Inquiry, 13,* 239-244.

Pargament, K. I. (2013). Searching for the sacred: Toward a nonreductionistic theory of spirituality. In K. I. Pargament (Editor-in-Chief), J. J. Exline, & J. W. Jones (Associate Editors), *APA handbook of psychology, religion, and spirituality: Vol. 1. Context, theory, and research* (pp. 257-273). Washington, DC: American Psychological Association.

Pargament, K. I., Koenig, H. G., & Perez, L. M. (2000). The many methods of religious coping: Development and initial validation of the RCOPE. *Journal of Clinical Psychology, 56,* 519-543.

Park, C. L. (2007). Religiousness/spirituality and health: A meaning systems perspective. *Journal of Behavioral Medicine, 30,* 319-328.

Park, C. L. (2010). Making sense of meaning literature: An integrative review of meaning making and its effects on adjustment to stressful life events. *Psychological Bulletin, 136,* 257-301.

Park, C. L. (2013). Religion and meaning. In R. F. Paloutzian & C. L. Park (Eds.), *Handbook of the psychology of religion and spirituality* (2nd ed., pp. 357-379). New York, NY: Guilford Press.

Park, C. L., Edmondson, D., & Hale-Smith, A. (2013). Why religion? Meaning as motivation. In K. I. Pargament (Editor-in-Chief), J. J. Exline, & J. W. Jones (Associate Editors), *APA handbook of psychology, religion, and spirituality. Vol. 1: Context, theory, and research* (pp. 157-171); Washington, D. C.: American Psychological Association.

Park, C. L., Holt, C. L., Le, D., Christie, J., & Williams, B. R. (2018). Positive and negative religious coping styles as prospective predictors of well-being in African Americans. *Psychology of Religion and Spirituality, 10,* 318-326.

Park, N., Peterson, C., & Seligman, M. E. P. (2004). Strengths of character and well-being. *Journal of Social and Clinical Psychology, 23,* 603-619.

Parsons, T. (1958). Religious perspectives in sociology and social psychology. In W. A. Lessa & E. Z. Vogt (Eds.), *Reader in comparative religion: An anthropological approach* (pp. 118-124). Evanston, IL: Row, Peterson and Company.

Parsons, W. B. (Ed.) (2018). *Being spiritual but not religious: Past, present, future(s).* New York, NY: Routledge.

Pasek, M. H., Kelly, J. M., Shackleford, C., White, C. J. M., Vishkin, A., Smith, J. M., Norenzayan, A., Shariff, A., & Ginges, J. (2023). Thinking about God encourages prosociality toward religious outgroups: A cross-cultural investigation. *Psychological Science, 34,* 657-669.

Paul, G. S. (2009). The chronic dependence of popular religiosity upon dysfunctional psychosociological conditions. *Evolutionary Psychology, 7,* 398-441.

Pearce, J. M. S. (2011). *The little book of unholy questions.* Fareham, United Kingdom: Ginger Prince Publications.

Pearson, H. I., Lo, R. F., & Sasaki, J. Y. (2023). How do culture and religion interact worldwide? A cultural match approach to understanding religiosity and well-being in the Many Analysts Religion Project. *Religion, Brain & Behavior, 13,* 329-336.

Pennycook, G., Cheyne, J. A., Koehler, D. J., & Fugelsang, J. A. (2020). On the belief that beliefs should change according to evidence: Implications for conspiratorial, moral, paranormal, political, religious, and science beliefs. *Judgement and Decision Making, 15,* 476-498.

Pennycook, G., Cheyne, J. A., Seli, P., Koehler, D. J., & Fugelsang, J. A. (2012). Analytic cognitive style predicts religious and paranormal belief. *Cognition, 123,* 335-346.

Pennycook, G., Ross, R. M., Koehler, D. J., & Fugelsang, J. A. (2016). Atheists and agnostics are more reflective than religious believers: Four empirical studies and a meta-analysis. *PLOS ONE, 11,* Article e0153039.

Peoples, H. C., Duda, P., & Marlowe, F. W. (2016). Hunter-gatherers and the origins of religion. *Human Nature, 27,* 261-282.

Peoples, H. C., & Marlowe, F. W. (2012). Subsistence and the evolution of religion. *Human Nature, 23,* 253-269.

Peri-Rotem, N. (2022). Global fertility and the future of religion: Addressing empirical and theoretical challenges. *Religion, Brain & Behavior, 12,* 413-417.

Perlin, J. D., & Li, L. (2020). Why does awe have prosocial effects? New perspectives on awe and the small self. *Perspectives on Psychological Science, 15,* 291-308.

Perry, S. L., Braunstein, R., Gorski, P. S., & Grubbs, J. B. (2022). Historical fundamentalism? Christian nationalism and ignorance about religion in American political history. *Journal for the Scientific Study of Religion, 61,* 21-40.

Perry, S. L., Whitehead, A. L., & Grubbs, J. B. (2020). Culture wars and COVID-19 conduct: Christian nationalism, religiosity, and Americans' behavior during the coronavirus pandemic. *Journal for the Scientific Study of Religion, 59,* 405-416.

Peterson, C., & Park, N. (2009). Classifying and measuring strengths of character. In S. J. Lopez & C. R. Snyder (Eds.), *The Oxford handbook of positive psychology* (pp. 25-34). New York, NY: Oxford University Press.

Peterson, C., & Park, N. (2012). Character strengths and the life of meaning. In P. T. P. Wong (Ed.), *The human quest for meaning: Theories, research, and applications* (2nd ed., pp. 277-295). New York, NY: Routledge.

Peterson, C., Park, N., & Seligman, M. E. P. (2005). Orientations to happiness and life satisfaction: The full life versus the empty life. *Journal of Happiness Studies, 6,* 25-41.

Peterson, C., Ruch, W., Beermann, U., Park, N., & Seligman, M. P. (2007). Strengths of character, orientations to happiness, and life satisfaction. *The Journal of Positive Psychology, 2,* 149-156.

Peterson, C., & Seligman, M. E. P. (2004). *Character strengths and virtues: A handbook and classification.* Washington, DC: American Psychological Association.

Petrican, R., & Burris, C. T. (2012). Am I the stone? Overattribution of agency and religious orientation. *Psychology of Religion and Spirituality, 4,* 312-323.

Petrovic, K., Chapman, C. M., & Schofield, T. P. (2021). Religiosity and volunteering over time: Religious service attendance is associated with the likelihood of volunteering, and religious importance with time spent volunteering. *Psychology of Religion and Spirituality, 13,* 136-146.

Pettazzoni, R. (1958). The formation of monotheism. In W. A. Lessa & E. Z. Vogt (Eds.), *Reader in comparative religion: An anthropological approach* (pp. 40-46). Evanston, IL: Row, Peterson and Company. (Reprinted from *Essays on the history of religion* [H. J. Rose, Trans.], Chapter 1, by R. Pettazzoni, 1954, Leiden: E. J. Brill)

Pew Research Center (n.d.). Religious landscape study: Political ideology. https://www.pewresearch.org/religion/religious-landscape-study/political-ideology/

Pew Research Center (2013). A survey of LGBT Americans. https://www.pewresearch.org/social-trends/2013/06/13/a-survey-of-lgbt-americans/

Pew Research Center (2014). Religious hostilities reach six-year high. https://www.pewresearch.org/religion/2014/01/14/religious-hostilities-reach-six-year-high/

Pew Research Center (2015). The future of world religions: Population growth projections, 2010-2050. https://www.pewresearch.org/religion/2015/04/02/religious-projections-2010-2050/

Pew Research Center (2017). More Americans now say they're spiritual but not religious. https://www.pewresearch.org/short-reads/2017/09/06/more-americans-now-say-theyre-spiritual-but-not-religious/

Pew Research Center (2018a). Being Christian in Western Europe. https://www.pewresearch.org/religion/2018/05/29/being-christian-in-western-europe/

Pew Research Center (2018b). Republicans turn more negative toward refugees as number admitted to U.S. plummets. https://www.pewresearch.org/short-reads/2018/05/24/republicans-turn-more-negative-toward-refugees-as-number-admitted-to-u-s-plummets/

Pew Research Center (2019). In U.S., decline of Christianity continues at a rapid pace. https://www.pewresearch.org/religion/2019/10/17/in-u-s-decline-of-christianity-continues-at-rapid-pace/

Pew Research Center (2020a). The global God divide. https://www.pewresearch.org/global/2020/07/20/the-global-god-divide/

Pew Research Center (2020b). What lessons do Americans see for humanity in the pandemic? https://www.pewresearch.org/religion/2020/10/08/what-lessons-do-americans-see-for-humanity-in-the-pandemic/

Pew Research Center (2021). More Americans than people in other advanced economies say COVID-19 has strengthened religious faith. https://www.pewresearch.org/religion/2021/01/27/more-americans-than-people-in-other-advanced-economies-say-covid-19-has-strengthened-religious-faith/

Pew Research Center (2022). Modeling the future of religion in America. https://www.pewresearch.org/religion/2022/09/13/modeling-the-future-of-religion-in-america/

Pew Research Center (2023a). Belief in five spiritual entities edges down to new lows. https://news.gallup.com/poll/508886/belief-five-spiritual-entities-edges-down-new-lows.aspx/

Pew Research Center (2023b). Many people in U.S., other advanced economies say its not necessary to believe in God to be moral. https://www.pewresearch.org/short-reads/2023/04/20/many-people-in-u-s-other-advanced-economies-say-its-not-necessary-to-believe-in-god-to-be-moral/

Pew Research Center (2024a). 8 in 10 Americans say religion is losing influence in public life.

https://www.pewresearch.org/religion/2024/03/15/8-in-10-americans-say-religion-is-losing-influence-in-public-life/

Pew Research Center (2024b). Globally, government restrictions on religion reached peak levels in 2021, while social hostilities went down. https://www.pewresearch.org/religion/2024/03/05/globally-government-restrictions-on-religion-reached-peak-levels-in-2021-while-social-hostilities-went-down/

Pew Research Center (2024c). Religious "nones" in America: Who they are and what they believe. https://www.pewresearch.org/religion/2024/01/24/religious-nones-in-america-who-they-are-and-what-they-believe/

Philpott, D. (2009). When faith meets history: The influence of religion on transitional justice. In T. Brudholm & T. Cushman (Eds.), *The religious in responses to mass atrocity: Interdisciplinary perspectives* (pp. 174-212). New York, NY: Cambridge University Press.

Piela, A. (2023, October 18). How the Catholic Church's crash in Poland brought down the Law and Justice Party. *Religion News Service.* https://religionnews.com/2023/10/18/how-the-catholic-churchs-crash-in-poland-brought-down-the-law-and-justice-party/

Piff, P., Dietze, P., Feinberg, M., Stancato, D. M., & Keltner, D. (2015). Awe, the small self, and prosocial behavior. *Journal of Personality and Social Psychology, 108,* 883-899.

Pinker, S. (2018). *Enlightenment now: The case for reason, science, humanism, and progress.* New York, NY: Penguin Books.

Piven, J. S. (2017). Psychological, theological, and thanatological aspects of suicide terrorism. In C. E. Stout (Ed.), *Terrorism, political violence, and extremism* (pp. 79-102). Santa Barbara, CA: Praeger.

Piven, S. D., Fischer, R., Shaver, J. H., Mogan, R., Karl, J. A., Kesberg, R., Richardson, A., Singh, P., Tewari, S., & Bulbulia, J. (2022). Kiwi Diwali: A longitudinal investigation of perceived social connection following a civic religious ritual. *Religion, Brain & Behavior, 12,* 235-253.

Plantinga, A. (2015). *Knowledge and Christian belief*. Grand Rapids, MI: William B. Eerdmans Publishing Company.

Plohl, N., & Musil, B. (2021). Modeling compliance with COVID-19 prevention guidelines: The critical role of trust in science. *Psychology, Health & Medicine, 26,* 1-12.

Polkinghorne, J. (2009). *Theology in the context of science.* New Haven and London: Yale University Press.

Post, J. M. (2007). The *mind of the terrorist: The psychology of terrorism from the IRA to Al Qaeda.* New York, NY: Palgrave MacMillan.

Powell, L. H., Shahabi, L., & Thoresen, C. E. (2003). Religion and spirituality: Linkages to physical health. *American Psychologist, 58,* 36-52.

Power, E. A. (2017). Discerning devotion: Testing the signaling theory of religion. *Evolution and Human Behavior, 38,* 82-91.

Preston, J. L., Ritter, R. S., & Hernandez, J. I. (2010). Principles of religious prosociality: A review and reformulation. *Social and Personality Psychology Compass, 4,* 574-590.

Preus, J. S. (1987). *Explaining religion: Criticism and theory from Bodin to Freud.* New Haven, CT: Yale University Press.

Price, M. E., & Launay, J. (2018). Increased wellbeing from social interaction in a secular congregation. *Secularism and Nonreligion, 7,* 1-9.

Public Religion Research Institute (2015). Nearly one in three support lifetime ban for football players who commit domestic violence. https://www.prri.org/research/prri-rns-ahead-of-super-bowl-nearly-three-in-ten-americans-support-lifetime-ban-for-football-players-who-commit-domestic-violence/

Public Religion Research Institute (2021). 2021 PRRI census of American religion, updates and trends: White Christian decline slows, unaffiliated growth levels off. https://www.prri.org/spotlight/prri-2021-american-values-atlas-religious-affiliation-updates-and-trends-white-christian-decline-slows-unaffiliated-growth-levels-off/

Purzycki, B. G., Apicella, C., Atkinson, Q. D., Cohen, E., McNamara, R. A., Willard, A. K., Xygalatas, D., Norenzayan, A., & Henrich, J. (2016). Moralistic gods, supernatural punishment and the expansion of human sociality. *Nature*, 530, 327-330.

Purzycki, B. G., Haque, O. S., & Sosis, R. (2014). Extending evolutionary accounts of religion beyond the mind: Religions as adaptive systems. In F. Watts & L. Turner (Eds.), *Evolution, religion, and cognitive science: Critical and constructive essays* (pp. 74-91). Oxford, UK: Oxford University Press.

Purzycki, B. G., Lang, M., Henrich, J., & Norenzayan, A. (2022). The Evolution of Religion and Morality project: Reflections and looking ahead. *Religion, Brain & Behavior, 12*, 190-211.

Purzycki, B. G., & Willard, A. K. (2016). MCI theory: A critical discussion. *Religion, Brain & Behavior, 6*, 207-248.

Purzycki, B. G., Willard, A. K., Kundtová Klocová, E., Apicella, C., Atkinson, Q., Bolyanatz, A., Cohen, E., Handley, C., Henrich, J., Lang, M., Lesorogol, C., Mathew, S., McNamara, R. A., Moya, C., Norenzayan, A., Placek, C., Soler, M., Vardy, T., Weigel, J., Xygalatas, D., & Ross, C. T. (2022). The moralization bias of gods' minds: A cross-cultural test. *Religion, Brain & Behavior, 12*, 38-60.

Putnam, R. D. (2000). *Bowling alone: The collapse and revival of American community.* New York, NY: Simon & Schuster Paperbacks.

Putnam, R. D., & Campbell, D. (2010). *American grace: How religion divides and unites.* New York, NY: Simon & Schuster.

Pyszczynski, T., Abdollahi, A., Solomon, S., Greenberg, J., Cohen, F., & Weise, D. (2006). Mortality salience, martyrdom, and military might: The great Satan versus the axis of evil. *Personality and Social Psychology Bulletin, 32*, 525-57.

Pyysiäinen, I., & Hauser, M. (2010). The origins of religion: Evolved adaptation or by-product? *Trends in Cognitive Science, 14*, 104-109.

Radcliffe-Brown, A. R. (1952). *Structure and function of primitive society: Essays and addresses.* Glencoe, IL: The Free Press.

Rappaport, R. A. (1999). *Ritual and religion in the making of humanity.* Cambridge, UK: Cambridge University Press.

Rattfield, B., Price, N., & Collard, M. (2019). Religious belief and cooperation: A view from Viking-age Scandinavia. *Religion, Brain & Behavior, 9,* 2-22.

Reddish, P., Tok, P., & Kundt, R. (2016). Religious cognition and behaviour in autism: The role of mentalizing. *The International Journal for the Psychology of Religion, 26,* 95-112.

Reddish, P., & Tong, E. M. W. (2023). A longitudinal investigation of religious prosociality: What predicts it and who benefits? *Psychology of Religion and Spirituality, 15,* 552-562.

Richerson, P., Baldini, R., Bell, A. V., Demps, K., Frost, K., Hillis, V., Mathew, S., Newton, E. K., Naar, N., Newson, L., Ross, C., Smaldino, P. E., Waring, T. M., & Zefferman, M. (2016). Cultural group selection plays an essential role in explaining human cooperation: A sketch of the evidence. *Behavioral and Brain Sciences, 39,* Article e30.

Richerson, P. J., & Newson, L. (2009). Is religion adaptive? Yes, no, neutral. But mostly we don't know. In J. Schloss & M. J. Murray (Eds.), *The believing primate: Scientific, philosophical, and theological reflections on the origin of religion* (pp. 100-117). Oxford, UK: Oxford University Press.

Riekki, T., Lindeman, M., Aleneff, M., Halme, A., & Nuortimo, A. (2013). Paranormal and religious believers are more prone to illusory face perception than skeptics and non-believers. *Applied Cognitive Psychology, 27,* 150-155.

Riekki, T., Lindeman, M., & Riaj, T. T. (2014). Supernatural believers attribute more intentions to random movement than skeptics: An fMRI study. *Social Neuroscience, 9,* 400-411.

Ritter, R. S., Preston, J. L., & Hernandez, I. (2014). Happy tweets: Christians are happier, more socially connected, and less analytical than atheists on Twitter. *Social Psychological and Personality Science, 5,* 243-249.

Rivera, G. N., Christy, A. G., Kim, J., Vess, M., Hicks, J. A., & Schlegel, R. J. (2019). Understanding the relationship between perceived authenticity and well-being. *Review of General Psychology, 23*, 113-126.

RNS Staff (2022, December 29). The most significant religion stories of 2022. *Religion News Service*. https://religionnews.com/2022/12/29/the-most-significant-religion-stories-of-2022/

Robbins, B. D., & Friedman, H. L. (2018). The unavoidable role of values in positive psychology: Reflections in light of psychology's replication crisis. In N. Brown, R. Lomas, & F. J. Eiroa-Orosa (Eds.), *The Routledge international handbook of critical positive psychology* (pp. 15-25). New York, NY: Routledge/Taylor & Francis Group.

Roberts, L. L. (2023). How exceptional is the West? An investigation of worldwide trends in societal-average levels of religiosity, 1981-2020. *Journal for the Scientific Study of Religion, 62*, 648-671.

Rochat, P., Morgan, R., & Carpenter, M. (1997). Young infants' sensitivity to movement information specifying social causality. *Cognitive Development, 12*, 537-561.

Rodell, J. (2024, January 31). Unprecedented times: Why humanists engage in interfaith dialogue. *Humanistically Speaking*. https://www.humanisticallyspeaking.org/post/unprecedented-times-why-humanists-engage-in-interfaith-dialogue

Roes, F. L., & Raymond, M. (2003). Belief in moralizing gods. *Evolution and Human Behavior, 24*, 126-135.

Rogers, C. R. (1961). *On becoming a person: A therapist's view of psychotherapy*. Boston, MA: Houghton Mifflin.

Root Luna, L. M., van Tongeren, D. R., & Witvliet, C. V. (2017). Virtue, positive psychology, and religion: Consideration of an overarching virtue and an underpinning mechanism. *Psychology of Religion and Spirituality, 9*, 299-302.

Rosmarin, D. H., Pirutinsky, S., Cohen, A. B., Galler, Y., & Krumrei, E. J. (2011). Grateful to God or just plain grateful? A comparison of religious and general gratitude. *The Journal of Positive Psychology, 6*, 389-396.

Rossano, M. J. (2007). Supernaturalizing social life: Religion and the evolution of human cooperation. *Human Nature, 18,* 272-294.

Rossano M. (2009). The African Interregnum: The "Where," "When," and "Why" of the evolution of religion. In E. Voland & W. Schiefenhövel (Eds.), *The biological evolution of religious mind and behavior* (pp. 127-141). Berlin: Springer-Verlag.

Rossano, M. J. (2012). The essential role of ritual in the transmission and reinforcement of social norms. *Psychological Bulletin, 138,* 529-549.

Rossano, M. J., & Vandewalle, B. (2021). Belief, ritual, and the evolution of religion. In J. R. Liddle & T. K. Shackelford (Eds.), *The Oxford handbook of evolutionary psychology and religion* (pp. 83-97). New York, NY: Oxford University Press.

Roth, P. (2001). *The dying animal.* New York, NY: Vintage International.

Rowatt, W. C. (2019). Associations between religiosity, political ideology, and attitudes toward immigrants: A mediation path-analytic approach. *Psychology of Religion and Spirituality, 11,* 368-381.

Rowatt, W. C., & Al-Kire, R. L. (2021). Dimensions of religiousness and their connection to racial, ethnic, and atheist prejudices. *Current Opinion in Psychology, 40,* 86-91.

Rowatt, W. C., Carpenter, T., & Haggard, M. (2014). Religion, prejudice, and intergroup relations. In V. Saroglou (Ed.), *Religion, personality, and social behavior* (pp. 170-192). New York, NY: Psychology Press.

Rowatt, W. C., LaBouff, J., Johnson, M., Froese, P., & Tsang, J. (2009). Associations among religiousness, social attitudes, and prejudice in a national random sample of American adults. *Psychology of Religion and Spirituality, 1,* 14-24.

Rowatt, W. C., Shen, M. J., LaBouff, J. P., & Gonzalez, A. (2013). Religious fundamentalism, right-wing authoritarianism, and prejudice: Insights from meta-analyses, implicit social cognition, and social neuroscience. In R. F. Paloutzian & C. L. Park (Eds.), *Handbook of the psychology of religion and spirituality* (2nd ed., pp. 457-475). New York: The Guilford Press.

Ruan, R., Vaughan, K. R., & Han, D. (2023). Trust in God: The COVID-19 pandemic's impact on religiosity in China. *Journal for the Scientific Study of Religion, 62*, 523-548.

Rudd, M., Vohs, K. D., & Aaker, J. (2012). Awe expands people's perception of time, alters decision making, and enhances well-being. *Psychological Science, 23*, 1130-1136.

Ruiter, S., & De Graaf, N. D. (2006). National context, religiosity, and volunteering: Results from 53 countries. *American Sociological Review, 71*, 191-210.

Ruiter, S., & van Tubergen, F. (2009). Religious attendance in cross-national perspective: A multilevel analysis in 60 countries. *American Journal of Sociology, 115*, 863-895.

Rumsey, A. (2016). Mana, power, and "pawa" in the Pacific and beyond. In M. Tomlinson & T. P. Kāwika-Tengan (Eds.), *New mana: Transformations of a classic concept in Pacific languages and cultures* (pp. 131-154). Canberra, Australia: Australian National University Press.

Ruse, M. (2014). Biologically evolutionary explanations of religious belief. In F. Watts & L. Turner (Eds.), *Evolution, religion, and cognitive science: Critical and constructive essays* (pp. 38-55). Oxford, UK: Oxford University Press.

Ruse, M. (2019). *A meaning to life.* New York, NY: Oxford University Press.

Russell, A. M., Yu, B., Thompson, C. G., Sussman, S. Y., & Barry, A. E. (2020). Assessing the relationship between youth religiosity and their alcohol use: A meta-analysis from 2008 to 2018. *Addictive Behaviors, 106*, 106361.

Russett, B. M., Oneal, J. R., & Cox, M. (2000). Clash of civilizations or realism and liberalism déjà vu? Some evidence. *Journal of Peace Research, 37*, 583-608.

Rutjens, B., van Harreveld, F., & van der Pligt, J. (2013). Step by step: Finding compensatory order in science. *Current Directions in Psychological Science, 22,* 250-255.

Rutjens, B., van Harreveld, F., van der Pligt, J., van Elk, M., & Pyszczynski, T. (2016). A march to a better world? Religiosity and the existential function of belief in social-moral progress. *The International Journal for the Psychology of Religion, 26,* 1-18.

Ryan, R. M., Curren, R. R., & Deci, E. (2013). What humans need: Flourishing in Aristotelian philosophy and self-determination theory. In A. S. Waterman (Ed.), *The best within us: Positive psychology perspectives on eudaimonia* (pp. 57-75). Washington, DC: American Psychological Association.

Ryan, R. M., & Deci, E. L. (2001). On happiness and human potentials: A review of research on hedonic and eudaimonic well-being. *Annual Review of Psychology, 52,* 141-166.

Ryan, R. M., Huta, V. A., & Deci, E. L. (2008). Living well: A self-determination theory perspective on eudaimonia. *Journal of Happiness Studies, 9,* 139-170.

Ryan, W. S., & Ryan, R. M. (2019). Toward a social psychology of authenticity: Exploring within-person variation in autonomy, congruence, and genuineness using self-determination theory. *Review of General Psychology, 23,* 99-112.

Ryff, C. D. (1989). Happiness is everything, or is it? Explorations of the meaning of psychological well-being. *Journal of Personality and Social Psychology, 57,* 1069-1081.

Ryff, C. D. (2013). Eudaimonic well-being and health: Mapping consequences of self-realization. In A. S. Waterman (Ed.), *The best within us: Positive psychology perspectives on eudaimonia* (pp. 77-98). Washington, DC: American Psychological Association.

Ryff, C. D., & Singer, B. H. (2008). Know thyself and become what you are: A eudaimonic approach to psychological well-being. *Journal of Happiness Studies, 9,* 13–39.

Ryrie, A. (2017). *Protestants: The faith that made the modern world*. New York, NY: Penguin Books.

Ryrie, A. (2019). *Unbelievers: An emotional history of doubt*. Cambridge, MA: The Belknap Press of Harvard University Press.

Sagan, C. (2007). *The God hypothesis*. In C. Hitchens (Ed.), *The portable atheist* (pp. 226-238). Philadelphia, PA: Da Capo Press. (Copyright © 2006 by Carl Sagan. Reprinted with permission from Democritus Properties, LLC.)

Saiya, N. (2017). Blasphemy and terrorism in the Muslim world. *Terrorism and Political Violence, 29*, 1087-1105.

Saleam, J., & Moustafa, A. A. (2016). The influence of divine rewards and punishments on religious prosociality. *Frontiers in Psychology, 7*, 1149.

Saliashvili (2024, February 15). Jordan Peterson wrestles with God. *Religion News Service*. https://religionnews.com/2024/02/15/jordan-peterson-wrestles-with-god/

Salsman, J. M., Brown, T. L., Brechting, E. H., & Carlson, C. R. (2005). The link between religion and spirituality and psychological adjustment: The mediating role of optimism and social support. *Personality and Social Psychology Bulletin, 31*, 522-535.

Salsman, J. M., Pustejovsky, J. E., Jim, H. S. L., Munoz, A. R., Merluzzi, T. V., George, L., Park, C. L., Danhauer, S. C., Sherman, A. C., Snyder, M. A., & Fitchett, G. (2015). A meta-analytic approach to examining the correlation between religion/spirituality and mental health in cancer. *Cancer, 121*, 3769-3778.

Samson, D. R. (2023). *Our tribal future: How to channel our foundational human instincts into a force for good*. New York, NY: St. Martin's Press.

Sandage, S. J., & Moe, S. P. (2013). Spiritual experience: Conversion and transformation. In K. I. Pargament (Editor-in-Chief), J. J. Exline, & J. W. Jones (Associate Editors), *APA handbook of psychology, religion, and spirituality: Vol. 1. Context, theory, and research* (pp. 407-422). Washington, DC: American Psychological Association.

Sanderson, S. K., & Roberts, W. W. (2008). The evolutionary forms of the religious life: A cross-cultural, quantitative analysis. *American Anthropologist, 110,* 454-466.

Saribay, S. A., & Yilmaz, O. (2017). Analytic cognitive style and cognitive ability differentially predict religiosity and social conservatism. *Personality and Individual Differences, 114,* 24-29.

Saroglou, V. (2002a). Beyond dogmatism: The need for closure as related to religion. *Mental Health, Religion & Culture, 5,* 183-194.

Saroglou, V. (2002b). Religion and the five factors of personality: A meta-analytic review. *Personality and Individual Differences, 32,* 15-25.

Saroglou, V. (2012). Is religion not prosocial at all? Comment on Galen (2012). *Psychological Bulletin, 138,* 907-912.

Saroglou, V. (2017). Culture, personality, and religiosity. In A. T. Church (Ed.), *The Praeger handbook of personality across cultures: Vol. 2. Culture and characteristic adaptations* (pp. 153-184). Santa Barbara, CA: Praeger.

Saroglou, V. (2021). *The psychology of religion.* London and New York: Routledge.

Saroglou, V., Clobert, M., Cohen, A. B., Johnson, K. A., Ladd, K. L., Brandt, P.-Y., Murken, S., Muñoz-Garcia, A., Adamovova, L., Blogowska, J., Çukur, C. S., Hwang, K.-K., Miglietta, A., Motti-Stefanidi, F., Roussiau, N., & Valladares, J. T. (2022). Fundamentalism as dogmatic belief, moral rigorism, and strong groupness across cultures: Dimensionality, underlying components, and related interreligious prejudice. *Psychology of Religion and Spirituality, 14,* 558-571.

Saroglou, V., & Craninx, M. (2021). Religious moral righteousness over care: A review and a meta-analysis. *Current Opinion in Psychology, 40,* 79-85.

Saroglou, V., Delpierre, V., & Dernelle, R. (2004) Values and religiosity: A meta-analysis of studies using Schwartz's model. *Personality and Individual Differences, 37,* 721-734.

Sartre, J.-P. (2007). *Existentialism is a humanism* (Carol Macomber, Trans.). New Haven, CT: Yale University Press. (Originally a 1946 lecture titled *L'Existentialisme est un humanism*)

Saslow, L. R., Willer, R., Feinberg, M., Piff, P. K., Clark, K., Keltner, D., & Saturn, S. R. (2013). My brother's keeper? Compassion predicts generosity more among less religious individuals. *Social Psychological and Personality Science, 4*, 31-38.

Saucier, G., & Skrzypińska, K. (2006). Spiritual but not religious? Evidence for two independent dispositions. *Journal of Personality, 74*, 1257-1291.

Schaap-Jonker, H., Sizoo, B., van Schothorst-van Roekel, J., & Corveleyn, J. (2013). Autism spectrum disorders and the image of God as a core aspect of religiousness. *The International Journal for the Psychology of Religion, 23*, 145-160.

Schachner, A., Zhu, L., Li, J., & Kelemen, D. (2017). Is the bias for function-based explanations culturally universal? Children from China endorse teleological explanations of natural phenomena. *Journal of Experimental Child Psychology, 157*, 29-48.

Scheepers, P., Gijsberts, M., & Hello, E. (2002). Religiosity and prejudice against ethnic minorities in Europe: Cross-national tests on a controversial relationship. *Review of Religious Research, 43*, 242–265.

Scheier, M. F., Swanson, J. D., Barlow, M. A., Greenhouse, J. B., Wrosch, C., & Tindle, H. A. (2021). Optimism versus pessimism as predictors of physical health: A comprehensive reanalysis of dispositional optimism research. *American Psychologist, 76*, 529-548.

Schjoedt, U., Stødkilde-Jørgensen, H., Geertz, A. W., & Roepstorff, A. (2009). Highly religious participants recruit areas of social cognition in personal prayer. *Social Cognitive and Affective Neuroscience, 4*, 199-207.

Schlegel, R. J., & Hicks, J. A. (2011). The true self and psychological health: Emerging evidence and future directions. *Social and Personality Psychology Compass, 5*, 989-1003.

Schlegel, R. J., Hirsch, K. A., & Smith, C. M. (2013). The importance of who you really are: The role of the true self in eudaimonia. In A. S. Waterman (Ed.), *The best within us: Positive psychology perspectives on eudaimonia* (pp. 207-225). Washington, DC: American Psychological Association.

Schloss, J. (2009). Introduction: Evolutionary theories of religion: Science unfettered or naturalism run wild? In J. Schloss & M. J. Murray (Eds.), *The believing primate: Scientific, philosophical, and theological reflections on the origin of religion* (pp. 1-25). Oxford, UK: Oxford University Press.

Schmidt, W. (1958). The nature, attributes and worship of the primitive high God. In W. A. Lessa & E. Z. Vogt (Eds.), *Reader in comparative religion: An anthropological approach* (pp. 24-39). Evanston, IL: Row, Peterson and Company. (Reprinted from *The origin and growth of religion: Facts and theories*, Chapter 16, by W. Schmidt, 1931, New York: NY: Lincoln MacVeach)

Schnabel, L., & Schieman, S. (2022). Religion protected mental health but constrained crisis response during crucial early days of the COVID-19 pandemic. *Journal for the Scientific Study of Religion, 61*, 530-543.

Schnell, T., de Boer, E., & Alma, H. (2023). Worlds apart? Atheist, agnostic, and humanist worldviews in three European countries. *Psychology of Religion and Spirituality, 15*, 83-93.

Schnell, T., & Keenan, W. (2011). Meaning-making in an atheist world. *Archives for the Study of Religion, 33*, 55-78.

Schnitker, S. A. (2012). An examination of patience and well-being. *The Journal of Positive Psychology, 9*, 264-275.

Schnitker, S. A., & Emmons, R. A. (2013). Spiritual striving and seeking the sacred: Religion as meaningful goal-directed behavior. *The International Journal for the Psychology of Religion, 23*, 315-324.

Schnitker, S. A., & Emmons, R. A. (2017). The psychology of virtue: Integrating positive psychology and the psychology of religion. *Psychology of Religion and Spirituality, 9*, 239-241.

Schnitker, S. A., Houltberg, B., Dyrness, W., & Redmond, N. (2017). The virtue of patience, spirituality, and suffering: Integrating lessons from positive psychology, psychology of religion, and Christian theology. *Psychology of Religion and Spirituality, 9*, 264-275.

Scholl, B. J., & Tremoulet, P. D. (2000). Perceptual causality and animacy. *Trends in Cognitive Science, 4*, 299-308.

Schotanus-Dijkstra, M., Pieterse, M. E., Drossaert, C. H. C., Westerhof, G. J., de Graaf, R., ten Have, M., Walburg, J. A., & Bohlmeijer, E. T. (2016). What factors are associated with flourishing? Results from a large representative national sample. *Journal of Happiness Studies, 17*, 1351–1370.

Schwartz, S. (2017). Individual values across cultures. In A. T. Church, (Ed.), *The Praeger handbook of personality across cultures: Vol. 2: Culture and characteristic adaptations* (pp. 121-152). Santa Barbara, CA: Praeger.

Sedikides, C., & Gebauer, J. E. (2010). Religiosity as self-enhancement: A meta-analysis of the relation between socially desirable responding and religiosity. *Personality and Social Psychology Review, 14*, 17-36.

Sedikides, C., & Gebauer, J. E. (2021). Do religious people self-enhance? *Current Opinion in Psychology, 40*, 29-33.

Seligman, M. E. P. (2011). *Flourish.* New York, NY: Free Press.

Seligman, M. (2018). PERMA and the building blocks of well-being. *The Journal of Positive Psychology, 13*, 333–335.

Seligman, M. E. P. (2019). Positive psychology: A personal history. *Annual Review of Clinical Psychology, 15*, 1-23.

Seligman, M. E. P., & Csikszentmihalyi, M. (2000). Positive psychology: An introduction. *American Psychologist, 55*, 5-14.

Seligman, M. E. P., Steen, T. A., Park, N., & Peterson, C. (2005). Positive psychology progress: Empirical validation of interventions. *American Psychologist, 60*, 410-421.

Sells, M. A. (2003). Crosses of blood: Sacred space, religion, and violence in Bosnia-Hercegovina. *Sociology of Religion, 64*, 309-331.

Shaman, N. J., Saide, A. R., & Richert, R. A. (2018). Dimensional structure of and variation in anthropomorphic concepts of God. *Frontiers in Psychology, 9*, article 1425.

Shariff, A. F. (2011). Big gods were made for big groups. *Religion, Brain & Behavior, 1*, 89-93.

Shariff, A. F. (2015). Does religion increase moral behavior. *Current Opinion in Psychology, 6*, 108-113.

Shariff, A. F. (2020). On balance. In A. B. Cohen (Ed.), *Religion and human flourishing* (pp. 189-205). Waco, TX: Baylor University Press.

Shariff, A. F., & Mercier, B. (2021). The evolution of religion and morality. In J. R. Liddle & T. K. Shackelford (Eds.), *The Oxford handbook of evolutionary psychology and religion* (pp. 246-264). New York, NY: Oxford University Press.

Shariff, A. F., & Norenzayan, A. (2007). God is watching you: Priming God concepts increases prosocial behavior in an anonymous economic game. *Psychological Science, 18*, 803-809.

Shariff, A. F., & Norenzayan, A. (2011). Mean gods make good people: Different views of God predict cheating behavior. *The International Journal for the Psychology of Religion, 21*, 85-96.

Shariff, A. F., & Rhemtulla, M. (2012). Divergent effects of beliefs in heaven and hell on national crime rates. *PLOS ONE, 7*, Article e39048.

Shariff, A. F., Willard, A. K., Anderson, T., & Norenzayan, A. (2016). Religious priming: A meta-analysis with a focus on prosociality. *Personality and Social Psychology Review, 20*, 27-48.

Sheldon, K. M. (2013). Individual daimon, universal needs, and subjective well-being: Happiness as the natural consequence of a life well lived. In A. S. Waterman (Ed.), *The best within us: Positive psychology perspectives on eudaimonia* (pp. 119-137). Washington, DC: American Psychological Association.

Sheldon, K. M. (2014). Becoming oneself: The central role of self-concordant goal selection. *Personality and Social Psychology Review, 18*, 349-365.

Sheldon, K. M., & Kasser, T. (2001). Goals, congruence, and positive well-being: New empirical support for humanistic theories. *Journal of Humanistic Psychology, 41*, 30-50.

Shenhav, A. S., Rand, D. G., & Greene, J. D. (2012). Divine intuition: Cognitive style influences belief in God. *Journal of Experimental Psychology: General, 141*, 432-428.

Sheridan, T. B. (2021). *Respectful atheism: A perspective on belief in God and each other.* Amherst, NY: Prometheus Books.

Sherkat, D. E. (2011). Religion and scientific literacy in the United States. *Social Science Quarterly, 92*, 1135-1150.

Sherkat, D. E. (2022). Race, gender, and the relationship between religious factors and verbal ability: An intersectional approach. *Journal for the Scientific Study of Religion, 61*, 609-618.

Shimron, Y. (2023, February 8). Poll: A third of Americans are Christian nationalists and most are white evangelicals. *Religion News Service.* http://religionnews.com/2023/02/08/a-third-of-americans-are-christian-nationalists-and-most-are-white-evangelicals

Shimron, Y. (2023, February 23). Poll: Support for abortion rights is strong, even among most religious groups. *Religion News Service.* https://religionnews.com/2023/02/23/poll-support-for-abortion-rights-is-strong-even-among-most-religious-groups

Shimron, Y., & Dell'orto, G. (2022, December 5). LGBTQ students wrestle with tensions at Christian colleges. *Religion News Service.* https://religionnews.com/2022/12/05/lgbtq-students-wrestle-with-tensions-at-christian-colleges

Shiota, M. N., Keltner, D., & Mossman, A. (2007). The nature of awe: Elicitors, appraisals, and effects on self-concept. *Cognition and Emotion, 21*, 944-963.

Shtulman, A., & Lindeman, M. (2016). Attributes of God: Conceptual foundations of a foundational belief. *Cognitive Science, 40*, 635-670.

Sibley, C. G., & Bulbulia, J. (2012). Faith after an earthquake: A longitudinal study of religion and perceived health before and after the 2011 Christchurch New Zealand earthquake. *PLOS ONE, 7*, Article e49648.

Silberman, I., Higgins, E., & Dweck, C. (2005). Religion and world change: Violence and terrorism versus peace. *Journal of Social Issues, 61*, 761-784.

Silver, C. F., Coleman, T. J., III, Hood, R. W., Jr., & Holcombe, J. M. (2014). The six types of nonbelief: A qualitative and quantitative study of type and narrative. *Mental Health, Religion & Culture, 17*, 990-1001.

Simpson, A., McCurrie, C., & Rios, K. (2019). Perceived morality and anti-atheist prejudice: A replication and extension. *The International Journal for the Psychology of Religion, 29*, 172-183.

Sin, N. L., & Lyubomirsky, S. (2009). Enhancing well-being and alleviating depressive symptoms with positive psychology interventions: A practice-friendly meta-analysis. *Journal of Clinical Psychology, 65*, 467-487.

Singh, M., & Henrich, J. (2020). Why do religious leaders observe costly prohibitions? Examining taboos on Mentawai shamans. *Evolutionary Human Sciences, 2*, e32.

Singh, P., Tewari, S., Kesberg, R., Karl, J. A., Bulbulia, J., & Fischer, R. (2020). Time investments in rituals are associated with social bonding, affect and subjective health: A longitudinal study of Diwali in two Indian communities. *Philosophical Transactions of the Royal Society B, 375*, Article 20190430.

Sirgy, M. J., Joshanloo, M., & Estes, R. J. (2019). The global challenge of jihadist terrorism: A quality-of-life model. *Social Indicators Research, 141*, 191-215.

Smietana, B. (2022, February 7). Woke war: How social justice and CRT became heresy for evangelicals. *Religion News Service*.

https://religionnews.com/2022/02/07/woke-war-why-social-justice-became-heresy-for-evangelicals-owen-strachan-crt-southern-baptists-trump/

Smietana, B. (2023, January 5). More Americans stay away from church as pandemic nears year three. *Religion News Service.* https://religionnews.com/2023/01/05/more-americans-stay-away-from-church-as-pandemic-nears-year-three/

Smietana, B. (2023, August 14). Parliament of the World's Religions hopes to harness faith to address world's ills. *Religion News Service.* https://religionnews.com/2023/08/14/parliament-of-the-worlds-religions-hopes-to-harness-faith-to-address-worlds-problems/

Smietana, B. (2023, August 28). White Christians think too many people see racism when it's not there, new survey finds. *Religion News Service.* https://religionnews.com/2023/08/28/white-christians-think-too-many-people-see-racism-when-its-not-there-new-survey-finds/

Smietana, B. (2024, March 25). Gallup poll: More than half of Americans rarely go to church. *Religion News Service.* https://religionnews.com/2024/03/25/gallup-poll-more-than-half-of-americans-rarely-go-to-church/

Smith, G. H. (2000). *Why atheism?* Amherst, NY: Prometheus Books.

Smith, J. M. (2017). Secular living: Many paths, many meanings. In P. Zuckerman & J. R. Shook (Eds.) (2017), *The Oxford handbook of secularism* (pp. 515-532). New York, NY: Oxford University Press.

Smith, J. M., Pasek, M. H., Vishkin, A., Johnson, K. A., Shackleford, C., & Ginges, J. (2022). Thinking about God discourages dehumanization of religious outgroups. *Journal of Experimental Psychology: General, 151,* 2586-2603.

Smith, T. B., McCullough, M. E., & Poll, J. (2003). Religiousness and depression: Evidence for a main effect and the moderating influence of stressful life events. *Psychological Bulletin, 129,* 614-636.

Smith, T. W. (2006). The National Spiritual Transformation Study. *Journal for the Scientific Study of Religion, 45,* 283-296.

Snow, N. E. (2019). Positive psychology, the classification of character strengths and virtues, and issues of measurement. *The Journal of Positive Psychology, 14,* 20-31.

Soenke, M., Landau, M. J., & Greenberg, J. (2013). Sacred armor: Religion's role as a buffer against the anxieties of life and the fear of death. In K. I. Pargament (Editor-in-Chief), J. J. Exline, & J. W. Jones (Associate Editors), *APA handbook of psychology, religion, and spirituality: Vol. 1. Context, theory, and research* (pp. 105-122). Washington, DC: American Psychological Association.

Soler, M. (2012). Costly signaling, ritual and cooperation: Evidence from Candomblé, an Afro-Brazilian religion. *Evolution and Human Behavior, 33,* 346-356.

Soler, M., Purzycki, B. G., & Lang, M. (2022). Perceptions of moralizing agents and cooperative behavior in Northeastern Brazil. *Religion, Brain & Behavior, 12,* 132-149.

Sommer, J., Musolino, J., & Hemmer, P. (2023). Counterintuitive concepts across domains: A unified phenomenon? *Cognitive Science, 47,* e13276.

Sorrentino, R. M., & Roney, C. J. R. (2000). *The uncertain mind: Individual differences in facing the unknown.* Philadelphia, PA: Psychology Press.

Sosis, R. (2006). Religious behaviors, badges, and bans: Signaling theory and the evolution of religion. In P. McNamara (Ed.), *Where God and science meet: How brain and evolutionary studies alter our understanding of religion: Vol. 1. Evolution, genes, and the religious brain* (pp. 61-86). Westport, CT: Praeger.

Sosis, R. (2023). Costly signaling: The ABCs of signaling theory and religion. In Y. Lior & J. Lane (Eds.), *The Routledge handbook of evolutionary approaches to religion* (pp. 209-226). London & New York: Routledge.

Sosis, R., & Alcorta, C. (2003). Signaling, solidarity, and the sacred: The evolution of religious behavior. *Evolutionary Anthropology, 12*, 264-274.

Sosis, R., & Bressler, E. R. (2003). Cooperation and commune longevity: A test of the costly signaling theory of religion. *Cross-Cultural Research, 37*, 211-239.

Sosis, R., Kress, H., & Boster, J. (2007). Scars for war: Evaluating alternative signaling explanations for cross-cultural variance in ritual costs. *Evolution and Human Behavior, 28*, 234-247.

Sosis, R., & Handwerker, W. P. (2011). Psalms and coping with uncertainty: Religious Israeli women's responses to the 2006 Lebanon war. *American Anthropologist, 113*, 40-55.

Sosis, R., & Ruffle, B. (2003). Religious ritual and cooperation: Testing for a relationship on Israeli religious and secular kibbutzim. *Current Anthropology, 44*, 713-722.

Speed, D. (2022). Godless in the Great White North: Assessing the health of Canadian atheists using data from the 2011/2012 Canadian Community Health Survey. *Journal of Religion and Health, 61*, 415-432.

Speed, D., Barry, C., & Cragun, R. (2020). With a little help from my (Canadian) friends: Health differences between minimal and maximal religiosity/spirituality are partially mediated by social support. *Social Science & Medicine, 265*, 113387.

Speed, D., & Edgell, P. (2023). Eternally damned, yet socially conscious? The volunteerism of Canadian atheists. *Sociology of Religion, 84*, 265-291.

Spencer, H. (1898). *The principles of sociology* (Vol. 1). New York, NY: D. Appleton and Company.

Spielmans, G. I., & Flückiger, C. (2018). Moderators in psychotherapy meta-analysis. *Psychotherapy Research, 28*, 333-346.

Stagnaro, M. N., & Rand, D. G. (2021). The coevolution of religious belief and intuitive cognitive style via individual-level selection. In J. R. Liddle & T. K. Shackelford (Eds.), *The Oxford handbook of evolutionary psy-*

chology and religion (pp. 153-173). New York, NY: Oxford University Press.

Stagnaro, M. N., Ross, R. M., Pennycook, G., & Rand, D. G. (2019). Cross-cultural support for a link between analytic thinking and disbelief in God: Evidence from India and the United Kingdom. *Judgment and Decision Making, 14,* 179-186.

Stanton, J., & Spratt, B. (2023, June 28). Bringing light without God: Humanist chaplain Anthony Cruz Pantojas. *Religion News Service.* https://religionnews.com/2023/06/28/bringing-light-without-god-humanist-chaplain-anthony-cruz-pantojas/

Stark, R. (1999). Secularization, R.I.P. *Sociology of Religion, 60,* 249-273.

Stark, R. (2007). *Discovering God: The origins of the great religions and the evolution of belief.* New York, NY: HarperOne.

Stavrova, O., Fetchenhauer, D., & Schlösser, T. (2012). Why are religious people happy? The effect of the social norm of religiosity across countries. *Social Science Research, 42,* 90-105.

Stavrova, O., & Siegers, P. (2014). Religious prosociality and morality across cultures: How social enforcement of religion shapes the effects of personal religiosity on prosocial and moral attitudes and behaviors. *Personality and Social Psychology Bulletin, 40,* 315-333.

Steadman, L. B., Palmer, C. T., & Tilley, C. F. (1996). The universality of ancestor worship. *Ethnology, 35,* 63-76.

Stedman, C. (2012). *Faitheist: How an atheist found common ground with the religious.* Boston, MA: Beacon Press.

Steger, M. F., & Frazier, P. (2005). Meaning in life: One link in the chain from religiousness to well-being. *Journal of Counseling Psychology, 52,* 574-582.

Steger, M. F., Frazier, P., Oishi, S., & Kaler, M. (2006). The Meaning in Life Questionnaire: Assessing the presence of and search for meaning in life. *Journal of Counseling Psychology, 53,* 80-93.

Steger, M. F., Pickering, N., Shin, J. Y., & Dik, B. J. (2010). Calling in work: Secular or sacred? *Journal of Career Assessment, 18,* 82-96.

Steger, M. F., Shin, J. Y., Shim, Y., & Fitch-Martin, A. (2013). Is meaning in life a flagship indicator of well-being? In A. S. Waterman (Ed.), *The best within us: Positive psychology perspectives on eudaimonia* (pp. 159-182). Washington, DC: American Psychological Association.

Stein, D. H., Hobson, N. M., & Schroeder, J. (2021). A sacred commitment: How rituals promote group survival. *Current Opinion in Psychology, 40,* 114-120.

Stein, S. (2011). Competing political science perspectives on the role of religion in conflict. *Politorbis, 52*(2), 21-27, Federal Department of Foreign Affairs.

Stenger, V. J. (2008). *God: The failed hypothesis: How science shows that God does not exist.* Amherst, NY: Prometheus Books.

Stephens, N. M., Fryberg, S. A., Markus, H. R., & Hamedani, M. G. (2012). Who explains Hurricane Katrina and the Chilean earthquake as an act of God? The experience of extreme hardship predicts religious meaning-making. *Journal of Cross-Cultural Psychology, 44,* 606-619.

Sterelny, K. (2020). Religion: Costs, signals, and the Neolithic transition. *Religion, Brain & Behavior, 10,* 303-320.

Stern, J. (2003). *Terror in the name of God: Why religious militants kill.* New York, NY: HarperCollins.

Stewart, E., Edgell, P., & Delehanty, J. (2018). The politics of religious prejudice and tolerance for cultural others. *The Sociological Quarterly, 59,* 17-39.

Stichter, M., & Saunders, L. (2019). Positive psychology and virtue: Values in action. *The Journal of Positive Psychology, 14,* 1-15.

Stolz, J. (2020). Secularization theories in the twenty-first century: Ideas, evidence, and problems. *Social Compass, 67,* 282-308.

Streib, H. (2021). Leaving religion: Deconversion. *Current Opinion in Psychology, 40,* 139-144.

Streib, H., Hood, R. W., Jr., & Klein, C. (2010). The Religious Schema Scale: Construction and initial validation of a quantitative measure for religious styles. *The International Journal for the Psychology of Religion, 20*, 151-172.

Streib, H., & Klein, C. (2013). Atheists, agnostics, and apostates. In K. I. Pargament (Editor-in-Chief), J. J. Exline, & J. W. Jones (Associate Editors), *APA handbook of psychology, religion, and spirituality: Vol. 1. Context, theory, and research* (pp. 713-728). Washington, DC: American Psychological Association.

Streib, H., & Klein, C. (2014). Religious styles predict interreligious prejudice: A study of German adolescents with the Religious Schema Scale. *The International Journal for the Psychology of Religion, 24*, 151-163.

Streib, H., & Klein, C. (Eds.) (2018). *Xenosophia and religion: Biographical and statistical paths for a culture of welcome.* Cham, Switzerland: Springer International Publishing.

Su, R., Tay, L., & Diener, E. (2014). The development and validation of the Comprehensive Inventory of Thriving (CIT) and the Brief Inventory of Thriving (BIT). *Applied Psychology: Health and Well-being, 6*, 251-279.

Swan, T., & Halberstadt, J. (2019). The mickey mouse problem: Distinguishing religious and fictional counterintuitive agents. *PLOS ONE, 14*, Article e0220886.

Swann, W., Buhrmester, M., Gómez, A., Jetten, J., Bastian, B., Vázquez, A., & Zhang, A. (2014). What makes a group worth dying for? Identity fusion fosters perception of familial ties, promoting self-sacrifice. *Journal of Personality and Social Psychology, 106*, 912–926.

Swanson, G. E. (1960). *The birth of the Gods: The origins of primitive beliefs.* Ann Arbor, MI: University of Michigan Press.

Tajfel, H., & Turner, J. C. (1986). The social identity theory of intergroup behavior. In S. Worchel & W. G. Austin (Eds.), *Psychology of intergroup relations* (pp. 7-24). Chicago, IL: Nelson-Hall.

Tangney, J. P. (2009). Humility. In C. R. Snyder & S. J. Lopez (Eds.), *The Oxford handbook of positive psychology* (2nd ed., pp. 483-490). New York, NY: Oxford University Press.

Tay, L., & Diener, E. (2011). Needs and subjective well-being around the world. *Journal of Personality and Social Psychology, 101*, 354-365.

Tay, L., Herian, M., & Diener, E. (2014). Detrimental effects of corruption and subjective well-being: Whether, how, and when. *Social Psychological & Personality Science, 5*, 193-208.

Tay, L., & Kuykendall, L. (2013). Promoting happiness: The malleability of individual and societal-level happiness. *International Journal of Psychology, 48*, 159-176.

Taylor, C. (2007). *A secular age*. Cambridge, MA: The Belknap Press of Harvard University Press.

Teehan, J. (2021). Religion and morality: The evolution of the cognitive nexus. In J. R. Liddle & T. K. Shackelford (Eds.), *The Oxford handbook of evolutionary psychology and religion* (pp. 117-134). New York, NY: Oxford University Press.

Terrizzi, J. A., Jr., & Shook, N. J. (2021). Religion: An evolutionary evoked disease-avoidance strategy. In J. R. Liddle & T. K. Shackelford (Eds.), *The Oxford handbook of evolutionary psychology and religion* (pp. 198-212). New York, NY: Oxford University Press.

Thomas, J. N., & Whitehead, A. L. (2015). Evangelical elites' anti-homosexuality narratives as a resistance strategy against attribution effects. *Journal for the Scientific Study of Religion, 54*, 345-362.

Tillich, P. (1957). *The dynamics of faith*. New York, NY: Harper & Row.

Tisby, J. (2019). *The color of compromise: The truth about the American church's complicity in racism*. Grand Rapids, MI: Zondervan.

Titus, C. S. (2017). Aquinas, Seligman, and positive psychology: A Christian approach to the use of the virtues in psychology. *The Journal of Positive Psychology, 12*, 447-458.

Tix, A. P., & Frazier, P. A. (1998). The use of religious coping during stressful life events: Main effects, moderation, and mediation. *Journal of Consulting and Clinical Psychology, 66,* 411-422.

Tix, A. P., & Frazier, P. A. (2005). Mediation and moderation of the relationship between intrinsic religiousness and mental health. *Personality and Social Psychology Bulletin, 31,* 295-306.

Tolstoy, L. (1983) *Confession* (David Paterson, trans.). New York, NY: W.W. Norton & Company. (A translation of *Ispoved'* as it appears in Tolstoy's *Polnoe sobranie sochinenii,* Volume 23, Moscow, 1957)

Tomlinson, M., & Kāwika-Tengan, T. P. (2016). Introduction: Mana anew. In M. Tomlinson & T. P. Kāwika-Tengan (Eds.), *New mana: Transformations of a classic concept in Pacific languages and cultures* (pp. 1-36). Canberra, Australia: Australian National University Press.

Tomlinson, M., & Makihara, M. (2009). New paths in the linguistic anthropology of Oceania. *Annual Review of Anthropology, 38,* 17-31.

Tooby, J., & Cosmides, L. (1992). The psychological foundations of culture. In J. H. Barkow, L. Cosmides, & J. Tooby (Eds.), *The adapted mind: Evolutionary psychology and the generation of culture* (pp. 19-136). New York, NY: Oxford University Press.

Torrey, E. F. (2017). *Evolving brains, emerging gods: Early humans and the origins of religion.* New York, NY: Columbia University Press.

Townsend, J. B. (1997). Shamanism. In S. D. Glazier (Ed.), *Anthropology of religion: A handbook* (pp. 429-469). Westport, CN: Greenwood Press.

Tsang, J.-A., Al-Kire, R. L., & Ratchford, J. L. (2021). Prosociality and religion. *Current Opinion in Psychology, 40,* 67-72.

Tsang, J.-A., McCullough, M. E., & Hoyt, W. T. (2005). Psychometric and rationalization accounts of the religion-forgiveness discrepancy. *Journal of Social Issues, 61,* 785-805.

Tse, D. C. K., Nakamura, J., & Csikszentmihalyi, M. (2021). Living well by "flowing' well: The indirect effect of autotelic personality on well-being through flow experience. *The Journal of Positive Psychology, 16,* 310-321.

Turchin, P., Whitehouse, H., Larson, J., Cioni, E., Reddish, J., Savage, P. E., Covey, R. A., Baines, J., Altaweel, M., Anderson, E., Bol, P., Brandl, E., Carballo, D. M., Feinman, G., Korotayev, A., Kradin, N., Levine, J. D., Nugent, S. E., Squitieri, A., Wallace, V., & François, P. (2023). Explaining the rise of moralizing religions: A test of competing hypotheses using the Seshat Databank. *Religion, Brain & Behavior, 13*, 167-194.

Turner, J. H., Maryanski, A. Petersen, A. K., & Geertz, A. W. (2018). *The emergence and evolution of religion by means of natural selection.* New York, NY: Routledge.

Turner, L. (2014). Introduction: Pluralism and complexity in the evolutionary cognitive science of religion. In F. Watts & L. Turner (Eds.), *Evolution, religion, and cognitive science: Critical and constructive essays* (pp. 1-20). Oxford, UK: Oxford University Press.

Tylor, E. B. (1958). *Religion in primitive culture.* New York, NY: Harper & Row (Chapters XI-XIX in *Primitive Culture*, originally published in 1871, by John Murray, London)

Unger, R. M. (2016). *The religion of the future.* London, UK: Verso.

Uzarevic, F., & Coleman, T. J., III (2021). The psychology of nonbelievers. *Current Opinion in Psychology, 40*, 131-138.

Uzarevic, F., & Saroglou, V. (2020). Understanding nonbelievers' prejudice toward ideological opponents: The role of self-expression values and other-oriented dispositions. *The International Journal for the Psychology of Religion, 30*, 161-177.

Vail, K. E., III, Juhl, J., Arndt, J., Vess, M., Routledge, C., & Rutjens, B. T. (2012). When death is good for life: Considering the positive trajectories of terror management. *Personality and Social Psychology Review, 6*, 303-329.

Vail, K. E., III, Rothschild, Z. K., Weise, D. R., Solomon, S., Pyszczynski, T., & Greenberg, J. (2010). A terror management analysis of the psychological functions of religion. *Personality and Social Psychology Review, 14*, 84-94.

Valdesolo, P. & Graham, J. (2014). Awe, uncertainty, and agency detection. *Psychological Science, 25,* 170-178.

Van Boven, L. (2005). Experientialism, materialism, and the pursuit of happiness. *Review of General Psychology, 9,* 132-142.

Van Cappellen, P. (2017). Rethinking self-transcendent positive emotions and religion: Insights from psychological and biblical research. *Psychology of Religion and Spirituality, 9,* 254-263.

Van Cappellen, P., Edwards, M., & Fredrickson, B. L. (2021). Upward spirals of positive emotions and religious behaviors. *Current Opinion in Psychology, 40,* 92-98.

Van Cappellen, P., Fredrickson, B. L., Saroglou, V., & Corneille, O. (2017). Religiosity and the motivation for social affiliation. *Personality and Individual Differences, 113,* 24-31.

Van Cappellen, P., & Saroglou, V. (2012). Awe activates religious and spiritual feelings and behavioral intentions. *Psychology of Religion and Spirituality, 4,* 223-236.

Van Cappellen, P., Saroglou, V., & Toth-Gauthier, M. (2016). Religiosity and prosocial behavior among churchgoers: Exploring underlying mechanisms. *The International Journal for the Psychology of Religion, 26,* 19-30.

Van Cappellen, P., Toth-Gauthier, M., Saroglou, V., & Fredrickson, B. L. (2016). Religion and well-being: The mediating role of positive emotions. *Journal of Happiness Studies, 17,* 485-505.

Van Cappellen, P., Zhang, R., & Fredrickson, B. L. (2023). The scientific study of positive psychology, religion/spirituality, and physical health. In E. B. Davis, E. L. Worthington, Jr., & S. A. Schnitker (Eds.), *Handbook of positive psychology, religion, and spirituality* (pp. 315-328). Cham, Switzerland: Springer.

Van den Bos, K., Van Ameijde, J., & Van Gorp, H. (2006). On the psychology of religion: The role of personal uncertainty in religious worldview defense. *Basic and Applied Social Psychology, 28,* 333-341.

van der Toorn, J., Jost, J. T., Packer, D. J., Noorbaloochi, S., & Van Bavel, J. J. (2017). In defense of tradition: Religiosity, conservatism, and opposition to same-sex marriage in North America. *Personality and Social Psychology Bulletin, 43, 1455-1468.*

Van Eyghen, H., & Bennett, C. T. (2022). Did natural selection select for true religious beliefs? *Religious Studies, 58,* 113– 37.

VanderWeele, T. J. (2017). Religious communities and human flourishing. *Current Directions in Psychological Science, 26,* 476-481.

VanderWeele, T. J. (2020a). Love of neighbor during a pandemic: Navigating the competing goods of religious gatherings and physical health. *Journal of Religion and Health, 59,* 2196-2202.

VanderWeele, T. J. (2020b). Spiritual well-being and human flourishing: Conceptual, causal, and policy relations. In A. B. Cohen (Ed.), *Religion and human flourishing* (pp. 43-54). Waco, TX: Baylor University Press.

Van Droogenbroeck, F., Spruyt, B., Siongers, J., & Keppens, G. (2016). Religious quest orientation and anti-gay sentiment: Nuancing the relationship between religiosity and negative attitudes toward homosexuality among young Muslims and Christians in Flanders. *Journal for the Scientific Study of Religion, 55,* 787-799.

van Elk, M., & Naaman, L. (2021). Religious unbelief in Israel: A replication study identifying and characterizing unbelievers using latent class analysis. *The International Journal for the Psychology of Religion, 31,* 51-56.

van Elk, M., Rutjens, T. T., van der Pligt, J., van Harreveld, F. (2016). Priming of supernatural agent concepts and agency detection. *Religion, Brain & Behavior, 6,* 4-33.

van Mulukom, V., Turpin, H., Haimila, R., Purzycki, B. G., Bendixen, T., Kundtová Klocová, E., Řezníček, D., Coleman, T. J., III, Sevinç, K., Maraldi, E., Schjoedt, U, Rutjens, B. T., & Farias, M. (2023). What do nonreligious nonbelievers believe in? Secular worldviews around the world. *Psychology of Religion and Spirituality, 15,* 143-156.

Van Ness, P. (Ed.). (1996). *Spirituality and the secular quest.* New York, NY: Crossroad Publishing.

Van Tongeren, D. R., Hakim, S., Hook, J. N., Johnson, K. A., Green, J. D., Hulsey, T. L., & Davis, D. E. (2016). Toward an understanding of religious tolerance: Quest religiousness and positive attitudes toward religiously dissimilar others. *The International Journal for the Psychology of Religion, 26,* 212-224.

Van Tongeren, D. R., Raad, J. M., McIntosh, D. N., & Pae, J. (2013). The existential function of intrinsic religiousness: Moderation of effects of priming religion on intercultural tolerance and afterlife anxiety. *Journal for the Scientific Study of Religion, 52,* 508-523.

Van Tongeren, D. R., Stafford, J., Hook, J. N., Green, J. D., David, D. E., & Johnson, K. A. (2016). Humility attenuates negative attitudes and behaviors toward religious out-group members. *The Journal of Positive Psychology, 11,* 199-208.

Vardy, T., Moya, C., Placek, C. D., Apicella, C. L., Bolyanatz, A., Cohen, E., Handley, C., Kundtová Klocová, E., Lesorogol, C., Mathew, S., McNamara, S. A., Purzycki, B. G., Soler, M., Weigel, J. L., Willard, A. K., Xygalatas, D., Norenzayan, A., Henrich, J., Lang, M., & Atkinson, Q. D. (2022) The religiosity gender gap in 14 diverse societies, *Religion, Brain & Behavior, 12,* 18-37.

Vernon, M. (2008). *After atheism: Science, religion, and the meaning of life.* London, UK: Palgrave Macmillan.

Vilchinsky, N., & Kravetz, S. (2005). How are religious belief and behavior good for you? An investigation of mediators relating religion to mental health in a sample of Israeli Jewish students. *Journal for the Scientific Study of Religion, 44,* 459-471.

Visala, A. (2011). *Naturalism, theism, and the cognitive science of religion: Religion explained?* Surrey, England: Ashgate Publishing Limited.

Visala, A. (2014). The evolution of divine and human minds: Evolutionary psychology, the cognitive study of religion and theism. In F. Watts & L.

Turner (Eds.), *Evolution, religion, and cognitive science: Critical and constructive essays* (pp. 56-73). Oxford, UK: Oxford University Press.

Vishkin, A. (2021). Variation and consistency in the links between religion and emotion regulation. *Current Opinion in Psychology, 40*, 6-9.

Voas, D. (2009). The rise and fall of fuzzy fidelity in Europe. *European Sociological Review, 25*, 155-168.

Voas, D. (2022). Linking the fertility and secular transitions. *Religion, Brain & Behavior, 12*, 425-430.

Voas, D., & Chaves, M. (2016). Is the United States a counterexample to the secularization thesis? *American Journal of Sociology, 121*, 1517-1556.

Volf, M., Croasmun, M., & McAnnally-Linz, R. (2020). Meanings and dimensions of flourishing (pp. 7-17). In A. B. Cohen (Ed.), *Religion and human flourishing* (pp. 1-6). Waco, TX: Baylor University Press.

Voytenko, V. L., Pargament, K. I., Cowden, R. G., Lemke, A. W., Kurniati, N. M. T., Bechara, A. O., Joynt, S., Tymchenko, S., Khalanskyi, V. V., Shtanko, L., Kocum, M. Korzhov, H., Mathur, M. B., Ho, M. Y., VanderWeele, T. J., & Worthington, E. L., Jr. (2023). Religious coping with interpersonal hurts: Psychological correlates of the Brief RCOPE in four non-western countries. *Psychology of Religion and Spirituality, 15*, 43-55.

Vukasović, T., & Bratko, D. (2015). Heritability of personality: A meta-analysis of behavior genetic studies. *Psychological Bulletin, 141*, 769-785.

Wade, N. G., Hoyt, W. T., Kidwell, J. E. M., & Worthington, E. L. (2014). Efficacy of psychotherapeutic interventions to promote forgiveness: A meta-analysis. *Journal of Counseling and Clinical Psychology, 82*, 154-170.

Wagner, L., Gander, F., Proyer, R. T., & Ruch, W. (2020). Character strengths and PERMA: Investigating the relationships of character strengths with a multidimensional framework of well-being. *Applied Research in Quality of Life, 15*, 307-328.

Waller, J. E. (2013). Religion and evil in the context of genocide. In K. I. Pargament (Editor-in-Chief), J. J. Exline & J. W. Jones (Associate Editors), *APA handbook of psychology, religion, and spirituality. Vol. 1: Context, theory, and research* (pp. 477-493). Washington, D. C.: American Psychological Association.

Walters, K. (2011). *Revolutionary deists: Early America's rational infidels.* Amherst, NY: Prometheus Books.

Ward, S. J., & King, L. A. (2016). Poor but happy? Income, happiness, and experienced and expected meaning in life. *Social Psychological & Personality Science, 7,* 463-470.

Warraq, I. (2020). *Why I am not a Muslim* (2nd ed.). Brooklyn, NY: Momus and Warraq Publishers, LLC. (First published in 1995 by Prometheus Books)

Washington-Nortey, M., Worthington, E. L., Jr., & Ahmed, R. (2023). The scientific study of religion/spirituality, forgiveness, and hope. In E. B. Davis, E. L. Worthington, Jr., & S. A. Schnitker (Eds.), *Handbook of positive psychology, religion, and spirituality* (pp. 361-377). Cham, Switzerland: Springer.

Waterman, A. S. (2013a). The humanistic psychology-positive psychology divide: Contrasts in philosophical foundations. *American Psychologist, 68,* 124-133.

Waterman, A. S. (2013b). Introduction: Considering the nature of a life well lived—intersections of positive psychology and eudaimonist philosophy. In A. S. Waterman (Ed.), *The best within us: Positive psychology perspectives on eudaimonia* (pp. 3-17). Washington, DC: American Psychological Association.

Waterman, A. S., & Schwartz, S. J. (2013). Eudaimonic identity theory. In A. S. Waterman (Ed.), *The best within us: Positive psychology perspectives on eudaimonia* (pp. 99-118). Washington, DC: American Psychological Association.

Watkins, P. C., Van Gelder, M., & Frias, A. (2009). Furthering the science of gratitude. In C. R. Snyder & S. J. Lopez (Eds.), *The Oxford hand-*

book of positive psychology (2nd ed., pp. 437-445). New York, NY: Oxford University Press.

Watson, D., & Clark, L. A. (1992). On traits and temperament: General and specific factors of emotional experience and their relation to the five-factor model. *Journal of Personality, 60*, 441-476.

Watson, P. (2016). *The age of nothing: How we have sought to live since the death of God.* London, England: Weidenfeld & Nicolson. (Originally published in 2014 as *The age of atheism: How we have sought to live since the death of God*).

Watson-Jones, R. E., Busch, J. T. A., Harris, P. L., & Legare, C. H. (2017, Suppl. 3). Does the body survive death? Cultural variation in beliefs about life everlasting. *Cognitive Science, 41*, 455-476.

Watts, F. (2014). Religion and the emergence of differentiated cognition. In F. Watts & L. Turner (Eds.), *Evolution, religion, and cognitive science: Critical and constructive essays* (pp. 109-131). Oxford, UK: Oxford University Press.

Watts, J., Greenhill, S. J., Atkinson, Q. D., Currie, T. E., Bulbulia, J., & Gray, R. D. (2015). Broad supernatural punishment but not moralizing high gods precede the evolution of political complexity in Austronesia. *Proceedings of the Royal Society B: Biological Sciences, 282*, 20142556.

Watts, J., Sheehan, O., Atkinson, Q. D., Bulbulia, J., & Gray, R. D. (2016). Ritual human sacrifice promoted and sustained the evolution of stratified societies. *Nature, 532*, 228-231.

Weber, M. (2003). *The Protestant ethic and the spirit of capitalism* (trans. Talcott Parsons). Mineola, NY: Dover Publications, Inc. (Unabridged republication of the work originally published by Charles Scribner's Sons, New York, in 1958; original German work published in 1904-1905)

Weinberg, S. (2007). What about God? From dreams of a final theory. In C. Hitchens (Ed.), *The portable atheist: Essential readings for the nonbeliever* (pp. 366-379). Philadelphia, PA: Da Capo Press. [From *Dreams of a final theory: The search for the fundamental laws of nature*, copyright © 1992 by

Steven Weinberg. Reprinted with permission of Pantheon Books, a division of Random House, Inc.]

Wellman, J. K., Jr. (2008). *Evangelical vs. liberal: The clash of Christian cultures in the Pacific Northwest*. New York, NY: Oxford University Press.

Wellman, J. K., Jr., Corcoran, K. E., & Stockly, K. J. (2020). *High on God: How megachurches won the heart of America*. New York, NY: Oxford University Press.

White, C. J. M., Baimel, A., & Norenzayan, A. (2021). How cultural learning and cognitive biases shape religious beliefs. *Current Opinion in Psychology, 40*, 34-39.

White, C. J. M., Kelly, J. M., Shariff, A. F., & Norenzayan, A. (2019). Supernatural norm enforcement: Thinking about karma and God reduces selfishness among believers. *Journal of Experimental Social Psychology, 84*, 103797.

White, C. J. M., & Norenzayan, A. (2022). Karma and God: Convergent and divergent mental representations of supernatural norm enforcement. *Psychology of Religion and Spirituality, 14*, 70-85.

White, C. J. M., Willard, A. K., Baimel, A., & Norenzayan, A. (2021). Cognitive pathways to belief in karma and belief in God. *Cognitive Science, 44*, e12935.

Whitehead, A. L., & Perry, S. L. (2020). *Taking America back for God: Christian nationalism in the United States*. New York, NY: Oxford University Press.

Whitehouse, H. (2005). The cognitive foundations of religiosity. In H. Whitehouse & R. N. McCauley, *Mind and religion: Psychological and cognitive foundations of religiosity* (pp. 207-232). Walnut Creek, CA: AltaMira Press.

Whitehouse, H. (2018). Dying for the group: Towards a general theory of extreme self-sacrifice. *Behavioral and Brain Sciences, 41*, Article e192.

Whitehouse, H. (2021). *The ritual animal: Imitation and cohesion in the evolution of social complexity.* Oxford, New York, NY: Oxford University Press.

Whitehouse, H., François, P., Savage, P. E., Hoyer, D., Feeney, K. C., Cioni, E., Purcell, R., Larson, J., Baines, J., ter Haar, B., Covey, A., & Turchin, P. (2023). Testing the Big Gods hypothesis with global historical data: A review and "retake." *Religion, Brain & Behavior, 13,* 124-166.

Whitehouse, H., & Hodder, I. (2010). Modes of religiosity at Çatalhöyük. In I. Hodder (Ed.), *Religion and the emergence of civilization: Çatalhöyük as a case study* (pp. 122-145). Cambridge, UK: Cambridge University Press.

Whitley, B. E., Jr. (2009). Religiosity and attitudes toward lesbians and gay men: A meta-analysis. *The International Journal for the Psychology of Religion, 19,* 21-38.

Wildman, W. J., Bulbulia, J., Sosis, R., & Schjoedt, U. (2020). Religion and the COVID-19 pandemic. *Religion, Brain & Behavior, 10,* 115-117.

Willard, A. K., Cingl, L., & Norenzayan, A. (2020). Cognitive biases and religious belief: A path model replication in the Czech Republic and Slovakia with a focus on anthropomorphism. *Social Psychological and Personality Science, 11,* 97-106.

Willard, A. K., Henrich, J., & Norenzayan, A. (2016). Memory and belief in the transmission of counterintuitive content. *Human Nature, 27,* 221-243.

Willard, A. K., & McNamara, R. A. (2019). The minds of god(s) and humans: Differences in mind perception in Fiji and North America. *Cognitive Science, 43,* e12703.

Willard, A. K., & Norenzayan, A. (2013). Cognitive biases explain religious belief, paranormal belief, and belief in life's purpose. *Cognition, 129,* 379-391.

Willard, A., & Norenzayan, A. (2017). Spiritual but not religious: Cognition, schizotypy, and conversion in alternative beliefs. *Cognition, 165,* 137-146.

Willard, A. K., Shariff, A. F., & Norenzayan, A. (2016). Religious priming as a research tool for studying religion: Evidentiary value, current issues, and future directions. *Current Opinion in Psychology, 12*, 71-75.

Wills, G. (2007). *Head and heart: A history of Christianity in America.* New York, NY: Penguin Books.

Wilson, D. S. (2002). *Darwin's cathedral: Evolution, religion, and the nature of society.* Chicago, IL: The University of Chicago Press.

Winell, M. (2017). The challenge of leaving religion and becoming secular. In P. Zuckerman & J. R. Shook (Eds.), *The Oxford handbook of secularism* (pp. 603-620). New York, NY: Oxford University Press.

Winkelman, M. J. (1990). Shamans and other "magico-religious" healers: A cross-cultural study of their origins, nature, and social transformations. *Ethos, 18*, 308-352.

Winkelman, M. (2015). Shamanism as a biogenetic structural paradigm for humans' evolved social psychology. *Psychology of Religion and Spirituality, 7*, 267-277.

Wissing, M. P., Schutte, L., Liversage, C., Entwisle, B., Gericke, M., & Keyes, C. (2019). Important goals, meanings, and relationships in flourishing and languishing states: Towards patterns of well-being. *Applied Research in Quality of Life, 16*, 573-609.

Witvliet, C. V. O., & Root Luna, L. (2018). Forgiveness and well-being. In D. S. Dunn (Ed.), *Positive psychology: Established and emerging issues* (pp. 129-152). New York, NY: Routledge.

Wixwat, M., & Saucier, G. (2021). Being spiritual but not religious. *Current Opinion in Psychology, 40*, 121-125.

Wong, P. T. P. (Ed.) (2012). *The human quest for meaning: Theories, research, and applications* (2nd ed.). New York, NY: Routledge.

Wong, P. T. P. (2014). Viktor Frankl's meaning-seeking model and positive psychology. In A. Batthyany & P. Russo-Netzer (Eds.), *Meaning in existential and positive psychology* (pp. 149-184). New York, NY: Springer.

Wong, P. T. P. (2017). Meaning-centered approach to research and therapy, second wave positive psychology, and the future of humanistic psychology. *The Humanist Psychologist, 45*, 207-216.

Wong, P. T. P., & Roy, S. (2018). Critique of positive psychology and positive interventions. In N. Brown, R. Lomas, & F. J. Eiroa-Orasa (Eds.), *The Routledge handbook of critical positive psychology* (pp. 142-160). New York, NY: Routledge/Taylor & Francis Group.

Wood, A. M., Froh, J., & Geraghty, A. (2010). Gratitude and well-being: A review and theoretical integration. *Clinical Psychology Review, 30*, 890-905.

Wood, A. M., Linley, P. A., Maltby, J., Baliousis, M., & Joseph, S. (2008). The authentic personality: A theoretical and empirical conceptualization and development of the Authenticity Scale. *Journal of Counseling Psychology, 55*, 385-399.

Wood, C. (2017). Ritual well-being: Toward a social signaling model of religion and mental health. *Religion, Brain & Behavior, 7*, 223-275.

Worthington, E. L., Jr. (2010). *Coming to peace with psychology: What Christians can learn from psychological science.* Downers Grove, IL: InterVarsity Press.

Worthington, E. L., Jr., & Allison, S. (2018). *Heroic humility: What the science of humility can say to people raised on self-focus.* Washington, DC: American Psychological Association.

Wright, B. R. E., Wallace, M., Wisnesky, A. S., Donnelly, C M., Missari, S., Wisnesky, A. S., & Zozula, C. (2015). Religion, race, and discrimination: A field experiment of how American churches welcome newcomers. *Journal for the Scientific Study of Religion, 54*, 185-204.

Wrzesniewski, A. (2015). Callings and the meaning of work. In D. B. Yaden, T. D. McCall, & J. H. Ellens (Eds.), *Being called: Scientific, secular, and sacred perspectives* (pp. 3-11). Santa Barbara, CA: Praeger.

Wunn, I. (2000). Beginning of religion. *NUMEN, 47*, 417-452.

Xygalatas, D. (2013). Effects of religious setting on cooperative behaviour: A case study from Mauritius. *Religion, Brain & Behavior, 3*, 91-102.

Xygalatas, D., Kundtová Klocová, E., Cigán, J., Kundt, R., Mano, P., Kotherová, S., Mitkidis, P., Wallot, S., & Kanovsky, M. (2016). Location, location, location: Effects of cross-religious primes on prosocial behavior. *The International Journal for the Psychological Study of Religion, 26,* 304-319.

Xygalatas, D., Kotherová, S., Mano, P., Kundt, R., Cigán, J., & Kundtová Klocová, E., & Lang, M. (2018). Big gods in small places: The random allocation game. *Religion, Brain & Behavior, 8*, 243-261.

Xygalatas, D., Mitkidis, P., Fischer, R., Reddish, P. Skewes, J., Geertz, A. W., Roepstorff, A., & Bulbulia, J. (2013). Extreme rituals promote prosociality. *Psychological Science, 24,* 1602-1605.

Xygalatas, D., Mano, P., Bahna, V., Kundtová Klocovà, E., Kundt, R., Lang, M., & Shaver, J. (2021). Social inequality and signaling in a costly ritual. *Evolution and Human Behavior, 42*, 524-533.

Yaden, D. B. (2015). Conclusion: Answering the call. In D. B. Yaden, T. D. McCall, & J. H. Ellens (Eds.), *Being called: Scientific, secular, and sacred perspectives* (pp. 275-282). Santa Barbara, CA: Praeger.

Yaden, D. B., Iwry, J., Smith, E. E., & Pawelski, J. O. (2017). Secularism and the science of well-being. In P. Zuckerman & J. R. Shook (Eds.), *The Oxford handbook of secularism* (pp. 554-570). New York, NY: Oxford University Press.

Yaden, D. B., & Newberg, A. B. (2015). Road to Damascus moments: Calling experiences as prospective epiphanies. In D. B. Yaden, T. D. McCall, & J. H. Ellens (Eds.), *Being called: Scientific, secular, and sacred perspectives* (pp. 27-46). Santa Barbara, CA: Praeger.

Yalom, I. (1980). *Existential psychotherapy.* New York, NY: Basic Books.

Yilmaz, O. (2021). Cognitive styles and religion. *Current Opinion in Psychology, 40,* 150-154.

Yilmaz, O., & Bahçekapili, H. G. (2016). Supernatural and secular monitors promote human cooperation only if they remind of punishment. *Evolution and Human Behavior, 37*, 79-84.

Yilmaz, O., Karadöller, D. Z., & Sofuoglu, G. (2016). Analytic thinking, religion, and prejudice: An experimental test of the dual-process model of mind. *The International Journal for the Psychology of Religion, 26*, 360–369.

Yonker, J. E., Edman, L. R., Cresswell, J., & Barrett, J. L. (2016). Primed analytic thought and religiosity: The importance of individual characteristics. *Psychology of Religion and Spirituality, 8*, 298–308.

Yonker, J. E., Schnabelrauch, C. A., & DeHaan, L. G. (2012). The relationship between spirituality and religiosity on psychological outcomes in adolescents and emerging adults: A meta-analytic review. *Journal of Adolescence, 35*, 299-314.

Zell, A. L., & Baumeister, R. F. (2013). How religion can support self-control and moral behavior. In. R. F. Paloutzian & C. L. Park (Eds.), *Handbook of the psychology of religion and spiritualty* (2nd ed., pp. 498-516). New York: Guilford Press.

Zuckerman, M., Li, C., & Diener, E. (2018). Religion as an exchange system: The interchangeability of God and government in a provider role. *Personality and Social Psychology Bulletin, 44*, 1201–1213.

Zuckerman, M., Li, C., Lin, S., & Hall, J. (2020). The negative intelligence-religiosity relation: New and confirming evidence. *Personality and Social Psychology Bulletin, 46*, 856-868.

Zuckerman, M., Silberman, J., & Hall, J. A. (2013). The relation between intelligence and religiosity: A meta-analysis and some proposed explanations. *Personality and Social Psychology Review, 17*, 325-354.

Zuckerman, P. (2008). *Society without God: What the least religious nations can tell us about contentment.* New York, NY: New York University Press.

Zuckerman, P. (2014). *Living the secular life: New answers to old questions.* New York, NY: Penguin Books.

Zuckerman, P. (2019). *What it means to be moral: Why religion is not necessary for living an ethical life.* Berkeley, CA: Counterpoint.

Zuckerman, P., Galen, L. W., & Pasquale, F. L. (2016). *The nonreligious: Understanding secular people & societies.* New York, NY: Oxford University Press.

About the Author

A. Timothy Church received a PhD in Psychology from the University of Minnesota and is Professor Emeritus in Counseling Psychology at Washington State University. He has an international reputation for his research on culture and personality and has published extensively in top scientific journals, including invited reviews in Current Opinion in Psychology, Advances in Culture and Psychology, Perspectives on Psychological Science, Social and Personality Compass, and Journal of Personality. Much of this research was conducted in collaboration with his wife Marcia S. Katigbak, PhD, and a network of international psychologists, with grant support from the National Science Foundation and National Institute of Mental Health in the United States. He edited the three-volume Praeger Handbook of Personality across Cultures (ABC-CLIO, 2017). He is a former associate editor for the Journal of Cross-Cultural Psychology and has served on the editorial boards for the Journal of Personality and Social Psychology, Journal of Personality, Journal of Research in Personality, Personality and Social Psychology Review, Psychological Science, European Journal of Personality, and Journal of Cross-Cultural Psychology. His scholarly interests include cross-cultural and indigenous psychology, personality and its measurement, multicultural issues in counseling and assessment, and the psychology and social science of religion and secularity.

www.ingramcontent.com/pod-product-compliance
Lightning Source LLC
Chambersburg PA
CBHW061041110426
42740CB00050B/2498